Ethnographic Research and Analysis

"I read this groundbreaking anthology with great interest. It captures a suspicion of mine. You cannot understand Being-in-the-world of doing organizational ethnography without also going deep into the inner spacetime of your own autoethnographic journey. It takes a double journey (inward and outward) otherwise it is merely creating more duality, avoidance of our own life of anxiety. Somehow the outer story-telling and the untold inner story must come into relationship in our qualitative methods."

—David Boje, *New Mexico State University, USA*

"This book offers rich bases for comparison, allowing an editorial focus on established practices and accepted problems in some disciplines and facilitating application to others. It is thus well set to present the personal dilemmas that ethnography inevitably presents, and to offer mutual learning from divergent experience.

The result is a rich collection of variations that could easily have produced an uncoordinated mishmash. This has been avoided by the skillful editing of its disparate inputs - all united by a demonstrated regard for ethnography. The result is a contribution to social science that should rightfully establish ethnography at the centre of social science endeavour."

—Gerald Mars, *Honorary Professor of Anthropology, University College London, UK*

Tom Vine • Jessica Clark • Sarah Richards
David Weir
Editors

Ethnographic Research and Analysis

Anxiety, Identity and Self

Editors
Tom Vine
University of Suffolk
Ipswich, UK

Jessica Clark
University of Suffolk
Ipswich, UK

Sarah Richards
University of Suffolk
Ipswich, UK

David Weir
York St John University
York, UK

ISBN 978-1-137-58554-7   ISBN 978-1-137-58555-4   (eBook)
https://doi.org/10.1057/978-1-137-58555-4

Library of Congress Control Number: 2017950217

© The Editor(s) (if applicable) and The Author(s) 2018
The author(s) has/have asserted their right(s) to be identified as the author(s) of this work in accordance with the Copyright, Designs and Patents Act 1988.
This work is subject to copyright. All rights are solely and exclusively licensed by the Publisher, whether the whole or part of the material is concerned, specifically the rights of translation, reprinting, reuse of illustrations, recitation, broadcasting, reproduction on microfilms or in any other physical way, and transmission or information storage and retrieval, electronic adaptation, computer software, or by similar or dissimilar methodology now known or hereafter developed.
The use of general descriptive names, registered names, trademarks, service marks, etc. in this publication does not imply, even in the absence of a specific statement, that such names are exempt from the relevant protective laws and regulations and therefore free for general use.
The publisher, the authors and the editors are safe to assume that the advice and information in this book are believed to be true and accurate at the date of publication. Neither the publisher nor the authors or the editors give a warranty, express or implied, with respect to the material contained herein or for any errors or omissions that may have been made. The publisher remains neutral with regard to jurisdictional claims in published maps and institutional affiliations.

Cover illustration: Jim Corwin / Alamy Stock Photo

Printed on acid-free paper

This Palgrave Macmillan imprint is published by Springer Nature
The registered company is Macmillan Publishers Ltd.
The registered company address is: The Campus, 4 Crinan Street, London, N1 9XW, United Kingdom

CONTENTS

1 Introduction   1
Tom Vine, Jessica Clark, Sarah Richards, and David Weir

2 Home-Grown Exoticism? Identity Tales from a New Age Intentional Community   13
Tom Vine

3 Wrestling with Online Avatars: Technology and Sexual Transformation   37
Paul Driscoll-Evans

4 Chóng ér fēi: Cultural Performances of Belonging in Intercountry Adoptive Families   53
Sarah Richards

5 Ethnographic Practices of Listening   77
Allison Boggis

6 Discussion and Collaboration in Diagnostic Radiography   97
Ruth Strudwick

7 Living with Uncertainty: The Ethnographer's Burden   113
Steve Barnes

vi CONTENTS

8 What Makes the Autoethnographic Analysis Authentic? 127
David Weir and Daniel Clarke

9 Saying the unsayable: An Autoethnography of Working in a For-Profit University 155
Katie Best

10 An Autoethnographic Account of Gender and Workflow Processes in a Commercial Laundry 171
David Weir

11 The Salience of Emotions in (Auto) ethnography: Towards an Analytical Framework 191
Ilaria Boncori

12 It's More Than Deciding What to Wank Into: Negotiating an Unconventional Fatherhood 217
John Hadlow

13 Hate the Results? Blame the Methods: An Autoethnography of Contract Research 233
Will Thomas and Mirjam Southwell

14 Collaborative Autoethnography: Enhancing Reflexive Communication Processes 253
Ngaire Bissett, Sharon Saunders, and Carolina Bouten Pinto

15 Methodology: From Paradigms to Paradox 273
Tom Vine

16 Conclusion 301
Tom Vine, Jessica Clark, Sarah Richards, and David Weir

Index 309

LIST OF FIGURES

Fig. 6.1	Outpatient journey through the DID	101
Fig. 6.2	Inpatient journey through the DID	102

LIST OF TABLES

Table 8.1	Delamont and authentic autoethnographic texts	130
Table 10.1	Dirty and clean areas	178
Table 10.2	Heavy and light areas	178
Table 10.3	Male and female areas	180
Table 10.4	Interface areas	183
Table 10.5	Zones of control	184

CHAPTER 1

Introduction

Tom Vine, Jessica Clark, Sarah Richards, and David Weir

The ideas for this book originated from a 2012 conference held at the University of Suffolk. What emerged from this conference was recognition that although our disciplinary backgrounds varied, there was significant value in establishing a shared platform for our ethnographic experiences, not least in the interests of mutual scholarship and reciprocal learning. Notably, and in spite of our disparate subject areas, it became clear that as ethnographers we were encountering similar challenges and epistemological anxieties. Moreover, there appeared to be mutual recognition in terms of the potential for advancing the ethnographic method in the future. In capturing the essence of this conference, this book is not intended as a 'how to guide', of which there are many, but rather a space to bring together and share the experiential aspects of ethnographic work. As such, this edited book presents these experiences from a wide range of disciplines including work and organisation studies, sociology, social policy, philosophy, management, health and human sciences, family studies, education, disability studies, and childhood studies.

This book seeks to devolve methodological themes and practices which are established in some subject areas but not in others. These

T. Vine (✉) • J. Clark • S. Richards
University of Suffolk, Ipswich, UK

D. Weir
York St John University, York, UK

© The Author(s) 2018
T. Vine et al. (eds.), *Ethnographic Research and Analysis*,
https://doi.org/10.1057/978-1-137-58555-4_1

include, for example, the rise of autoethnography and the role of story-telling. Additionally, the chapters contained within interrogate and reframe long-standing ethnographic discussions including those concerning reflexivity, while exploring evolving themes such as the experiential use of technologies. This book thus demonstrates the value and versatility of ethnography as a method in a diverse range of rarely combined disciplines. In further emphasising our transdisciplinary objectives, each chapter includes a brief biographical preamble in which the author reflects on the existing character and impact of ethnographic research within their native discipline.

Ethnography is widely considered to have emerged as part of anthropology and is considered both its trademark (e.g. Schwartzman, 1993) and textual product (e.g. Atkinson, 1990). However, in this book we acknowledge that the practice of ethnography long predates its formal canonisation in anthropology and reflect on this significance. This historical precedent notwithstanding, ethnography has traversed changing dynamics of how and why research is conducted across the social sciences and remains a pivotal method through which the rich context and complexity of the human condition is revealed. As such, ethnography remains as relevant to contemporary social science as it did to historical anthropology. In this book, we explore ethnography as a research tool in online endeavours, visual methods, autoethnography, performance theory, and collaborative techniques. However, from the diversity of perspectives presented, commonalities are revealed in respect of both the challenges of ethnographic encounters and the opportunities these bring. The recurring narratives of ethnography thus remain among the contemporary topics explored. Each writer rediscovers these themes and wrestles with their implications. These include positionality, the researcher–researched relationship, identity, liminality, subjectivity, presentation of self, and the role of storytelling. This historical 'baggage' of ethnography remains acutely relevant and topical to contemporary conversations. To this end we urge the reader to consider an alternate history of ethnography; one that *pre-dates* anthropology. Here the concept of a 'proto-ethnographer' is pertinent, both noted (e.g. Herodotus) and lay (since ethnographic research can be considered instinctive as well as schooled; this is because schooling invariably involves social construction and so can *constrain* as well as enable creativity). Second, the relationship between teaching and learning is to some degree characterised by contradiction and paradox; see, for example, Ackoff and Greenberg (2008). We therefore suggest that ethnography can be usefully conceptualised as pre-formal and intuitive. Furthermore, given that ethnography seeks not to distil human behaviour into abstract or schematised models, the parameters and preferences for which vary from academic discipline to academic discipline, but to prioritise experiential data collection and analysis, ethnography is here conceptualised as a relevant research tool which *transcends* the normative and expected parameters of social science.

At this point, it is worth noting the difference between qualitative methods and ethnography. While numerous social scientific projects lay claim to using one or more qualitative methods (such as interviewing, photography, discourse analysis, etc.), far fewer are representative of ethnography per se. In its purest (anthropological) sense, ethnography is only achieved where the researcher immerses herself in a participatory observational context in the proposed environs for as long a period as possible. For Moeran (2009, p. 150), 'ethnographic fieldwork should last between six months and one year'. The advantages of a full year's research—or perhaps even several years'—are relatively obvious: it affords the researcher experience of both annual rituals and seasonal variations in environmental conditions and associated behaviour. Studies of this nature are less numerous, not because the method is inappropriate or ineffective; rather they require commitment and time which is off-putting for many academics who today work in an environment where there exists an emphasis on quantity with regard to publications (Schwartzman, 1993). It is hoped, therefore, that the ethnographies presented in this book go some way to redressing the balance.

We take the position that collections of ethnographic work are better presented as transdisciplinary bricolage than as discipline-specific series. As such this volume provides a space where the plurality of ethnographic approaches is illustrated through the varied ways that researchers apply its principles to diverse disciplinary contexts. This book therefore delineates (1) the continued relevance of ethnography in contemporary research, (2) the opportunities to apply ethnographic approaches across diverse spaces, and (3) open and honest accounts in which the perennial questions ethnographic research produces can be re-examined. The importance of the 'ethical subject' notwithstanding, we note that the pressure to conform to 'sanitised' methods is pervasive—even in ethnography—and this presents myriad challenges. Indeed, although ethics does not constitute an explicit theme for this book, many of the chapters reveal subtleties, complexities, and paradoxes associated with 'ethical research'.

TRANSDISCIPLINARITY

Under the guise of social anthropology, ethnography was 'linked to the spread of colonial empire and its administrative, missionary and commercial needs' (Evans-Pritchard, 1969, p. x). It fell out of favour in the wake of the decline of colonial rule across the globe and became a niche method and methodology, largely limited to anthropologists and a few quirky sociologists. However, it regained popularity in the UK and elsewhere in the 1960s and 1970s. As part of this resurgence, serious attempts were made to listen to the voices and view the worlds of those considered marginalised. These included the fields of poverty (Wilson & Aponte, 1985), sexuality (Sonenschein, 1968), crime and deviance (Hamm, Ferrell, Adler, & Adler, 1998), and latterly children (Montgomery, 2007). While retaining its niche status, its resurgence has in many ways seen it transformed beyond its original applications of anthropology and marginalised groups. Ethnographic approaches are now a relatively common site in disciplines as diverse as management, radiography, childhood studies, education, and disability studies. This suggests that ethnography is a flexible and reflexive methodological tool that can be effectively applied in many research contexts regardless of topic, participants, or indeed discipline. This book is a response to these developments whereby authors present ethnographic tales of their diverse research experiences and the application of such methodologies in their respective fields. The extent to which ethnography retains its original features and characteristics through such diverse applications is a debate that this book opens rather than closes. Many of the authors reflect explicitly on the place of ethnographic methodologies in their native discipline and the role they play in unsettling the extant knowledges of that subject area. This is particularly interesting when such disciplines are traditionally associated with the natural sciences, such as radiography, and are therefore built upon different epistemological assumptions.

Although this is a transdisciplinary book, it does not include a contribution from the field of anthropology. Is this significant in any way? Does it indicate that ethnography has successfully made the transition into other areas of social science? The fact remains that, as editors, we would have certainly considered contributions from anthropologists, but received none. Perhaps this implies a reticence on the part of anthropologists to publish in applied areas? We can conclude with more confidence that this underlines the point that ethnography has spread beyond its origin. However, this gives our book discernible direction. It is this very dispersal that interests us foremost since, inevitably, the methodology has developed in divergent ways in each discipline; the specific ethnographic techniques and preferences vary between contributors, and we reflect on this as part of the concluding chapter.

And why transdisciplinarity? Why not interdisciplinarity? Or multidisciplinarity? We considered these alternate terms but decided ultimately that our endeavour did not sit 'between' different disciplines nor was it simply about lending voice to a 'multiplicity' of different disciplines. Rather, we wanted to demonstrate the ways in which ethnography can and does transcend disciplinary boundaries and, more importantly, how its application in each differs. Ultimately, since practice does vary, this is configured as a pedagogical venture whereby disciplines are able to learn from one another. You are very much encouraged to read the ethnographic accounts from disciplines different to your own and reflect on them from the perspective of your native world. Where do analytical emphases differ? Is language used differently? How might the insights cross-pollinate your own research? Is there scope for further collaborative, cross-disciplinary work in the future?

Finally, the book was led by a team from the University of Suffolk. In many respects young universities in the UK are at extraordinary disadvantages, not least in terms of reputation and—by implication—their ability to recruit students. However, one clear advantage of universities such as Suffolk is their small size. Unlike most established institutions in which exist clear architectural and cultural divides between academic departments, at Suffolk scholars from different disciplines sit cheek by jowl in open-plan offices. Although this certainly brings its own challenges, it creates an environment which readily enables collaborative, transdisciplinary dialogues.

The 'Researcher Self'

In each chapter of this book regardless of discipline, topic, and subject matter, what emerges—almost subconsciously—is the 'ethnographer'. The ethnographer, it would seem, is inseparable from the ethnography. Part of the reason for this is the way in which ethnography is regulated. The expectation for reflexivity and the recognition of positionality within the research process are key tenets within ethnographic work whereby compliance produces the 'ethical subject' (Danaher et al. 2006, p. 131). What the chapters in this book reveal is a variance in the continuum of this revealing of self. This revelation extends from the full and confident immersion of the researcher in their subject matter and respective fields to tentative and often overt anxiety about finding oneself in one's own research. Perhaps because of the continued pressure to conform to sanitised methods across all social research, we are reluctant to engage in the explicit 'revealing of self'. However, what these chapters do reveal is that ethnography inevitably contributes to the construction of the researcher. They constitute a reflection that reveals who we are. Regardless of whether or not the researcher actively self-discloses, what emerges in each chapter is a recognisable researcher role and identity. Arguably, this is an integral part of knowledge construction in *any* method, irrespective of ontological position. The critical difference is that ethnographers, it seems, are more attentive to it.

The First-Person Pronoun

Drawing on novelist, Ursula Le Guin's (1989) reference to the third-person voice as 'the father tongue', Bochner and Ellis (2016, p. 82) suggest that the conventional use of the third person denotes a high-minded mode of expression that seeks and embraces objectivity. 'Spoken from above', they say, 'the father tongue distances the writer from the reader, creating a gap between self and other'. They suggest that 'autoethnographic writing resists this kind of emotional distancing'. This is certainly a persuasive argument, but it feels rather one sided.

For others, the first-person pronoun can be construed as a discernibly modern construct. The concept of the individual's self-identity (and, by implication, the use of the first-person pronoun) has been a key concern for Giddens. He writes, '[s]elf-identity is not a distinctive trait, or even a collection of traits, possessed by the individual. It is the self as *reflexively understood by the person in terms of his or her biography*' (Giddens, 1991, p. 53, original emphasis). Important here is the notion of biography. Giddens suggests that in contemporary society the continuity, predictability, and security associated with premodern life have had to be substituted. In Giddens' eyes, this substitution is provided by the self in terms of establishing and maintaining a sense of personal history. This particular theorisation is justified in terms of an internalisation of scientific reflexivity. By way of clarification, Giddens continues:

> in the context of a post-traditional order, the self becomes a reflexive project. Transitions in individuals' lives have always demanded psychic reorgani-

zation. ... But in some cultures, where things stayed more or less the same from generation to generation *on the level of the collectivity*, the changed identity was clearly staked out—as when an individual moved from adolescence to adulthood. In the settings of modernity, by contrast, the altered self has to be explored and constructed as part of a reflexive process of connecting personal and social change. (ibid. 32–33, emphasis added)

We are reminded here that the notion of the 'individual' is a modern invention: 'the 'individual', in a certain sense, did not exist in traditional cultures, and individuality was not revered as it is today. Only with the emergence of modern societies and, particularly, with the differentiation of the division of labour, did the individual as a distinct entity become a focus of attention (Durkheim, as cited in Giddens, 1991, p. 75). Ironically, perhaps, the external institutionalisation of reflexivity is mirrored internally at the level of the individual. Giddens identifies 'the lifespan as a distinctive and *enclosed* trajectory' (ibid., p. 146: emphasis added). He goes on to suggest that the individual is reified by 'turning his back' on external sources of meaning such as the life cycle of generations, the ties of kinship, other pre-existing relationships, and the permanence of physical place. For Giddens, then, the 'self as reflexive project' is understood as the means by which we are each compelled to 'narrativise' our own life so as to sustain some semblance of meaning and existential security in an uncertain world.

In the field of critical psychology too, there is an overriding concern that in the fold of free market economics, western history has systematically prioritised the analytical category of the individual over and above that of the collective (Carrette, 2007). In this way, 'knowledge framed in terms of individualism is prioritised over and above that framed in social or communal terms'. (Vine, 2011, p. 185). An emphasis on the first-person pronoun might therefore reinforce this bias.

So where does this leave us as ethnographers? On the one hand, ethnography—particularly when configured as autoethnography—is about the effective articulation of subjective, individual experience. In this way, its use of the first-person pronoun appears to be perfectly justified. On the other, and as we have seen, the use of the first-person pronoun reflects a specific linguistic tradition, emergent in some (but not all) cultures and languages in which the concept of the individual is lent primacy over that of the collective. Finally, an added complication arises when autoethnography is co-produced, ostensibly as a 'single voice'. Is it appropriate to use the first-person pronoun in these cases? These are certainly interesting questions, and we very much hope they will generate discussion beyond the confines of the text. Ultimately, we decided to leave the manner in which the first-person pronoun was used—if indeed at all—to each of our contributors. However, as editors we were sure to point out that in going to significant lengths to avoid the fallacy of misplaced concreteness (Whitehead 1967 [1925]), authors should be mindful not to fall prey to the ethnographic fallacy (Duneier, 1999) in which observation is overly subject centred and taken at face value. Inevitably, ethnography is a balancing act.

Anxiety and Uncertainty (of Self)

The final theme that connects the chapters of this book is that of anxiety and uncertainty. Indeed, during the aforementioned 2012 conference, one of the overriding experiences of the research discussed was that of uncertainty. Some of those presenting (and many more in the audience) were early career researchers and the sense of anxiety that comes with that most likely compounded the issue further. Ethnography is investigative (Fetterman, 1988). Ethnography is messy (Crang & Cook, 2007). Ethnography is problematising (Schwartzman, 1993). And ethnography is largely boundaryless and non-linear; it involves 'flying by the seat of your pants' (Van Maanen, 1988, p. 120). For all these reasons, it is no surprise that ethnography invokes anxiety and uncertainty. But rather than focus on means of mitigation, the chapters in this book explore—and celebrate—these experiences for their own sake. It is here that existential doubts in respect of our honesty, empathy, culture, sexuality, competence, and intellect are brought into the open and explored. A generation ago, Rose speculated on the implications of what he called 'multigenre ethnography':

> a new sort of enculturated student will be formed who will conceptualize fieldwork differently from now. *Above all, their inquiry might well have a narrative sort of quality, that is, students will seek to place themselves in unfolding situations, to live through complex ongoing events—the stuff of stories—* rather than looking for the meaning of gestures, the presentation of selves, class relations, the meaning of rituals, or other abstract, analytical category phenomena on which we have historically relied. (Rose, 1990, p. 58, original emphasis)

This advice has come of age. Our book is dedicated to exploring the ramifications of conducting research immersed within the complex, unfolding situations Rose contemplates. Unsurprisingly, then, most of the ethnographies presented in this book are inevitably multi-sited and, in some cases, collaborative.

CHAPTER OUTLINES

This book begins with chapters most akin to traditional ethnography but as it unfolds we transition into autoethnographic work and the emerging field of collaborative ethnography.

In Chap. 2, Tom Vine recounts his experience of living and working in a New Age commune. The appeal of such communities is typically presented in terms of the unfamiliar or 'exotic'. Ironically, upon closer investigation, Tom concludes that the appeal is very much in the mundane: Findhorn provides for its participants a palpable sense of organisational and familial belonging. Reflecting these findings back on the macrosociological shifts of the past generation, Tom notes that this sense of belonging has been surrendered in the mainstream as our work lives have become increasingly contingent and domestic living arrangements continue to depart from the nuclear 'norm'.

In Chap. 3, Paul Driscoll-Evans, a nursing clinician-academic, reflects on a decade working in the field of sexual health and HIV care. As part of this experience, he undertook ethnographic fieldwork among men who have sex with men (MSM) in Norfolk. He explores, in particular, the effects of the internet in facilitating homosexual encounters and the challenge they present to traditional concepts of personhood and psychosocial geography.

In Chap. 4, Sarah Richards explores the consumption of 'authentic' identities among intercountry adoption families. Reflecting on the experiences of her subjects, together with her own as an adoptive mother, she explores the imperative for English adoptive parents of Chinese children to provide them with mediated cultural experiences. In one sense, it is a well-intentioned response to policies, but a response that inevitably leads to tensions and challenges regarding the performance of 'authentic' identities.

In Chap. 5, Allison Boggis reflects on her experience using ethnography to assist in the researcher's ability to identify and interpret the voices, experiences, and opinions of disabled children. Disabled children have, traditionally, been voiceless; their voices are proxied by their parents and mediating professionals. With the assistance of high-tech Augmentative and Alternative Communication Systems (AACS), Alison demonstrates one of the myriad advantages of adopting an ethnographic approach in her native field.

In Chap. 6, clinical radiographer, Ruth Strudwick, departs from the methodological norms of her field and engages in participant observation of other radiographers working in the National Health Service. On the one hand, her work reveals the mundanity of a clinical environment. On the other, like that of Van Maanen (1973, 1975) in respect of US Police Departments, her data reveal the salience of socialisation in respect of mastering the profession.

In Chap. 7, Steve Barnes grapples with existential angst. He comes from a background in positivist methods where uncertainty is mitigated by means of reassuring boundaries. He discovers that no such boundaries exist in ethnography. His five-year journey through his doctoral thesis is presented as a series of anxieties about himself, his abilities, the methodological shortcomings, and the fact that nothing seems to happen. In this sense, Steve's experience is a narrative of two selves, from 'who I was' to 'who I am', demonstrating 'how a life course can be reimagined or transformed by crisis' (Bochner & Ellis, 2016, p. 213). However, as you will see, Steve still remains to be convinced of the validity of this journey.

In Chap. 8, David Weir and Daniel Clarke wrestle with the authenticity of autoethnographic analysis. By way of a response to Delamont's (2007) infamous critique, they each present a personal retrospective to lend empirics to their defence of the method.

In Chap. 9, Katie Best reflects on the schizophrenic nature of working in a 'for-profit' university. As a scholar accustomed to Marx (at least from the relative comfort of a leather-clad armchair) and more contemporary critical accounts of management, she finds herself having to play the corporate game. Strangely, she quite enjoys it. But this serves only to further aggravate her sense of intellectual integrity and personal narrative. The chapter taps into the insecurities, doubts, dualities, and endemic frustrations many of us in the world of academia—and beyond—share.

In Chap. 10, David Weir reminisces about his experiences working as an impressionable teenager in a commercial laundry in the 1950s. Gendered workflow patterns, backroom coitus, and flying turds come together to form a truly evocative account of post-war work life in northern England.

In Chap. 11, Ilaria Boncori argues that, in spite of its influence elsewhere in the academy, emotional content continues to take a back seat in ethnographies set in the worlds of business and management. For Ilaria, this is a source of perennial frustration. Determined to address this shortcoming, she presents a model from which future scholarship may take precedence.

In Chap. 12, John Hadlow renders explicit his own experiences as an informal sperm donor to a lesbian couple and the unusual conceptualisation of fatherhood this constructs. As part of this passage, he reveals anxiety about his use of autoethnography, not least because of the lasting effects the printed word has on those involved, irrespective of procedural anonymity. In this way, a significant complexity in respect of ethnographic ethics is revealed.

In Chap. 13, Will Thomas and Mirjam Southwell recount for us a painful experience of rejection in the world of commercial research. As befitted their remit, they conducted qualitative research. Presented with the unanticipated results of their research, the client reacted by rejecting the findings on the basis of their non-quantitative methods. Their narrative explores their journey of reflection to try to understand where, if anywhere, they went wrong.

In a truly collaborative venture, for Chap. 14, Ngaire Bissett, Sharon Saunders, and Carolina Bouten Pinto present personal vignettes reflecting on their experiences both in academia and in industry. Although decidedly different, they forge a pattern from which they are able to learn from one another and hone their pedagogical skills accordingly. Indeed, given the focus on mutual learning from one another's divergent experience, this chapter echoes in microcosm, the guise of this book in its entirety.

In Chap. 15, in the final contribution to this volume—'Methodology: From Paradigms to Paradox'—Tom Vine explores the ontological tensions inherent to the research process, including the rarely challenged claim that empirics must be underpinned by a supposedly sublime honesty. This chapter reflects on ethnography by recourse to paradox as a means of reinterpreting the experiences presented by the preceding contributors.

REFERENCES

Ackoff, R., & Greenberg, D. (2008). *Turning Learning Right Side Up: Putting Education Back on Track*. Upper Saddle River, NJ: Prentice Hall.

Atkinson, P. (1990). *The Ethnographic Imagination: Textual Constructions of Reality*. London: Routledge.

Bochner, A., & Ellis, C. (2016). *Evocative Autoethnography: Writing Lives and Telling Stories*. London: Routledge.

Carrette, J. (2007). *Religion and Critical Psychology: Religious Experience in the Knowledge Economy*. London: Routledge.

Crang, M., & Cook, I. (2007). *Doing Ethnographies*. London: Sage.

Danaher, G., Schirato, T., & Webb, J. (2006). Understanding Foucault. London: Sage.

Delamont, S. (2007). *Arguments Against Auto-Ethnography*. Paper Presented at the British Educational Research Association Annual Conference (Vol. 5, September p. 8).

Duneier, M. (1999). *Sidewalk*. New York: Farrar, Strauss and Giroux.

Evans-Pritchard, E. (1969). Preface. In J. Degerando (Ed.), *The Observation of Savage People*. Berkeley: University of California Press.

Fetterman, D. (1988). *Ethnography: Step by Step*. London: Sage.

Giddens, A. (1991). *Modernity and Self-Identity*. Cambridge: Polity Press.

Hamm, M., Ferrell, J., Adler, P., & Adler, P. A. (1998). *Ethnography at the Edge: Crime, Deviance and Field Research Paperback*. New England: Northeastern University Press.

Le Guin, U. (1989). Bryn Mawr Commencement Address. In *Dancing At The Edge of the World: Thoughts on Words, Women, Places* (pp. 147–160). New York: Harper & Row.

Moeran, B. (2009). From Participant Observation to Observation Participant. In S. Ybema, D. Yanow, H. Wels, & F. Kamsteeg (Eds.), *Organizational Ethnography: Studying the Complexities of Everyday Life*. London: Sage.

Montgomery. (2007). Working with Child Prostitutes in Thailand: Problems of Practice and Interpretation. *Childhood, 14*(4), 415–430.

Rose, D. (1990). *Living the Ethnographic Life*. London: Sage.

Schwartzman, J. (1993). *Ethnography in Organizations*. London: Sage.

Sonenschein, D. (1968). The Ethnography of Male Homosexual Relationships. *The Journal of Sex Research, 4*(2), 69–83.

Van Maanen, J. (1973). Observations on the Making of Policemen. *Human Organizations, 32*, 407–418.

Van Maanen, J. (1975). Police Socialization. *Administrative Science Quarterly, 20*, 207–228.

Van Maanen, J. (1988). *Tales of the Field*. Chicago: Chicago University Press.

Vine, T. (2011). A Review of Jeremy Carrette's Religion and Critical Psychology: Religious Experience in the Knowledge Economy. *Journal of Management, Spirituality & Religion, 8*(2), 184–189.

Whitehead, A. (1967 [1925]). *Science and the Modern World*. New York: Simon & Schuster.

Wilson, W. J., & Aponte, R. (1985). Urban Poverty. *Annual Review of Sociology, 11*, 231–258.

CHAPTER 2

Home-Grown Exoticism? Identity Tales from a New Age Intentional Community

Tom Vine

I like to describe myself as a 'work and organisation academic'. However, when networking on behalf of the University or liaising with a prospective MBA student, I present myself as a 'business and management lecturer'. Circumstances determine which label I use. Sometimes, however, my selection is motivated by a desire to challenge preconceptions. For example, a school friend of mine recently died and, at the funeral, I got cornered by our old headmaster, a profoundly conservative Oxbridge graduate. 'Vine', he said, 'what are you doing these days?' 'I'm a lecturer', I responded. 'Which university?' he said, most likely hoping that I would proclaim affiliation to a prestigious Russell Group institution. 'Suffolk', I responded. He scoffed. 'What do you lecture?' 'Work and organisation', I said. 'What? That sounds suspiciously like sociology'. 'Well, yes, it's a multidisciplinary subject area, a key component of most management degrees'. 'Ah! So you work in a business school?' 'Yes'. 'Why didn't you say so? You don't want to give people the impression you're a bloody sociologist!' That was, of course, precisely what I was trying to do.

Ethnography is reasonably well received in the domain of work and organisation, but finds rather less traction in the commercially oriented world of business and management. However, it's worth noting that to

T. Vine (✉)
University of Suffolk, Ipswich, UK

© The Author(s) 2018
T. Vine et al. (eds.), *Ethnographic Research and Analysis*,
https://doi.org/10.1057/978-1-137-58555-4_2

> *some extent the practice of management consultancy (which is as commercially oriented as it gets!) involves ethnography. The parameters in management consultancy are very different and we're probably some way off seeing 'participant observation' itemised on an invoice. A very different vocabulary is deployed too: 'on-site specialist research', for example, or 'leveraged professional advice'. Nevertheless, there is an underexplored kinship between the two approaches.*

In one sense, the research presented in this chapter runs contrary to the turning tide of ethnography. Twentieth-century ethnography sought to distance itself from the imperialist anthropology of the Victorian era. Whereas British adventurers of the 1800s lavished us with accounts of life from 'exotic' corners of the earth, the twentieth century witnessed a shift in empirical focus—to 'ordinary' life: street corners, police departments, prisons, amusement parks, and so on. However, the Findhorn Foundation in Scotland, the focus of this chapter, apparently represents a New Age way of life at odds with the 'ordinary' cultures in which it is embedded and might legitimately be considered 'exotic'. Others have concluded the same of comparable sites. Prince and Riches (2000, p. 9) suggest that 'for most New Agers in Glastonbury, the existential experience is departure from the mainstream'. Ironically, and at least in the case of Findhorn, the purpose of this chapter is to persuade you otherwise. I follow a strategy delineated by Silverman (2007): to reveal the mundane in the remarkable. However, here I focus on a particular mundanity, one which the mainstream has surrendered.

The Findhorn Foundation, as it is known today, is sometimes described as a commune. Its members, however, prefer the term 'community' or 'intentional community'. The Findhorn community was established in 1962 by Eileen and Peter Caddy, with Dorothy Maclean. Five years previously, working as hoteliers, the Caddys had been entrusted with the management of the Cluny Hill Hotel in the nearby town of Forres. Eileen allegedly received guidance in her meditations from an inner divine source she called 'the still small voice within', and Peter ran the hotel according to this guidance and his own intuition. Cluny Hill which had up until this point been relatively unsuccessful won the praise of the inspectorate and was awarded four-star accreditation. Impressed at the speed at which they had improved the profitability of the hotel, the owners of the hotel chain decided to relocate the Caddys to another of their failing hotels in the hope that they would do the same there. Following identical spiritual techniques, the two were unable to replicate success in this new setting. They were sacked a few years later. With no immediate source of income and no permanent lodgings, they moved with their three young sons and Dorothy to a caravan on a plot of wasteland adjacent to the village of Findhorn on the Morayshire coast. The community was born.

Although modest in its inception, the community has grown steadily. The founders cultivated a vision which, though subject to both contestation and controversy, retains a central theme: a life premised on an apparently synergetic blend of spiritual and ecological sensitivity. Today, the community is spread over two main sites (*Park Campus*, the original site, and *Cluny Campus*, the site of what was the Cluny hotel, acquired by the Foundation in the 1970s). Additionally, the community includes settlements on two smaller island outposts located off the west coast of Scotland. Collectively, it is home to approximately 300 people, most of whom work for the community either directly or in the form of related business ventures providing both conventional and esoteric products and services for the thousands of visitors to the Foundation each year.

The Foundation is the largest intentional community in Europe and is a powerful 'brand' within New Age circles (for an extensive discussion of the New Age, see Heelas, 1996). Typically, visitors to the community enrol on focussed group-based residential programmes. These include 'Experience Week' (which offers participants a taste of community living and is a prerequisite for other courses); 'Ecovillage training' (a practical sustainability course for planning and constructing settlements); and 'Spiritual Practice' (for meditative and related techniques). In addition, Findhorn also offers residential workweeks where participants work alongside community members on dedicated cleaning, maintenance, building, and horticultural projects. Of my six residential visits to Findhorn, three were on such programmes. These included Experience Week, a workweek for the housekeeping department, and a workweek for the maintenance department.

During my ethnography, I experienced a life far removed from conventional society: sweet-smelling homes fashioned from old whisky barrels; a widely shared belief that work at Findhorn is 'love in action'; ritualised mourning prior to the felling of trees; decision-making via 'attunement' (feeling internally drawn to a particular outcome); a system of servant leadership in which stewards (described as 'focalisers') practise 'responsibility without authority'; hot tub bathing in the nude; the exchange of fairy stories between like-minded adults; and monastic-style singing sessions in Tolkienesque woodland lodgings. All constitute interesting phenomena, but in this chapter I explore Findhorn's appeal by recourse to participant biographies.

My approach has afforded conclusions which non-immersive research methods are unlikely to have yielded. What appears to be 'exotic' is, in practice, both organised and formalised. Findhorn's attraction is *not* its exoticism (which is the presumed appeal when invoking 'escapist' interpretations). Its appeal is better understood in terms of more prosaic desires, particularly *familial belonging* and *organisational security*, qualities which participants have been unable to realise satisfactorily in mainstream society. The stories conveyed represent a corollary of the New Capitalism in which and by contrast to the relative stability of the post-war period—life in the neo-liberal West is experienced as precarious, itinerant, fragmented, solitary, and economically insecure (Barley & Kunda, 2004; Boltanski & Chiapello, 2006; Giddens, 1991; Sennett, 1998). Gradually, our experience of organisations is increasingly characterised by 'an array of short-term arrangements including part-time work, temporary employment, self-employment, contracting, outsourcing, and home-based work' (Barley & Kunda, 2004, p. 9). Therefore, identifying with an employer, let alone securing a sense of job security, has been dealt a serious blow. Of the nuclear family, Weigert and Hastings (1977, p. 1172) described it as a device which harbours:

> a socially and personally defined reality with a unique history, a recognizable collective identity, and mutual claims projected into the future. In a word, a family is a 'world', albeit a little one, in which selves emerge, act, and acquire a stable sense of identity and reality.

However, by 1988 Popenoe had concluded that the institution of the nuclear family was now in permanent decline and with it came significant ramifications in respect of identity and stability. Although my intention is certainly not to reify the nuclear iteration of family, the perception of the existential security once afforded to many by the nuclear family has—like that of the traditional workplace—undoubtedly shifted.

WHY ETHNOGRAPHY?

My research is framed around generating a more nuanced understanding of identity. Glynn (1998) theorised people's 'need for organisational identification' ('nOID'). Having established that we are predisposed to identify with organisations, she asked: 'How can we operationalize and measure nOID?' (ibid., p. 243). However, Glynn was unable to offer an appropriate means of undertaking this venture. Sveningsson and Alvesson (2003, p. 1165) suggest that 'identity lacks sufficient substance and discreteness to be captured in questionnaires or single interviews'. Glynn's inability to answer her own question was due to identity being ill suited to quantitative methodologies. For Van Maanen, such pursuits are better paired with ethnography:

> Studies of organizational identity and change are often—perhaps most often—ethnographic in character. Because symbolic meaning and unfolding history are critical to any account of collective identity, there is perhaps no other substantive area for which ethnography is more suitable as a method of study. (Van Maanen, 1988, p. 244)

Identity and change were fundamental concerns for my investigation, not least because New Age discourses are typically characterised by changing lifestyles, identity (re)formation, and maintenance (see Heelas, 1996). Furthermore, there is an interesting relativist dynamic to ethnography which offers additional justification for its choice here as appropriate method: 'Ethnographies are as much about the culture of the student as they are of the studied' (Herbert, 2000, p. 563). Auto-ethnography requires us to *intentionally* blur the boundary between the researcher and the researched. I chose to orient my study at the juncture where studies of organisation engage with the social scientific rendering of family, religion, and spirituality. The latter has constituted an interest dating back to my conservative education at a Jesuit school where any attempts to develop skills of critical thinking were rapidly quashed. More recently, my mother had embraced the New Age culture with gusto, and I was fascinated if somewhat concerned by this turn of events. Burrell has commented that as scholars we are 'predisposed to study our insecurities' (personal communication, 2001). In line with the rationale proffered by Herbert (ibid.), this ethnography probably imparts as much about me as it does of my subjects.

Although full immersion is impractical (and, given the potential for institutionalisation, not always advantageous), I was able to dedicate a full year to my ethnographic endeavours. Over the course of this period, I stayed with the community on six different occasions (ranging in duration from four nights to two weeks) and maintained regular contact with participants on email forums throughout the entire period. Significantly, with the exception of the long-term residents (who constitute a minority), this sporadic participation is not dissimilar to how the majority of participants experience Findhorn.

FINDHORN: EXPLORING THE APPEAL

On 16 February 2009, I sent an email to Findhorn introducing myself as a doctoral student interested in studying their community. I received the following response:

> Dear Tom. Thank you for your enquiry. The best start here is to participate in Experience Week. It is the basic building block upon which our other programmes and explorations are built. You will find much about us on our website www.findhorn.org. I hope this is helpful. Donald (For Findhorn Foundation Enquiries)

I was struck at the apparent modularity and formality of involvement: 'Experience Week ... is the basic building block upon which the other programmes and explorations are built'. This sounded light years away from my preconceptions: communes were supposed to be *informal* counter-cultural collectives! But unlike the vast majority of communes established in the 1960s and 1970s, of which very few survived, Findhorn *had* survived.

The formality, however, did necessitate a financial outlay on my part. Even with a discount for those on low income (including students, such as myself), the fee for 'Experience Week' was £395, paid online. The whole transaction was comparable to booking a hotel or flight. For Carrette and King (2005, p. 15) this would undoubtedly constitute evidence of the 'commodification of religion'; for me, however, it was my first taste of the formalisation of New Age spirituality. All particulars (full name, date of birth, address, nationality, contact details, and so on) were required before the transaction was complete. I was also required to submit a personal statement which described my 'spiritual background' and rationale for enrolling on Experience Week. Suffice to say, as a doctoral researcher, I had plenty to declare.

Upon arrival in Scotland for Experience Week there was continued evidence of this formalised approach to organisational life, as recorded in my field notes:

HOME-GROWN EXOTICISM? IDENTITY TALES FROM A NEW AGE... 19

> I arrived at the Visitors Centre at the Findhorn Foundation (Park Campus) at the time stipulated. I introduced myself to the woman at the desk. Her appearance was entirely conventional; I think I had been expecting tie-dye attire and facial piercings. With an air of no nonsense professionalism, any remaining prejudice began to fade. Without prompting, she asked me if I was Tom Vine. I was, apparently, the last to arrive. They were expecting me. 'Before proceeding any further', she said, 'I must ask you to verify [and, it transpired, sign off] the personal details you supplied online'.

Her insistence that the details for next of kin must be accurate made me feel a little uneasy; my private prejudices momentarily resurfaced as I contemplated the grisly fate of Howie in *The Wicker Man*.

Over the course of my research, I met—and in some cases got to know very well—many different people. As my relationship with participants grew stronger, and where circumstances permitted, I oriented our conversations to get a feel for their lives prior to and beyond Findhorn. This was relatively straightforward: most were more than happy to talk about themselves. Indeed, in one case, conversation appeared to double as a form of therapy. I collected life historical data for 31 subjects in total. I focus on three of these as case studies and draw upon data from the other subjects where relevant in the subsequent analysis. Emma is a self-employed divorcee; Andy is an unmarried single man on indefinite leave from work; and Sofie is in full-time employment and is in a committed relationship.

Emma

I first met Emma on Experience Week, at which point we were both new to the community. She had just turned 50. She has one adult son and is separated from his father. She said to me early on in our acquaintance:

> Tom, you really remind me of my son.

She laughed raucously. I learned that this sort of affectionate familiarity was typical of participants. Emma was from London, like me, and apparently her son and I 'sound alike'. Emma adopted a maternal demeanour when I was present and didn't seem to tire of telling the other participants how much she enjoyed 'mothering Tom'. I could have probably allowed this to piss me off, but I actually got quite used to it. Emma's cheeriness was, however, punctuated with periods of negativity. Emma suffers from migraines and they seemed to plague her most days, so much so that she was unable to participate in some of the scheduled activities during Experience Week. Following our Experience Week, however, Emma and I stayed in touch online (as did the entire of the group). When I next returned to Findhorn, in October 2009, Emma had arranged her second visit too. I got to know her very well because it was just the two of us this time. As we walked through the community gardens, I asked Emma what constitutes the attraction for her:

> It's two-pronged. First … well, I see the community as a forum which allows me to [she pauses] … *objectify* my spirituality … it is an opportunity to relax with like-minded people. Second, I am looking to buy a home here.

She looks at me awkwardly as if to convey a sense of concession; is it appropriate to speak of conformist matters such as property acquisition, at Findhorn? Later, Emma takes a call on her mobile phone from a woman trying to sell her a small two-bed house on the 'Field of Dreams' (a development of privately owned eco-houses on Park Campus). Her earlier concerns at whether or not such materialist intentions are appropriate give way to pecuniary practicalities. Emma comments, '£190,000 is outrageous!' Having ended the phone call, she says to me:

> You know, I thought my money would go much further up here. But property here is almost as expensive as it is at home!

Home, of course, is London. Emma is not the first participant to mention to me a desire to purchase property in the Findhorn area, but with Emma I am able to witness first hand her unfolding plans to move.

Two days later, we arrange to meet for lunch again. We spend a further two hours together, over which I learn more about her past and motivation for visiting Findhorn, as well as her plans to settle here.

> When I was 17 I won a recording contract. But then shortly afterwards I fell pregnant with my son. This really rocked me and of course I had to put my singing ambitions on the backburner.

'You know, you remind me of my son', she says, again lending voice to her maternal convictions. Emma was a single parent, but beyond this she didn't go into details. She tells me that with her 'singing on the backburner', she trained as a Shiatsu healer and has fashioned a career in this mould. With her son now long 'flown the nest', her Shiatsu work beginning to 'exhaust' her, and her 'migraines getting worse', she has decided she would like to resurrect her music career. Findhorn it seems is the perfect home in this regard since it has its own recording studios, and, apparently, 'offers *real* artistic inspiration'. Such was its inspirational appeal, Emma explained that the lead singer of the Waterboys recorded an album here. Emma then showed me an enormous collection of her photographs, many of which were shot in the gardens when we were here in the summer for Experience Week. Singling out the images she wanted to incorporate as part of her album sleeve artwork and promotional material, she said again:

> You know, I would *really* love to live here.

Our conversation was interrupted by another phone call. It was another estate agent. Emma's reflective and considered tone once again gave way to business-like decorum. She was offered a three-bedroom house in Findhorn village (which is outside the geographical remit of the Foundation) for £175,000 which was, apparently, 'more reasonable' than what was quoted on Sunday. She planned to take some time to ponder the offer. Following the phone call, she appeared contemplative. Thinking through the finances, she then said:

> My London flat requires some work but even at these prices I would be able to sell it, pay off the rest of my mortgage, buy the Findhorn place, and have some leftover to live on.

Andy

I met Andy for the first time on a housekeeping workweek. Over the years, this particular workweek has affectionately become known as 'Sprinklings of Light'. At 48 Andy is an ex-nuclear engineer. He was required to take indeterminate leave from work because of illness. He suffers from mental health problems and is unmarried. Early on, Andy and I discover that we are both without girlfriends and this opens up a mutual likeness:

> I'm always on the lookout, Tom!

He chuckles with a sense of bravado. The next day we sit next to each other on the minibus that shuttles between the two campuses and resume our conversation. Yesterday's bravado is gone. In its place Andy reveals vulnerability:

> I've had a rough time lately, Tom. The relationship with my girlfriend broke down recently. ... I use prescription drugs to control my stress level and to help me sleep.

Perhaps conscious that this statement might lead to a sombre conversation, he then said more enthusiastically:

> But I soon plan to buy a small plot of land within 15 miles of the Foundation. Ideally, it will be south facing, big enough to support a wind turbine ... or have a sufficiently fast flowing river for the generation of hydroelectricity ... and will have outline planning permission for a small dwelling.

He invites me to accompany him on Wednesday afternoon (which is time-tabled as our 'free' session) to view some potential plots.

After work the following day, I sat down in the communal area of our lodge with Andy and Cherie, another Experience Week participant. Andy really opened up to us. He told us that he was having a 'wobbly day'. Over the years, he's been prescribed both anti-depressants and anti-psychotics. It seems his main problems are stress, insomnia, and a lack of 'energy' (a term which, I come to learn, has an interesting poignancy in New Age discourses). Towards the end of the evening, it was just myself and Andy left chatting in the kitchen. He first experienced mental health problems in his early twenties which were, at the time, corrected with medication. Of his teenage years, he spoke about a love of motorbikes and how much he enjoyed studying physics, a passion which led him into nuclear engineering. His love of machines continued into his late twenties, in spite of his worsening health. He talked about gaining his pilot's licence, after which he bought a microlight, and was proud to tell me that on one occasion he flew over the Hebrides and as far as Northern Ireland. However, his microlight, motorbike, and Audi TT sports car were sold when he had his breakdown (which he referred to as his 'crash'). Reminiscing about his professional work, prior to his 'crash', he said:

> I really enjoyed my work. In that line of work, you are forever on courses and conferences ... in fact, to be honest, it was a bit like being at Findhorn ... if you know what I mean!

This was an extremely insightful revelation and constituted an important watershed moment in my research. This is because it lent credence to a thesis I was developing that organisational participation not only carries existential currency, but is substitutable between different forms of organisation.

Andy then went on to talk about his eventual departure from work.

> [T]here was a fair bit of ill feeling.

He explained how his relationship with both colleagues and family—his brother in particular—was strained at this time because they had difficulty understanding the legitimacy of his condition. In a later conversation, he and Luke (another Sprinklings of Light participant) were discussing the same period of his life. Andy said:

> I often half wish I was missing a leg … because then my problem would be manifestly obvious to others. … It was difficult … especially at work.

In spite of this, Andy speaks fondly of his work. Indeed, he later spoke of a moment of clarity which involved him recounting his time at work.

> For years I felt de-personalised … de-realised and detached. It's like being asleep, but unpleasant. And then one day, I woke up.

I asked what he meant.

> Last year I was staying at Jamie's house in Ireland.

Jamie was another of our co-participants this week. Both Andy and Jamie had met previously on a workweek.

> I was chatting with Jamie's son. He asked me about the work I did before my crash [and subsequent indeterminate leave]. I was talking about the nuclear power plant and he was asking me lots of questions. We spoke for hours about something I was passionate about, and at that moment I realised I had woken up!

This comment triggered in Andy a reminiscence of work. He genuinely missed it. I was beginning to understand.

The next afternoon we went to view the potential plots he'd mentioned earlier in the week. As we drove through the Scottish countryside, Andy

24   T. VINE

spoke at length about how he had met his last partner on his Experience Week (which was in 2001), but that it hadn't worked out. This had clearly upset him.

Following the Sprinklings of Light workweek, and in response to a message I had sent, I received the following email:

> 'Hi Tom! I go back to Findhorn on Saturday ... yippee ... for another month. I enjoyed it so much I just don't want to be anywhere else to be honest and at the moment see myself spending most of this year—if not my life—there! I guess in many ways I have connected with things inside and out that are truly worth living for. ... Cluny [Campus] is a great place to spend time, there are such nice folks there, just a big loving family ... lots of people to have fun [and] sing with. I lived there and 'worked' in Maintenance in the Park [Campus], though it was just really pure fun for me. ... My old stresshead did play up quite a lot so there were quite a few days 'off sick' but I received lots of support and impromptu massages and of course many hugs which helped lots; and I made lots of friends. ... I really am changing in many ways, all for the better. ... I am definitely in a healing and transformational process, I have made some beautiful breakthroughs. ... I think for me the most important thing is just to be there regardless of quite what I am doing! Love, Andy.

I saw Andy briefly again over the summer. He had met another woman and was sharing his new caravan with her. He and I didn't spend and see much of one another this time round; I was committed to another workweek. In any event, the distractions of his new girlfriend were clearly preferable to those of an inquisitive male doctoral student.

Sofie

Like Andy, I met Sofie for the first time during the Sprinklings of Light workweek. Sofie is 31 and Dutch. She is attractive and very friendly, a combination which seemed to elicit unwanted attention from older male admirers at Findhorn. However, in spite of this, she regards Findhorn as the 'panacea' to her problems. Her problems, it seems, stem from a history of work dissatisfaction. Midway through the week, I joined Sofie in the community's hot tub. After 15 minutes or so, it was just the two of us. I took the opportunity to steer the conversation towards Sofie's work history. Her first job was working with TNT.

> 'It was a big company', she told me. 'I loved the job'.

However, four years later, and in the interests of career advancement, she decided to leave. She got a job at a smaller company. However,

> After about a year and half, I went to see a job counsellor.

Sofie says that her relationship with her parents was strained at the time, but felt that her bigger concern was that she wasn't getting the satisfaction in her new job that she so craved. The counsellor suggested that Sofie should visit Findhorn. This was probably a risky strategy for a therapist, but Sofie didn't hesitate.

> I had my leaving party on the Friday and was booked on a flight out to Scotland the following morning.

Sofie had agreed with the counsellor that she would stay at Findhorn for a fortnight. She ended up staying for two years and, even though she is now resident once again in the Netherlands, regularly visits Findhorn for short periods. Upon her return to the Netherlands, she got a job at a gas and metering company. I asked whether she is happier at work now. 'Not really'. But since she met her current partner there she tells me: 'every cloud has a silver lining'. Her partner is her boss.

Following the Sprinklings of Light workweek, I visited Sofie in Antwerp, not far from her home in the Netherlands. She told me she was planning to leave her job very soon, and that it 'just isn't right for me at this time'. She explained that she used to be artistic and would 'quite like to pursue a career in that'. I asked whether she felt a sense of insecurity moving in and out of jobs all the time. She replied:

> Well, I always have Findhorn. Findhorn is my rock.

Interpretation and Analysis

In establishing a contextual frame of reference, interpretation of the life historical data I have collected (not just of the three cases cited but of the 28 other participants I got to know well) is first considered in terms of demographics. These data in relation to nationality, gender, and age are significant in respect of the work life histories examined further on.

Riddell, who wrote about the community in the 1980s, reported the following:

> At present our guests come from mainly northern Europe, the United States and Australia, with a sprinkling from other areas. Most are white and middle class. We have never done a survey, but my sociologically trained eye reads that the majority are between 30 and 45, in various kinds of caring professions, already concerned with ... their own identity ... there are more than average single and divorced people. (Riddell, 1991, p. 112)

Of the 1990s, Sutcliffe—who wrote about Experience Week—imparted similar findings:

> [The] members of my group came from England, Germany, the United States, Brazil and Switzerland. We numbered 14, with a typical Findhorn profile: ten women, four men, all white Euro-Americans, and three-quarters in their 30s and 40s. ... [Most] were highly educated (nearly two thirds had attended university). (Sutcliffe, 2000, pp. 217, 218)

Of my own research, in terms of nationality, there was the same occidental bias as reported by both Riddell and Sutcliffe. In terms of gender, my data suggest that participation is not as biased towards women as it once was. Of the 18 participants on my Experience Week, 11 were women and 6 were men. In terms of ethnicity, the situation appears to be much the same as it was in the 1980s and 1990s. Although there were two non-white people on my Experience Week, there was none on the workweeks, and over the course of the entire year, I only encountered another three non-white people visiting or staying within the community. In terms of age, my data gave a mean of 46; hence somewhat older than that previously reported by both Riddell and Sutcliffe.

In all three accounts, participants come from those nations which are most 'advanced' economically. On a practical level, this means their subjects are more likely to have the money to travel to communities such as Findhorn but, perhaps more importantly, it is 'advanced' economies which are increasingly composed of contingent and precariously employed labour (DiPrete, Goux, Maurin, & Quesnel-Vallee, 2006; Hitt, Keats, & DeMarie, 1998). In terms of gender, although both Riddell and Sutcliffe report an overwhelming bias towards female participants, my data suggest this is no longer the case. Interestingly, women have long occupied precarious positions in the labour market (particularly in part-time and temporary capacities), but the New Capitalism bestows this arrangement on men too. It may be that the increasing participation of men at Findhorn can be understood, at least in part, by this change.

Familial Identity

Sutcliffe does not explore the familial profiles of his Findhorn subjects, but Riddell comments that there is a high proportion of single and divorced people. My own research corroborates this. Of the 31 subjects I got to know well (18 from Experience Week, 9 from Sprinklings of Light, and 4 from the maintenance week) only four were married and of these, two had been previously divorced. Of my subjects, 13% were married compared to a British national average of 51% (ONS, 2010a). A further six were in cohabiting relationships. Of the remaining 21, all were either divorced (and had not remarried) or were single. In sum, two thirds of all participants were single and lived alone.

Of the three case studies presented, all (but particularly those of Emma and Andy) convey a sense of familial anomie. In the case of Emma, she is separated from her grown up son's father. Emma is fairly typical of many Findhorn participants in that she is single, and with her adult son having 'flown the nest', she lives alone. Furthermore she had affected a maternal demeanour through her interactions with others, particularly to me (having reminded her of her son). Finally, she was actively trying to buy a new home in the vicinity such that she could spend her days with 'like-minded people'. In the case of Andy, at 48, he has never married nor had children. However, he did speak fondly of the relationship he established with a woman he met on his Experience Week in 2001. Andy explicitly mentions the strain his psychological problems placed on his relationship with his family; he is especially regretful about the situation with his brother. For Andy, Findhorn is described as just 'a big loving family', which as a childless single man in his late forties is something apparently absent in Andy's own life. Like Emma, Andy is seeking to buy a home nearby. Finally, her work concerns notwithstanding, Sofie also describes the strained nature of her relationship with her parents. Interestingly, in spite of her dislike of her current appointment, it is justified—to some extent at least—on the basis that she is now dating her boss ('every cloud has a silver lining').

Of the other participants, Jamie (Sprinklings of Light); Rochelle (maintenance workweek participant); and Harvey (maintenance workweek focaliser) all described life histories that resonate in a similar way. Jamie, from Ireland, separated from his wife in 1988. I asked Jamie what had first brought him to Findhorn:

> Well, I'd been vaguely interested in spiritual things and ... er ... well, my children had flown the nest.

As a divorcee and now living alone, he commented of his new circumstances during a group session later that week:

> For me, this community is my family now.

For Rochelle, when asked what had prompted her to visit Findhorn, she conveyed a sense of motherhood engendered through her discovery of Findhorn. She recounted this 'discovery' for our benefit: 'I do not have children myself ... but when I returned home from Findhorn, it was like I'd *given birth* to so much important information'. Rochelle placed significant emphasis on the words 'given birth'.

Finally, Harvey describes a series of historical events from which we can identify a pattern:

> I separated from my partner seven years ago. I decided I wanted to go to China because I realised I was fed up with the Western world. I taught English as a foreign language and had a little group of friends ... it was the perfect arrangement ... we lived together and cooked for each other and had such fun ... but after two years I wanted more. ... I wanted to go to Findhorn. At that point, I received a letter from my ex-wife suggesting we try it again. So I flew to Germany. But when she saw me at the airport, she said it wasn't going to work. My decision was made ... and I flew straight to Findhorn. That was three years ago and I've been here ever since.

Following his divorce, Harvey sought a sense of kinship in the close knit group of friends he had in China. He reconsidered 'conventional' family life thereafter (upon receiving the letter from his ex-wife), but since that wasn't going to work, he headed straight for Findhorn. On each subsequent occasion (initially his divorce and then later the unrealised possibility that he and his ex-wife might rekindle their marriage), Harvey sought and found a sense of kinship elsewhere.

More explicitly still, on my visit to see Sofie in Antwerp, we briefly discussed the familial qualities of Findhorn. To emphasise how significant this role was at Findhorn, she commented:

> I have a friend who says that if she ever got divorced she'd go and live in Findhorn—for the family feel.

In this way, familial history—and recognition that the nuclear family is a fragile institution—appears to be commensurate with the predisposition to visit or live in Findhorn. Indeed, beyond historical/biographical circumstance, the familial feel of Findhorn was widely acknowledged by my subjects. Rochelle's metaphor of 'giving birth' is certainly interesting, but more usually the term 'family' itself is used metaphorically at Findhorn. Such occasions include Cherie regretting one morning that she attuned to work in the kitchen while the rest of our group were cleaning the lodges. By way of expressing this, she said to us when we were reunited at lunchtime: 'I'm missing my family today!' Bruno regularly began his emails to us writing 'To my dear Findhorn Flowers' ...; Leanne notably began one of her emails: 'To my Beautiful Extended Family'. As the eldest members of our group, Louis and Janine (husband and wife) regularly described themselves as 'grandparents' to the rest of us. Anna, one of our focalisers during the Sprinklings of Light week, passed a similar sentiment. She had noticed, for example, that I was quite taken with one of the member's babies, and suggested that I would make 'a good father one day'. She explained how she herself wasn't a parent in the conventional sense, but is a 'grandparent to many children'.

At Findhorn, it seems, biological precedent holds no monopoly over the terminology. In this sense, then, participants at Findhorn adopt the terminology of conventional familial roles but apply them in non-conventional contexts. For Emma, it was a maternal demeanour; for Louis and Janine it was a grandparental role as regards the rest of our group; for Anna—and despite never having married or borne children herself—it was a grandparental role as regards the various children born to younger community members. The importance of broadening our understanding of family beyond its biological, conventional framing was illustrated by Bruno who, following our Experience Week, emailed us a web link to the footage of the opening performance at the infamous Woodstock festival in 1969. It was Richie Havens singing 'Freedom'. Bruno sent the link to mark the 40th anniversary of the festival, but implied that this song was relevant to our lives. The lyrics are as follows:

> Freedom, freedom, freedom ... (refrain)
> Sometimes I feel like a motherless child ...

A long way from my home …
Sometimes I feel like I'm almost gone …
A long, long, long, way, way from my home.

The pertinence of the lyrics to the apparently dislocated situation in which many of the participants found themselves was remarkable. As Goode (1964) argues, family is a cultural construct; its nuclear iteration is a relatively recent configuration. It is tempting to view Findhorn as a kind of *surrogate* family for those lacking a conventional familial background. Certainly, Christiano (1986) in his study *Church as a Family Surrogate* finds some legitimacy to this relationship in the field of religious studies. More recently, Cao (2005) reports similar findings. In practice, however, surrogacy implies a default or 'proper' referent. The nuclear family is certainly conventional (although increasingly less so), but to suggest it is in some way 'proper' would imply a bias towards a particular cultural norm. The question as to whether Findhorn serves as a family surrogate makes too many assumptions. However, we can say with greater confidence that the concept of 'family' at Findhorn is a powerful thematic and is used both metaphorically (e.g., Anna describing herself as a 'grandmother' to every child in the community, in spite of never having borne children herself) and romantically (e.g., Bruno addressing us as his 'Dear Findhorn Flowers'). Of their study of Glastonbury, Prince and Riches (2000, p. 118) commented that:

> Family was a word with many meanings. It certainly did not imply an adult male and adult female living in the same residential unit with varying numbers of children parented by both. Family could equally be applied to a group of adults living together with no blood ties; … or to a spiritual group which meets regularly; or, clearly in a metaphoric sense, to describe the feelings in the whole Glastonbury area.

The understanding of family at Findhorn is very similar. Findhorn does not offer a surrogate for the lost or fragmented nuclear family, but a distinct alternative, an alternative which apparently resurrects the some of the familial identity associated with its nuclear iteration, but with a very different guise.

Organisational Identity

The vocabulary that describes economic organisation—*company*, *firm*, and *corporation*—has generic meanings beyond the parameters of their economic application. Of *company*, the first entry listed in the Oxford

English Dictionary is 'companionship, fellowship, society'. The second entry describes 'a number of individuals assembled or associated together'. As regards *firm*, the same dictionary notes the word's etymological precedence to the Latin *firmare*, 'to strengthen'. Finally, 'corporation' is described as 'the action or result of incorporating', which is itself defined as a means to 'combine or unite into one body ... to form a whole'. With these more nuanced interpretations, it becomes easier to conceptualise the workplace as a site of organisational identity and belonging. However, given the culture of flexibility and fragmentation that has dominated recent discourses of organisation, it is implied that economic organisations no longer reflect these definitions. This section therefore explores Findhorn as a company/firm/corporation and hence an *alternative* source of organisational identity.

Sutcliffe does not explore his participants' work backgrounds. Riddell (1991, p. 132) comments simply that 'the majority [of participants] ... are in various kinds of caring professions'. My own data depart somewhat from this observation. Of the 31 subjects I asked about their work backgrounds, only two can in any sense be considered working in the caring professions. Interestingly, Elizabeth who is unemployed, but described herself as a social worker, has had enough working in her industry: 'I'm fed up of social work; I don't want to help people anymore. I want to help myself'. Her comment is said dryly, but this should not betray its revelation. Findhorn, as we have seen, is a forum in which—through the opportunities for identity work afforded by togetherness and human interaction—participants are able to 'help themselves'.

Each of the three case studies presented above conveys a sense of organisational anomie. In the case of Emma, she has a history of changing occupation and hasn't really established a career path in an identity-defining sense. Most recently she has followed an entrepreneurial path and provides Shiatsu services for individual clients. She works alone and lacks the support, security, and predictability of a conventional workplace and its tenure. In the case of Andy, he spoke fondly of his previous work as a nuclear engineer but forced into early retirement on health grounds, now lacks *any* sense of workplace collective. Notably, Andy parallels the communal element of his earlier work (in particular 'courses and conferences') to the communal element of Findhorn. Later, his description of the scene and circumstances in which he describes his 'waking up' from a mental existence characterised as 'de-personalised, de-realised, and detached' is of salience too since it occurred when he was reminiscing about his work life.

32   T. VINE

The case of Sofie is, perhaps, most remarkable. She has had a variety of jobs in different industries but has struggled to find the enthusiasm her contemporaries apparently feel. Although this tendency is attributed to her choices (rather than exogenous factors), it is nonetheless significant. There are several characteristics of Sofie's case which are noteworthy. First, she enjoyed working in a large company (TNT); but does not share the same enthusiasm working as part of smaller entrepreneurial start-ups. Second, her career counsellor recommended Findhorn as a means of ameliorating her condition. It is interesting that the counsellor himself acknowledged that her cure was not going to be found through the interface of one-to-one therapy but that it was the focus on groups at Findhorn that appeared to elicit the desired change. Third, when we met in Antwerp and I enquired whether her proposal to switch jobs once again would not bring with it a sense of insecurity, she described Findhorn as her 'rock', and in so doing attributed to it the sense of permanence and continuity others may seek in a single, enduring, place of work.

I discussed work histories with 24 of my subjects. Of these, just 5 (or 21%) were in full-time permanent employment. This compares to the national average of 44% (ONS, 2010b). The other 19 are contingent workers (9), unemployed (6), or retired (4). Furthermore, of the whole sample, only two suggested that they were happy in their work. At one point during my research, I worked alongside Yuuka weeding and performing various other horticultural tasks in the Findhorn Gardens. Weeding was, for Yuuka, a form of 'bliss'. She contrasted it to her job in Japan which she 'hated'. Her English was broken, but I understood that her dissatisfaction stemmed from the intensity of the Japanese working culture. An email received from Yuuka following our Experience Week is relevant in this regard:

> It feels like ages since we were [at Findhorn]. I am sure Tokyo has the same effect as London or even more. I have already worked for some days having commuted squeezed in jam-packed train car. Findhorn life was a paradise as compared with this reality.

Of those unemployed or engaged in contingent work, many (including, of course, Emma) hinted at the negative effects of organisational isolation. On the evening of the first day of my Experience Week, I spoke to two women who, interested in my research, described for me their work histories. My field notes from that evening read as follows:

> In the hot tub, I get chatting to two women who are not on our course. It transpires that one of them is a Findhorn veteran, and the other now resident at the site for over a year. The veteran tells me how she ran a shop and that was how she 'engaged' with her community but when she sold the shop she quickly got bored and felt isolated, hence joining the Findhorn community. The younger woman told of how she had lived and worked at Findhorn for over a year now and how it was the longest she'd stayed put in her adult life and—like the veteran—attributed this to the 'communal strength of Findhorn'.

Of course, running a [small] shop is fundamentally different from working in a [large] organisation. However, typically they both involve communal interaction. The 'communal strength' of Findhorn is thus proffered as salving the negative effects of communal isolation. In a similar vein, this time on the Sprinklings of Light workweek, I chatted with Jamie as we cleaned the windows in pairs, he on the inside, and myself on the outside. My field notes for that day read as follows:

> Working with him like this, I got to know Jamie a bit better and once again steered the conversation towards his work history. ... As regards his work, he is a draughtsman; he does drawings mainly of roofs, but he is self-employed and has been since 1980. He tells me that he rarely works on site but typically works alone at home.

Isolation at work is something Bud, another of our maintenance week focalisers, also imparted in recounting his work history:

> Originally I worked for the railroad ... I had to travel a lot for work ... I lost a couple of relationships as a result ... I've done all sorts.

He then becomes self-employed. In his own words, 'I was a handyman, a jack of all trades ... occasionally I would bring somebody else in [to help on particular jobs], but predominantly I worked alone'. Bud's work life has been classically contingent. Although he had a single employer early on, he had to travel extensively and, as he admits, this took its toll on his personal relationships. After that, he did 'allsorts' of jobs, before eventually becoming self-employed where he mostly worked alone. In this way, it is easy to see the appeal the community of Findhorn holds for Bud.

Summary

Life at Findhorn is frequently represented as 'exotic', at least by comparison to the everyday realities of a conventional Western existence. The ethnography presented here suggests instead that the appeal is very much built on prosaic factors, the very factors which were once a cornerstone of that conventional existence. Findhorn presents an alternative for absent or fragmented familial and workplace lives. In the interests of clarity, I have analysed family and organisation separately. In practice, however, they are not especially dissimilar from one another. The 'decline' of the nuclear family—to some extent at least—parallels the 'decline' of the conventional workplace. These findings add credence to the New Capitalism thesis. Whereas commune participants in the 1960s and 1970s had 'opted out' of mainstream society for what they regarded as the creativity-stifling trappings of workplace bureaucracies and the constraints—both institutional and sexual—of the nuclear family, comparable communities today attract participants for precisely the opposite reason: these participants are searching for the existential security of the collective. They seek the sense of routine, familiarity, and belonging that both family and employment once provided. Ironically, then, the exotic is *not* the whisky barrel houses, the fairies, the nude bathing, the servant leadership, or the Tolkienesque woodland lodgings but that which was once both conventional and conformist: familial and organisational identity.

I gained enormously by living and working at Findhorn—and not just in terms of the ethnographic data imparted in this chapter. The experience enhanced my view of the world; I am now a passionate gardener, for example, and more sensitive to the spiritual and effervescent aspects of the human condition. I can only hope that my participants gained in some way from my involvement too.

References

Barley, S., & Kunda, G. (2004). *Gurus, Hired Guns, and Warm Bodies: Itinerant Experts in a Knowledge Economy*. Princeton: Princeton University Press.
Boltanski, L., & Chiapello, É. (2006). *The New Spirit of Capitalism*. London: Verso.

Cao, N. (2005). The Church as a Surrogate Family for Working Class Immigrant Chinese Youth: An Ethnography of Segmented Assimilation. *Sociology of Religion, 66*(2), 183–200.

Carrette, J., & King, R. (2005). *Selling Spirituality: The Silent Takeover of Religion.* London: Routledge.

Chistiano, K. (1986). Church as a Family Surrogate: Another Look at Family Ties, Anomie, and Church Involvement. *The Social Scientific Study of Religion, 25*(3), 339–354.

Crang, M., & Cook, I. (2007). *Doing Ethnographies.* London: Sage.

DiPrete, T., Goux, D., Maurin, E., & Quesnel-Vallee, A. (2006). Work and Pay in Flexible and Regulated Labor Markets: A Generalized Perspective on Institutional Evolution and Inequality Trends in Europe and the US. *Research in Social Stratification and Mobility, 24*(3), 311–332.

Giddens, A. (1991). *Modernity and Self-Identity: Self and Society in the Late Modern Age.* Cambridge: Polity Press.

Glynn, M. (1998). Individuals' Need for Organizational Identification (nOID): Speculations on Individual Differences in the Propensity to Identify. In D. Whetton & P. Godfrey (Eds.), *Identity in Organizations: Building Theory Through Conversations.* London: Sage.

Goode, W. (1964). *The Family.* Upper Saddle River, NJ: Prentice Hall.

Heelas, P. (1996). *The New Age Movement: The Celebration of Self and the Sacralization of Modernity.* Oxford: Blackwell.

Herbert, S. (2000). For Ethnography. *Progress in Human Geography, 24*(4), 550–568.

Hitt, M., Keats, B., & DeMarie, S. (1998). Navigating in the New Competitive Landscape: Building Strategic Flexibility and Competitive Advantage in the 21st Century. *The Academy of Management Executive, 12*(4), 22–42.

Office of National Statistics. (2010a). It Should Be Stressed That While My Own Ethnographic Data Is Transnational. This Source is Based on British Data. Retrieved from http://www.statistics.gov.uk/CCI/nugget.asp?ID=1652&Pos=6&ColRank=2&Rank=1000

Office of National Statistics. (2010b). This Figure is Calculated from Data Sourced from the December 2010 Statistical Bulletin. Published by the Office of National Statistics. Retrieved from http://www.statistics.gov.uk/pdfdir/lmsuk1210.pdf

Popenoe, D. (1988). *Disturbing the Nest: Family Change and Decline in Modern Societies.* New York: de Gruyter.

Prince, R., & Riches, D. (2000). *The New Age in Glastonbury: The Construction of Religious Movements.* Oxford: Berghahn.

Riddell, C. (1991). *The Findhorn Community: Creating a Human Identity for the 21st Century.* Findhorn: Findhorn Press.

Sennett, R. (1998). *The Corrosion of Character: The Personal Consequences of Work in the New Capitalism*. New York and London: W.W. Norton & Company.

Silverman, D. (2007). *A Very Short, Fairly Interesting and Reasonably Cheap Book About Qualitative Research*. London: Sage.

Sutcliffe, S. (2000). A Colony of Seekers: Findhorn in the 1990s. *Journal of Contemporary Religion, 15*(2), 215–231.

Sveningsson, S., & Alvesson, M. (2003). Managing Managerial Identities: Organizational Fragmentation, Discourse and Identity Struggle. *Human Relations; Studies Towards the Integration of the Social Sciences, 56*(10), 1163–1193.

Van Maanen, J. (1988). *Tales of the Field*. Chicago: Chicago University Press.

Weigert, A., & Hastings, R. (1977). Identity Loss, Family, and Social Change. *American Journal of Sociology, 82*(6), 1171–1184.

CHAPTER 3

Wrestling with Online Avatars: Technology and Sexual Transformation

Paul Driscoll-Evans

As a registered nurse, I spent the best part of a decade working in the field of sexual health and HIV care. During this time I saw first-hand the extent to which the stigma associated with HIV, and sexual ill-health in general, resulted in significant negative psychosocial impacts on those diagnosed. I also gained an appreciation that well-tailored health care services are essential to improving the experiences of those affected. However, it became apparent that the majority of sexual health services adhere to a medical model of service provision which places health professionals at the centre of service design as opposed to the users of the services themselves. As a consequence, upon transitioning from clinical practice to my first academic post I opted to dedicate my research to uncovering narratives related to the practice of unsafe sex by straddling queer-theory and health research. As a methodology, ethnography provides me with the ideal lens through which sexual conduct narratives can be explored. It enables me to focus on individual narratives while reflecting analytically on a much wider conceptual landscape.

P. Driscoll-Evans (✉)
University of Suffolk, Ipswich, UK

© The Author(s) 2018
T. Vine et al. (eds.), *Ethnographic Research and Analysis*,
https://doi.org/10.1057/978-1-137-58555-4_3

INTRODUCTION

This chapter uses ethnographic fieldwork to gain insight into sexual risk taking within Norfolk's Lesbian, Gay, Bisexual, and Transgender (LGBT) community. Particular attention is given to examining men who have sex with men's (MSM) use of social/sexual networking sites.

In framing the ethnographic research on the experiences of MSM, a conscious decision was made to reject boundaried classifications of sexual orientation such as gay or bisexual, thus enabling the consideration of more fluid sexual identities and practices. As a man who has sex with men myself, I share Boellstorff's (2011, p. 287) concerns that the MSM classification can negatively influence the perception of sexual action between men by stripping it of romantic potential. While acknowledging this stance, the parameters of the research were set to avoid the alienation of potential participants.

In referencing time spent with Norfolk's LGBT community, this chapter will explore how the internet can present a challenge to traditionally held concepts of personhood and human geographies. Central to this chapter's argument will be the view that the internet provides individuals with the opportunity to use multi-modal practices to write themselves into being online and the implications of this to the ethnographer (Beneito-Montagut, 2011; Livingstone, 2009). A hybrid of Van Maanen's (2011), p. 74) 'realist-confessional' ethnographical approaches will be used in the analysis and presentation of findings.

METHODOLOGY

In recognition of Inhorn and Brown's (1990) suggestion that the examination of factors influencing the incidence of infectious diseases (in this case those transmitted via unprotected sexual intercourse) requires a macro- and microethnographic approach, a variety of methods for data collection were utilised in this project. The primary method adopted was to carry out an extended period of participant observation within a non-governmental organisation (NGO) focusing on health promotion in the MSM community in Norfolk. This approach enabled a broad overview of attitudes towards intentional condom-free sexual intercourse to be gained. This was to be complimented by the use of semi-structured interviews focusing on micro-scale components of the phenomenon, specifically the more intimate narratives on the subject. A research placement was secured with Norfolk's LGBT Project as a volunteer MSM worker in order to facilitate access to narratives from the local MSM community. The organisation was enthusiastic and supportive regarding the possibility of fieldwork being carried out through their service. An overt, consent-led research approach was operated with full disclosure of the research intentions to all participants, as was my status as a man who has sex with men. All those encountered during the period of participant observation were receptive to this approach with the project's management team acting as key gatekeepers to the local MSM community.

I spent seven months working with the LGBT Project. This involved twice weekly contact with the Project, usually during evenings and weekends when the Project is most active. Activities undertaken as part of participant observation included health promotion work in commercialised MSM venues, the facilitation of support groups, and even assisting with the LGBT youth group's Christmas party.

The ethnographic approach of studying and gaining understanding through action (Murchison, 2010, p. 5) formed a sound basis for my study. While, at times, the period of participant observation proved to be demanding, the research process proved to be highly rewarding. It also enabled a natural evolution of the parameters of the research project to incorporate consideration of wider themes as they emerged. My observations in respect of the pervasive presence of mobile technologies resulting in transformative effects on sexual personhood, action, and spacialities is a prime example of this.

The Smartphone

They lurk on tables between pints of lager throughout Norfolk's gay bars. They are never far from the sweaty palms of the LGBT youth. Their presence is announced through perpetual vibrations, chirpings, and the pale blue glow emitted from their screens. Mobile devices were ever-present during this fieldwork; they are in constant use. Norfolk's MSM, it seems, is nothing without his smartphone. At times, it seems that Norfolk's LGBT community is abuzz with the exchange of tweets, status updates, and the thrum of instant message replies.

The use of the internet as a conduit through which interpersonal relationships can be formed is evidenced in the popularity of gay dating and hook-up websites. It has been observed that the popularity of these has grown dramatically in the last decade (Hall, Park, Song, & Cody, 2010, p. 117; Mowlabocus, 2010), and as a result in a society with a proliferation of mobile internet-accessing technologies and a robust Wi-Fi/3G/4G network, MSM have myriad ways in which they can render themselves online.

Online Avatars and Virtual Spacialities

While from a programming perspective, social network and dating websites are perfunctory databases which encourage users to act as straight forward 'data miners', I here explore the wider social significance of these sites. In common with Livingstone (2009, p. 93), it is suggested that the internet, and social networking sites specifically, provide the opportunity for the MSM to use multi-modal practices to write himself into being online. To achieve this, the MSM creates an online profile, populating it with personal information, text, photographs, and, occasionally, video content consequently keying themselves into the digital space. This process allows for the formation of online avatars. I contend that online avatars should not be seen as passive database constructs but rather they should be viewed as a challenge to traditional concepts of personhood in that they possess a degree of independent agency and present an idealised totality of personal identity in the virtual space which other users are able to examine and interact with. Notably, a Facebook profile (an online avatar), for example, exists even when its creator is offline; it does not blink out of existence when the user logs off. It remains available to those who may wish to discover it and will indiscriminately share, based on predetermined privacy settings, personal information. Over the course of my research, I discovered that there is a clear expectation that avatars will fully disclose personal details of those being embodied. Those which failed to do this were treated with caution.

Through construction of an online avatar, the MSM generates a dual social presence, inhabiting two spacialities simultaneously. This presents a challenge to the ethnographer; failure to acknowledge the presence and impact of virtual geographies will result in limited ethnographic insight. In order to contextualise a discussion addressing MSM's use of virtual space, it is beneficial to first consider the mercurial nature of the human geographies that they have generated. It is not my intention to present a totality of the history of queer geographies but to provide an illustration of the dynamic nature of the socio-political changes endured by men who have sex with men (Hall et al., 2010, p. 17) and the impact this has had upon their spacialities.

As a manifestation of heterocentric hegemonic discourses framing male same-gender sexual intercourse as immoral and damaging to both the individual and wider society (Kitchin, 2002, p. 208), prior to the late 1960s, sexual contact between two men was classified as illegal in the United Kingdom. This status was rigorously enforced, resulting in prosecution of hundreds of individuals, profoundly impacting the intimate lives of gay men and resulted in the creation of a unique network of sexualised geographical spaces. During this period, the homosexual was not considered a member of society; he was an outcast and without legal rights was denied the ability to seek 'legitimate pleasures' (Weeks, 2000, p. 217). Under constant threat of imprisonment, MSM were unable to freely enact their intimate selves, instead forced to inhabit an existence of clandestine interaction and secrecy. As the reach of the law extended into the 'private' sphere, furtive encounters in public spaces were often regarded as the safest and, for the majority, the only means of experiencing same-sex intimacy. This resulted in the sexualisation of the United Kingdom's landscape with many spaces cultivating a hybrid identity: lay-bys on motorways, public toilets, prisons, dormitories, and park land all becoming conduits for sexual exploration and the enactment of homosexuality (Hubbard, 2001). Homosexual sex and the public setting became inextricably linked; homosexual sex *was* public sex (Califia, 1994), and for those able to read hidden cultural coding, homosexual sex spaces could be found in both rural and metropolitan settings.

Following the publication of the 1967 Sexual Offences Act, male same-gender sexual contact was no longer classified as 'indecent' in the United Kingdom, a move which resulted in significant legislative changes to the civil and legal rights afforded to men who have sex with men. Consequently homosexuals were able to experience and organise themselves outside of the 'closet' for the first time; this politicised the hitherto invisible cohort, with organisations such as the Gay Liberation Front emerging in the early 1970s and seeking to position homosexuality as a 'political issue', actively campaigning for civil rights awards (Weeks, 1991, p. 186). As politically empowered individuals, MSM began to experience increased visibility in all socio-political arenas; from a human geography perspective, this was most acutely manifested in the rise of the commercialised MSM space that occurred in the 1970s and 1980s.

Legal recognition enabled men to have sex with men legitimately for the first time in modern British history. They were provided with permission to experience legitimate desires for sex, for community, and for a voice. This heralded the discreet but widespread emergence of publicly identified 'gay' social spaces across the United Kingdom, environments catering for those with same-gender attraction which facilitates identify formation and promoted social cohesion. The commercialised transformation of public space into homo space is evidenced in every major city in the West. However, despite the increasing visibility that MSM experienced in the 1970s and 1980s, Joseph Bristow (1989, p. 74) noted:

> In Britain it is possible to be gay [only] in specific places; notably the club scene and social networks often organised around campaigning organisations.

Publication of the Sexual Offences Act in 1967 did not result in instantaneous equality in civil rights affordances between MSM and their heterosexual peers; homosexuals could claim space for their own and demonstrate intimacy but only in silos on the margins of society.

Liberation from the fear of prosecution did not lessen the demand for spaces that enabled anonymous sexual contact for some members of the MSM community. Indeed, in response to this demand, many commercialised MSM social spaces cultivated a hybrid identity by incorporating 'dark/back rooms' into their premises, erotising social spaces to cater for those seeking anonymous sexual encounters (Parker, 1999). It should be noted that those who continued to use public space (dark/back rooms included) for sexualised means persisted in putting themselves at risk of prosecution under public indecency law; it is, therefore, valid to question why, when provided with freedom from one form of prosecution, MSM continued to engage in this high-risk activity.

As this discussion demonstrates, the spacialities inhabited by MSM are innately shaped by, and tied to, the socio-political evolution this group has undergone. In 2016 MSM living in the United Kingdom are experiencing unprecedented equality in civil rights entitlements and visibility in the mainstream media. Despite this a heterosexual hegemony remains, and as such Foster (2001) suggests homosexuals have been drawn to the allure of cyberspace as a means of exploring an alternative to this. Lying beyond the physical world, this digital space provides an opportunity for the MSM to use multi-modal practices to write himself into being online (Livingstone, 2009, p. 93). This is an illuminating process empowering even the most 'fully formed' homosexual to construct and declare (out) himself in this setting. Furthermore, in digital space MSM can experience an enhanced state of sexual agency, autonomy, and equality online; both heterosexuals and MSM can construct themselves.

The impact of the digital space on MSM has evolved as the technology itself has developed; where once relatively impersonal desktop computers were the only means through which individuals could go online, digital space is now, of course, accessible through a variety of means: laptop computers, tablets, smartphones, smart televisions, and even smart-watches provide MSM with increasingly intimate personal relationships with—and mediated by—technology. Prime examples of this are the applications (apps) that harness the power of geographical positioning software to inform users where their closest available potential sexual partners are located. Accessible principally through mobile technologies, this software allows for users to create profiles online, complete with photos, demographic information, and sexual preferences, facilitating both transient and lasting interpersonal relationship formations. The apps add to the growing list of dating and 'hook-up' sites targeting the MSM cohort: gaydar.co.uk, squirt.org, ladslads.net, and thecruisingground.com representing just a small selection. Sexually explicit in nature, many of these websites and apps ensure that the nature of the service being provided is overt. The Grindr app, for example, proudly boasts that users should 'Log on to get off', and Squirt.org advertises itself as being the United Kingdom's top site for 'Hot 'n' Horny Hook-ups'. They present a highly sexualised virtual spatiality which challenge traditional concepts of gay spaces. This is a sentiment openly recognised by Squirt.org which, in composing global positioning system (GPS)-powered listings of local public sex spaces, actively positions itself as the evolution of the traditional cruising ground. Adhering to public sex etiquette, Squirt.org is one of the few MSM-centric sites that encourages anonymous sexual contact (member's profiles routinely do not include face pictures) and provides virtual connectivity as a means of arranging sexual encounters in public sex spaces (Mowlabocus, 2008). In offering a new model of sexual connectivity which straddles the established cruising experience and social networking, Squirt.org demonstrates the impact of technology on intimate practices. These networks exhibit a transformative effect on the ontologies of everyday objects, with the telephone being transformed into a sexualised object, woven into the creation of a subcultural space (Bell, 2006, p. 397), and the computer hardware itself becoming a conduit for erotic potential. These online networks have also transformed the way in which MSM geographies are constituted; gone are the days when homosexual spacialities could be mapped in the material world by those possessing knowledge of even the most hidden of enclaves. Virtual spaces in the form of the intimate networking site (INS) and the 'physical, communicative, and social mobility' these provide (Barton, 2009, p. 93) are gaining increased prominence in the lives of men who have sex with men, and it is imperative that the digital arena is considered in any discussion of contemporary homosexual geographies.

As the borders between digital and physical spaces become blurred, the work of Mowlabocus (2010, p. 193) and de Souza (2006, p. 264) suggest that the virtual spaces created by INS should be regarded as *hybrid* spaces. This new category of space, created through the 'constant movement of users carrying portable devises with them', rearticulates existing relationships with space and subject and is born out of the connectivity enabled by the technology (de Souza, 2006, p. 262). This hybrid space provides users with a spatiality which, through both instantaneous and asynchronous communication, challenges traditional notions of temporality (Hearn, 2006, p. 949; Stokes, 2012, p. 377) and through which identities are constructed, relationships formed, and intimacy enacted.

A case is presented for a shift in perception away from viewing online as artificial to regarding it as, in a phrase coined by Waskul et al. (2004, p. 43), *a layer of reality*, with the interactions that occur online regarded as being as impactful and valid as those occurring offline. This epistemological position demands that virtual enclaves and the impacts of social/sexual interactions in the fluid, liminal, and heterotopic digital space (Attwood, 2009, p. 280) are considered key components of homosexual geographies.

The importance of the epistemological shift being proposed here can be demonstrated through a reflection on how users interact with the website Squirt.org. This online domain represents a hybrid space, accessible through both portable technology and desktop computers; it is highly mobile in utilising GPS with instant messaging; it 'folds' distance and renders unseen contacts visible. The MSM accessing Squirt.org is able to communicate with other MSM across the globe and view and post attendance information to cruising site listings. Both actions exponentially increase his social/sexual connectivity. In this scenario the hybrid space the website facilitates is a direct analogue for the connectivity (albeit enhanced by the far reach of the online space) an offline homosexual space would provide. Postings made on the message boards of Squirt.org replace the hand-written graffiti advertising opportunities for sexual liaisons that can be found in most offline public sex spaces; this demonstating that the interactions occuring in the digital space should be seen as carrying equal value and meaning.

Digital space offers the potential for new patterns of social order and conduct to be created (Hum, Chamberlin, Hambright, et al., 2011, p. 1832), enabling users to explore/create fantasies (Mowlabocus, 2008, p. 434). This is particularly meaningful for those residing in settings where accessing spacialities enabling social inclusion in the homosexual community is challenging; online they are able to conduct themselves without restriction in a transnational geography. In this space, increased connectivity also provides endless relationship possibilities, both with individuals and communities (Mowlabocus et al, 2013, p. 259). Those potential contacts hidden by physical geographies are visible on intimate networking sites and thus increased possibilities are also uncovered. In this setting greater fluidity of identity is also experienced with each interaction the individual is required to write himself into being, allowing the construction of a variety of selves (Bryson & MacIntosh, 2010, p. 114; Gudelunas, 2012, p. 351; Zhao, Grasmuck, & Martin, 2008, p. 1832) and the ability to select the terms of their engagement. The digital homosexual space enables increased liberation in terms of conduct, relationship formation, and identity and has benefitted the rights, experiences, and sexual citizenship of MSM.

My ethnography revealed that Norfolk's homosexual community inhabits virtual spacialities and forms interpersonal relationships via the internet normatively. Routinely, long-term and casual partners are met via this medium with no social stigma being felt. Among Norfolk's LGBT community, every MSM encountered engaged in technology as a form of social or sexual networking, it has become an integral part of relationship formation. As previously mentioned participants routinely reported that those not possessing an online avatar (or an avatar displaying no face picture/limited personal information) were regarded with suspicion:

> *Iain—If I don't see a face pic on a Grindr profile or a blank profile I assume he has a boyfriend or wife or something. Same thing happens if they say they need 'discretion'; I just think cheater and avoid.*

Transforming Sex Lives

I challenge the view that the internet should be viewed as simply a tool for the facilitation of sexual behaviour (Grosskopf et al., 2011, p. 378). Instead, in line with a Hackian perspective, the internet itself forms a 'moveable' component in the creation of different 'kinds' of people. To clarify: it is argued that the internet can provide a lens through which individuals can view themselves in new ways. It can act as a transformative catalyst resulting in a shift of sexual identity and conduct, prompting people to experience themselves as revised 'kinds'. My ethnography adheres to Hacking's core argument (1999, p. 223) that through the process of classification, new ways for 'people to be' are created and suggests that in relation to sexual identity, the internet can play a significant role in this. While this can occur as a broad societal movement, I argue that this effect can be best evidenced by examining it occurring on a micro-scale. A narrative gathered from James, a fellow LGBT Project worker, provides an ideal illustration of this effect in practice. Quiet and somewhat reserved, James lived with his parents until the age of 36. Growing up he had felt he was 'asexual'. Despite initially describing himself as having no overt attractions for either gender, in later conversations, James did acknowledge that he always felt a sexual attraction to the same gender. From a strict Catholic family, he was in denial about his orientation.

James: It was so frowned upon that I don't think I really admitted it to myself for years, it just wasn't an option. I think my parents just assumed … well, I don't know what they assumed [laughs]. Living in the sticks [rural Norfolk] I didn't know anyone who was gay, didn't know any gay bars. I didn't know how to be gay.
PDE: So what changed?
James: I got really low, depressed but I never went to the doctor. In the end I decided to move out of my parents' place and into a flat of my own. I ended up living in a one-bedroom flat, near the Cathedral, and I got the internet; my parents had never wanted it installed at home. The first thing I did was to check out Gaydar and set up a profile. It's like the world opened up to me. I would have never been able to walk into a gay bar and meet people; I would have been terrified but sat in my flat with my computer I felt brave! I met guys, my first boyfriend, it changed everything.

Access to technology provided James with a revised way of experiencing himself and through this facilitated a shift in his sexual identity. Accessing Gaydar.com provided him a conduit through which he could access sexual experiences, find his current long-term partner, and ultimately connect him with Norfolk's LGBT Project. Without the internet, James would not have been able to experiment with his sexual identity; the technology catalysed action. At this point it should be acknowledged that Hacking himself views the internet as an 'immoveable object' in relation to the creation of new 'kinds' of people, an inanimate object unaffected by and unable to impact social forces. Notwithstanding the use of his theories as a lens through which to view the ways in which the internet impacts person-hood, this chapter challenges this particular perspective.

It has already been claimed that the anonymity attached to computer-mediated communication and the instantaneous nature of computer-mediated communication (CMC) results in users making intimate disclosures about repressed desires (Bauermeister et al., 2011, p. 272). Described as being akin to the 'passing stranger' effect (Gibbs et al., 2006), it could be argued that this is relatively harmless in most virtual settings. However, online dating or 'hook-up' websites are qualitatively different. Unlike sites such as Facebook or Twitter, dating websites focus specifically on the transition from online dialogue to an offline, face-to-face encounter. In fact this is the key objective for most of those engaging in the process (Ellison et al., 2006, p. 416). Members of the MSM community in Norfolk, at times, seemed to be almost obsessive in the frequency that they would check for messages from the various dating websites on which they had avatars. The triaging, engagement with, or discarding of prospective sexual and romantic partners through mobile apps or dating websites was witnessed on numerous occasions. This process was discussed openly in social settings with MSM seeking approval from their peers regarding their most recent 'chat partner'. During this period of fieldwork, a sense of positive liberation provided by online dating was witnessed; MSM seemed to be exhilarated at the relationship possibilities provided by cyberspace-mediated communication. It was only through in-depth interviewing that the more complex ramifications associated with online avatar agency as well as the transformative effects of the internet on sexual conduct was uncovered.

It was during an interview with a member of the Men's Group that the arguably negative impact of internet use on sexual conduct was first acknowledged. Warren is in his late 20s and has been 'out' since he was 16 years old; he describes himself as being empowered and 'quite streetwise'. During the interview he disclosed:

Warren: I've had a Gaydar profile for years, used it on and off, met a few guys off there, nothing major though, didn't meet the love of my life through it or anything. I mostly used it to check out profiles.

PDE:	Check out?
Warren:	Yeah, kind of lurk, just look at the pictures, like real-life porn. I found I like the kinkier stuff [laughs] ... I liked that they were real guys, it was horny.
PDE:	What sort of 'kinkier stuff'?
Warren:	[Hesitates] I liked the guys who said they were into barebacking and stuff, I was well vanilla but I got turned on by the thought of bare. My little option box always said 'safe sex only'.
PDE:	You said '*was* vanilla'. Has that changed?
Warren:	[Laughs] Yeah, well no. [Hesitates] I started lurking on more hardcore websites, kinkier ones, like Squirt. I wasn't meeting guys but just liked chatting, flirting, mostly with the guys into bareback, like I was living out fantasies. Trouble was few of them were interested in chatting to me because I always listed that I was into safe stuff only, so I ended up changing the box to 'Into bareback' or something like that. People were more interested then, I uploaded a new picture, more revealing. Chatted lots. Then I met one guy on there who was really hot, don't even remember his name... how bad is that? He wanted to meet, wanted to do bareback and I got carried away, we chatted, exchanged pictures and I agreed to meet him. I drove to his place and had sex, it was my first time with no condoms, never saw him again.
PDE:	How did you feel afterwards?
Warren:	[Hesitates] Like shit, I took such a massive risk, never even asked if he was clean. I had always been really careful but when I got to his I didn't feel like I could ask to use condoms. I mean I wanted it, it wasn't like I was raped but I just felt backed into a corner. Once I said I was into barebacking there was no going back, I hadn't expected that. I am lucky; I tested myself afterwards and was all clear.

Use of the internet provided Warren with the opportunity to experiment with his sexual preferences and ultimately had a profound impact on his offline conduct. The seemingly innocuous act of declaring his interest in unprotected intercourse (barebacking) via his online avatar enabled him to experience and construct himself in the digital space as a sexual risk taker. In presenting this as a self-fulfilling prophecy, Warren demonstrates the power of the online world on offline action. This was not the sole example provided. It was regularly reported that MSM living in Norfolk found themselves in encounters where sexual or personal safety risks were taken due to connections made through the internet: intercourse had with a stranger enabled by the fact that Grindr informed that he was only metres away and the flirtatious online chat which led to a drinks date where sex was an expected chaser were two such examples shared with me. With the exception of Warren, these were treated with levity, being seen as of little consequence, and almost exclusively it was found that these incidents were linked to the sense of liberation and disinhibition provided by the internet.

Self-disclosure

The time spent with the MSM community in Norfolk illustrated the potency of online avatar construction in respect of the offline world and enabled an exploration of the internet as a liminal domain. In sharing their stories, the participants enabled me to explore the impact of virtual spaces in shaping sexual norms and behaviours, a trend that public health bodies need to consider.

The cultural insight I gained through the use of ethnography proved to be hugely advantageous. However, it also presented challenges. The most significant of these was the perceived risk to my personal safety when visiting strangers in their homes to carry out interviews. While I ensured a third party always knew of my whereabouts, on several occasions I experienced a sense of acute vulnerability and anxiety. This subsided as I gained more experience in the field. I also came to the late realisation that my participants, too, were taking a risk by inviting me into their homes. A further challenge was the reconciliation of my status as a sexual health professional with the narratives of sexual risk-taking behaviour being shared by participants. I was conscious not to preach messages of safer sex for fear this would fundamentally undermine my relationship with participants but equally felt a professional responsibility to ensure that my participants were aware of the risks they were taking. Ultimately, I managed this during interviews by passively establishing whether or not the participant was aware of the risks. For those who demonstrated a lack of understanding, I discreetly signposted them to online sexual health resources.

I consider myself incredibly fortunate to have been given significant access to the MSM community in Norfolk through securing placement with the County's LGBT Project. I am in debt to the gatekeepers I encountered who enabled much of this research to take place. I also recognise that openly disclosing my sexual preferences enabled easier access to the community and allowed me to elicit more frank disclosures from those interviewed (see Richards, this volume). Furthermore, as an MSM I also had insight into the coded language use in the cohort which enabled aided reflections and relationship formation. The benefits of a shared position with research participants is recognised by some (Irvine, 2014, p. 634; Phoenix, 2008; Richards et al., 2015), and while this research has been enhanced by an approach of self-disclosure, it was crucial that clear boundaries were established throughout. On numerous occasions during the fieldwork, I was sexually propositioned both in person and online; this was managed by clearly stating my status as a researcher and reiterating ethical boundaries. A lesson learnt from this was that limited personal disclosures are beneficial in gaining narratives of intimacy and sexual practices from participants, but in doing so the researcher can become vulnerable to challenges to ethical conduct within research relationships.

Plummer's (2003, p. 77) view is that the pseudo-independent agency of the online avatar and the role digital spacialities play in identity and relationship formation is imperative. My own experience in the field corroborates this. I acknowledge that the sexual/social networking websites and apps considered as part of this research are all UK-centric. It is also recognised that it could be argued that this can limit transferability. However, I propose that all the findings herein are applicable to other Wi-Fi/3G/4G-enabled countries with comparable civil rights entitlements for MSM. Beyond this the possibilities to sexual agency created by digital spacialities could be framed as more impactful in cultures with restricted sexual/civil rights entitlements for MSM. Exploring the themes presented in this chapter through a framework of globalisation would provide a significant contribution to this field and would benefit the formation of public health policy and, by extension, the health and well-being of men who have sex with men.

References

Attwood, F. (2009). 'Deepthroatfucker' and 'Discerning Adonis'—Men and Cybersex. *International Journal of Cultural Studies, 12*(3), 279–294.

Barton, B. J. (2009). iPhone City. *Architectural Design, 79*(4), 90–97.

Bauermeister, J. A., et al. (2011). Mr Right and Mr Right Now: Romantic and Casual Partner-Seeking Online Among Young Men Who Have Sex with Men. *AIDS Behaviour, 15*, 261–272.

WRESTLING WITH ONLINE AVATARS: TECHNOLOGY AND SEXUAL... 51

Bell, D. (2006). Bodies, Technologies, Spaces: On 'Dogging'. *Sexualities, 9*(4), 387–407.

Beneito-Montagut, R. (2011). Ethnography Goes Online: Towards a User-Centered Methodology to Research Interpersonal Communication on the Internet. *Qualitative Research, 11*(6), 716–735.

Boellstorff, T. (2011). But Do Not Identify As Gay: a Proleptic Genealogy of the MSM Category. *Cultural Anthropology, 26*(2), 287–312.

Bristow, J. (1989). Being Gay: Politics, Identity and Pleasure. *New Formations, 9*(Winter), 61–81.

Bryson, M. K., & MacIntosh, L. B. (2010). Can We Play Fun Gay? *International Journal of Qualitative Studies in Education, 23*(1), 101–124.

Califia, P. (1994). *Public Sex: The Culture of Radical Sex*. San Francisco: Cleis Press.

De Souza e Silva, A. (2006). From Cyber to Hybrid: Mobile Technologies as Interfaces of Hybrid Spaces. *Space and Culture, 9*(3), 261–278.

Ellison, N., Heino, R., & Gibbs, J. (2006). Managing Impressions Online: Self-Presentation Processes in the Online Dating Environment. *Journal of Computer-Mediated Communication, 11*(2), 415–441.

Foster, T. (2001). Trapped by the Body? Telepresence, Technologies and Transgendered Performance in Feminist and Lesbian Rewriting to Cyberpunk Fiction. In D. Bell & B. Kennedy (Eds.), *The Cybercultures Reader*. London: Routledge.

Gibbs, J. L., Ellison, N. B., & Heino, R. D. (2006). Self-Presentation in Online Personals. *Communication Research, 33*(2), 152–177.

Grosskopf, N. A., Harris, J. K., & Wallace, B. C. (2011). Online Sex-Seeking Behaviours of Men Who Have Sex With Men in New York City. *American Journal of Men's Health, 5*(5), 378–385.

Gudelunas, D. (2012). There's an App for That: The Uses and Gratifications of Online Social Networks for Gay Men. *Sexuality & Culture, 16*, 347–365.

Hacking, I. (1999). *The Social Construction of What?* London: Harvard University Press.

Hall, J. A., Park, N., Song, H., & Cody, M. J. (2010). Strategic Misrepresentation in Online Dating: The Effects of Gender, Self-Monitoring and Personality Traits. *Journal of Social and Personal Relationships, 27*(1), 117–135.

Hearn, J. (2006). The Implications of Information and Communication Technologies for Sexualities and Sexualised Violences: Contradictions of Sexual Citizenships. *Political Geography, 25*, 944–963.

Hubbard, P. (2001). Sex Zones: Intimacy, Citizenship and Public Space. *Sexualities, 4*(1), 51–71.

Hum, N. J., Chamberlin, P. E., Hambright, B. L., et al. (2011). A Picture Is Worth a Thousand Words: A Content Analysis of Facebook Profile Pictures. *Computers in Human Behaviour, 27*, 1828–1833.

Inhorn, M. C., & Brown, P. J. (1990). The Anthropology of Infectious Disease. *Annual Review of Anthropology, 19*, 89–117.

52   P. DRISCOLL-EVANS

Irvine, J. M. (2014). Is Sexuality Research 'Dirty Work'? Institutionalised Stigma in the Production of Sexual Knowledge. *Sexualities, 17*(5/6), 632–656.

Kitchin, R. (2002). Sexing the City: The Sexual Production of Non-Heterosexual Space in Belfast, Manchester and San Francisco. *City, 6*(2), 205–218.

Livingstone, S. (2009). *Children and the Internet.* London: Polity Press.

Mowlabocus, S. (2008). Revisiting Old Haunts Through New Technologies: Public (Homo)sexual Cultures in Cyberspace. *International Journal of Cultural Studies, 11*(940), 419–439.

Mowlabocus, S. (2010). *Gaydar Culture: Gay Men, Technology and Embodiment in the Digital Age.* Surrey: Ashgate Publishing.

Mowlabocus, S., Harbottle, J., & Witzel, C. (2013). Porn Laid Bare: Gay Men, Pornography and Bareback Sex. *Sexualities, 16*(5/6), 523–547.

Murchison, J. M. (2010). *Ethnography Essentials—Designing, Conducting and Presenting Research.* London: Wiley.

Parker, M. (1999). HIV Transmission in Urban Environments: London and Beyond. In L. Schell & S. Ulijaszek (Eds.), *Urbanisation and Human Biology in Industrialised Countries.* Cambridge University Press: Cambridge.

Phoenix, A. (2008). Analysing Narrative Contexts. In M. Andrews, C. Squire, & M. Tamboukou (Eds.), *Doing Narrative Research.* London: Sage.

Plummer, K. (2003). *Intimate Citizenship: Personal Decisions and Public Dialogues.* London: University Washington Press.

Richards, S., Clark, J., & Boggis, A. (2015). *Ethical Research with Children: Untold Narratives.* London: Palgrave Macmillan.

Stokes, P. (2012). Ghosts in the Machine: Do the Dead Live on in Facebook? *Philosophy and Technology, 25*, 363–379.

Van Maanen, J. (2011). *Tales of the Field: On Writing Ethnography* (2nd ed.). London: University of Chicago.

Waskul, D., Douglass, M., & Edgley, C. (2004). Outercourse: Body and Self in Text Cybersex. In D. Waskul (Ed.), *Net.seXXX: Readings of Sex, Pornography and the Internet.* London: Peter Lang.

Weeks, J. (1991). *Against Nature: Essays on History, Sexuality and Identity.* London: Rivers Oram Press.

Weeks, J. (2000). *Coming Out: Homosexual Politics in Britain from the Nineteenth Century to the Present.* London: Quartet Books.

Zhao, S., Grasmuck, S., & Martin, J. (2008). Identity Construction on Facebook: Digital Empowerment in Anchored Relationships. *Computers in Human Behaviour, 24*, 1816–1836.

CHAPTER 4

Chóng ér fēi: Cultural Performances of Belonging in Intercountry Adoptive Families

Sarah Richards

I first encountered ethnography as a student of social policy. The scope and application of the approach to researching the impact of particular social policies on social groups attracted me to the method. I was determined that ethnography would underpin my doctoral study on intercountry adoption policy. When disclosing this to other PhD students, one took me aside and confided a secret wish to embrace this 'dark side' of research himself but had resisted such temptation as he wanted his PhD 'to be taken seriously'. Now, as a senior lecturer in Childhood Studies, I encourage students to see the relevance of ethnography to their own research with children. I demonstrate the ways in which ethnography can enable meaningful connection with their participants as well as aid self-reflection in terms of their own positionality within the research process. I can only wonder whether that fellow PhD student ever released his inner ethnographic self and, if so, how it was received in his academic world.

S. Richards (✉)
University of Suffolk, Ipswich, UK

© The Author(s) 2018
T. Vine et al. (eds.), *Ethnographic Research and Analysis,*
https://doi.org/10.1057/978-1-137-58555-4_4

Introduction

The existence of intercountry adoption policy which facilitates the removal of children from birth country for the purpose of adoption is unsurprisingly controversial. Much has been written about its practice and perhaps even more about its malpractice. The risks it may pose to children, their development and wellbeing along with the supposed attributes and characteristics of those who adopt are also common themes within this complex discourse. Yet, Selwyn and Wijedasa (2008) argue that little research has taken place with adoptive families to identify how ethnicity, culture, and belonging are facilitated. This 'lack of knowledge and insight into racial and cultural issues' portrayed by intercountry adopters is a valid cause of concern according to Allen (2007), p. 125). My research provides insight into ways in which the complexities of belonging (Yuval-Davis, 2011) are managed, displayed (Finch, 2007), and performed by intercountry adoptive families (Richards, 2013). The intention of this chapter therefore is to use specific cultural practices of a group of intercountry adoptive families to explore how their performed rituals and collective activities reproduce dominant identity narratives which relate to prevailing themes within contemporary intercountry adoption policy. Such an ethnography obviously does not seek or claim to capture the entirety of this group's cultures or the many and diverse 'ways of life therein' (Denzin, 1997, p. 247) but rather selects and highlights 'interpreted slices' (Denzin, 1997) of social interaction whose performances can reflect the policy texts which make intercountry adoptions possible. The selected performances used here, like the policy they represent, are situated and temporally specific but not temporally distant (Conquergood, 1992, p. 85). My aim is not to capture or reproduce the exotic from another time and place but to 'meet the Other on the same ground, in the same time' (Fabian, 1983, p. 165). This methodological value is enhanced by my positionality within this group as an intercountry adoptive mother. The intertwining of my roles as researcher, mother, and fellow performer are threads that weave through the vignettes presented and analysed here. Throughout this discussion, I endeavour to recognise that a storied reality such as the one told here has me as a narrator whose inflections and presentation of the data shape what is told (Coffey, 1999; Madden, 2010).

Using performance theory, I illustrate the strategies employed by families who live in the UK and have adopted children from China to address the deficit of origin and belonging narratives for their adopted daughters. My intention was not just to explore the stories of daughters but only families with girls participated in the research. This ethnography explores how these families construct and reinforce familial and cultural belonging across ethnic, cultural, and biological boundaries. I argue here that these families display and perform their own adoptive belonging narratives whilst simultaneously using strategies to connect their daughters to the culture of China and an absent biological family. By these means they conform to the policy expectations representative of the 'good adoptive parent' explicit in the Hague Convention on Intercountry Adoption (1993) ratified by the UK in 2005. They also concur with current domestic adoption policy where the best interests of the child dictum based upon familial ideology situates children within a family, preferably biological with adoptive as a subordinate and secondary option.

Through biological connections between parent and child, a sense of continuity, connection, and identity is constructed through a 'narrative of generational succession' (Warner, 1991). Such inherited connections are commonly connected to nation state and are perceived by some to create a formal bond linking biological and familial belonging, essentialised as integral to identity (Bartholet, 1999). The British television programme *'Who do you think you are?'* encapsulates this perspective succinctly through a discourse which implies we can learn about ourselves through the occupations, traits, and tribulations of our recent ancestors. This 'essential essence' narrative informs social work practice in adoption (Cohen, 1995). Adopted children and adults are socially constructed as holding incomplete identity narratives, a deficit which is argued to pose a risk to the development of an authentic identity (Richards, 2012). Sants describes its absence as being 'genealogical bewilderment' (cited in Volkman, 2005, p. 26). This risk must be compensated for throughout the life of an adopted person. 'Long Lost Family', as another television programme, neatly encapsulates this social anxiety by following individuals as they attempt to reconnect their severed 'generational succession' (Warner, 1991). Meeting a person responsible for our receding hairline, pungent feet, or bulbous nose is thus constructed as essential in understanding who we are, who we can be, or indeed who we are allowed to be. Such a preordained narrative extends to intercountry adoptees, but, in the absence of a known biological or genetic family link (as is common in intercountry adoption), the narrative has to be constructed from the known history of their life course. For girls adopted from China, issues such as abandonment, orphanage care, deprivation, and poverty become focal points of their early narratives. These themes script the stories which are told to the girls.

The complexity surrounding the movement of children through intercountry adoption should not be underestimated; however, there are certain issues which are typically emphasised to the extent that they have become synonymous with the process. These fundamental principles have become the canonical narratives (Bruner, 2004) of adoption and have informed national and international policy development. Hollingsworth (1998) usefully articulates these concerns by outlining five broad professional principles which have emerged as a result of the emphasis on 'race' and 'ethnicity' in social work practice. These principles typify what can be said, written, and practised in adoption work currently and in intercountry adoption specifically (Richards, 2012). The first relates to the significance of an ethnic heritage, the second to the preference that biological parents or relatives should raise children, the third stresses that economic circumstance alone should not deprive children of their biological families, the fourth that effort and preference for same-race adoption should be pursued, and the fifth that alternative arrangements (such as intercountry adoption) are only acceptable and can only be made when a child is otherwise deprived of a permanent family and home. Through a process of governmentality (Foucault, 2003), these principles have become constructed as objective knowledge and 'truths' (Rose, 1999) about the best interests of children in need of adoption and thus shape the policies through which the welfare subjects of adoptee, intercountry adoptee, and adoptive parent are constructed. Adoption literature generally emphasises the imperative to connect and maintain links to birth country and culture for adoptive children. The expectation to connect intercountry adopted children with birth country, heritage, and culture is part of a policy script which governs the welfare subjects involved and sets out the role of 'good adoptive parent'. The 'cultural capital' of parents in this regard is the subject of 'fierce debate' (Barn, 2013, p. 1273). It is a contested topic, yet little is known of the strategies and activities engaged of intercountry adoptive families in England.

Geertz (1980) suggests that every society has some form of 'metacommentary' which forms the 'story a group tells itself about itself' (cited in

Turner, 1982, p. 104). The performances explored here are situated in the metacommentary about intercountry adoption. The issues highlighted above provide the social and political context through which intercountry adoption is discussed, explained, constructed, and indeed researched. This discussion therefore highlights three origin and belonging narratives crucial to the contemporary discourse of intercountry adoption. First on the primacy of the biological family, second on birth as a point where ethnicity and cultural belonging is fixed, and third how the loss of birth family and birth culture risks an incomplete and inauthentic identity, a risk which must be managed by adoptee and adoptive family on an ongoing basis.

Performance studies in this context are construed as being human actions in everyday life which enact 'gender, race, and class roles' where 'any action that is framed, presented, highlighted, or displayed is a performance' (Schechner, 2006, p. 2). The application of performance ethnography to critically analyse social policy is not usual. Policy research has gradually embraced qualitative approaches, but the role of quantitative research has traditionally dominated. However, Li (2007) argues that there is a tradition of ethnographic methods being deployed to analyse discursive practices within social policy in order to avoid what Marston (2002) depicts as the tendency to construe situated practices from meta-narrative analysis. Performance ethnography is also perhaps the road less travelled. Turner (1986) claimed that the performed text is the last remaining boundary for ethnography to span. Part of the emerging narrative in this chapter is to consider the efficacy of this approach as a research tool in exploring specific dictums of a policy or set of policies. Performance ethnography is used here to highlight the ways that certain aspects of adoption policy are practised by its users and thus illustrates the relevance of ethnography and performance in providing evidence-based discussions about the practice of social policy by those whose lives are regulated by it (McKee, 2009). Before outlining the research context from which these performances are drawn, a clarification of performance ethnography as applied here is a useful place to begin.

Bruner (1986) argues that culture is an enduring performance where its uncertainties and inconsistencies can be emphasised. Conquergood (1992), p. 80) claims performance to be the 'nexus between playful and the political', 'a way of knowing' through 'embodied practice ... bound up with cultural discourses' (Taylor, 2004, p. 382; see also Butler, 1993). Gender, sexual identity, and citizenship to name but a few are identity

58   S. RICHARDS

traits, (Taylor, 2004, p. 381), rehearsed and performed daily in the public domain. The term performance therefore is not restricted to the arts and their performance but is also representative of 'the ways of doing' culture (Blackmore, 2000, p. 65). Performance can illustrate what Singer (1959, p. xii) referred to as particular 'instances of cultural structure'. These structures can reveal the normative expectations and compelled behaviours ascribed to each of us through the many roles we perform. Each of us perform multiple socially constructed roles simultaneously, mother, 'good adoptive parent role', group member, researcher, and author to name but a few of mine performed in this account. What constitutes such cultural performance is very diverse, suggested by Taylor to involve 'dance, theater, ritual, political rallies and funerals, that encompass theatrical, rehearsed, conventional or event-appropriate behaviors' (2004, p. 381). In this chapter, performed rituals, dance, and song highlight particular events—appropriate behaviour within and by this small cultural group that tells the stories of individual families whilst simultaneously reproducing dominant narratives embedded in intercountry adoption policy.

RESEARCH CONTEXT

The data used in this chapter are drawn from a wider PhD study which aimed to explore the belonging narratives of adoptive families in England and their daughters adopted from China. As part of this study, I engaged in participant observation. These observations took place at CACH (Children Adopted from China) organised events over a three-year period. CACH is a charitable organisation, and through the activities that it organises, it serves as a location of support (see e.g. Caballero, Edwards, Goodyer, & Okitikpi, 2012; Harman, 2013) for families who have adopted from China. It holds annual national events twice a year one being a three-day annual reunion/AGM. CACH is also active regionally. These regional groups hold events throughout the year which include Christmas parties, Chinese New Year celebrations, and spring and autumn festivals. A magazine and website is also part of the way in which the members of this organisation communicate and are communicated with. Adoption applicants are encouraged to join the group by social workers, and it serves as a source of information and support through the application process and into the adoptions. The events discussed in this chapter include two national reunion/AGM meetings each lasting three days and attended by about 150 families. I also observed one summer school lasting four days and attended by about 100 families. The summer school takes place each year in a rural primary school and is designed so that older Chinese adoptees (16 years and over) can interact with younger girls in group settings. Each group participates in dance, Mandarin lessons, art, and cookery, but the main aim is to facilitate friendship and companionship between the girls. The activities of summer school and CACH are representative of what Gillis describes as 'symbolic universes':

> biology alone cannot provide a habitable world and that people create cultures [in part] to foster a sense of security. These 'symbolic universes', become 'populated' with our significant others, with meaningful objects, and with the times and places we hold sacred. (Gillis, 1996, p. 61)

Through these activities CACH also performs as location for disparate families to connect and network, defined by Britton (2013) as:

> sets of social relationships between people who understand themselves to share specific social ties; they usually involve friendship, advice and information exchange and practical and emotional support.

The actors here share similar familial structures, and this similarity along with their compliance with, and knowledge of, specific 'scripted' roles, allows for a particular 'symbolic universe' to be created. Membership of this group brings an effective understanding of issues around intercountry adoption and an ability to communicate easily not necessarily available elsewhere (Yuval-Davis, 1994). Solidarity within this group is in part constructed through the social and political positioning of these families as different to other families. Particular characteristics, performances, and rituals can reveal that which is meaningful to this group, what is valued, sacred, and profane; however, belonging to this group should not be assumed to create a homogeneous universe. Whilst holding what Geertz (1988, p. 147) calls an 'endless connection', these individuals nevertheless hold disparate interests and diverse economic status and power. It can therefore be demonstrated that they interpret the ascribed script of 'good adoptive parent' individually and in diverse ways.

60   S. RICHARDS

The following vignettes taken from my PhD research (Richards, 2013) demonstrate the multiple ways that members of this group perform their roles as parent, daughter, friend, and group member. All performances respond to the policy values through which these adoptions occur. The first took place at meal time:

> They made Chinese fruit salad with lychees and none of the children would eat them because they didn't know what they were.

On the arrival evening of the reunion/AGM, a buffet supper is provided in one of two massive conference rooms. The other room has a young children's entertainer setting up for the evening and a dance floor ready for music and entertainer/disc jockey with balloons for the dancers. Tables and chairs are set out on the periphery for parents to sit and chat as the girls take part. The food available is a mixture of noodles, rice, meat, and vegetables with an assumed 'Asian' influence. One mother explained to another who had arrived later, with a degree of ironic humour that the hotel was trying to better accommodate the group than they had in past years and that this year they were offering a dessert which included lychees. She explained that many of the children and a number of the adults would not try it as they did not recognise the fruit. This provides an interesting aspect to explore the contradictions and diversities in this group as well as the expectations placed upon them.

Analysing this observation through the good adoptive parent script, it is possible to regard it as being evidential of identity construction both through grand gestures such as travelling to China, sustained and committed acts such as families learning Mandarin, through to the mundane and ritualistic such as particular cultural choices of food. I argue however that it better demonstrates the tension between the script that parents are prescribed through policy to perform and the other narratives within these families related to individual lifestyle choices and socio-economic status. This tension itself can provide humorous family narratives. Lisa (aged 8 years) identified her favourite family story being the one where her mother ate duck's feet in China. She laughed as she told me about this typical Chinese food that is evidently not typical within their family.

My favorite family story

I love to hear the story about

Mummy eating ducks feet.

Lisa (8yrs.)

The assumed homogenisation of families who adopt intercountry (Anagnost, 2000) has done little to reveal these families beyond the stereotypical whilst at the same time dictates that they perform stereotypical and tokenistic cultural depictions of the birth culture of their children. A lack of knowledge of a particular fruit consumed in China (as well as many other countries) should not be simplistically construed as a failure on the part of such parents to effectively bestow a Chinese cultural narrative for their children or provide an explicit example of such construction occurring through the presence of the fruit and other Asian food at the table. Rather, it can be said to reveal the diversity of these families and the multiple ways in which they interpret and perform the compulsion to connect their daughters to their birth heritage. Yet in an environment where all parents are displaying and performing their fulfilment of this expectation to each other, the lack of knowledge about a lychee on the part of either child or parent becomes evidence of an implied failure on the part of some and also an aspect to judge others by. The cultural literacy of these girls is assessed through the knowledge and consumption of a piece of 'Chinese fruit', and the parenting skills in facilitating this literacy is judged by others through their daughter's willingness to eat it. The rather preposterous nature of recognition (or otherwise) of fruit in a salad bowl is not lost on those who laughingly participate in this conversation (including me). Yet none of us questions the validity of the script itself. The surveillance of other parents becomes a part of self-regulation, where the 'good adoptive parent script' has become so conventionalised and natural within this group that it goes unquestioned and unchallenged.

Consumption of China Through Ritual and Celebration

Being Chinese as a cause for celebration is a recurring theme in CACH events and can be keyed to the wider overall need to foster and facilitate a strong ethnic and cultural identity for the adopted children. Attention is given to certain aspects of being Chinese whilst also obscuring others. Every reference to China offered to the girls is framed in positive, playful, happy, and colourful ways. China as a country where girls are abandoned is inextricably linked to the reason for the event itself but absent. A particular reality is thus constructed through the activities of these events as much by what is absent or considered profane by what is included. Santino (2004) claims that definitional ceremonies are significant events chosen from culture to be public and relate to how a particular cultural group wishes to be perceived. The Lion Dance is a case in point. The official opening of each AGM/reunion is done in a traditional way each year. A lion dances to the beat of a large Chinese drum as all the families are gathered around in one of the two large conference rooms. The lion dancers begin with the young children sitting around the edge of a large circle area with parents sitting or standing around behind them in close proximity. As the drum starts to beat loudly and the large lion starts to jump and prance around the edge leaning over the young children, a few of the smaller ones begin to cry and show signs of being scared. They are comforted or removed by their parents. The Lion Dance culminates with him eating a lettuce and tossing shredded leaves into the audience to the laughter and anticipation of the children as they call to and encourage the lion to come closer to them or shy away from him. The dance finishes and there is a large round of cheering and applause. As the crowd disperses children gather around the lion costume and the drum with permission to touch the lion's head and beat the drum.

The Lion Dance is symbolic of Chinese celebration; here it is also imbued with feelings of collective belonging to something; it is also symbolic of excitement and fun activities loosely based around China and things Chinese, for the girls. As the opening event, it is indicative of what is to come, a vibrant, active, and noisy weekend. As Santino (2004) contends, this ritualistic definitional ceremony draws in the observers as active participants interacting with the lion through laughter, fear, anticipation, and being drawn into the dance. There is a fluidity in the performance as children respond to the prancing, leaping lion with fear, excitement, and bravado. Children throw lettuce back at the lion during the dance and shout for him to come to them, shrinking back and clutching parents as he approaches. It is reminiscent of Chinese culture but also symbolic of this cultural group where two cultures merge into something liminal whilst continuing to embody aspects of each. The ritual remains in its performance and context unique to this group, performed annually at the same time in the same room with parents forming the same shape and position of protective circle around the lion in the middle, standing and facing inwards with children sitting at their feet.

I am standing close to a mother and notice that she is crying. When I ask if she is okay, she replies that she's fine, but this event enables her to see all these girls in one place looking happy, healthy, sharing the event and she says that it, 'gets her every time'. For her and her family, this date in the annual calendar is fixed and regarded as sacrosanct. This touches on the significance it holds for the adults present, more than just a social occasion where one can meet up with friends and acquaintances, it is seen as a culturally significant event. The Lion Dance in its symbolism depicts a celebration, of colour, noise, a clash of symbols and drums, which evoke the size and volume of this group, metaphorically as strong and fierce as a lion in protecting family members. Visually it speaks powerfully of substance, vibrancy, identity, and the sustainability of these families.

A significant adoptive parenting role which preoccupies many present at these CACH events is that of ensuring a cultural identity for the children, as outlined in intercountry adoption policy. The challenge of

64   S. RICHARDS

securing this for the children in these families is daunting and indeed perhaps one that these families work very hard towards, but can never really achieve, and which leaves parents open to accusations of failure (see e.g., Anagnost, 2000). A common criticism of these parents is that the cultural picture offered to the girls is one which is purely celebratory and devoid of history (Anagnost, 2000). This is demonstrated by a young participant called Amy who, when she was five years old, attended the event for the first time and made the following remark:

> Girls must be very special in China to have a party like this for them.

THE CONSUMPTION OF CHINA

The extent, to which the reunion event emphasises the celebratory element, was made explicit through the contrasting narrative of a Chinese flautist invited to attend and perform. In the midst of the event finale where prizes were handed out for best fancy dress, the money raised through the raffle was identified and applauded and those whose hard work had made the event possible were profusely thanked, a middle aged man holding a flute was invited up on to the stage and began to speak of the inspiration for his music. He spoke of his impoverished childhood in revolutionary China and detailed the loss of his mother when she was branded an intellectual and sent to the countryside for a number of years, returning, as he described, a broken woman. The contrast of this man's China with the one being consumed elsewhere in the weekend's performance was stark. It is argued by some that celebratory narratives, devoid of history, may cause problems for the 'adopted child' in developing an understanding of their racialisation (Anagnost, 2000). I argue that these families are set up to fail in this regard. On the one hand, they are tasked with creating a secure and confident adoptive narrative, a story where the girls are able to feel a connection to, and pride, in their ethnic identity. However, in attempting to perform this role, parents are also accused of a failure to offer a 'warts and all' cultural narrative, one more indicative of that told by the flautist. Whilst such events as those depicted in this chapter can be seen to err on the side of China as a celebration, perhaps to the detriment of other important narratives of China, I contend that the task of ensuring the cultural wellbeing of these girls is uppermost in the thoughts and actions of many parents at these events. Indeed an accusation of colonialism (Smolin, 2004) and racial blindness (Barn, 2013), never far from the discourse around these families, might be evoked by a cultural narrative of China which cast this culture in a less than favourable light. Both of which resonate historically in interracial adoption practice.

Sullivan (1986) claims that successful theories of performance all attempt to separate culturally performed acts from other social interaction and interpret them through analysis which seeks to identify the symbolism expressed. Symbolic action is performed in this context in part through language, dance, play, music, and education. It therefore requires an explanation of synaesthesia, where such areas of cultural display evoke symbolic meaning, for example, through music. An example of this is where the flautist played his music from the soundtrack of a renowned documentary which captured the hardship and romance of life in a remote mountain village in rural China in the early 1990s. As he played the haunting music, the room grew silent and still. Some mothers were quietly weeping by the end of the rendition. One mother suggested to me afterwards that it evoked memories of their adoption trip, thoughts of a lost biological family and the idea of a beautiful and disappearing China that she wished to convey to her daughter, and in doing so she articulated Said's (1978, p. 1) explanation of 'Orientalism' and its associated ascribed characteristics (1978, p. 201). The music evoked a romantic and fantasy narrative of a lost country and synthesised aspects of what this group collectively hold and understand as valuable: China as a country to be proud of, China with a long heritage that can be tapped into and form part of the identity of the girls. Such symbolism is manifest through music, or as Sullivan (1986, p. 24) describes, by 'performance of symbolic sounds' such as the Chinese flute. Music, he argues, structures society but also its performance forms the script of social order.

Such symbolic expression and influence is also evident when some of the girls sing 'Chóng ér fēi translated as 'Fireflies', at Chinese summer school (2010). This gentle and equally haunting melody, chosen by the organisers/teachers of the school to teach the girls (aged from 5 to 11 years) to sing, once again captures that which is held sacred and valuable by this group. Sung in Mandarin by the whole school in front of their parents, like the previous example, it reduces some mothers to tears as girls play musical instruments and collectively sing a song of lost but enduring friendship which cannot be severed by time or distance. It is symbolic of the relationship that the girls may have (or parents ascribe to them and may wish them to have) not only with a birth country but perhaps a birth

66   S. RICHARDS

family too. The song itself is emblematic of all that the children are deemed to have lost, an absence which cannot be filled but which the girls themselves (and their parents) must somehow come to terms with. Such ideas held as sacred by this group are evoked and performed through a collective 'unity of senses' (Sullivan, 1986, p. 6). The Lion Dance as music (Frith, 1996), ritual, and collective performance provides further example of the synthesis of symbolic values and meanings of the group. But, in contrast to previous examples, it is the traditional loud, celebratory sounds of the drum beat as the lion dances, interacting with the audience in boisterous and mischievous ways which carries the expressions of that which is valued by this group and specific to the reunion.

'I JUST WANT TO SHOP': CONSUMING AN AUTHENTIC IDENTITY

The imperative to pursue an 'authentic identity' has generated significant economic opportunities around these families. Paying for someone to archive a child's life story is one example where families produce material artefacts and pay another to build their daughter's life history into a book. CACH reunion activities offer numerous other examples. Selling China to families eager to purchase it as part of how they perform and display family would seem to be a potentially successful business opportunity. CACH reunion events are not alone in this. Jacobson (2008, p. 2) suggests that extensive industries have developed to support parents 'keep culture' for their children.

The consumption of China at these events can be keyed (Goffman, 1974) into a wider adoptive role of performing the good adoptive parent, in this case by making China accessible and part of the life experiences of the girls which reflects the adopted child's right to ethnic, religious, cultural, and linguistic background (Hague Convention on Intercountry Adoption, 1993; United Nations Convention on the Rights of the Child, 1989). The consumption of products which are in some way linked to China is an accessible and attractive opportunity for parents to fulfil this expectation and for children to acquire a variety of new toys and gifts. However, the diversity of how this is achieved is something that I wish to emphasise. The cultural and economic disparities within this group are as evident in this cultural consumption as in the consumption of Asian food. For some the consumption is achieved by being at the event itself; for others it is the purchase of a

Chinese fan, for yet others it is return trips to China, and for a few it is all of these. At these two events, the engagement of both parents (where relevant) in window shopping and actual purchase of Chinese products is marked.

During each of the observed AGM/reunions and the summer school, there are stalls (often charitable) selling goods from China. At the AGM/reunion, the main atrium is filled around the edge with sprawling stalls and stands adorned with a colourful array of products connected by an overall Asian theme. The colour and vibrancy of these stands adds to the atmosphere of expectation and excitement. There is also an element of ritualism in that many of the stalls are regular to the event, some through the involvement of some of the parents attending the event as members of CACH. The scene also reflects the celebratory focus of the event itself, where this rather bland open space in the hotel is festooned with brightly coloured sometimes unusual and perhaps even exotic products. As one family pass through the atrium, a mother asks her child, 'Shall we go for a swim when we have found our room?' the daughter responds by saying 'No, I just want to shop'. Whilst these stands perhaps represent China and a cultural connection (however tenuous) for the parents, it would seem for at least one of the girls, that the event represents one akin to a birthday or Christmas through the opportunity to acquire toys and gifts.

A prominent stall at this event is a book stand where specific themes inform the books available to purchase. China is a dominant theme with historical, cultural, political, linguistic, and social texts available to inform the adult reader about the country, its people and languages, including language courses. Children's books are also on sale here. One of the themes is adoption and the stand offers creative and factual books across the age range. Many of these books are specific to adoption from China. Parents around this stand discuss books and offer advice about which books they have found useful in some way and which books their children have enjoyed. This stand does a brisk trade throughout the event. It also provides a location for parents to display and perform their knowledge of China, adoption and raising the adopted child. Keyed (Goffman, 1974) into the social activity surrounding, this stand is a display of the scripted role for the 'good adoptive parent'. Near the book stall are stands selling clothes for children (particularly girls). There is a Chinese theme in the pyjamas and traditional dresses on display. As with other stands, the colours

68   S. RICHARDS

are vibrant and attract attention. As the event progresses, girls wearing the clothes from these stalls can be seen having their photograph taken by the professional photographer whose stand is a dominant feature at the centre of the shopping experience. The girls in traditional clothes are predominantly the younger ones as are those who throng around the stands selling trinkets, toys, and gifts. One mother admires these girls as they run past, saying:

> I wish my daughter would still wear these dresses; she won't even come to Chinese New Year celebrations any more as she's too busy with her horse riding.

The above account echoes parental perceptions in Thomas and Tessler's (2007) study where parents suggest that older children become less interested in Chinese cultural activities as they grow older and engage in other activities. Tension between parent and older children concerning clothes exist in any family. But in this context the clothes are connected to the parent's obligation to provide cultural literacy and, like the eating lychees, daughters in traditional dresses display parent's commitment to this task.

There is also a regular second-hand clothes stall where clothes are not only purchased but also donated and the proceeds go towards charitable causes raising money for children in orphanages in China. There is a recurrent emphasis on charitable causes throughout each of these events. At summer school there are numerous stands selling Chinese products on two mornings and each afternoon. All of these stands represent individual charities related to children in China. These charities are either UK based or China based. At the Christmas event, there is a raffle held to raise money for a particular charity; a different one is selected each year. A charity which sends children's second-hand winter coats to orphanages in China is also collecting at this Christmas event. Being involved in such charity even if it is no more than donating money or clothes to the second-hand stall, is a normative aspect of parenting in this group and part of how these parents display family roles. The charities represented here are personal to these families, sometimes involving the orphanages where daughters have been adopted and frequently concern the province where their daughters were born. Involvement becomes part of what these families do and is performed here as part of how China is consumed by these families.

The Ties That Bind: Return Trips to China

A discussion point for many of the adults present at these events is taking children back to China to visit the country, province, orphanage, and sometimes, too, foster families. Such visits are recommended by social workers (Carstens & Julia, 2000; Hollingsworth, 2008) and have become part of *doing* Chinese adoptive parenting and displaying it to others. In one of the AGM/reunion events a company from the USA offering to facilitate and organise such trips ran a seminar on the subject and had a stall at the event selling Chinese gifts to raise money for their specific charity. Parents who have already made such a trip offer insights to those seeking to make it, and those who have returned recently speak of their diverse experiences. The opportunity to connect with others through offering support, gaining information, and displaying the good adoptive family are all present in these return trip discussions: How to contact and correspond with respective orphanages, how to find a suitable facilitator in China, how to handle abandonment site visits, how individual children may or have responded to such trips. All these themes are explored allowing good parenting to be displayed and judged and reproduced in this group.

The opportunity to connect through common interest, socialise through a common topic, and offer support and advice to others on a theme relevant to all seem at work here. The consumerism can perhaps be argued to be straightforward consumption (perhaps most evident with the young girls who 'just want to shop'). However, I argue that it is more complex than this. The stalls offer a degree of ritualism in their annual presence at the event and the goods that they sell. Continuity in the location of these stands at the event and the presence of the regular stall holders themselves as well as the products offer a sense of normative activity, personal connection, and belonging for the individual members present at this event. The activities presented here demonstrate cultural performance which is possible to key into adoption discourse, but this group have ritualised and refined this consumerism to meet the assumed needs of those present, and as such this consumerism fosters cultural belonging, enables family to be displayed, and becomes another example of performance in this cultural group.

Another way in which the good parent is displayed and performed at the reunion/AGM events is to attend at least some of the seminars which run throughout the two days. A crèche is available for those who need it,

70 S. RICHARDS

but many parents decide between them who will monitor children and who will participate in the seminars.

PARENTING THE DAMAGED CHILD: 'IT'S MORE THAN JUST PIANO LESSONS ISN'T IT?'

The above quotation is taken from a conversation that I had with a mother as a result of her disclosure in a seminar where she asked for help in understanding and coping with her eight -year-old daughter's violent behaviour. The seminar was run by a psychologist whose argument was that adopted children would only ever have a weak attachment to adoptive parents and, though this could be compensated for through adoptive parenting, was nevertheless a permanent scar for the child. The deficit stance here reminded me of Bowlby's depiction of the adopted child from the 1960s. The emotional impact of this scar (the psychologist suggested) is manifest in the daily behaviour of the children. This generated a significant amount of intimate disclosure and discussion and some anxiety on the part of the parents. One mother tearfully spoke of the violence that her daughter showed towards her and asked for help in how to reduce this. This violence was linked by the professional presenter to a graph on the power point slide, a depiction of a cycle of emotions involving concepts of loss, fear, anger; and the presenter agreed with the mother that her daughter's behaviour was indicative of weak attachment, anger, and insecurity related to the loss of her birth family and subsequent adoption. Greene et al. (2007, p. 18) provide a counter balance to the perspective above by arguing that adoption professionals commonly identify children's symptoms through 'diagnostic boxes which do not fit' and explain individual children's behaviour through the child's early experiences. 'Good adoptive parents', however, will not want to ignore such professional input no matter how flawed, those in the seminar are no exception.

I asked the mother who had been rather distraught if she was okay the following day. She said that she had spoken to the seminar presenter after the event and had got some helpful advice but that she felt it was important to speak up about the problems because as she said:

Parenting these girls is more than just piano lessons isn't it?

I need to reflect on my own personal values towards the depiction of children at this point and the influence it has on how I discuss this observation.

As a childhood scholar and an adoptive mother, I am uncomfortable about the ways in which these girls are simplistically constructed through the ideas and concepts presented at the seminar as described above. The following related exchange with Ruth (who, when this discussion took place, had recently taken part in my research) occurred at a regional event to celebrate Christmas. The exchange illustrates the deterministic nature of the 'damaged child' identity as well as my distrust of it. Her two-year-old daughter (adopted at eight months old) was running around the room and Ruth drew my attention to her by saying:

Ruth: Look at her; she has these uncontrollable spurts of frenetic energy which can be very destructive; she can destroy a room if we let her.
Sarah: She looks like she is having fun; two year olds are not always known to contain their emotions are they?
Ruth: No, this level is not normal; she has too much cortisol in her system due to the noise and the stress of the orphanage.
          I remain silent
Ruth: I know that this is not normal; my birth son was never like this.

The final remark was made perhaps in response to my passive resistance to describing an exuberant two-year-old waiting for Father Christmas to arrive, as abnormal in some way as a result of care prior to adoption. An interesting insight was her use of the authority of a birth mother status to support her position as an adoptive one. Ruth seeks to authenticate her judgement of her daughter's behaviour through her role as a birth mother that others in the room (including me) do not have. I do not dispute Ruth's interpretation of her daughter's behaviour, though my silence may have indicated that I did. Nor do I challenge that behavioural and emotional problems can and do occur for children separated from birth parents, or in institutional care, or as a result of adoption. However, such problems seem to be rather deterministic in nature and on occasion casually applied by experts and parents alike.

The cultural events discussed here are explored through the notion of performance of roles which are socially regarded as normative, mother, father, daughter, family, yet the very enactment of such performances here highlights the otherness of the families on this particular stage (including my own). These seminars are not only stages to perform the scripts in this overall cultural performance, they are also productive in constructing and ascribing particular identities related to adoption which are used by parents to parent by. In the seminar the good parent of the adopted child is reinforced, reascribed, with little questioning of the sweeping and, at times simplistic generalisations through which a young girl is diagnosed and advice through this diagnosis subsumed. This left me to reflect on ways that policy rationalities inevitably construct particular welfare subjects and to wonder whether the narratives of the girl's lives must always be first and foremost understood through adoption and loss. As Frank (2010, p. 2) eloquently argues about the power of the narrative, the 'story is less her choice than her fate'.

The expectation on adoptive parents to perform a specific parenting script is explicit in adoption policy and professional social work practice. This script reflects some of the contemporary canonical narratives of intercountry adoption policy highlighted earlier by Hollingsworth (1998) which, under the policy dictum of the best interests of the child (Richards, 2014), specific knowledge and institutions become privileged—birth family, birth culture, and birth place being paramount in this. Absence of such knowledge is argued to damage the 'authentic identities' (Cheng, 2004) of adopted children. Such a deficit model of adoption is normative, powerful, and unquestioned within adoption discourse, and thus the fate and identities of adoptees is ascribed along with the expectation that they will perform these identity roles. The performances presented in this chapter reveal the compliance and endeavours of intercountry adoptive parents to follow this identity-driven script by linking their daughters and sons to China and its culture and by helping them to recognise and then manage the loss of birth family whilst simultaneously securing successful attachments to adoptive family, culture, and country. In doing so the group create their own 'symbolic universe' (Gillis, 1996, p. 61) a culture with rituals which represent neither birth nor adopted culture exclusively but something more than the sum of its parts. In doing they inevitably resist and transcend the limits of such a simplistic policy rational which perceives culture, ethnicity, and belonging as somehow static and fixed at birth rather than dynamic, emerging, and performative.

As with many ethnographic research relationships, the ones I developed as a result of this research are multifaceted and ongoing. In my interactions with the group, I am on occasion the academic that did research with some of the families; sometimes I am my daughter's mother, sometimes a friend, and sometimes I am one of many intercountry adoptive parents trying to do what is argued to be in the best interests of my daughter. I often feel compelled to perform the adoptive mothering script even as I critique it. My relationships and commitment with this group ensure that they remain central to the ways I write about them and I remain well aware that there is no exit in this research field. The participants and CACH are inextricable from how I perform family, making my positionality both academically fruitful and ethically nuanced.

Ethnography and social policy research are not necessarily close companions. Policy development commonly relies on nomothetic data with seemingly little room for qualitative participant observation (Marston, 2002). Yet the performances explored above provide narratives where the implementation of policy and its impact on the subjugated populations it constructs is explicit. Performative ethnography can make visible situated knowledge concerning the effects of governing practices through illustrating the behaviours of those regulated by the dictates of policy. Its wider application would enhance social policy debate concerning the efficacy and application of welfare provision.

REFERENCES

Allen, N. (2007). *Making Sense of the New Adoption Law a Guide for Social and Welfare Services*. Lyme Regis: Russell House Publishing.

Anagnost, A. (2000). Scenes of Misrecognition: Maternal Citizenship in the Age of Transnational Adoption. *Positions, 8*(2), 241–389.

Barn, R. (2013). Doing the Right Thing: Transracial Adoption in the USA. *Ethnic and Racial Studies, 36*(8), 1273–1291. https://doi.org/10.1080/01419870.2013.770543

Bartholet, E. (1999). *Family Bonds: Adoption, Infertility and the New World of Child Production*. Boston: Beacon Press.

Blackmore, S. (2000, October). The Power of Memes. *Scientific American, 283*(4), 64–73.

Britton, J. (2013). Researching White Mothers of Mixed-Parentage Children: The Significance of Investigating Whiteness. *Ethnic and Racial Studies, 36*(8), 1311–1322. https://doi.org/10.1080/01419870.2013.752101

Bruner, E. M. (1986). Experiences and Its Expressions. In V. M. Turner & E. M. Bruner (Eds.), *The Anthropology of Experience* (pp. 3–30). Urbana: University of Illinois Press.

Bruner, J. (2004). Life as Narrative. *Social Research, 71*(3), 691–710.

Butler, J. (1993). *Bodies that Matter*. London: Routledge.

Caballero, C., Edwards, R., Goodyer, A., & Okitikpi, T. (2012). The Diversity and Complexity of the Everyday Lives of Mixed Racial and Ethnic Families:

Implications for Adoption and Fostering Practice and Policy. *Adoption & Fostering, 36*(3–4), 9–25.

Carstens, C., & Julia, M. (2000). Ethnoracial Awareness in Intercountry Adoption: US Experiences. *International Social Work, 43*(1), 61–73.

Cheng, V. J. (2004). *Inauthentic, The Anxiety over Culture and Identity*. London: Rutgers University Press.

Coffey, A. (1999). *The Ethnographic Self Fieldwork and the Representation of Identity*. London: Sage.

Cohen, P. (1995). Yesterday's Worlds, Tomorrow's World: From Racialisation of Adoption to the Politics of Difference. In I. Gaber & J. Aldridge (Eds.), *In the Best Interests of the Child: Culture Identity and Transracial Adoption* (pp. 43–76). London: Free Association Press.

Conquergood, D. (1992). Ethnography, Rhetoric, and Performance. *Quarterly Journal on Speech, 78*, 80–123.

Denzin, N. K. (1997). *Interpretive Ethnography, Ethnographic Practices for the 21st Century*. Thousand Oaks, CA: Sage.

Fabian, J. (1983). *Time and the Other: How Anthropology Makes Its Object*. New York: Columbia University Press.

Finch, J. (2007). Displaying Families. *Sociology, 41*(1), 65–81.

Foucault, M. (2003). Governmentality. In P. Rabinow & N. Rose (Eds.), *The Essential Foucault: Selections from Essential Works of Foucault 1954–1984* (pp. 229–245). London: The New Press.

Frank, A. W. (2010). *Letting Stories Breathe a Socio-Narratology*. Chicago: The University of Chicago Press.

Frith, S. (1996). Music and Identity. In S. Hall & P. Du Gay (Eds.), *Questions of Cultural Identity* (pp. 108–127). London: Sage.

Geertz, C. (1988). *Works and Lives*. Stanford: Stanford University Press.

Gillis, J. R. (1996). *A World of Their Own Making Myth, Ritual, and the Quest for Family Values*. New York: Harper Collins.

Goffman, E. (1974). *Frame Analysis*. Cambridge: Harvard University Press.

Greene, S., Kelly, R., Nixon, E., Kelly, G. Borska, Z., Murphy, S., et al. (2007). *A Study of Intercountry Adoption Outcomes in Ireland Summary Report*. Retrieved April 3, 2013, from http://www.tcd.ie/childrensresearchcentre/assets/pdf/Publications/Adoptionsummary.pdf

Hague Conference on Private International Law. (1993). Retrieved April 26, 2013, from http://www.hcch.net/index_en.php?act=conventions.status&cid=69

Harman, V. (2013). Social Capital and the Informal Support Networks of Lone White Mothers of Mixed-Parentage Children. *Ethnic and Racial Studies, 36*(8), 1323–1341. https://doi.org/10.1080/01419870.2013.752100

Hollingsworth, L. D. (1998). Promoting Same-Race Adoption for Children of Color. *Social Work, 43*(2), 104–116.

Hollingsworth, L. D. (2008). Does the Hague Convention on Intercountry Adoption Address the Protection of Adoptees' Cultural Identity? And Should It? *Social Work, 53*, 377–379.

Jacobson, H. (2008). *Culture Keeping.* Nashville: Vanderbilt University Press.

Li, T. (2007). *The Will to Improve: Governmentality, Development and the Practice of Politics.* London: Duke University Press.

Madden, R. (2010). *Being Ethnographic: A Guide to the Theory and Practice of Ethnography.* London: Sage.

Marston, G. (2002). Critical Discourse Analysis and Policy-Orientated Housing Research. *Housing Theory and Society, 19*(2), 82–91.

McKee, K. (2009). Post-Foucauldian Governmentality: What Does It Offer Critical Social Policy Analysis? *Critical Social Policy, 29*(3), 465–486.

Richards, S. (2012). What the Map Cuts up the Story Cuts Across: Narratives of Belonging in Intercountry Adoption. In J. Simmonds & A. Phoenix (Eds.), *Multiculturalism, Identity and Family Placement,* in *Adoption & Fostering, 36* (3–4): 104–111.

Richards, S. (2013). Stories of Paper and Blood: Narratives of Belonging in Families with Daughters Adopted from China. PhD diss., Institute of Education University College, London.

Richards, S. (2014). *HCIA Implementation and the Best Interests of the Child.* ISS Working Paper Series/General Series, vol. 597, 1–18. International Institute of Social Studies of Erasmus University (ISS). Retrieved from http://hdl.handle.net/1765/77407

Rose, N. (1999). *Governing the Soul: The Shaping of the Private Self.* London: Free Association Books.

Said, E. (1978). *Orientalism.* London: Penguin Books.

Santino, J. (2004). Performative Commemoratives, the Personal, and the Public: Spontaneous Shrines, Emergent Ritual. In H. Bial (Ed.), *The Performance Studies Reader* (pp. 125–133). London: Routledge.

Schechner, R. (2006). *Performance Studies an Introduction* (2nd ed.). New York: Routledge.

Selwyn, J., & Wijedasa, D. (2008). *'The Language of Matching', Why Am I Waiting? 7 July 2008 LVSRC.* London: British Association Adoption & Fostering Conference.

Singer, M. (Ed.). (1959). *Traditional India; Structure and Change* (Vol. X). Philadelphia: American Folklore Society.

Smolin, D. M. (2004). Intercountry Adoption as Child Trafficking. *Valparaiso University Law Review, 39* (2): 281–325. Retrieved from http://scholar.valpo.edu/vulr/vol39/iss2/1

Sullivan, L. E. (1986). Sound and Senses: Toward a Hermeneutics of Performance. *History of Religions, 26*(1), 2–14.

Taylor, D. (2004). Translating Performance. In H. Bial (Ed.), *The Performance Studies Reader* (pp. 381–386). London: Routledge.

Thomas, K. A., & Tessler, R. C. (2007). Bicultural Socialization Among Adoptive Families: Where There Is a Will There Is a Way. *Journal of Family Issues, 28*(9), 1189–1219. https://doi.org/10.1177/0192513X07301115

76   S. RICHARDS

Turner, V. (1982). *From Ritual to Theatre: The Human Seriousness of Play*. New York: Performing Arts Journal Publications.

Turner, V. (1986). *The Anthropology of Performance*. New York: Performing Arts Journal Publications.

United Nations Convention on the Rights of the Child. (1989). Retrieved August 13, 2013, from http://www.unicef.org.uk/UNICEFs-Work/Our-mission/UN-Convention/

Volkman, T. A. (2005). Embodying Chinese Culture Transnational Adoption in North America. In T. A. Volkman (Ed.), *Cultures of Transnational Adoption* (pp. 81–113). Durham: Duke University Press.

Warner, M. (1991). Introduction: Fear of a Queer Planet. *Social Text, 29*(4), 3–17.

Yuval-Davis, N. (1994). Identity Politics and Women's Ethnicity. In V. M. Moghadam (Ed.), *Identity Politics and Women Cultural Reassertions and Feminisms in International Perspective* (pp. 408–424). Boulder: Westview Press.

Yuval-Davis, N. (2011). *The Politics of Belonging Intersectional Contestations*. London: Sage.

CHAPTER 5

Ethnographic Practices of Listening

Allison Boggis

My apprenticeship into ethnography began as I started my PhD studies in 2008 whereupon I undertook research with disabled children and young people who had little or no speech. As I engaged with the young participants, my skills as an ethnographer developed and my sensorial acclimatisation to social practices began. By paying close attention, my ability to listen to voices that were different became much more acute. As an embodied knowledge of these young participants began to emerge, I started talking and writing about personal accounts of doing social research and sharing my stories of interactions with others.

This chapter continues with this practice and shares some aspects of my research journey, drawing on the sensory experiences of ethnographic practices of listening that I have encountered thus far.

INTRODUCTION

Whilst the recognition of children's rights has led to prioritising their active participation in research (Veale, 2005), Franklin and Sloper (2009) argue that growth in this area has been slower in respect of disabled children. Indeed, Stalker and Connors (2003) suggest that the majority of studies relating to disabled children continue to rely on data collected from parents and professionals. Equally, Abbott (2013) contends that the

A. Boggis (✉)
University of Suffolk, Ipswich, Suffolk

© The Author(s) 2018
T. Vine et al. (eds.), *Ethnographic Research and Analysis,*
https://doi.org/10.1057/978-1-137-58555-4_5

77

emphasis on much of the research is evaluative, applied, and service-orientated. However, there has been a notable increase in recent research where disabled children and young people's views and experiences have been included (see e.g. Curran & Runswick-Cole, 2013; Goodley, 2011; Goodley & Runswick-Cole, 2011; Priestly, 1999; Wickenden, 2011). This shift is encouraging because it goes some way towards recognising the importance of including the voices of those who have hitherto been excluded. However, less critical attention has been paid to methodological issues that arise when researching with disabled children and young people. This chapter helps to redress this balance by offering an evaluation of how ethnography can be used successfully to recognise and interpret voices, experiences, and opinions.

Arguably, hard-to-reach children, such as those with little or no speech, present researchers with significant challenges, and facilitating their inclusion requires a considerable investment of time, resources, and skills. The exclusion of populations based on assumptions of vulnerability, incapacity, or incompetence is highly problematic creating a void of information relating to disabled children's experiences. Their inclusion calls for adaptations to traditional research designs and methodologies.

My journey into ethnography was influenced by a commitment to recognising strength-based perceptions of children, regarding them as experts on their own lives (James & Prout, 1997), as active citizens with participation rights (UNCRC, 1989) and within principles of ethical symmetry (Christensen & Prout, 2002). This chapter considers a methodological approach that encompasses ethnographic practices of listening. In doing so, it pays attention to specific aspects of research with disabled children and young people and offers a critical response to conventional, interpretive conceptions of voice in qualitative inquiry. Indeed, adopting a sensory approach that pays close attention to communication which does not rely predominantly on words enabled me to listen, observe, and interpret disabled children and young people's experiences of using high-tech communication aids in their everyday lives. I found that including a range of voices in research expanded the soundscape to incorporate other forms of communication such as body language, facial expression, sign, vocalisation, and utterances. Extending our understanding of voice to encompass different pitches and tones not only acknowledges the importance of including *all* social agents within social and political realities of society but also acknowledges that a range of views and experiences contributes to our depth of understanding of the variety of childhoods.

The voices of my participants were braided with others including teachers, support staff, and my own. This brings a number of distinct advantages (Richardson, 1990). It liberates diverse perspectives, offers a nuanced understanding of social relations and their construction, and recognises voices as interdependent and context specific (Richards, Clark, & Boggis, 2015).

The choice of working alongside the participants as a voluntary classroom helper was intentional for it required not only what Reinharz (1992) terms as closeness *with* rather than distance *from* participants but also demanded a critical examination and analytical reflection on the nature of the research and my own position within it. Therefore, in order to disrupt humanly constructed boundaries of voice, I adopted a feminist-based research enquiry which embraces and actively encourages ongoing concerns with silencing, marginalisation, absences, and boundaries. Whilst this chapter is not written from an explicitly feminist perspective, much of the material drawn on is from that canon. The intention here, however, is not to provide a detailed confession of personal experiences of conducting the research but to recognise the impact that my own perspectives might have had on the relationship with the participants, the production, and interpretation of the data and the form in which the research is presented (see Richards et al., 2015, Chap. 5, for a more in-depth exploration of the ramifications of category entitlement).

A Note on Terminology

The children and young people who agreed to participate in this study are registered as disabled and all use high-tech augmentative and alternative communication systems (AACS). Whilst it is recognised that the disabled population is not a homogeneous one, it is argued that researching a social category necessitates a definition of the population about whose lives are being reviewed. However, the contentiousness of terminology regarding disability has been the cause for much academic discussion, and clearly, it means different things to different people. Oliver notes that 'it has been suggested that the term "people with disabilities" should be used in preference to "disabled people" because this prioritizes people rather than disability' (1983, p. 261), but he goes on to explain that 'disabled people' is the preferred terminology of those within the disabled movement because it makes a political statement: they are not people 'with' disabilities, but people who are disabled or disadvantaged by soci-

80   A. BOGGIS

ety's response to their differences (Oliver, 1990). The intention of this chapter is not to add to the ongoing debate of the tension created by the value placed on either term of reference. Therefore, the terms 'disabled children' and 'children with disabilities' are used interchangeably and intentionally with 'disability' placed purposefully either before or after 'children' to emphasise social barriers and/or individual impairment. In addition, the terms 'children' and 'young people' are used to describe the participants aged 18 and under. All participants agreed to share their stories with you, but I have preserved their identities through the use of pseudonyms.

Exploring Disabled Children's Childhoods

My understanding of childhood is that it is far from straightforward. I believe that it is not simply the outcome of the particular structured conditions in which children find themselves at in any one point in time. Nor is it merely the function of cultural determinants or the outcome of discourses produced by adults to preserve and recreate their own childhoods. It is also a product of the everyday actions of children themselves. Therefore, in order to contemplate disabled children and young people's positions within a social context and gain an understanding of where they stand as actors and how they are acted upon, the interplay of agency and structure emphasised within this chapter is guided by Giddens' (1984) theory of structuration. Rather than making a clear distinction between theory and ethnography, however, I will underpin my interpretation of this theoretical framework with the young participants' everyday experiences. Engaging with the ordinary (see Vine, 2017), I found that quite remarkable things occurred in their everyday lives in school and slowly, my awareness of how agency and structure co-exist, interact, and engage with each other began to develop. By retuning my ears and listening more carefully, I was able to explore these relationships through the young people's narratives, those who work closely with them in school, and the narratives of my own. In brief, the empirical research space gave me a platform from which I could examine the duality of structuration *and* gain an understanding of how specific contexts influence disabled children and young people's voices and the ways in which they used their voices to achieve agency.

Children's agency has been explored in terms of their competence and knowledge (e.g. Corsaro, 1997; Haugen, 2008; MacNaughton, Hughes, &

Smith, 2007). Children have shown that they are quite capable of making decisions about their medical treatment (Alderson & Montgomery, 1996), in living with terminal illness (Bluebond-Langner, 1978), responding to their parents' divorce (Smart, Neale, & Wade, 2001), and talking about their own experiences of disability (Stalker & Connors, 2003). However, whilst they are increasingly described as agents, it should be recognised that there are divergent understandings of agency. Mayall's (2002), p. 21) distinction between 'actor' and 'agency' is instructive here, with the former implying that children are of the social world (beings rather than becomings) and the latter taking 'action' forward, implying that children make a difference and that their views should be taken seriously. Within my own research, agency was taken not simply to imply the liberation of children but as an opportunity for opening up possibilities for hearing children, consulting with them and creating new spaces for their voices. Given the current emphasis of articulation, rationality, and strategy on agency, however, I believe, like others such as Prout (2000), that failure to incorporate a critical, embodied, and engendered account of agency into childhood studies serves only to reinforce a model in which the privileged are accorded more agency than those who do not demonstrate rationality and choice in conventional ways. I therefore argue that children's agency should be more carefully conceptualised to accommodate the diversity within childhoods. The absence of disabled children's voices not only fails to represent their experiences; it also distorts their representation. Therefore, in accordance with Gilligan's (1993) ideas about relational resonances of voice in terms of taking serious account of the distinctive character of the young participants' knowledge and capabilities, my ethnographic study was grounded in listening and in scrutinising the privileging of one voice over another.

The concept of voice was considered important to this study because disabled children and young people who have little or no speech may be perceived as not having a voice in either physical or metaphorical senses. Conventional meanings of voice assume naturally produced speech as a means of expression. The question here is whether unconventional voices are recognised and heard in the same way or if having a different voice has implications for participation. Whilst the social studies of childhood regard the child's voice as a matter of need, right, and skill and worthy of being listened to and studied in its own right (James & Prout, 1997), the complex debates relating to children's competencies, age, and maturity and the credibility of their statements have excluded children who have unconventional voices. I argue that assumptions of disabled children and young people's lack of competence have hitherto denied their agency and participation. Therefore, in terms of rethinking the social positions that disabled children and young people may hold, I draw again on Gilligan's (1993) study of women's knowledge here. Not only does she consider how each unique characteristic of knowledge provides us with distinctive experiences but she also offers a detailed examination of the ways in which it might be instructive in reshaping social theory. In order to incorporate these ideas into my own work and uphold the need to take disabled children and young people's rights of participation seriously, I adopted a methodological approach whereby I could critically appraise the issues relating to the socially embedded nature of rights in situ. Drawing out these ambiguities and tensions further and critically appraising them allowed for what Gilligan (1993) describes as interpretations of the social order. It did not mean, however, that I sought new ways to present voices but just that I tried to look at things in a different way.

Ethnographic Vantage Points

As I worked alongside the disabled children and young people, I was able to secure a vantage point within specific social relations. As we got to know each other, with them I was able to unravel their narratives and develop what Stones (2005) refers to as an internal critique of their lives. Whilst my concern was not to question disabled children's competencies, I was curious to understand how their voices were acknowledged and expressed or disguised and controlled. As a mother of a disabled child myself, I could draw on my personal experiences of the ways in which 'superordinate parties', usually the official and professional authorities (see Becker, 1967) treated my son as incapable and incompetent due to what some might term as inefficiency of voice. By resisting fixed notions of competence and capability, and insisting on seeking out personal experiences, I did as Morris (1993) suggested and tried to pay attention to the ways in which such homogeneity is assumed. Through critiquing accepted 'facts' that surround disability and emphasising flexibility and inclusivity rather than rigidity and exclusivity, and having insider experiences of disability, I felt able to deconstruct concepts in a way that neither negated nor dismissed: it merely opened them up in a way that has previously not been considered.

Adopting an Ethnographic Approach

I found that researching with disabled children and young people using an ethnographic approach was 'messy and emergent' (Huber & Clandinin, 2002, p. 787). As the young participants had little or no speech, I became aware that there was a limited amount of spoken information that could be directly gathered from disabled children and young people themselves (Morris, 1998). I therefore gathered information from a range of sources and in a variety of ways in order to gain more detailed knowledge about the participants' lives. As a result, I created what Eisner (1991), p. 72) described as a 'collage' where pieces of descriptive information were patched together to make a recognisable 'whole'. Therefore, drawing on a multiplicity of methods of data collection, sources included academic literature, situational research, observations, semi-structured interviews, and focus groups. In addition, research conversations were conducted with school staff who were familiar with the young participants and who were skilled in facilitating communication.

Immersing myself within the culture of a community in order to study it raised tensions in respect of distance and the maintenance of objectivity. Observing, listening, recording, and facilitating participant's voices enabled me to piece together multiple stories and from a variety of perspectives. Becoming 'interconnected and involved in the changing social and cultural relations under study' (Crang & Cook, 2007, n9), familiarisation with the participants' worlds, and seeing their lives from the inside afforded an otherwise unobtainable view. That is not to say, however, that I did not question my own credibility, acquired sympathy and judgement throughout the research. Equally, I cannot deny that my own position as a mother of a disabled child persuaded me to take 'sides' with what Becker (1967, p. 243) describes as 'subordinates'. At the same time, however, I wrestled with the dilemma as to whether ethnographers can ever fully become an 'insider', heeding Phillips' warning of the importance to appreciate that 'almost any utterance in any language carries with it a set of assumptions, feelings and values that the speaker may or may not be aware of but that the fieldworker, as an outsider, usually is not' (1960 cited in Temple & Young, 2004, p. 165). With this in mind, becoming a 'good enough' ethnographer, that is 'someone willing and able to become a more reflexive and social version of him or herself in order to learn something meaningful about other people's lives' (Cloke et al., 2004, p. 170) was what I continuously strived for.

In Recognition of the Role of the Researcher

Emond (2000) believes that when researching with children, collecting the data and analysing it, one cannot be considered disconnected from the research. The researcher too has attributes, characteristics, history and gender, class, race, and social attributes that constitute part of the research interaction. My own role as a researcher was inextricably bound with roles such as volunteer-helper and mother of a disabled son. Rose (1997, p. 308) captures this by describing the researcher as a 'multiple self' where one's existing subject knowledge and understanding becomes entangled with experience. In the light of multiple positions, selves, and identities at play within the research process, Komarovsky voices concerns that subjectivity comes 'too close ... to a total elimination of the inter-subjective validation of description and explanation' (Komarovsky, 1988, p. 592). Whilst I have highlighted questions of objectivity, validity, and reliability and the nature of positionality both within this chapter and elsewhere (see Boggis, 2011; Richards et al., 2015), rather than to try to dislocate the author from the research or ignore the impact I may have on the participants or the research itself, I made a conscious decision to try to understand the nature of subjective enquiry. Indeed, as Stanley and Wise suggest:

> Whether we like it or not, researchers remain human beings complete with the usual assembly of feelings, failings and moods. All of these things influence how we feel and understand what is going on. Our consciousness is always the medium through which research occurs; there is no method or technique of doing research other than through the medium of the researcher. (Stanley & Wise, 1993, p. 157)

Generational issues, developmental perspectives, and power differentials have featured prominently in research involving children and young people, reinforcing the general belief that adults have superior knowledge. However, consistent with the view of Clarke and Moss (2001), I recognised disabled children and young people as experts in their own lives and challenged the concept of competence that has dominated research with children. I focussed on facilitating disabled children's active participation, encouraging them to speak out, enabling their voices to be heard and endeavouring to draw on their strengths instead of focussing on what they are unable to do. I believe that this, in itself, goes some way towards addressing issues of power and social exclusion.

Authenticity of Voice

Whilst careful consideration was given to issues of researcher power and representation throughout the research, the authenticity of the voices of those represented within the research was questionable. At times, the research became complex and confusing because listening to disabled children's voices and other indicators of expression often exceeded my own ways of hearing, knowing, and understanding. Clearly, 'voice' occurred in spoken utterances as well as within silence, behaviour, body language and facial expression, and therefore, as a listener, I adopted what Mazzei (2009) proposes as attentiveness and openness to different sounds in order to render silent voices as valuable contributors to the soundscape. I found that children with few words could not easily articulate answers without their augmentative and alternative communication systems (AACSs) and, as Mascia-Lees, Sharpe, and Cohen (1989) suggest, there may be problems of control when devices are borrowed to express voice. As mentioned previously, I expanded the notion of soundscape to incorporate other forms of communication and, in doing so, became responsible for being more attentive to what goes unsaid (Booth & Booth, 1996), paying attention to body language, eye contact, eye pointing, and facial expression as additional means of communication.

Observing the young AACS users in school whilst they went about their daily business, I noted that all of them had individual means of communicating simple yes/no answers. Without the high-tech communication aids however, many of them had little opportunity to expand on this. I soon became aware that whilst their AACSs 'lent' them voices, it was adults who programmed the majority of the aids with vocabulary that they deemed appropriate for general use or curriculum purpose. The 'spoken' word was severely limiting and did not (and in many cases, could not) answer the questions posed in the interviews or elaborate meaning within research conversations. This inefficiency of voice could therefore perpetuate the concept of disabled children as incompetent. Furthermore, the authenticity of the young participants' choice of words was questionable. Making their voices heard without exploiting or distorting them posed what Alcoff terms a 'crisis of representation' (2009, p. 12)—not only was the authenticity of voice a concern but I also experienced an acute insecurity of speaking *about* others or *for* others either adequately or justifiably. Arguably, facilitating voices and representing disabled children and young people's voices do not overcome the problem of representation, because

86   A. BOGGIS

the respondent's comments are already mediated by the situation in which they occur and the interview in which they take part. Whilst I recognised that it was me that had the final responsibility for the text, I felt that I needed to make clear my positionality in relationship to the voices that were represented. Indeed, as Fine (1992, p. 217) urges, researchers should 'articulate how, how not and within what limits' voices are framed and used.

Careful Listening

A defining characteristic of Giddens' (1984) theory of structuration is its emphasis on the interrelationships and interdependencies of social structures and agency. Put simply, social structures are the products of past practices of agents, and agents' practices are the result of direct experiences of structures. Therefore, I use the term 'quiet voices' in literal and metaphorical terms because I feel this describes not only the young disabled participants' voices but also their social status. As I see it, the pitch and tone of their voices and the silence they keep is a reflection of the world they see and their position within it. However, the ontological positioning of the disabled children and young people is far from simplistic. My research established that their agentic positions were not only influenced causally by independent social structures which identify them as vulnerable, dependent, and incompetent, but in phenomenological terms, the external forces of control often left them feeling unable to resist the practices of adults. However, as I spent time familiarising myself with the young participants and understanding their unique methods of communication, I became aware of the ways in which they actively drew on their knowledge of social structures as they engaged in social practices. Whilst traditionally disabled children and young people are constructed as 'becoming', dependent, and incompetent typically characterising them as vulnerable and passive, I found the opposite to be true. Without exception, they were all active, independent, and competent social agents. Adopting a strategy of careful listening (which not only concentrated on verbal utterances but included observing body language and movement, facial expression, and sign language) as they went about their daily business in school, I noted the young participants competently engaging socially with peers and support staff, making independent choices and resisting school rules. In addition, the young participants chose to engage in research conversations with me and talked openly and honestly about their experiences of using high-tech communication systems. As they actively engaged in the research interviews and focus groups, I discovered that they appreciated a platform from which their voices could be heard and were recognised as powerful, interesting, and reliable. Therefore, rather than applying a broad brush stroke approach when trying to understand disabled children's lives and accepting what Archer (1995, p. 167) identifies as 'causal powers of external structures that set out general directions and expectations' of disabled children and young people, by creating spaces and allowing time to express their views, the discussions we had were insightful. Indeed, by listening carefully, I was able to re-examine the interrelationships between the context of control and the conduct of the participants. This allowed me to gain a more nuanced understanding of the ways in which their voices were affected. Drawing on Gilligan's work (Gilligan, 1993) with different voices, and Back's (2007) suggestions of artful listening, I was able to focus more fully on the situated experiences of disabled children and young people themselves.

Contexts of Silence

Interviews as a method of data collection are firmly established in contemporary qualitative research, part of normative ethnographic practice and talking plays a pivotal role within them (Pink, 2015). However, I argue that the emphasis on talking limits the ways in which meanings can be conveyed and understood. The narratives I collected were not always spoken but they were shaped by my own interpretation as listener. The scrutiny of the data therefore relied not only on being sufficiently reflexive about the 'type' of voice and the best ways of collecting them but also on becoming proficient in what Lewis (2010) describes as advanced listening skills, which include hearing silences that are neither neutral nor empty. Indeed, Pink (2015, p. 73) argues that ethnographic engagement should be a sensorial event within a context of emplaced knowing. Through prolonged engagement with the disabled children and young people, I learned that they all had developed alternative informal ways of expressing themselves (e.g. facial expression, vocalisation, gestures, and eye-and-body pointing), which they supplemented with signing or using picture and symbol books. They complemented their overall sensorial-based communication style by using their voice-synthesised high-tech communication aids. Most used more than one method of communication, with some being favoured over others for pragmatic reasons. For example, some of the participant's reported that the high-tech aids were much slower to use and more physically tiring than some of the other communication options and so opted for the latter when talking to people who knew them well enough to understand them.

I also observed that many AACS users depended on their conversational partner to co-construct their intended meaning from a small number of keywords. During my time in the field as a researcher, I learned that this takes good judgement skills of the partner about when to guess and when to wait. For example, on one occasion, I waited 20 minutes for one of the female participants to compose a sentence using her AACS. However, once I got to know her and she trusted me to interpret her facial expression and her vocalisation, we adopted our own Creole style conversation and it became much speedier. It was far less taxing for her than relying on her high-tech communication system exclusively. During our research conversations, she told me that she was not overly keen on the choice of electronically generated voice options: '*Not keen voice*' *(made an unhappy facial expression and gestured with thumbs down towards her AACS)*. She demonstrated this by playing a number of options of available voices (age and gender appropriate, American or British accents, and some other aspects of style)—expressing the ones she liked (with a thumbs up and a smile) and those she disliked (with a thumbs down and a grimace). Using this bespoke conversation style, we chatted away and I agreed that the electronic voices she played lacked naturalness in terms of the subtle variations in tone and voice quality that physiological voices have. Even with the present level of technology, I discovered that the voices had a 'robotic' quality which was neither unique nor natural.

This sensorial approach resonates with what Sherman Heyl (2001, p. 367) describes as an 'established, respectful and ongoing relationship' which engages with a genuine exchange of views, allowing sufficient time for the interviewer and interviewee to purposefully explore the meanings they place on events in their lived experiences. Whilst I agree with Beresford (1997) who argued that we should not assume that disabled children and young people with little or no speech have nothing to say, I am suggesting that conventional meanings of 'voice' need further expansion, for whilst the young participants in my study had much to say, their voices were significantly different from those of 'natural' speakers. Our conversations were undeniably effective, but they were different. The question here is whether alternative voices are recognised and heard in the same ways as others or whether having a different voice implies other kinds of difference. As Paterson and Hughes suggest, we live in a verbal world, where those with 'vocal bodies' are often exclusionary in the ways that they structure society and 'norms of communication and norms of inter-corporeal interaction reflect the carnal needs of non-disabled actors' (Paterson & Hughes, 1999, p. 604). Supporters of the social model of disability would argue that exclusionary barriers to voices that are different are oppressive and that notions of difference, incapacity, and incompetence stem from the individualised medical model of disability. This not only symbolises restrictions of freedom and choice for disabled children and young people but also defines them in terms of difference and (dis)ability, highlighting what they cannot do, rather than celebrating what they could do. Expected 'norms' of conversational style do likewise.

It is the combination of these factors that engender what Stones (2005) terms as independent causal influences which effectively silence disabled children's voices. I also argue that when such causal influences combine, they shape disabled children and young people's positions as vulnerable, incompetent, and dependent. Weinberg's (2006) work with street drug users can be usefully employed here to illustrate how the context and circumstances in which we live shapes us. For example, one of his participants described his collective descent into the world of drugs at length and Weinberg (2006, p. 108) concluded that the phrase 'I couldn't take it' was the product of defeat which resulted from an environmentally induced relinquishing of self-control, rather than a deliberate exercise of self-control. Parallels regarding contexts that shape and determine disabled voices can be drawn here. As witnessed, adults often made decisions on behalf of the disabled children and young people, authenticating their own presence, conferring legitimacy and credibility on themselves. By default, this confers illegitimacy and discredit on 'inarticulate' children and young people. It follows, then, that the voices of the young participants in my study were environmentally induced by structures of control. However, instead of descending in 'quasi-Hobbesian order' like Weinberg's participants (Weinberg, 2006, p. 108), the voices of the disabled children and young participants often descended into silence.

Adopting an ethnographic approach offered me an opportunity to get close to the participants, and as I spent time with them, it was clear that all could communicate, and, even to an inexperienced listener, those who had little or no speech had unique ways of making their voices heard. It was surprising to me that their views were not readily heard or listened to and acted upon. Failure to include them in decisions that affect them or to listen to their voices supports general expectations or what Archer terms as 'situational tendencies' (Archer, 1995, p. 167) whereby disabled children and young people are conceptualised as vulnerable, dependent, and incompetent. Further to this, Oliver (1990, 2009) argues that society is organised around an able-bodied paradigm that constructs disability as a deficit or lack. The following example can be usefully employed here to illustrate this point further.

During a research conversation with a member of staff, I was told about a young female's non-use of her AACS. Apparently, she had just about given up on it because it was physically exhausting to use and the time it took to compose a response meant that she could not keep in sync with situational conversations. I had previously observed that she was an infrequent AACS user but one day when I was working in the classroom with another child, I heard her becoming increasingly distressed as a teaching assistant was trying to fix her AACS to the lap tray of her wheelchair. She began to cry and shout loudly. I observed her wriggling in her wheelchair as she tried to push the teaching assistant's arm away. This attracted much attention and a second teaching assistant joined her. As the behaviour continued, the teacher also attempted to calm her down. The majority of the pupils in the class did not seem overly concerned but one boy covered his ears, walked into the corner of the room and faced the wall as if to shield himself from this outburst. My field notes described how the staff asked *lots of questions in a variety of ways, but elicited no change in response. The teaching assistant then moved her wheelchair to the far corner of the room where she was joined by the second teaching assistant and the teacher resumed the lesson.* The two members of staff were trying to figure out why she was so distressed and spoke together loudly above the screaming. Whilst I was unable to hear the whole conversation, I understood that one of the teaching assistants was more familiar with this pupil than the other. After some discussion, they decided that the episode was just a case of her *'going off on one again because she didn't want to use her AACS'.* The AACS was taken off the lap tray but the young person continued to cry and shout. The teaching assistant, who was less familiar with her, explained that she thought she saw her sign 'toilet' and she was concerned that she looked uncomfortable. The wheelchair was reclined and she quietened momentarily. She signed 'toilet' again which was dismissed with *'we can't take you yet 'cos toilet break isn't for another 30 minutes. If we take you now, Terry will be shorthanded in the classroom'* upon which the teacher looked up and waved them away with a nod, giving them permission to take her to the toilet. She stopped crying and shouting as she was taken down the corridor to the toilet. The lesson resumed.

During break time, I met one of the teaching assistants in the playground as she was pushing this young person in her wheelchair into the shade. I asked how she was feeling. I got no response and she did not lift her head to look at me or acknowledge that I had asked her a question. The teaching assistant replied on her behalf, telling me that she was fine and that she had been making all that fuss because she had a tummy ache and had just started her period. Later, when I wrote up my observations, I reflected on the situation and wondered how other female teenagers would have reacted in a similar situation. Clearly, this young female relied on others for personal, intimate care. She had little or no speech but found her AACS physically tiring to use. She relied on help to set it up and I had been told that she had just about given up using it. Without this voice prosthetic, she had used other means of communicating—signing, vocalising, and body language. When her signing voice did not get the required response, she vocalised and used body language voice to communicate. Even then, it took some time for the conveyed message to be understood and acted upon. In addition, intimate and personal information was relayed to me in the playground at break time in earshot of others.

I reflected that a combination of irresistible internal and external structures had overlapped here, resulting in silence. She had rationalised her action based on her previous attempts to make her voice heard and reflexively used her knowledge to monitor her conduct. Despite dominant assumptions of incompetence and dependence, she chose not to use her AACS, opting for a more powerful form of communication to get her message across. Whilst her choice was purposeful and successful, the outcome was that over time, she became less inclined to use her voice prosthetic. I noted that she began to use her other voices less frequently and then only in relation to pain or frustration. Having previously observed that this young person was more than capable of conveying her message, it would seem that it is listening rather than speaking that is problematic here. As Back (2007) suggests, the art of listening lies in paying attention to the fragments of voices that are often passed over or ignored. In this case those fragments included body language, sign, facial expression, and vocalisation. Actively listening means retuning our hearing and paying attention. This will not only give us an opportunity to engage with the world differently but will also provide new directions for thought and critique.

Another young AACS user told me that she found her high-tech communication system '*very time consuming and physically tiring to use*'. However, she persisted in using it. She explained, '*I like it [the AACS]. It helps me to speak*'. She also told me she '*felt lost without it*'. The young participant did not sign or vocalise, but she did use a communication book and other forms of bodily communication '*because it is quicker*'. Whilst she was a prolific AACS user, she told me that she felt that her voice was undervalued, for when she was asked if people listened to what she had to say, she replied, '*No, not really. Mostly, they usually can't be bothered to wait for my answer*'. She took great care to compose sentences with precision and this was often a lengthy process. Consequently, during some conversations with peers and staff I noted that they did not wait for her to catch up and consequently stopped listening. Her voice was disregarded. Their conversations moved on at a pace that was quicker than this young person could manage and so, after being left behind on several occasions, her active participation became less frequent. This not only illustrates the ways in which the disabled children and young people's voices can be subjugated as incompetent and inefficient but also about the ways in they are socially positioned. Whilst I acknowledge that processes of exclusion and perceptions of incapability and incompetence are patterned by historical concepts of children as 'objects of concern rather than persons with voice' (Prout & Hallett, 2003, p. 1), I would argue that unconventional voices receive less attention than mainstream voices, and unless we adopt progressive ways to listen to multiple representations of voice, these misconceptions will continue. If it remains unchallenged, children and young people will be assigned to a pre-ordained habitus which categorises them by their impairment. The outcomes will remain the same and the voices of disabled children and young people will gradually be silenced and they will continue to be marginalised.

Summary

Disabled children and young people are often subjected to multiple forms of assessment and judgement within a service-led system that assesses their needs. Due to both time and financial constraints, these are usually carried out by professionals on a 'one-off' basis. However, within this chapter, I have illustrated how spending time with the young participants builds reciprocal relationships of trust and understanding. This, I would argue, is one of the many advantages of adopting an ethnographic approach.

Listening to children who have little or no speech is not an easy task, and hearing and understanding multifarious voices requires developing careful listening skills. The time required to accomplish skills of listening should not be underestimated, and whilst it is concluded that not only is it important, both morally and from a rights-based perspective to include disabled children and young people in research, it is imperative that researchers become more aware of the diversities of childhood and give serious consideration to incorporating reflexivity into methodological approaches. Participatory research and the use of innovative, responsive methods demonstrate how disabled children's childhood research can create spaces for young people to share their experiences (see Goodley, 2011; Goodley & Runswick-Cole, 2011; Priestly, 1999; Wickenden, 2011) and go some way to reshaping social constructions of disability. Indeed, I believe that it is important to remember that the 'problem' of researching with participants with little or no speech is a function of the limitations of researcher and not of the children and young people themselves. The 'one size fits all' approach to research simply will not do. It is therefore recommended that future ethnographic studies encourage researchers to adopt a range of skills that will enable them to utilise techniques that relate to participant's abilities in order to gather rich data about their lived experiences.

This chapter is not intended to be a 'how to guide' to researching with disabled children and young people, rather I have shared some of the things that I have reflected upon in this process. I cannot make claims that the research methods I adopted were particularly new or original. However, if one is to consider that *every* child can participate not only within the research arena but in every day circumstances, we must ensure that their participation is properly planned and not reliant on short-term adult-driven assessments and agendas.

References

Abbott, D. (2013). Who Says What, Where, Why and How? Doing Real-World Research with Disabled Children, Young People and Family Members. In T. Curran & K. Runswick-Cole (Eds.), *Disabled Children's Childhood Studies.* Basingstoke: Palgrave Macmillan.

Alcoff, L. M. (2009). The Problem of Speaking for Others. In A. Y. Jackson & L. A. Mazzei (Eds.), *Voice in Qualitative Inquiry. Challenging Conventions, Interpretive and Critical Conceptions in Qualitative Research.* London: Routledge.

94   A. BOGGIS

Alderson, P., & Montgomery, J. (1996). *Healthcare Choices: Making Decisions with Children*. London: Institute for Public Policy Research.

Archer, M. (1995). *Realist Social Theory: The Morphogenetic Approach*. Cambridge: Cambridge University Press.

Back, L. (2007). *The Art of Listening*. Oxford: Berg.

Becker, H. (1967, Winter). Whose Side Are We On? *Social Problems, 14*(3), 239–247.

Beresford, B. (1997). *Personal Accounts: Involving Disabled Children in Research*. Norwich: Social Policy Research Unit.

Bluebond-Langner, M. (1978). *The Private World of Dying Children*. Princeton, NJ: Princeton University Press.

Boggis, A. (2011). Deafening Silences: Researching with Inarticulate Children. *Disability Studies Quarterly, 31*(4), 1–7.

Booth, T., & Booth, W. (1996). Sounds of Silence: Narrative Research with Inarticulate Subjects. *Disability and Society, 18*(Pt. 4), 431–442.

Christensen, P., & Prout, A. (2002). Working with Ethical Symmetry in Social Research with Children. *Childhood, 9*(4), 477–497.

Clarke, A., & Moss, P. (2001). *Listening to Young Children: The Mosaic Approach*. London: National Children's Bureau.

Cloke, P., Cook, I., Crang, P., Goodwin, M., Painter, J., & Philo, C. (2004). *Practicing Human Geographies*. London: Sage.

Corsaro, W. A. (1997). *The Sociology of Childhood*. Thousand Oaks, CA: Pine Forges Press.

Crang, M., & Cook, I. (2007). *Doing Ethnographies*. London: Sage.

Curran, T., & Runswick-Cole, K. (Eds.). (2013). *Disabled Children's Childhood Studies. Critical Approaches in a Global Context*. London: Palgrave Macmillan.

Eisner, E. (1991). *The Enlightened Eye: Qualitative Inquiry and the Enhancement of Educational Practice*. Toronto: Collier Macmillan Canada.

Emond, R. (2000). *Survival of the Skilful: An Ethnographic Study of Two Groups of Young People in Residential Care*. Unpublished doctoral thesis, University of Stirling.

Fine, M. (1992). Passions, Politics and Power: Feminist Research Possibilities. In M. Fine (Ed.), *Disruptive Voices: The Possibilities of Feminist Research*. Ann Arbor: University of Michigan Press.

Franklin, A., & Sloper, P. (2009). Supporting the Participation of Disabled Children and Young People in Decision-Making. *Children and Society, 23*, 3–15.

Giddens, A. (1984). *The Constitution of Society*. Cambridge: Polity Press.

Gilligan, C. (1993). *In a Different Voice* (2nd ed.). London: Harvard University Press.

Goodley, D. (2011). *Disability Studies: An Interdisciplinary Introduction*. London: Sage.

Goodley, D., & Runswick-Cole, K. (2011). Cyborgs: Photovoice and Disabled Children. Presentation to ESRC Seminar Series: Researching the Lives of Disabled Children with a Focus on their Perspectives Seminar 4. Recent Research, University of Bristol, 21st January. Retrieved January 14, 2016, from http://www.strath.ac.uk/humanities

Haugen, G. M. D. (2008). Children's Perspectives on Everyday Experiences of Shared Residence: Time, Emotions and Agency Dilemmas. *Children and Society, 11*, 71–94.

Huber, J., & Clandinin, D. J. (2002). Ethical Dilemmas in Relational Narrative Enquiry with Children. *Qualitative Inquiry, 8*(Pt. 6), 785–803.

James, A., & Prout, A. (1997). Re-presenting Childhood: Time and Transition in the Study of Childhood. In A. James & A. Prout (Eds.), *Constructing and Reconstructing Childhood*. London: Falmer Press.

Komarovsky, M. (1988). The New Feminist Scholarship: Some Precursors and Polemics. *Journal of Marriage and Family, 50*, 585–593.

Lewis, A. (2010). Silence in the Context of 'Child Voice'. *Children and Society, 24*, 14–23.

MacNaughton, G., Hughes, P., & Smith, K. (2007). Young Children's Rights and Public Policy: Practices and Possibilities for Citizenship in the Early Years. *Children and Society, 21*, 458–469.

Mascia-Lees, F. E., Sharpe, P., & Cohen, C. B. (1989). The Postmodern Turn in Anthropology: Cautions from a Feminist Perspective. *Signs, 15*, 7–33.

Mayall, B. (2002). *Towards a Sociology for Childhood. Thinking from Children's Lives*. Maidenhead: Open University Press.

Mazzei, L. A. (2009). An Impossibly Full Voice. In A. Y. Jackson & L. A. Mazzei (Eds.), *Voice in Qualitative Inquiry*. London: Routledge.

Morris, J. (1993). *Independent Lives: Community Care and Disabled People*. Basingstoke: Macmillan.

Morris, J. (1998). *Don't Leave Us Out! Involving Disabled Children and Young People with Communication Impairments*. York: Joseph Rowntree Foundation.

Oliver, M. (1983). *Social Work and Disabled People*. Basingstoke: Macmillan.

Oliver, M. (1990). *The Politics of Disablement*. Basingstoke: Macmillan.

Oliver, M. (2009). *Understanding Disability: From Theory to Practice* (2nd ed.). Basingstoke: Palgrave Macmillan.

Paterson, K., & Hughes, B. (1999). Disability Studies and Phenomenology: The Carnal Politics of Everyday Life. *Disability and Society, 14*(Pt. 5), 597–611.

Pink, S. (2015). *Doing Sensory Ethnography* (2nd ed.). London: Sage.

Priestly, M. (1999). Discourse and Identity: Disabled Children in Mainstream High Schools. In M. Corker & S. French (Eds.), *Disability Discourse*. Buckingham: Open University Press.

Prout, A. (2000). *The Body, the Childhood and Society*. Basingstoke: Macmillan Press.

Prout, A., & Hallett, C. (2003). Introduction. In *Hearing the Voices of Children: Social Policy for a New Century*. London: RoutledgeFalmer.

Reinharz, S. (1992). *Feminist Methods in Social Research*. Oxford: Oxford University Press.

Richards, S., Clark, J., & Boggis, A. (2015). *Ethical Research with Children. Untold Narratives and Taboos*. Basingstoke: Palgrave Macmillan.

Richardson, L. (1990). *Writing Strategies: Researching Diverse Audiences*. Thousand Oaks, CA: Sage.

Rose, G. (1997). Situating Knowledges: Positionality, Reflexivities and Other Tactics. *Progress in Human Geography, 21*(Pt. 3), 305–320.

Sherman Heyl, B. (2001). Ethnographic Interviewing. In C. Seale (Ed.), *Researching Society and Culture*. London: Sage.

Smart, C., Neale, B., & Wade, A. (2001). *The Changing Experience of Childhood: Families and Divorce*. Cambridge: Polity Press.

Stalker, K., & Connors, C. (2003). Communicating with Disabled Children. *Adoption and Fostering, 27*(1), 26–35.

Stanley, L., & Wise, S. (1993). *Breaking Out: Feminist Consciousness and Feminist Research*. London: Routledge and Kegan Paul.

Stones, R. (2005). *Structuration Theory*. Basingstoke: Palgrave Macmillan.

Temple, B., & Young, A. (2004). Qualitative Research and Translation Dilemma. *Qualitative Research, 4*(Pt. 2), 161–178.

United Nations. (1989). *Conventions on the Rights of the Child*. Geneva: United Nations.

Veale, A. (2005). Creative Methodologies in Participatory Research with Children. In S. Green & D. Hogan (Eds.), *Researching Children's Experience: Approaches and Methods*. London: Sage.

Weinberg, D. (2006). The Language of Social Science: A Brief Introduction. In P. Drew, G. Raymond, & D. Weinberg (Eds.), *Talk and Interaction in Social Research Methods*. London: Sage.

Wickenden, M. (2011). 'Give Me Time and I Will Tell You': Using Ethnography to Investigate Aspects of Identity with Teenagers Who Use Alternative and Augmentative Methods to Communication. In S. Roulstone & S. McLeod (Eds.), *Listening to Children and Young People with Speech, Language and Communication Needs*. Guildford: J&R Press.

CHAPTER 6

Discussion and Collaboration in Diagnostic Radiography

Ruth Strudwick

In 2011 I completed my doctoral thesis titled 'An ethnographic study of the culture in a Diagnostic Imaging Department'. I was interested in studying the culture of my own profession and ethnography was the obvious choice.

I am a diagnostic radiographer with 21 years' experience. I worked as a clinical radiographer for eight years, then I moved into education and I am currently an associate professor at a university in the East of England. I have had close involvement with many diagnostic radiographers working in placement hospitals associated with the university. The hospital where this research was carried out is one of these placement hospitals.

My perspective is therefore not one of a detached, objective researcher. I am familiar with the working practices and culture of diagnostic radiographers and how the departments in which they work function on a day-to-day basis. I am also familiar with current challenges within the profession of radiography, both in clinical practice and in education. As an educator at the university, I have contact with many of the diagnostic radiographers in the region due to the student radiographers being placed at hospitals within the region. I am conscious about the way in which I write; as a diagnostic radiographer, I have been taught

R. Strudwick (✉)
University of Suffolk, Ipswich, UK

© The Author(s) 2018
T. Vine et al. (eds.), *Ethnographic Research and Analysis*,
https://doi.org/10.1057/978-1-137-58555-4_6

97

to write in a factual, 'evidence-based' way, presenting information in an objective manner with little emotional involvement so that my work is open to scientific scrutiny. The production of an ethnographic text was therefore a real challenge to me, and one with which I continue to grapple. There is, of course, an ever-present danger that ethnographic research such as this may be seen as un-scientific in a field such as radiography. I sincerely hope I can persuade you otherwise.

Introduction

This chapter outlines the role of discussion and storytelling between diagnostic radiographers (DR) within the Diagnostic Imaging Department (DID) in an National Health Service (NHS) hospital in the East of England. My doctoral study reflected upon here explored the workplace and professional culture in a DID, examining how DRs work and interact with one another, as well other medical professionals and patients. Ethnography was the methodology deployed. I was the lead researcher and took on the role of 'observer as participant' (Gold, 1958) during the four-month observation period. This was supplemented by semi-structured interviews with ten staff working in the DID. The data were analysed using thematic analysis (Fetterman, 1989). Discussion and collaboration emerged as core themes: DRs discuss their work with one another and share experiences through storytelling. I argue that this collaboration can be competitive but is also an essential mechanism for learning and professional development within practice.

Ethnographic Research in Healthcare and Diagnostic Radiography

Ethnographic research is slowly gaining traction within healthcare, and there have been multiple studies carried out by healthcare professionals examining the culture of their native professional group. In their seminal study, Becker, Geer, Hughes, and Strauss (1961) studied trainee doctors as they became immersed in the medical profession in the 1960s. More recently authors such as Annandale, Clark, and Allen (1999) and Batch and Windsor (2015) have explored the professional cultures within nursing (see also Cudmore & Sondermeyer, 2007; Goransson, 2006; Wolf, 1988). Notably, Goodson and Vassar (2011) argue that the complexity of healthcare lends itself to ethnographic research. However, there remains very little written about the professional culture within diagnostic radiography or about radiographers and how they work and interact. Consequently, the work of DRs is not widely understood.

DRs work in many acute settings. In the UK, the majority are employed by the NHS, working in acute NHS hospital trusts. They are responsible for producing diagnostic images using various imaging modalities and technologies. They work in mainly uni-professional teams in the DID. DRs also interact with other healthcare professionals and NHS employees. They can also carry out diagnostic imaging in other parts of the hospital such as in Accident and Emergency. In these situations they work within a multidisciplinary team and interact with patients of all ages and abilities. This element of human interaction is a frequently unseen aspect of the radiographer's role and is explored in this chapter.

Radiography has a very short track record in research with much of its knowledge contingent on the research of medical practitioners and physicists rather than radiographers themselves (Adams & Smith, 2003). The profession of diagnostic radiography is now realising its own research and knowledge base. This is largely due to the emphasis on professional development and, notably, that radiography became a graduate profession in the early 1990s. Much of the research in radiography has been and still is quantitative, as the profession is seen to be science- and technology-driven. However, qualitative research in radiography is becoming more important as a means of realising a more holistic understanding of the profession (Adams & Smith, 2003; Ng & White, 2005).

My work sits within a limited group of ethnographic studies which explore diagnostic radiography. Much of the existing ethnographic work in this field focuses on technological practices (see Larsson et al., 2007; Larsson, Lundberg, & Hillergard, 2008). However, I argue ethnography as a methodology can be very useful in investigating the culture of the profession and revealing some of the hitherto hidden aspects of it. Ethnography can highlight norms, values, and beliefs within a profession and provide insight into the group, its cultural artefacts, hierarchies, and structures (O'Reilly, 2005).

The issue of role and identity became a major consideration in my research. All researchers are to some degree connected to, or a part of, their research setting (Aull-Davis, 2008). As I felt more accepted within the group, the radiographers would ask my opinion about their practice. I therefore had to consider the nature of my role. This was a real challenge. I knew that I was present as a researcher and therefore I wanted to gain information from the participants, but how much should I ask? How much should I participate? Should I simply observe? The participants were obviously aware of who I was and my current role and job title. Before the research commenced, I spoke to all of the staff about my study. Seeking and giving consent is complex (Sin, 2005) and in my ethnography, participants perhaps inevitably considered my position and impartiality when making their decision to take part. Given the nature of my position, it may be that those who did choose to participate had to consider what they were willing to share with me. This made my rapport with participants particularly relevant (Oakley, 1981).

My professional knowledge and experience gave me an advantage over a non-radiographer investigating this topic (Roberts, 2007), as the participants did not need to provide detailed explanations about what they were doing (Aull-Davis, 2008). However, I am aware that I entered into this research with some preconceived ideas. Because of personal history and closeness to the subject being studied, ethnographers 'help to construct the observations that become their data' (Aull-Davis, 2008: 5). I intentionally developed a rapport with my participants, which inevitably influenced how I presented their stories.

INTRODUCTION TO THE DID

The DID where the research was carried out is located within a medium-sized district general hospital which performed 113,034 radiological examinations in the 2007–2008 financial year.

The main DID houses general X-ray, fluoroscopy, computed tomography (CT), ultrasound, and radionuclide imaging (RNI). Accident and Emergency (A&E) X-ray is located in the A&E department with magnetic resonance imaging (MRI) and breast imaging located elsewhere in the hospital. The DID employs 25 full-time (FT) and 27 part-time (PT) diagnostic radiographers. There is also a range of clinical and non-clinical support staff and student radiographers on clinical placement.

Of the DRs studied within the DID, five are male and seven are female. The manager is male. The radiographers work a 37.5 hour week, doing a variety of shifts to cover the 24 hour period (9am–5pm, 1–8pm, 3–10pm, or nights). During each shift the radiographer normally has 60 minutes for lunch and two 20-minute tea breaks. I noted the radiographers stuck rigidly to their breaks and most of them went to the staff room where they would engage in storytelling. These stories form the empirical basis of this chapter.

There is a set proforma for admitting patients for radiographic examination.

Please see Figs. 6.1 and 6.2: Patient journeys through the DID.

The role of the DR could be seen as routine with patients coming and going from the DID for imaging examinations. Radiographic tasks can be learnt quickly, and the X-ray equipment is relatively simple to learn to operate now that most of it is computerised (Murphy, 2006). The work can be mundane and repetitive. Once a radiographer has mastered the psychomotor skills and dexterity required to use the X-ray equipment, its operation becomes relatively routine. It is the human interactions, however, which generate the variety in the work; communication with patients and colleagues is an important but sometimes unseen aspect of the role. The dichotomy between the mundane and everyday tasks of imaging patients and the importance of decision-making and human interactions provides some explanation for the collaboration between radiographers.

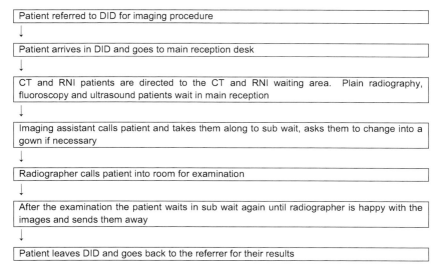

Fig. 6.1 Outpatient journey through the DID

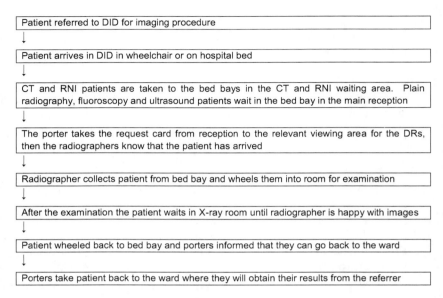

Fig. 6.2 Inpatient journey through the DID

The DRs discuss their tasks as they carry them out and in consequence support one another by sharing experience and expertise. This constitutes informal professional development. This network of professional support (Southon, 2006) provides 'communities of practice' (Lave & Wenger, 1991) and allows for social learning, support, and collaboration in the workplace. Decker and Iphofen (2005) also argue they can alleviate some of the mundane tasks, but Southon (2006) reminds us that cliques may develop within such staff groups.

Discussion About Work

In every area of the department during the period of observation, it was noted that the diagnostic radiographers discussed their work with one another as they were doing it. The radiographers discussed their patients, the request cards for imaging examinations, their images, the patient's previous images, colleagues, the rota, and general technical know-how. This discussion about work mainly occurred in the viewing areas of the department where I spent increasing amounts of time, as radiographers

DISCUSSION AND COLLABORATION IN DIAGNOSTIC RADIOGRAPHY   103

talked about their work as they were doing it. This appeared to be a normal part of the culture within the DID.

Discussions about work often occurred in order to gain positive reassurance from colleagues. My fieldwork notes provided many examples of this:

> The radiographers discuss their patient and their images in the viewing area. One radiographer has a patient who cannot turn their leg for an image of their knee and so asks another radiographer for help in positioning the patient and then they look at the resultant image together and decide if it shows the fracture clearly enough.
>
> Observation 13/8/08, viewing area

This is a fairly routine example of the supportive environment described by Southon (2006). As noted in my field notes, radiographers often discussed unusual situations with colleagues, frequently to ask for specific advice but also to share relevant experiences.

> One of the radiographers checks the clinical history on a request card with a colleague. This was a particularly quiet time in the department and so all of the radiographers want to find out what pathology was on the request card; this resulted in a search on Google and a discussion about the unusual condition that the patient had. The radiographers then went on to discuss some of the unusual pathologies that they had come across and some of the interesting cases they had recently seen. This discussion all took place in the viewing area.
>
> Observation 20/8/08, viewing area

Part of the diagnostic radiographer's role is to ensure that the images of patients that they produce provide an answer to the relevant clinical question. Therefore the radiographers would check the diagnostic acceptability.

> This conversation would be something like this:
> Questions: What do you think? Is that okay? Do I need to do it again?
> Responses: I think that's okay, let's have a look at your request card? Yes, that's fine,
> Or
> I would have another go at that and see if you can get a better image. This was observed many times during the course of a day.
>
> Observation 2/10/08, viewing area

104　R. STRUDWICK

Challenging patients were also discussed, often prior to examination to decide the best course of action.

> The radiographer and the student look at images in the viewing area and discuss the position of the patient to decide if they could improve the images at all. This was a patient with dementia who had been a real challenge. The discussion that followed was a dialogue about whether they could have done any better with this patient. The radiographer and student carrying out the examination were scrutinising their images, and then the other staff working in the area also came over and looked at the images and they all decided as a group that these were probably the best that they could do. Once the patient had left the department one of the radiographers then proceeded to talk about a patient with dementia who had been in the department a few weeks before and how this patient had thought that she was her daughter, she talked about how she had felt and how she had gone along with this in order to avoid the patient's distress, but how it had made her feel, and how she was quite upset about it. This started a discussion about how best to manage patients with dementia and how the radiographers found such patients to be very difficult to manage when they knew very little about them and had not had a lot of training.
>
> Observation 23/10/08, viewing area

A further example from my field notes provides further evidence of collaboration:

> A request for a baby to have skull X-rays has been received. The radiographers discuss together how to best position the baby for these images. They use their collective expertise and experience to decide on the best course of action. After the event there was further discussion about imaging children and how difficult it could be to keep the child still for the X-ray examination. Radiographers talked about children they had tried to keep still and some of the techniques they had employed to distract the child during the X-ray examination.
>
> Observation 17/10/08, viewing area

These two examples can also be seen as practice learning, where the radiographers are using the expertise of others to provide support and advice in order to improve their practice. The manager offered an explanation for this behaviour:

> Well you have got that immediate availability of the other person's experience, ... and I think that's a very positive thing ... there is lots of integration of the team in that area and it is part of the supportive network that they build up.

Hafslund, Clare, Graverholt, and Nortvedt (2008) when writing about evidence-based radiography comment that the practice of diagnostic radiography is reliant on tradition and on subjective experience. On a day-to-day basis, radiographers tap into that experience by asking the opinions of their colleagues and discuss their work as they are doing it. This provides support and the sharing of professional expertise for staff development.

Other ethnographers have described this knowledge-sharing. Hunter, Spence, McKenna, and Iedema (2008) found that nurses in a neonatal unit often sought guidance from one another and more experienced staff. Street (1992) and Wolf (1988) also found that in the hospital ward environment that nurses would refer to other colleagues for advice. Wolf (1988) also comments that staff would normally go to their colleagues rather than written policies. This was true for my study where radiographers appeared to find it easier to ask a trusted colleague rather than use a textbook, or written protocols.

I was also involved in these discussions about work, as the radiographers were aware of my professional role as a radiographer and an educator (Aull-Davis, 2008). This meant that I was asked about my professional opinion when I was present in the viewing area. I felt that I could participate in these discussions and it seemed to be accepted that my expertise could inform this collaboration. I took this as a compliment and evidence of rapport. Once more this raised questions for me about positionality and my influence on the research situation (Aull-Davis, 2008).

The DID appears to be an environment conducive to learning from and with one another. The way in which this occurs demonstrates the theory about experience and expertise from Benner (2001). She argues that expertise develops when the practitioner tests and refines propositions, hypotheses, and expectations, and that experience is a requisite for expertise. She concludes that experience is the refinement of preconceived notions and theory through encounters and situations. Radiographers do this by tapping into the expertise of their colleagues.

The Role of Storytelling as Support and Collaboration

Storytelling was commonplace within the department, particularly during quiet periods or at break time. It usually occurred in the staff room. Storytelling did also occur within the viewing area, but was normally restricted to quiet times as in this area staff could potentially be heard by patients, relatives, and other staff members. This is important as to the outsider some of these conversations about patients and colleagues could be seen to be unprofessional and also a breach of patient confidentiality if heard by others. I decided at an early stage in my study that the staff room would be an important place to be, I knew that radiographers would use their 'downtime' to 'sound off' to one another.

> Whilst sitting in the staff room during their break the radiographers tell stories about the patients they have seen this morning, on-call and in out-of-hours situations. Each radiographer appears to take their own turn to discuss how their morning has gone and share something that has happened. This ranged from complaining about a rude patient, to talking about a nurse on one of the wards who had not been very helpful. The stories told within the staff tended to be derogatory or complaining about others, there were rarely any positive stories told.
>
> Observation 11/8/08, staff room

These stories were often about other staff members or about difficult situations.

> One radiographer tells the other radiographers about a patient in A&E who had a cervical collar badly fitted and how the nurses didn't understand why this was problem and made imaging him difficult. The radiographer had gone to talk to the nursing staff about it and had not really had a very positive response to their questions. This radiographer was particularly annoyed that this showed that the A&E staff were not aware of the role of the radiographer.
>
> Observation 13/8/08, staff room

A lack of understanding of the role of the DR emerged during storytelling and this was a constant source of frustration. As a fellow DR professional (with insider knowledge) I could empathise with this. However, I found that the discussion about bodily fluids whilst eating my lunch (recorded next) was a step too far for me, thus demonstrating my outsider status (Bonner & Tolhurst, 2002) now I am predominantly an educator.

> There was a discussion about nasty experiences and about bodily fluids. One of the radiographers started to talk about a pus-filled abscess whilst one of the other radiographers was eating some custard! It was pointed out that the custard and pus were similar in colour ...
> This did not appear to faze the radiographer eating the custard and in fact she proceeded to talk about a patient who had vomited that morning. None of the radiographers were bothered that they were talking about pus and vomit whilst eating. I was actually uncomfortable and this made me realise that I wasn't used to this sort of conversation at lunch time anymore!
>
> Observation 3/9/08, staff room

Humour can also be a useful strategy in storytelling to reconstruct emotionally draining or painful memories (Norrick, 2006; Strudwick, Mackay, & Hicks, 2012) or deal with the mundane nature of some of the work. Goleman (2004, p. 135) says that 'being able to pick up on emotional clues is particularly important in situations where people have reason to conceal their true feelings'. So radiographers often provide a way for a colleague to talk about what they have been through by speaking to them on the level that they have chosen to use, which is often humour. Dean and Major (2008) discuss the supportive use of dark humour on an Intensive Therapy Unit (ITU) to relieve the tension created by life-and-death situations. Storytelling sessions often also became competitive, particularly in respect of who could tell the most disturbing or unpleasant story. Allen (2004) argues that a repertoire of stories and the ability to identify appropriate occasions for telling them are important requirements in becoming a competent member of an occupational group. I was drawn as a participant into the storytelling. Disclosure of experiences and the telling of stories allowed me to be recognised as a legitimate member of the group. This rapport enhanced my capacity to gather data (Aull-Davis, 2008). Such friendships between researchers and participants are an important element in obtaining good data (Oakley, 1981).

My field notes provided a plethora of examples of this competitiveness:

> When we get together it's well 'we've had all this', 'we've seen all this, that and the other' and all of the stories come out. It appears to me that the radiographers are competing with each other to tell the worst story and to

see who has experienced the worst patient or who has had the busiest night shift or dealt with the rudest referring doctor. It all seems to be a big competition.

Interview with student

This student felt that the radiographers competed with one another to tell the 'best' stories or to see who had had the 'worst' experiences, but she also confided that as a third year student she felt herself being drawn into this competitive storytelling as she too now had a collection of anecdotes to tell about her experiences. She felt that this allowed her to become part of the group and be seen as a legitimate group member. I argue that the benefits of this were that the radiographers were able to learn from one another's experiences and provide advice to one another. However, I also consider that this could actually lead to the perpetuation of poor practice (Lave & Wenger, 1991).

In discussing difficult or challenging situations, the radiographers were perhaps able to use storytelling as a way to manage and explore their emotions. Radiographers were able to express their emotions in the safer environment of the staff room, away from the patients, and thus experience the support of colleagues (Murphy, 2009). The front stage (Goffman, 1959) in a DID is where the radiographer interacts with the patients and the public. In these areas they have a professional persona and demeanour, remaining calm and not showing their emotions; these are termed 'display rules' (Goleman, 2004). The back stage is a place where it is acceptable for this persona to slip (Goffman, 1959) to talk about patients and to express emotions. This also aligns with the professional responsibility that radiographers (along with all other healthcare professionals) have to maintain patient confidentiality. The opportunity to discuss experiences with colleagues is critical to the mental health and wellbeing of staff. Staff members cannot discuss such things with their families and friends, and so their colleagues play a crucial role in facilitating this sharing and storytelling. Knowing that you are all bound by the same confidentiality requirements enables you to talk in a safe environment, whereas you cannot always do this at home. This can assist staff members in dealing with death or with some of the unpleasant things that they have seen during their working day. This further validates the importance of the professional culture within allied healthcare professions in order to understand the constraints that professionals face and how they manage to work through these difficult issues.

Leaving the Field

I experienced a sense of overriding sadness at having to leave the DID at the end of my research. I really felt that I had became part of the team and I had made some lasting friendships with some of the radiographers. Chesney (2001) reflects on this issue at the end of her study expressing a similar feeling. Coffey (1999) takes this further suggesting that researchers will always have an emotional involvement with their first set of participants; she goes as far as calling them the 'first love'. She says that 'ethnographers rarely leave fieldwork totally unaffected by their research experience' (p. 7), and that this is rarely talked about in the research texts; it is a 'silent space' (p. 8). I also felt the tension between the friendships I had developed and the dissemination of my results. I was concerned about how to ensure that I did not betray the participants who had become my friends (Becker, 1967; Oakley, 1981). However, I was optimistic that my research would have a positive effect on the DID. I have truly never really left the field. Yes, I am no longer collecting data in that one DID, but I am still fully immersed in the profession. I teach diagnostic radiography students and have contact with the DID where I carried out my research. That feeling of connectedness towards the participants remains: I recognise that I am still a diagnostic radiographer at heart.

Collaboration and storytelling are an important part of the professional culture within diagnostic radiography. DRs gain reassurance and support from colleagues and use stories to offload to one another. They tell stories and discuss ongoing work in order to become accepted as a legitimate group member (Lave & Wenger, 1991). In the process they receive peer support, and storytelling becomes a means of collaboration, competition, and learning.

References

Adams, J., & Smith, T. (2003, August). Qualitative Methods in Radiography Research: A Proposed Framework. *Radiography, 9*(3), 193–199.

Allen, D. (2004). Ethnomethodological Insights into Insider-Outsider Relationships in Nursing Ethnographies of Healthcare Settings. *Nursing Inquiry, 11*(1), 14–24.

Annandale, E., Clark, J., & Allen, E. (1999). Interprofessional Working: An Ethnographic Case Study of Emergency Health Care. *Journal of Interprofessional Care, 13*(2), 1999.

Aull-Davis, C. (2008). *Reflexive Ethnography, a Guide to Researching Selves and Others* (2nd ed.). London: Routledge.

Batch, M., & Windsor, C. (2015). Nursing Casualization and Communication: A Critical Ethnography. *Journal of Advanced Nursing, 71*(4), 870–880.

Becker, H. S. (1967). Whose Side Are We On? *Social Problems, 14*(3), 239–247.

Becker, H. S., Geer, B., Hughes, E. C., & Strauss, A. L. (1961). *Boys in White—Student Culture in Medical School.* New Brunswick: Transaction Publishers.

Benner, P. (2001). *From Novice to Expert—Excellence and Power in Clinical Nursing Practice.* Upper Saddle River, NJ: Prentice Hall.

Bonner, A., & Tolhurst, G. (2002). Insider-Outsider Perspectives of Participant Observation. *Nurse Researcher, 9*(4), 7–19.

Chesney, M. (2001). Dilemma of Self in the Method. *Qualitative Health Research, 11,* 127–135.

Coffey, A. (1999). *The Ethnographic Self.* London: Sage.

Cudmore, H., & Sondermeyer, J. (2007). Through the Looking Glass: Being a Critical Ethnographer in a Familiar Nursing Context. *Nurse Researcher, 14*(3), 25–35.

Dean, R. A., & Major, J. E. (2008, April). From Critical Care to Comfort Care: The Sustaining Value of Humour. *Journal of Clinical Nursing, 17*(8), 1088–1095.

Decker, S., & Iphofen, R. (2005). Developing the Professional of Radiography: Making Use of Oral History. *Radiography, 11,* 262–271.

Fetterman, D. J. (1989). *Ethnography—Step by Step.* Basingstoke, CA: Sage.

Goffman, E. (1959). *The Presentation of Self in Everyday Life.* Middlesex: Penguin Books.

Gold, R. L. (1958). Roles in Sociological Fieldwork. *Social Forces, 36,* 217–223.

Goleman, D. (2004). *Emotional Intelligence and Working with Emotional Intelligence—Omnibus.* New York: Bloomsbury.

Goodson, L., & Vassar, M. (2011). An Overview of Ethnography in Healthcare and Medical Education Research. *Journal of Education Evaluation for Health Professions, 8*(4), 1–5.

Goransson, K. (2006). Registered Nurse-Led Emergency Department Triage: Organisation, Allocation of Acuity Ratings and Triage Decision-Making. PhD thesis, unpublished. Orebro University, Sweden.

Hafslund, B., Clare, J., Graverholt, B., & Nortvedt, M. W. (2008). Evidence-Based Radiography. *Radiography.* https://doi.org/10.1016/ j.radi.2008.01.003

Hunter, C. L., Spence, K., McKenna, K., & Iedema, R. (2008). Learning How We Learn: An Ethnographic Study in a Neonatal Intensive Care Unit. *Journal of Advanced Nursing, 62*(2), 657–664.

Larsson, W., Aspelin, P., Bergquist, M., Hillergard, K., Jacobsson, B., Lindskold, L., et al. (2007). The Effects of PACS on Radiographer's Work Practice. *Radiography, 13,* 235–240.

Larsson, W., Lundberg, N., & Hillergard, K. (2008). Use Your Good Judgement—Radiographers' Knowledge in Image Production Work. *Radiography.* https:// doi.org/10.1016/j.radi.2008.09.003

Lave, J., & Wenger, E. (1991). *Situated Learning. Legitimate Peripheral Participation*. Cambridge: Cambridge University Press.

Murphy, F. (2009). Act, Scene, Agency: The Drama of Medical Imaging. *Radiography, 15*, 34–39.

Murphy, F. J. (2006). The Paradox of Imaging Technology: A Review of the Literature. *Radiography, 12*, 169–174.

Ng, C. K. C., & White, P. (2005, August). Qualitative Research Design and Approaches in Radiography. *Radiography, 11*(3), 217–225.

Norrick, N. (2006). Humour in Oral History Interviews. *Oral History, 32*, 85–94.

O'Reilly, K. (2005). *Ethnographic Methods*. London: Routledge.

Oakley, A. (1981). Interviewing Women: A Contradiction in Terms. In H. Roberts (Ed.), *Doing Feminist Research*. London: Routledge.

Roberts, D. (2007). Ethnography and Staying in Your Own Nest. *Nurse Researcher, 14*(3), 15–24.

Sin, C. H. (2005). Seeking Informed Consent: Reflections on Research Practice. *Sociology, 39*(20), 277–294.

Southon, G. (2006). The Role of Professional Networks in Radiology Services. *Rev Panam Salud Publica, 20*(2/3), 99–103.

Street, A. F. (1992). *Inside Nursing—A Critical Ethnography of Clinical Nursing Practice*. Albany: State University of New York Press.

Strudwick, R., Mackay, S., & Hicks, S. (2012, February). Cracking Up? The Use of Dark Humour in the Radiography Department. *Synergy*, 4–7.

Strudwick, R. M. (2011). *An Ethnographic Study of the Culture in a Diagnostic Imaging Department (DID)*. DProf thesis, Unpublished, University of Salford.

Wolf, Z. R. (1988). *Nurses' Work, the Sacred and the Profane*. Philadelphia: University of Pennsylvania Press.

CHAPTER 7

Living with Uncertainty: The Ethnographer's Burden

Steve Barnes

I didn't enjoy learning woolly subjects at school. They didn't feel like 'real knowledge'. I enjoyed maths and science because they carried with them the security that even if I got the answer wrong there was still a correct answer out there somewhere. My subject choices throughout my schooling reflected this need for closure and I really couldn't get interested in subjects that left me with a heft of 'perhaps' and 'maybes'.

Much later, I developed an interest in fictional writing. However, it took a long time for me to realise that I enjoyed writing (or what Alan Bennett calls 'talking to yourself') precisely because it involves exploring the uncertain and the inconclusive. When I later began ethnographic research, the giving of a voice to ambiguity and complexity led me to a Kuhnian rebellion against quantitative research and its theoretical presuppositions. Am I a born-again ethnographer? I'm not sure. My research (and I) remain a work-in-progress.

INTRODUCTION

Uncertainty occurs during most studies, and some argue that this is both expected and necessary because uncertainty is 'a potent and powerful force that motivates research' (Holden, 2015, p. 1). My position is not

S. Barnes (✉)
University of Suffolk, Ipswich, UK

© The Author(s) 2018
T. Vine et al. (eds.), *Ethnographic Research and Analysis*,
https://doi.org/10.1057/978-1-137-58555-4_7

that uncertainty is bad or unwanted. Rather, in my experience it appears to be a greater burden in the field of ethnography than in research employing positivist research methods. This observation is based on my ethnographic study which spanned five years, as contrasted with my experience with two previous degree-based courses using quantitative research methods. Notably, there was scant acknowledgement of uncertainty either by myself, my supervisor, or indeed in the extant literature, at the time of my ethnographic study. I use my published thesis to support this claim.

The high level of uncertainty about the outcomes of my Doctorate in Education (Ed.D.) caused me to reflect upon its nature, and so questions arose like 'why was the uncertainty greater than I had previously experienced?' and 'Was the uncertainty mostly related to the method of study (ethnography) or was it the study environment itself?' By highlighting the potential factors relating to uncertainty, it is hoped that some understanding can be reached about why I experienced such persistently high levels: perhaps because of the interpretive nature of ethnography but also perhaps because of a previous preference for quantitative (positivistic) research methods.

BACKGROUND

My study focussed on the transitioning of the business school, originally part of a further education college (Suffolk College), to its new-found status as a university (University Campus Suffolk—now the University of Suffolk). Such a change has never happened before in the UK so it had the potential to be interesting. It was also achievable because I worked at the College and so had access to people and documentation in the organisation at the time. The research question that underpinned the research focussed on what it meant to be a lecturer in a 'new university'. The study followed the changing guise of the Business School over a period of 5 years.

The research programme undertaken was a 'Doctor of Education' (Ed.D.), which had a research focus 'designed to meet the needs of professionals in education, and related disciplines, who wish to enhance their knowledge and understanding of educational issues, keep abreast of a range of educational topics, and refine and develop their research skills' (Leeds, 2016, p. 1).

What Was Uncertain?

Uncertainty in the context of my doctoral research was initially confined to the choice of methodology, the methodological design, how to ensure the quality of the data collected, how to analyse the data and present it, and how to interpret the findings. It became clear during the study that, as well as these, a different kind of uncertainty was presenting itself, because the positivistic concepts of objectivity and 'proof' that I was familiar with in quantitative research did not seem to be part of an ethnographic methodology.

What was warranted, according to practitioners in ethnography, was 'description' and 'interpretation' of the cultural group or system under study (Creswell, 1998). This meant that the 'findings' and 'results' of my investigations were not going to 'prove' anything, nor would they help establish or even corroborate any cultural laws or principles that I might expect to see. What I also found was that ethnography was a demanding activity requiring diverse skills, including the ability to make decisions in conditions of considerable uncertainty, as I negotiated and often renegotiated my role as a participant observer.

The result of this great and increasing uncertainty resulted in anxiety not just about what to look at and how to interpret what I saw, but a growing feeling that perhaps there was nothing to see. As the study progressed, there seemed to be no significant behavioural changes, no rebellion against change, few negative comments, and none of the stages of the Kubler-Ross coping cycle (Kubler-Ross, 1969) that might be expected from a business school going through fundamental organisational and ideological change.

How Uncertainty Presented Itself

No extreme changes to behaviour or even language seemed to take place for several years after the change of status of the HE department of the further education college (Suffolk College), even though I had studied many public, private, formal, and informal conversations during the period. The strategic 5-year plan for the organisation was publicly available, and it spelled out clearly its ambition for increases in student population and the reforming of the whole organisation to one that was more like a business than an educational institution (Deem, 1998).

Yet there appeared to be no significant cultural changes that might reveal how the lecturers in the business school were coping and perhaps adapting to changes in its organisational structure, including increased class sizes and teaching delivery through a virtual learning environment (VLE). Significantly, job descriptions changed to include, for the first time, the requirement for lecturers to have 'contemporary experience in the discipline relevant to the post' (Suffolk, 2007, p. 3), as many had never worked in the academic area in which they taught.

For a period, this lack of change caused my research to shift towards finding out what factors might be responsible for such a seemingly small response to a momentous and unique change, beginning with considerable introspection and reflexivity. Questions arose about whether I was, as part of the team, incapable of seeing cultural changes and had just accepted them at face value because I had become an insider. If this were so, then my ability to study change would be rendered even more uncertain.

My hope was that being an insider did not mean that change was impossible to see, but rather that I simply had access to different sorts of information (Hammersley & Atkinson, 2007). I expected, according to experienced practitioners (Wolcott, 1994; Tedlock, 2000), that my (insider) interpretation of the situation would be different to that of an outsider, and that I would be less sensitive to cultural change, but I didn't expect it to be invisible.

Looking at field notes and open-ended interview questionnaires that I produced at the time of the study, I note that, under the heading 'Organisational change in a new university', there is a question 'Is there evidence of any cultural norms? If so what?' (Barnes, 2010, Appendix D) It seemed as if, at the time, I was expecting a cultural norm to be found hiding amongst the data, perhaps embedded in a 'normal' distribution curve. This and other material in the finished doctorate shows a researcher struggling to find answers about culture and how it was captured, measured, and analysed. Some relief came in the form of Creswell's suggested use of the 'data analysis spiral' (Creswell, 1998, p. 143), which stated that 'data' could be collected, managed, analysed, and then represented, and for me this eased the feeling of uncertainty greatly.

The use of the 'data spiral' together with Miles and Huberman's notion of collecting data in bins (Miles & Huberman, 1994) gave me a structure that felt solid and that would produce reliable results and, reflecting upon my mood at the time, allow me to resume a positivistic, evidence-based approach to research.

Methodology and Uncertainty

The course of study (Ed.D.) that I was enrolled on was situated in the Faculty of Social Sciences at the University of East Anglia with a stated 'preference for research that adopts qualitative methodologies' (Husbands, 2004, p. 10). My research was undertaken using ethnography because, after consideration, it was felt more likely to result in an understanding of a changing culture. My first task was to understand ethnography as a methodology and how it could help me to study the business school at the university. Ethnography has been described as 'the integration of first hand empirical investigation and the theoretical and comparative interpretation of social organisation and culture' (Hammersley & Atkinson, 2007, p. 1). It was clear to me from the beginning that the challenge would be in the 'theoretical and comparative interpretation' of the culture that I observed and gradually came to understand in the new university. I also knew from previous academic courses that it would have been possible to study the same situation as a case study through a quantitative, scientific research methodology. However, I was aware that this was not an option at UEA's Social Sciences faculty.

In a quantitative research study, the research question is likely to have included 'the description of a theoretical framework and the logical deduction of a hypothesis from the results; known as the hypothetico-deductive method' (Sekaran, 2010, p. 17). My preference for a hypothetico-deductive approach came from my previous working experience in technology research and development but also from previous studies where I had used a quantitative research methodology on an MBA degree (Barnes, 1999). In that study, organisational behaviour was examined to try to deduce the relationship between the antecedents (or starting conditions) and the outcomes of customer loyalty (up to eleven different types) using quantitative research methods. In the loyalty study, questionnaires were used to record a group of buyers' beliefs about, and their attitude towards, their supplier so that a relationship between their attitudes (antecedents) and types of loyalty could be deduced. This approach is clearly positivistic; collecting data about 'variables' such as gender, length-of-service, marital status, and then measuring other 'dimensions' such as whether workers were work-driven, feedback-seeking, or needy-for-challenge. Often, in quantitative organisational research design, variables are identified, given a name and scale by which they are measured, and then positioned within a theoretical framework. The variables can then be measured, often through questioning of the target group, and analysed in terms of the 'goodness' of the data found, before being tested by recourse to a hypothesis. This contrasts with a qualitative approach where 'only rarely are sociological models sufficiently well developed for hypothesis to be derived and tested' (Hammersley & Atkinson, 2007, p. 165). The results of the loyalty study were plotted on a five-point Likert scale and then interpreted using statistical tools including analysis of variants, t-tests, and multiple regression analysis. The results of this process were used to propose a hypothesis, namely, 'the null hypothesis', that could be either proved (substantiated) or not proved (unsubstantiated). For example:

Proposition P1 That there is a high correlation between trust and loyalty in the study's customer group.

In my study the hypothesis was (statistically) substantiated.

But what does any of this have to do with uncertainty? Well, in the hypothetico argument, uncertainty is dealt with in several ways, including, for example, measuring the validity of a statistically derived outcome by assigning it a 'p' value or probability value. 'p' values reveal 'whether the findings in a research study are statistically significant, meaning that, if they are significant then the findings are unlikely to have occurred by chance' (Forbes, 2012, p. 34). Uncertainty is therefore managed by interpreting the results using probability and then giving it a value, and by doing so, containing uncertainty.

Another term used to describe the quality of the data collected and how it was measured, is 'goodness', and this is explained in terms of the validity and reliability of the data, helping to identify the level of uncertainty. For example, validity is used to describe whether the data collected measured what it was intended to measure. Another 'goodness' test for data is whether it is reliable, that is, that the stability and consistency with which the instrument is measuring the concept is reliable (stable under differing conditions). Using these ideas of validity and reliability, it is possible to contain uncertainty about the data's ability to test a concept by referring to the 'goodness' with which it was measured. Quantitative researchers in organisational research are encouraged to use one of several instruments that have already been developed and shown to have a high level of 'goodness' (Sekaran, 2010).

It is possible to conclude therefore that my uncertainties were not rooted just in the differences in my experience of quantitative and qualitative methodologies alone, but also in my expectations of a clearer and less messy outcome. This is because of the way that uncertainty is 'specified' and 'contained' in quantitative research methods.

Notably, the one method that was shared across my previous quantitative and current qualitative experiences was questionnaires. Historically, it was a key medium for data collection. As part of my ethnography, it was a relatively minor technique used to compliment techniques more usual to the methodology. However, even here, I noted significant discrepancy in terms of uncertainty. My experiences using questionnaires revealed that the way in which a subject interprets a question was dealt with differently in my quantitative and qualitative research. In my quantitative research, potential errors in the interpretation of questions were dealt with by issuing a pilot questionnaire and then reviewing the returns to assess any misunderstandings. Questions were then reformed so that 'ambiguities' did not occur, often by asking 'individuals who are likely to be sympathetic to your work' (Munn & Drever, 1990, p. 75) to review the questions and make clear what answers were required (these were often multiple choice answers). In my ethnographic studies, however, the interpretation of the subject's response to the questionnaire is regarded as additional information that helps in 'studying the meaning, behaviour, language, and interactions of the culture-sharing group' (Creswell, 1998, p. 58). Questions that caused problems for the subject would not be modified or reformed, but rather would be probed deeper to perhaps elicit information that might be left untouched in a quantitative study.

Vignettes and Uncertainty

Vignettes had been constructed in my thesis as a useful way to reflect the issues that were present in the changing environment and to avoid 'privileging the self' (Coffey, 1992) in the presentation of what it means to be a lecturer. I state in the thesis that they were also used to 'improve the validity of accounts describing the observed cultural behaviour' (Barnes, 2010, p. 76). The notion of improved validity appealed to me at the time. The concept of validity is a seductive one, offering the certainties that are associated with quantitative research. On reflection, I'm not sure that validity was improved. However, the use of vignettes did enhance my *own* understanding of the research process. I was beginning to understand that accounts produced by people under study 'should not be treated as valid

120   S. BARNES

in their own terms and thus beyond assessment and explanation' (Hammersley & Atkinson, 2007, p. 120).

The vignettes were developed using stories taken from interviews and 'field' conversations and mixed with the experiences of the researcher (myself) during the period of change, to construct a historical record of the conditions at the institution at the time. The way in which they were constructed was by using 'evidence' to piece together a story that could then be justified by information in an appendix. For example, the following vignette was constructed about a lecturer resistant to change, and is meant to be —as such—representative of all those resistant to change:

Jonathan Teach—Lecturer in Business Studies

Although I have been teaching for 25 years now, it has been rare for me to have to resort to using computers to get the message across to students. Having worked in Human Resources for a while in industry, it was clear to me that people relate to other people much more easily than they relate to technology. We had some bad experiences in the 1980s when some of the older staff had to do their job by computer instead of face-to-face or using paper records, or worse, they ended up using both because they weren't confident with a computer. Some of them were actually afraid of the keyboard, because they thought they would break the system, or because they just didn't understand it. Others, like secretaries, thought it was a plot to put them out of a job because now anybody could do their own typing.

Personally, I prefer to use overhead slides, or acetates as they used to be known, as it gives me the chance to face the class whilst talking to them about my subject. This means that I have built up a tremendous library of OHP slides that I am loath to get rid of, just so that we can say that we are using the new VLE (Virtual Learning Environment). And, in any case, I am very suspicious about this new VLE system, because although we can see what students are viewing on the system (although I don't know how to do that yet), managers can also see what we are doing on the system.

I am really unhappy with the computer system on so many levels. Firstly, it keeps breaking down, and we lose access to the module content that we have spent ages loading onto the system. This has occurred a couple of times, just as the lecture is about to start at 9am, and it means that all my material that has been loaded onto the system in readiness for the lesson is now inaccessible, so I bring in a memory stick now with all my notes on it, just in case.

This vignette was presented as a 'voice' of the lecturer and how they felt about the changing nature of their work, and some of the 'evidence' used to support this interpretation included (1) the CV of the lecturer being studied (called Jonathan Teach to preserve anonymity) and (2) a certificate

LIVING WITH UNCERTAINTY: THE ETHNOGRAPHER'S BURDEN 121

showing that I worked alongside Jonathan Teach in a previous environment in the 1980s. On reviewing the process, the description of the lecturer's viewpoint in the vignette carried with it the possibility of foreclosing other, perhaps more interesting areas, by channelling the interviewee's responses into just thinking about, in this case, the IT system. This is one reason why I am uncertain about my use of vignettes. Notably, these uncertainties went unacknowledged in my first encounter with the method. Furthermore, I did not mention in the doctorate that there are 'few detailed accounts about the use of vignettes, particularly within qualitative research' (Barter & Renold, 1999) so that uncertainties about my interpretation were unacknowledged at that time.

Participant Observation and Uncertainty

One of the key objections to relying upon participant observational (PO) data is that it raises the question about how effectively a participant observer can observe the group if they are participating fully (Punch, 2005). Was it the case, then, that in my research journey, the interpretation of my PO data did not fully take account of this? For example, on one occasion, I had arrived at a regular monthly business school team meeting intent on recording it with a digital voice recorder. I began by openly asking if anybody objected to my recording the session, to gather data for my doctorate, and all agreed to allow it. Ten minutes after the start of the meeting, the Dean of the Business School arrived and quickly noticed that I had a recorder on the desk and asked whether it was recording the meeting. I said that it was, so she asked me to immediately turn off the recorder and wipe any material recorded so far, as I did not have her explicit permission and the data would therefore be inadmissible.

Although I cannot corroborate my view, as the recording is lost, I noticed immediately that I and others spoke differently after the voice recorder had been switched off. Those sat in the meeting seemed to relax as evidenced by their body posture. Even my contributions to the meeting were less formal. Each of us used slang and shorthand words were used more liberally. Notably, I would not have noticed this but for an abrupt change in the circumstances. It was clear that being surveilled (by the visible presence of the recorder) had had an effect: something that I recognised only upon reflection.

This event only serves to exacerbate my uncertainty about the extent to which I have relied upon participant observation that was apparently adversely affected by my presence. I was constructing a historical record about the changing culture at my university (a university which was, of course, my employer as well), and some—perhaps all—of my subjects' responses were being 'staged'!

Liminality

As well as the uncertainty associated with the methods used to interpret a changing culture during the doctorate, there is also the uncertainty created by the development of the doctoral student, that is, myself. Uncertainty in doctoral research is not new, but studying it and dealing with it is. Latterly the notion of liminality has been introduced (Keefer, 2013). Derived primarily from anthropology, a liminal state is a period of transition during a rite of passage that points to where an identity shift occurs. More comprehensively, it might be described as an awareness threshold since a person who enters the rite is no longer the same, nor have they yet transitioned into their new life as a result of completing their rite (Turner, 2011).

One view of doctoral studies is that students undergo a transformation in thinking as they pursue their chosen discipline, and relatively recently, the notion has been introduced that learning occurs in stages passing through several thresholds of understanding, or liminal states. A threshold, once passed, 'leads to a qualitatively different view of the subject matter and/or learning experience and of oneself as a learner' (Kiley & Wisker, 2009, p. 18). Liminality in this context can be understood as the period that precedes the actual 'crossing' of the threshold, and this transformation may be sudden or protracted over a considerable period.

An example of a threshold in ethnography is 'otherness', as students understand themselves and their learning from different perspectives, and this may lead to changes in self-perception and perhaps their perception of the subject. The liminal state might involve considerable oscillation, confusion, and uncertainty, and whilst in the liminal state students may mimic the language and behaviours that they perceive are required of them, prior to gaining a fuller understanding. It is whilst in this state that doctoral students are often likely to feel 'stuck', depressed, unable to continue, challenged, and confused, and it is the understanding of the threshold concept and the liminal state in research education that can help students to understand that their uncertainty is justified but also that it is likely to be time-limited. It is possible that my feelings of uncertainty were related

LIVING WITH UNCERTAINTY: THE ETHNOGRAPHER'S BURDEN   **123**

to one or more liminal states that I was passing through, and added to the intensity of the insecurity that was being felt.

According to Keefer (2013), regardless of discipline, nationality, age, type of doctorate, or any other demographic qualifier, liminal experiences fall into at least one of three thematically distinct, though related, categories. These include a lack of confidence related to impostor syndrome (or not being good enough), a sense of loneliness and isolation, and potentially a misalignment between the methodological perspectives of the learner and their institution. On approaching a liminal state, uncertainty will dominate the student's mind and they will be prone to a lack of motivation.

It may be that part of the uncertainty that I experienced related to my transition from a background in quantitative research to the requirement to familiarise myself with qualitative research. It is also possible that my uncertainty about the lack of obvious changes in culture at the university were not about questions of methodology, or about techniques, or even liminality, but that perhaps changes were suppressed by lecturers because of the calming influences of the 'advocates of restraint' (Wolcott, 1994, p. 146).

SUMMARY

There are likely to be many reasons for the uncertainty I felt during the process of research for my doctorate. These range from the simple-but-expected methodological choices to the more difficult-to-show concepts like interpretation and the presence of liminality. It is important to note here that it was my *feeling* that things were more uncertain than I had ever experienced, rather than an epistemological or doxastic argument that this was so.

It may be that my journey from positivism to interpretivism was the main cause for my uncertainty, although for some both quantitative and qualitative data can been treated as complementary in the field of ethnography (e.g. Deegan, 2001). It does seem that a scientific approach to research and analysis has fewer uncertain outcomes because of the way in which they are achieved: 'in a deductive fashion by appeal to universal laws that state regular relationships between variables, holding across all relevant circumstances' (Hammersley & Atkinson, 2007, p. 5). In such an approach, uncertainties are often given a name and a value (number) and then set to one side in the explanation of a law, principle, or axiom (see Einstein's gravitational constant, and many others). Conversely interpretivist approaches seem to include such uncertainties in its explanations, as 'it resists schemes or models which over-simplify the complexity of everyday life' (Denzin, 1971).

The degree of uncertainty felt during the course of my ethnography was considerably higher than that during those prior, positivist research projects. I struggled to interpret culture using vignettes, participant observation, and other well-regarded techniques. Ethnographers will know that this is, in part, because of the difficulty of interpreting behaviour that is infused by individual motives, beliefs, values, and intentions. Equally, the passing through one or more liminal states inevitably contributed to my feelings of uncertainty, though I resist the temptation to using this by way of explanation. Schooled now in interpretivism, I know better than that.

It is possible that I will never be comfortable with the level of uncertainty that the ethnographer endures because there are no clear boundaries and we are expected to perpetually speculate. Even my suggestion that 'it may be that my journey from positivism to interpretivism was the main cause for my uncertainty' might seem, to some, as too linear or too positivistic. Perhaps it is enough that I have described my experience in arguments that have ethnographic underpinnings. But, I am not certain about that either.

References

Barnes, S. J. (1999). *Establishing a Relationship Between the Antecedents and the Outcomes of Loyalty Using Customer Segmentation.* Master in Business Administration (MBA), University of East Anglia.

Barnes, S. J. (2010). *What Does It Mean to Be a Lecturer at a New University? An Ethnographic Study of Organisational Change in a University Business School.* Doctor of Education (EdD), University of East Anglia (UEA).

Barter, C., & Renold, E. (1999). The Use of Vignettes in Qualitative Research. *Social Research Update* 25: 1–7.

Coffey, A. (1992). *The Ethnographic Self: Fieldwork and the Representation of Identity.* Thousand Oaks, CA: Sage.

Creswell, J. W. (1998). *Qualitative Inquiry and Research Design: Choosing Among Five Traditions.* London: Sage.

Deegan, M. J. (2001). The Chicage School of Ethnography. In P. Atkinson, A. Coffey, S. Delamont, J. Lofland, & L. Lofland (Eds.), *Handbook of Ethnography.* London: Sage.

Deem, R. (1998). New Managerialism and Higher Education: The Management of Performances and Cultures in Universities in the United Kingdom. *International Studies in Sociology of Education, 8,* 47–56.

Denzin, N. K. (1971). The Logic of Naturalistic Enquiry. *Social Forces, 50,* 166–182.

Forbes, D. A. (2012). What Is a p Value and What Does It Mean? *Evidence Based Nursing, 15,* 34.

Hammersley, M., & Atkinson, P. (2007). *Ethnography: Principles and Practice.* London: Routledge.

Holden, S. S. (2015). *Oh, the Uncertainty: How Do We Cope?* [Online]. Retrieved from http://theconversation.com/oh-the-uncertainty-how-do-we-cope-32155

Husbands, C. (2004). *Research Degree Programmes 2004–2005.* Norwich: University of East Anglia.

Keefer, J. M. (Ed.). (2013). *Navigating Liminality: The Experience of Troublesome Periods and Distance During Doctoral Study.* Lancaster: Lancaster University.

Kiley, M., & Wisker, G. (2009). Threshold Concepts in Research Education and Evidence of Threshold Crossing. *Higher Education Research & Development, 28,* 431–441.

Kubler-Ross, E. (1969). *On Death and Dying.* New York: Collier Books.

Leeds, U. O. (2016). *Doctor of Education* [Online]. Leeds. Retrieved November 17, 2016, from http://www.education.leeds.ac.uk/postgraduates/research-postgraduates/edd

Miles, M. B., & Huberman, A. M. (1994). *Qualitative Data Analysis: An Expanded Sourcebook.* London: Sage.

Munn, P., & Drever, E. (1990). *Using Questionnaires in Small Scale Research.* Scottish Council for Research in Education, Edinburgh.

Punch, K. (2005). *Introduction to Social Research.* London: Sage.

Sekaran, U. (2010). *Research Methods for Business: A Skill Building Approach.* New York: John Wiley & Sons.

Suffolk, U. C. (2007). Job Description. *Lecturer (Teaching and Scholarship).* University Campus Suffolk, Human Resourves Management Department.

Tedlock, B. (2000). Ethnography and Ethnographic Presentation. In N. Denzin & Y. Lincoln (Eds.), *Handbook of Qualitative Research.* London and Thousand Oaks: Sage.

Turner, V. (2011). *The Ritual Process: Structure and Anti-structure.* New Brunswick: AldineTransaction.

Wolcott, H. F. (1994). *Transforming Qualitative Data: Description, Analysis and Interpretation.* Thousand Oaks, CA: Sage.

CHAPTER 8

What Makes the Autoethnographic Analysis Authentic?

David Weir and Daniel Clarke

David—My mother died when I was six and my father while in my second term at University. My autoethnography is helping me to realize the lasting significance of these events. Academia aside, I am a practising performance poet. My poem "Journeyman" won none less than the Shetland Islands Libraries' "Bards in the Bog" competition (2008).

Daniel—My main research interests revolve around understanding the ways people experience and attribute meanings to places and organized spaces over time. Exploring how different people connect with place has brought me to the realization that identity plays a significant role in how people act, make sense of and feel in places; so too does the non-human aspects of the environments through which people move. Having developed a subsequent interest in the dynamics of human and non-human relations, sensory experience and affect, I have observed a growing trend in the use of digital devices and relational concepts by researchers interested in studying organizational space and place. It seems that the desire to develop evocative forms of understanding through the use of imaginative, creative, and expressive representations

---

D. Weir (✉)
York St John University, York, UK

D. Clarke
University of Dundee, Dundee, UK

© The Author(s) 2018
T. Vine et al. (eds.), *Ethnographic Research and Analysis*,
https://doi.org/10.1057/978-1-137-58555-4_8

127

128   D. WEIR AND D. CLARKE

including videography, autoethnography, and poetry has particularly captured the imagination of spatial researchers; I am no different. I am, however, possibly the only Scouser living in Scotland trying to make sense of the interconnections between body/heat/balance/speed/ proprioception/place/machine/people/mud on the grass track cycling circuit in the Scottish Highland Games.

Introduction

We position autoethnography (AE) in the mainstream ethnographic canon *and* related to storytelling (Boje, 1991, 2008). Van Maanen's (2011) framing of "ethnography as work" incorporates three constitutive overlapping tasks—field, head, and textwork.

Autoethnography is "anthropology carried out in the social context which produced it" (Strathern, 1987, p. 17) or "anthropology at home" (Jackson, 1987). It is "a thing all on its own, not just an 'auto' linked to an 'ethnography' ..." (Ellis, 2013, p. 9) a qualitative enquiry, reframing experience (Reed-Danahay, 1997; Tolich, 2010) associated with emotion and reflexivity (Anderson, 2006).

In this chapter we deal with the critiques of Delamont (2007) of AE as literally and intellectually lazy and refute that we have been lazy in our literary and intellectual work. The energy requirements needed to do our field/head/textwork is tough, rather than lazy work. Through presenting our work at conferences and obtaining relevant feedback, our research becomes "comprehensive, well-argued, and full of passion and conviction" (Adams, Holman Jones, & Ellis, 2015, p. 100). It is through respecting key *principles* (Ellis & Adams, 2014, p. 260) and upholding the *goals* of AE (Adams et al., 2015, p. 102) that our autoethnographic analyses achieve *authenticity*.

Daniel analyses the demands of taking up an academic position while writing scholarly articles, detailing the successions of framing within which AE was created and shared. David details the framing (Goffman, 1974) of a retrospective analysis of farming practices in which the first insights came from poetic representation subsequently validated from other accounts and secondary data.

We argue that reflexivity is not singular (Alvesson, Hardy, & Harley, 2008) but multivocal, so choices of voice have to be made (Derrida, 2001), not privileging one account over another (Derrida, 1988, p. 256). Reflexivity is processual rather than absolute and reflexion and critique are evolved rather than skills claimed by assertion (Alvesson & Skoldberg, 2000). Part of the craft of achieving multivocality is that of presenting versions of text and listening to feedback that subverts as well as supports. Storytelling permits variety and evolution and creates opportunities for anguish (Roth, 2002) and cathartic and therapeutic benefits (Wright, 2009), externalizing internal conversations (Archer, 2003).

"AE is not a solution to our organizational research problems. Rather it is just one more piece ..." (Buchanan & Bryson, 2009, p. 699). The generic criteria of narrative apply: it must be parsimonious, readable and cogent and above all "engaging" as "screenplay for a historical documentary" (ibid., p. 698).

REVIEWING DELAMONT'S EVALUATION OF AE

Evaluations seek to "contest or reach out" (Gingrich-Philbrook, 2013, p. 618) explicitly incorporating emotional as well as rational response (Ellis, 2009). Delamont states that her critique of AE is *deliberately controversial* and the discourse of "pernicious," "objections," "cannot," "wrong," "entirely," "essentially," "dead ends," "lazy," "abrogates," "abuse" to contest AE, makes for more than a challenge. Presenting six arguments against AE (see Table 8.1), her evaluation constitutes an outright objection and absolute denial of authenticity in *any* of the "work" involved in the practice of it, concluding that AE is essentially harmful and our energy is best "put to work" doing other kinds of research. Delamont risks throwing some important and promising scholarly babies out with the bathwater of disdain. By demonstrating "evaluative flexibility" (Ellis & Adams, 2014, p. 270) we offer hope for the future of AE as authentic.

We accept that "budding autoethnographers may very well want the reassurance of a checklist" to ensure their text meets all the criteria and recognize there may be a "desire to know what the rules are in order to avoid the punishment of breaking them", but because "there is no 'blueprint' for [auto]ethnography" (Humphreys & Learmonth, 2012, p. 326) we fear an "increased focus on formulaic papers," and "evaluations based on tick-box processes" (Alvesson & Spicer, 2016, p. 33). It is more important to have something interesting or relevant to say than rigorous compliance with external standards (Gabriel, 2016; Alvesson & Spicer, 2016) or strict adherence to any recipe or formula (Van Maanen, 2011).

We do not comprehensively review the criteria appropriate to evaluate AE texts (see Adams et al., 2015, p. 104 for an overview) but note that

130   D. WEIR AND D. CLARKE

Table 8.1   Delamont and authentic autoethnographic texts

Delamont	Daniel's story	David's story
1. AE cannot fight familiarity	Tries to make sense of a sudden dislocation when the familiar becomes suddenly unfamiliar. Writing of Mother's death "disturbs but also activates the self-world relation" (Stewart, 2013, p. 661)	Starts with what had been familiar but had been forgotten or overlain. Attempts to make sense of the unfamiliarity of the recent past by reworking material through diverse available methods
2. AE is almost impossible to write and publish *ethically*	No one else's rights are compromised, especially since Mother is not here anymore "… and the dead can't be libelled because they cannot suffer as a result of damaged reputations" (Ellis, 2007, p. 14, citing Couser, 2004, p. 6)	No one else's rights are compromised. Secrecy and failure to bear witness are equally heinous offences against truth. The ethical canons of today's contemporary practice are equally open to debate and challenge
3. Research is supposed to be analytic not merely experiential. AE is all experience and is noticeably lacking in *analytic* outcome	A principle of AE is to *value* and *use* the personal and experiential (Adams et al., 2015). The analytical emerges from the narrative.	Various analytic frameworks are available, but no other scientist so far has touched this topic though it disrupts simplistic rational economic action paradigms frameworks
4. AE focuses on the powerful and not the powerless to whom we should be directing our sociological gaze	I became sentient to what was happening; exploring how the force of loss can hit my body; trying to understand how sensibilities circulate and become, perhaps delicately or ephemerally, collective (adapted from Stewart, 2013, p. 661). But this did not make me powerful	Not correct: Anyway this is a strong value judgement about who is powerful. Are autoethnographers/ sociologists/ ethnographers powerful? Are the farmers in my story *the powerful?* We doubt this

(continued)

WHAT MAKES THE AUTOETHNOGRAPHIC ANALYSIS AUTHENTIC?   131

Table 8.1   (continued)

Delamont	Daniel's story	David's story
5. AE abrogates our duty to go out and collect data: we are not paid generous salaries to sit in our offices obsessing about ourselves. Sociology is an empirical discipline and we are supposed to study *the social*	These data came as a product of an unplanned experience, "part of the life process" (Brinkmann, 2014, p. 722). Where does the "field" start and end, anyway? In AE, "fieldwork is a bit different [...] everyday experience can serve as relevant 'data'..." (Ellis & Adams, 2014, p. 266). Further still, during my scheduled weekly "drop-ins" when Advisees suffering loss sometimes come to talk with me about coping with writing deadlines, events of the world and "unbearable atmospheres" (Stewart, 2013, p. 666), my office becomes *the social* with "no division, in practice, between work and life" (in Brinkman 2012, citing Ingold, 2011 who cites CW Mills). A link is forged between self and world, the "fuzzy or smudged yet precise" (Stewart, 2013, p. 667) and, everyday life becomes "part of an ambiguous and ever-changing field" (Ellis & Adams, 2014, p. 266)	These data came, quite legitimately as a consequence of a field experience" (Brinkmann, 2014, p. 722). Scholars don't get "generous salaries"?
6. The important questions are *not* about the personal anguish (and most AE is about anguish)	But important and personally, meaningful research questions can start there. As autoethnographers, we must then move from the "personal anguish" to a more generic framing. AE is a "...'what if' practice—a method for imagining, living into, and sharing our collective future" (Adams et al., 2013, p. 674).	No anguish. Perhaps some sentimentality in the recall or genuine mourning for the loss of a way of life?

(continued)

132   D. WEIR AND D. CLARKE

Table 8.1   (continued)

Delamont	Daniel's story	David's story
Sociologists are a privileged group … AE is an abuse of that privilege—our duty is to go out and research the classic texts of 2050 or 2090—not sit in our homes focusing on ourselves	"Most scholarly work … generates little excitement and rarely gets much attention even in the domain in which it is hatched" (Van Maanen, 2011, p. 230), "exemplary … high quality work in any domain is … by definition, rare" (p. 231). No sane person ever thinks they are going to create a "classic text." WF Whyte didn't (1955, 1994). E. Goffman might have thought on these lines. Anyway, what is this about "duty"? Our duty as scholars of the social is to reveal lives and acknowledge multiple truths, *wherever, however.* No scholarly work is incontestable	

evaluations of AE, "capture efforts of real people and deploy them in arguments advancing the evaluator's own paradigm, psyche, and professional identity-work" (Gingrich-Philbrook, 2013, p. 615). No evaluation enjoys an entitlement to remain untroubled (Adams et al., 2015) and we *use* our evaluation as a way to continue our "commitment to trouble the disequilibrium in the distribution of entitlements" (Gingrich-Philbrook, 2013, p. 625).

We have an entitlement to tell our story and respect the "right to write" but AE does not have, *per se*, an epistemic advantage over what it evaluates (Gingrich-Philbrook, 2013, p. 618). We "must still make its points by pretty much the same means that were available before these contingencies were recognized and absorbed … the appeal of any single work remains tied to the specific arguments made in a given text and referenced to particular, not general, substantive, methodological, and narrative matters" (Van Maanen, 2011, p. 226). It would be "narcissistic to think that we are somehow outside our studies and not subject to the same social forces and cultural conditioning as those we study or that somehow our own actions and relationships need no reflexive thought …" (Ellis & Adams, 2014, p. 267).

AUTHENTICITY AS RESPECTING THE *PRINCIPLES* AND UPHOLDING THE *GOALS* OF AE

Adams et al. (2015) note four goals of AE:

- Making contributions to knowledge
- Valuing the personal and experiential

WHAT MAKES THE AUTOETHNOGRAPHIC ANALYSIS AUTHENTIC? 133

- Demonstrating the power, craft, and responsibilities of stories and storytelling
- Taking a relationally responsible approach to research practice and representation

So how does a situation ripe for AE analysis achieve authenticity? And how does such an evaluation of autoethnographic production become genuinely useful? Rather than seeing authentic AE as a one-off accomplishment, achieved through measuring text against a closed set of criteria, we, like Adams et al. (2015), see authenticity as *an emergent property of text*, stemming from how completely the value of AE has been realized through the writing *and* how successfully the core *goals* of AE have been achieved. "To evaluate autoethnography in a genuinely useful way you have to open yourself up to being changed by it, to heeding its call to surrender your entitlement" (Gingrich-Philbrook, 2013, p. 618)

Personal experience, even anguish, can be an appropriate starting point for a sociological analysis and can link with structural issues, and although we accept that w*e are not interesting enough to ourselves be the prime subject matter* (Delamont, 2007), nonetheless our field of experience *may be*. In order "to pull a subject on to the stage of the world, to world the subject, to subject a world", personal anguish can provide a way of sidling up to "a hinge onto a moment of some world's legibility" (Stewart, 2013, p. 667), thus "worlding" the subject, presenting a plausible jumping-off point to "research and write for the betterment of all" (Barley, 2015, pp. 6–7).

The use of personal experience and the need to develop a familiarity with existing research are "features that cut across almost all autoethnographic work" (Ellis & Adams, 2014, p. 260). A further five elements (using personal experience to describe and critique cultural experience; taking advantage of and valuing insider knowledge; breaking silence, (re) claiming voice; healing and manoeuvring through pain, confusion, anger and uncertainty; writing accessible prose) "are more specific goals, advantages, and rewards to using AE in research" (Ellis & Adams, 2014, p. 260).

Daniel's Story and His Field/Head/Textwork

In late 2009 I started work on a paper to introduce Lomography (Hall, Jones, Hall, Richardson, & Hodgson, 2007) into organizational analysis, planning to submit to the Research Methods track at the EURAM conference in Rome in 2010. However, the title (and my writing aim) soon changed.

My mother died while I was writing the paper. Though I wanted to keep on writing to meet the deadline for submission, it became very difficult. With so much grief and emotion it was hard to concentrate. But I pushed on. "Don't give up now. Failing to meet the deadline is not an option", I told myself and continued to write.

In my attempt to write up an "insider account" of developing a novel research method, writing after my mother's funeral to show my situatedness in a cultural context and shine a strange light on what I was up to (Van Maanen, 2011), I wrote:

> I don't know what to do. I want to visit my Mum's grave at the cemetery, but I know it will make me cry again. It will make me sad and I won't be able to concentrate in order to write. I want to visit my Grandma and I want to be there for her, but I also want to visit my Dad and be there for him too, [...] but I have to mark transcripts. I want to visit my Girlfriend, but I have to write that invited chapter. I want to [...] do a 3 hour hill run [...] but I have to write this paper. The EURAM 2010 deadline is fast upon us and I am not ready to submit. Will I ever be ready? Are you ever ready to submit a conference paper?

Drawing inspiration from Wall (2008), using illustrative vignettes (Humphreys, 2005), my aim shifted and I began writing a "writing story". To articulate my new focus I noted:

> This is an ethnographic memoir that describes what goes on in the backstage of struggling to develop a novel [research] method. I am studying myself in order to make cultural sense of myself.

Questioning my decision to keep on writing, I wrote:

> I want to forge a name for myself in 'arts-based' research methods (Taylor & Ladkin, 2009) and eventually come to be known as an authority on developing 'creative' research methods for organization and management studies ... [...] ... its where, in the long term, I want to be. Therefore, I must write, get published and get cited!

I was living in the thick of academic probation in my first academic appointment, so learning an answer to the question *why write when I ought to be grieving and my family needs me more than ever* rested "more on a logic of discovery and happenstance than a logic of verification and plan" (Van Maanen, 2011, p. 220). Because "for the autoethnographer, fieldwork is a bit different" (Ellis & Adams, 2014, p. 266). By writing about continuing to write when I felt I had other important things to be getting on with, such as grieving the loss of my mother and writing a conference paper, being a fieldworker in my everyday life with a cultural identity, observing my own actions and social patterns around me, I and the field became one.

On the subject of textwork, as a newly qualified lecturer and early career academic, trying to find a way in the academy, I did not go to the field to ask of probationers experiencing loss "How do they live? What do they do? How do they get by?" (Van Maanen, 2011, p. 226). Respecting the *principle* of using personal experience, pursuing self-therapy (Haynes, 2006) at my desk—where writing became a therapeutic experience, I found myself doing the textwork that would lead to an answer to these three questions. Rather than "reduce the indignity of speaking for others that some ethnographers feel" (Van Maanen, 2011, p. 225), I argue it is better to let the textwork show what goes on in the background of writing yet another conference paper; after all, isn't an individual experiencing it "best suited to describe his or her own experience more accurately than anyone else" (Wall, 2006, p. 3)? This is where I thought the potential contribution of my AE might lie.

"Tinkering" (Van Maanen, 2011, p. 223) with concepts and theories, my headwork involved positioning the paper as a therapeutic journey, reflecting on the effects that undertaking research was having on my identity construction (Haynes, 2006). To reflect this, in early 2010, I gave the paper a new working title (Clarke, 2010), offering details on the personal, identifying multiple identities, and locating myself in order to contextualize the situation: an early career academic, struggling to write a conference paper while experiencing an "emotionally demanding phase of adult life" (borrowed and adapted from Reviewer 1 of the submitted conference paper).

However, now I recognize that I did not do enough headwork to situate my story among the relevant scholarly literature (Ellis & Adams, 2014, p. 267). On this, I feel I was somewhat unsuccessful in respecting the second *principle* of needing to develop a familiarity with existing research. However, now that I am more aware of the literature on becoming academic and academic literacies, I feel more confident in my ability to continue writing in this vein. Gray and Sinclair (2006, p. 449) observe

136 D. WEIR AND D. CLARKE

that "We write because it has become our way of being, our way of reassuring ourselves about our own significance. I'm cited, therefore I am!" so, writing in my research diary, I noted how the experience of writing was beginning to affect me:

> I am yet to experience how I have been transformed and to gain new insight on how I have been transformed. I know that I am still yet to gain knowledge on how I have been transformed because all I know at present is that my life is no longer the same as it once was: I am without a mother. (January 16, 2010)

I then went on to write in the paper "… my first year as an academic became more significant when my mother died". While this, I believe, demonstrates the "unbearable slowness of ethnography" (Van Maanen Van Maanen, 2011, p. 220) because I observe that I am yet to learn how I have been shifted by my experience of writing through the loss of my mother; even though I tried to show how I had changed, I believe now that I was unsuccessful in showing then how this experience shifted me.

Academic "culture" is "shape shifting" (Van Maanen, 2011, p. 220) and while my autoethnographic writing had been "self-full," it seems that my textwork fell down in demonstrating the processes and outcomes of the ways in which my reflecting on my experiences was "self-altering" (Berry, 2008, p. 158). I was not explicit enough in articulating where my introspection had taken me to: my exposure of the self who is also a spectator failed to take us somewhere we couldn't have otherwise got to (Adams et al., 2015, p. 40). While my writing was therapeutic in that it helped me to go on living and to make sense of my loss, I now believe it was also self-altering because it prevented me from mourning properly.

To give authoritative voice to my loss, I sought to enable readers to "vicariously share" (McMahon & Dinan-Thompson, 2011, p. 24) my experience of writing yet another conference paper and, wanting to create a research text that "leaves readers feeling changed by what they read", I also wanted to encourage epiphany in the reader (Nicol, 2008, p. 323, citing Van Maanen, 1997). So, in an effort to leave readers feeling changed by reading what I had written, I penned the following paragraph in summary to my paper:

> This is a story of transition. I know that I am now a different person but I have not yet fully experienced how I have been transformed. Therefore,

WHAT MAKES THE AUTOETHNOGRAPHIC ANALYSIS AUTHENTIC? 137

> I am yet to gain knowledge on how I have been transformed by this experience. Dealing with my loss, creating a place for myself in academia, developing stronger connections with my family and my intimate others, developing [a new research] method are all works in progress. That this paper was written and submitted shows that it can be done.

I made the conference submission deadline. But in doing so, I missed the opportunity to accomplish the AE *goal* of breaking silence on two fronts: first, about the limiting construct of the idealized academic identity of the four-star researcher (Harding, 2008; Harding, Ford, & Gough, 2010) and second, about the potential for harm that the pursuit can entail for an individual. As for the *goal* of AE in taking a relationally responsible approach to research practice, while writing that my submission "shows that it [i.e. submitting a conference paper on time] can be done", making me a survivor of my own loss, it conceals my failure to experience "good grief".

My writing is perhaps the least successful in terms of the *principle* of reclaiming voice. In light of more recent critiques on "compliance" with the "myopic focus on publishing in highly ranked journals" (Alvesson & Spicer, 2016, p. 32), by not obsessing about writing a methodology paper for presentation at a conference and for eventual publication, taking heed of Adams et al.'s (2015, p. 114) plea to "not focus on or worry about publication" but instead "concentrate on doing the best AE work", and, by not taking the "compassionate leave" that was made available to me by my employer to grieve and be with my family, I failed to demonstrate social change "one person at a time" (Ellis & Adams, 2014, p. 261).

Asking the question, how is it possible I should obsess about writing when my mum is in hospital/she has just died/on the day of her funeral/ when I might otherwise be mourning our loss with my family—had I gone far and deep enough in my reflexivity, given the estranging sensitivity, mystery, breakdown, and lack of a separation between the living of life, work, research, theory, methods, AE, data, then I might have *stumbled* upon my determination to submit that paper as an occurrence that is evidence that the *machinery for its production is currently available* (adapted from Brinkmann, 2014, p. 723 my emphasis in italics). Breaching this everyday "requirement" (and identity-affirming experience) to write might constitute a deliberate contrast, or breach, of academic custom (Berry, 2008). Recognizing my failure to breach draws explicit attention to the possibility for myopic thinking, complacency, uniformity (Berry, 2008), and compliance (Alvesson & Spicer, 2016) in academic writing culture.

I now read my writing, however, as successful in conveying an experience of what goes on in the background of writing yet another conference paper and when I share my story of loss with other mature and early career academics, their responses bear witness to that. But perhaps one of the most important ways in which the text falls short in upholding the *goals* of AE is in that I did not realize the potential to use the power of my story about loss to critique *culture*, not going far enough in my headwork, tinkering with concepts of fear of failure (Haynes, 2006), inadequacy (Holt, 2003; Ogbonna & Harris, 2004), and fear of failing to achieve an idealized academic identity (Harding et al., 2010) to critique the culture of compliance with the idea of universities as "Four by four factories" (Alvesson & Spicer, 2016, p. 32). Subsequently, I was unable to "go the distance" in my textwork, writing to allow my text to "do" the work of ending "harmful cultural beliefs" (Adams et al., 2015, p. 114).

To use a sporting analogy, by writing through my loss I obeyed one of the many mantras I have since come to realize that I live(d) my life by: "Pain is only temporary, failure is forever." Continuing to write was to the longer-term detriment of family relations and self-care. At a time when it hurt the most, while I gained some*thing* (i.e. conference paper acceptance), by continuing to write I also suffered loss and failure. I lost the opportunity to fully experience my pain and to grieve, something which I now wish I had given myself more time and space to do. Writing prevented me from mourning properly. I failed to mourn my loss and be with my family when compassion, communion, and togetherness are perhaps most needed and rewarding. That kind of failure *is* forever.

It is now 2016 and although I have failed to achieve the idealized academic identity of the four-star researcher through publication of that conference paper, there is the delicious irony (Van Maanen, 2011) of this chapter which is potentially much more meaningful and capable of doing more "work" in the world. Unlike the conference paper I submitted, the point of doing this AE is "not for the academic career reward that might result" from it, but it is "to figure out 'how things work' in some specified domain and get the word(s) out as best we can" (Van Maanen, 2011, p. 230). That I deem myself partially unsuccessful—in my original piece— in presenting a compelling and convincing argument to end harmful cultural beliefs is not so much a sign of being intellectually lazy, rather it is more an indicator of the unbearable (for some) slowness to learn answers through sustained tinkering and work on the craft of writing good auto-ethnographic texts.

In my current textwork, as in my role of Academic Advisor to some 50 undergraduate students, I write to lessen harm done by the similar orienting stories and limiting constructs such as "I am the journals in which I have published in" (Alvesson & Spicer, 2016, p. 39) and "I'm cited, therefore I am!" (Gray & Sinclair, 2006, p. 449). I regularly dispense advice with my Academic Advisees who are demonstrably suffering with loss and write to help make sense of how one can make life better and offer companionship (Ellis & Adams, 2014) to those who feel troubled about spending time grieving with their family instead of writing for their next assignment. I regularly remind students that this is what an Extenuating Circumstances Committee, External Examiners, and Examination Boards are for ... The grades students get in their exams can affect the rest of their lives, but so too can failing to experience "good grief". Making sense of my personal anguish helps me to "*move* and *live into*" the world with others to try to shape a future together (Adams, Holman Jones, & Ellis, 2013, p. 669 original emphasis in italics).

Embarking on AE carries significant personal and professional risk for scholars (Boyle & Parry, 2007); however, I did and, I continue to do, what I had to. Trying to make sense of my experiences and convey the meanings I attached to those experiences so the reader could feel and think about my life and their life in relation to mine (Ellis, 1999, p. 674, adapted); *I had to write.* Although I made the deadline, AE is never something that "can be knocked off over night" (Humphreys & Learmonth, 2012, p. 326).

Ellis (2010) notes that by writing about her 9-year relationship with her partner who died, his illness and her caregiving, she felt the need to tell her story to achieve an "interior liberation"; she also observes that she "wrote her way through grief and loss" (Ellis, 2007, p. 16, adapted). In pursuit of this and along with Ellis, "I felt I had to tell my story to move on in my personal and professional life" (p. 16). Considering my extrospective-out-hereness by writing about how my experience of loss relates to other people's loss, and writing for publication within the academy, I argue that my AE goes beyond the merely experiential providing social analysis.

David's Story and How a Sudden Vision of His Life and Work Led on to Head and Textwork

One late hot summer afternoon in the 1990s found me on a train journey from London's Kings Cross station to Leeds after an "important" committee meeting in the corridors of power. When the train stopped unexpectedly, I caught sight of a man in overalls picking his way through a recently combine-harvested field, and a gut-wrenching start of recognition told me that I knew that man, that I had worked with him in such fields and that something in me was stumbling with him through that dead landscape needing to find its voice. The words of a poem flowed to my pen. Something had happened and some irreversible corner had been turned.

The poem stands or falls by its merits but did win a prize in an international competition. There was a conflicted nature to my understanding nonetheless for the poem lay in a drawer for a few years until I read it one day to my daughter and her children as a means of telling them what it had been like working on a farm in the 1950s: she asked for a copy. The next I heard of it was a message out of the blue that the poem had won a competition. This was a surprise because as far as I was aware it had never been entered in a competition: but it had of course by my daughter.

A few weeks later I was as usual on a Monday evening in a Liverpool pub preparing for a vocal evening of a folk and Irish night when my friend suddenly stood up and said "we have an award winning poet in the house and he will now read you his poem." I demurred safe in the knowledge that the poem was not in my pocket. It was in his however and it was read. The following week the guitarist said "have you another poem for us then?" This became my Monday evening life pattern. One evening a bunch of lads carried on talking through my recitation. An older man suddenly stood up and in broadest Scouse shouted "Come on now lads, Respect in the house for the Poet!" A year after that a genuine, published poet joined us for a Monday evening session: he strutted his stuff and I did mine. As we broke up he said, "keep on with this. You gave a voice, you know."

A new pattern started and I became another person at least on a Monday. There had been no anguish but there was now serious disruption in my self-image and aspirations. My "inner conversation" (Archer, 2003) now contained more questions than answers: my poetry writing found its place in a cycle driven by the demands of a Monday night audience of

WHAT MAKES THE AUTOETHNOGRAPHIC ANALYSIS AUTHENTIC? 141

fellow performers to be original, entertaining, and authentic in respect of a new self, an identity long covered in structural constraints, that clamoured for release. In Dennett's terms, the centre of narrative gravity of my self-hood had changed or was enabled to pursue a new path (Dennett, 1988). My autobiographical self was now differently located, like it or not (Damasio, 2000).

An epiphany is an event after which life never seems quite the same (Ellis and Adams, 2014, p. 264), initiating an autoethnographic process by presenting an object for further study, reflection, and analysis of celebration as much as a "lament for a lost order of things" (Macklin, 1998, p. 20), and it became clear that this experience had changed a central understanding of my life and career. My role-set changed, not towards liminality or "somewhere in-between" (Daskalaski, Butler, & Petrovic, 2016) but towards contradiction and the need for subsequent life choices to allow suddenly available space for another way of grasping and communicating experience.

The identity change that had occurred was brought sharply to me by a small incident at the pub where I had by now become the poet in residence. One evening one of the whistle players asked over a pint "I think I met a chap who knows you: but he says that you are a Prof at the University. He lives near us and he was talking about someone and I said that sounds like our Poet but I didn't know if that could be you, but is that right? Is that what you do?" This small conversation brought home to me the extent of the transition I had made, because I had been an academic pretty much since leaving University and a Professor since 1974, and this fact was inscribed on my cheque book so it had to be true, but now in the eyes of another constituency of interest it was a secondary role to my existence as a poet. Shortly after that incident, one of the really good instrumentalists told me that he had accepted a booking for a Benefit Night for the Marie Curie Care Home "it will be me backing your poems, I have some ideas about tunes and riffs: it will be a good night and this would work great, Dave". But at the University nobody called me "Dave."

That poem (not reproduced here but I will send it to anyone interested) was a first response to being suddenly heaved out of the rut of cognitive habit (Weir, 2008). Now again my central role as a social scientist took over for I needed to recover by scholarly means what else could be known about this experience and present it in more conventional terms: a time for "headwork." So I followed my usual practice by creating a file

142   D. WEIR AND D. CLARKE

(Mills, 1959) and sought "the literature" to position what I could add to an authentic tradition of scholarship.

I thus joined the Agricultural History Society and circulated drafts of a paper. But the comparative literature of this genre that I sought was not to be found there so I dared to create some by writing a paper presented at several conferences describing farm work in a 1950s mixed farm in East Yorkshire (Weir, 2009a, 2009b). Some scholars said how much they had enjoyed and learned from my paper; others warned that such material had no place in their journals ... and advised that if it had been related to medieval farm work, if it had a stronger statistical base or if the data had comprised other regions with maybe a European comparison ... if there were a link to Foreign Direct Investment in the agricultural sector, if I had undertaken a survey of older and retired farm workers, etc. etc. That was not my stuff/it would have compromised authenticity to put my old wine into these unfriendly new bottles however much they could have facilitated the task of "getting published and into the literature."

So I wrote my paper as a descriptive retrospective piece of recovered ethnography and gave papers at conferences as an example of "autoethnography a posteriori" (Boncori & Vine, 2014) or "retrospective autoethnography" (Potkins & Vine, forthcoming).

One day an excited Scotsman called from an agricultural museum in Perth. "Davie," he said, "your paper made me jump for joy. This is how it was on the farms when I was sent tattie pickin' in Fife and naebody kens it noo, naebody cares." When I gave the paper at a Critical Management Studies conference, the room was shocked when a senior Professor of OB suddenly broke down into tears as I told my story (Weir, 2009b). Afterwards, presuming that my portrayal was erroneous, I asked her "how did that compare? Have I got it wrong?" She answered that she had been brought up on a farm like that in South Yorkshire and that I had indeed got it right, and that what had moved her to tears was not criticism but the sudden shock of shared accurate reminiscence. What had been epiphanic for me was validated by an expert listener.

There is no claim that the account presented (Weir, 2009a) is *incorrigible*: but it *has not in fact been corrected*, nor been shown to be substantially inaccurate by other testimony or further and better particulars. But it attempts to position a testimony of recollection in a pattern that one would not have been able to do better (or maybe at all) at the time of those experiences.

WHAT MAKES THE AUTOETHNOGRAPHIC ANALYSIS AUTHENTIC?   143

The voyage of the self does not have to be the introverted self-obsessed self so feared by Delamont but rather the self in society for ... "here" is something we never discover ... .we inherit a going concern ... We know nothing about any of it until it is well under way ... everything that has happened to us since then constitutes what is already a life. .... but to begin with, at any rate, our consciousness is not a consciousness of self ... The process moves in the opposite direction: we start by being aware of things outside ourselves ... and it is only by degrees that we become aware of ourselves as centres of these experiences" (Magee, 2004, p. 2).

The memoir is an *authentic* and well-established genre (Verney, 1955, p. 20), since "*life histories are exceptionally effective historical sources* because through the totality of lived experience they reveal relations between individuals and social forces which are rarely apparent in other sources" (Lummis, 1988, p. 108) (my italics). The memoir is not presently "institutionalized and taken-for-granted as constitutive of the trade" (Van Maanen, 2011, p. 219), but perhaps it ought to be a more current issue in ethnography, for the utility, authenticity, and reliability of the memoir is currently seriously debated in the disciplines of historical research. A good memoir does not privilege the solitary, solipsistic self: one comes to knowledge or understanding of self through reflecting on what happens in interaction with others (Weir, 2015).

My writing included small stories, vignettes, recollections of specific events that had made their mark at the time, following Boje's account of story as "an oral or written performance involving two or more people interpreting past or anticipated experience" (Boje, 1991, p. 111), within the overall narrative of life and work on the farm. Here is one such mini-story:

> One day when we were stooking in the big field that bordered on the main road a Ford Popular stopped at the roadside and the driver shouted something to the gang in the field. Ron walked steadily over to speak to him and he stayed speaking to him for about fifteen minutes. Then he picked up his place with his partner, Bernard. After a respectful pause Bernard said to him 'Does ta know 'im, Ron?'
> 'Aye' replied Ron 'But aa've not seen 'im fer a while'
> 'What's a while, then?'
> 'Sin' t'war ended A think, ... Aye not sin t'war ended'
> 'Does 'e live local?'
> 'No it's a long way off,'
> 'Where's that, then? London way?'

144 D. WEIR AND D. CLARKE

'Ossforth, near Leeds, but 'es off to Brid fer 'is holidays an 'e thought e'd call by'
'oo 'is he then?'
'e's me brother'.
This was in 1954. The war had ended in 1945. (Weir, 2009a)

That "story" illuminates the changing reality of time, distance, travel, family, and consumerism between the 1950s and the 2000s as well as many a statistical account. But although I do not privilege this story above others, nonetheless I *claim* this story. No more do I wish to preload the analytic or sense-making attempts of others by classifying this story or others in such macro-categoric schemes as "performativity" (Lyotard, 1984) or as exemplary of a panoptic gaze or illustrative of power relations (Foucault, 1977, 1980). All cannot be sucked retrospectively into one super schema. Recasting these materials into other analytical frames and currently fashionable discourse may make them less rather than more valuable. They are shards, not yet whole pots, but to the archaeologist the shard can tell a story (Woolley, 1929), and maybe it will be the task of other scholars to more completely reconstruct these shards.

This is another story from that paper:

On the last stint of the day, yours is the privilege of riding back to the farmyard on top of the laden cart. One day from this vantage point as we turned from the Big Field towards the lane, at around seven o'clock in the evening glow, I saw a field pattern across several miles of Wold farmland that still gleams in my inner eye. We had been reading Gerard Manley Hopkins at school and I suddenly saw 'Landscape plotted and pieced—fold, fallow, and plough" and if I thought myself not yet a tradesman worthy of "áll trádes, their gear and tackle and trim' (Hopkins, 1918), this was a landscape that I had learnt albeit temporarily to be part of. That emotion has never left me.

I knew instantly that this was one of those moments where 'a door opens and lets the future in' (Greene, 1939, ch 1) and that these fields and that pattern were something precious to be experienced but something complex and evolving to be grasped and explained. (Weir, 2009b)

That story illustrates the power of the present to better illuminate and pattern a remembered past and an example of where heartwork rooted my headwork analysis because that framing conceptualisation of a landscape as a palimpsest and of ones lived life experience as being that of clambering through a layered matrix searching for connections has through my career been central to my scholarly stuff.

WHAT MAKES THE AUTOETHNOGRAPHIC ANALYSIS AUTHENTIC? 145

A third story relates to taking our morning "lowance" in the Top Field that dropped down to a dip in the Wold with a sunken streambed below the field end (the Wolds are chalk hills and there is little surface water), dividing it from the neighbour's land:

> We sat on hay bales to eat our bacon cake and took our mugs of tea (it is customary in these kinds of recollection to describe the tea as 'steaming' but 'steaming' it never was because it had come a mile up the farm on the tractor.) As we sat we heard a groaning, clanking noise from Cayley's field and a huge engine came into view: we observed in silence. Then Ron said 'its Cayley's combine.' It was my first sight of the machine that was to take all our work away. (Weir, 2009b)

This story refers to the potential of technological change to recast social structures, but although I can see that now, this was not apparent to me then, and it could not have been because I did not have the mental equipment, the theories, the models, the comparative frameworks to put that observation into a wider perspective. Maybe even now I am uncertain as to what framework best contains this shard: I should like more time to reflect, to study, to read around the topics, reworking the patterns as craft workers always do.

Recollection and recording is part of the craft of research, and part of the analytic value of my recalled experience is the purely circumstantial one that not many people now living, even on farms, remember a time before the combine harvester. If the presence of sentiment as a trigger of recall signals lack of authenticity, I argue that sentiment is always present in craft and the objectivity that claims to eradicate sentiment may itself be inauthentic. An acceptance of the ultimate honesty of others may not be a necessary condition of positive science, but it is an essential bedfellow of worldly wisdom.

One insight often underplayed in scientific writing is that the experience of recall is a total experience, involving more than one sense. As I write I can smell the corn, hear the clack-clack of the Reaper and Binder, and a Mantovani melody and its sweeping strings come to ears (Auric, 1952) for "the perception, preservation and presentation of personal histories and memories is by no means solely linguistic, given that our experience of the world, especially in early childhood days, is primarily sensual" (Hecht, 2001, p. 129). Smell is a powerful sense (Lindstrom & Kotler, 2010), if perhaps the least esteemed among social scientists (Synott, 1991).

Pat, the Irish haytime and harvest man who was my oppo the first year on the farm liked Mantovani as did Ron, the Wag or leader of the field gang who also claimed to have a soft spot for "Mantovani and 'is Band." The title "Wag" is an abbreviation of "Waggoner" as the senior man in the field would at one time have had local control over the horse-drawn carts that took the sheaves back to the farm yard.

My mind's eye replays Bernard the stockman, who could run a rabbit down as it scampered from the last uncut area of wheat before the reaper and binder cut it down and still sees that last hapless rabbit break for cover, the uncouth way he ran after it, legs splayed apart and the little sharp crack as he broke its neck. Sparkes (2009, p. 34) reminds us that "*all* the senses deserve serious attention in ethnographic work if we are to better understand the life world of others and our own locations in relation to these". The totality of a set of experiences over a period of time when senses were perhaps more awake than they are now is significant.

Recall is not perfect, but neither is contemporaneous observation and *the one does not substitute for the other nor is necessarily of higher epistemologic value. Both are necessary* (Bernard-Donals, 2001). The past is a whole bundle of structures, both analytical and affective, "so information about the past comes completely with evaluations, explanations and theories which often constitute a principal value of the account and are intrinsic to its representations of reality" (Lummis, 1988, p. 107). Over time the mind sifts, but it is not only the dross that remains nor is retrospective interrogation of field material from a richer and more refined and rich set of mental constructs necessarily inferior to naïve contemporaneous observation. Sense-making is an achieved craft, not a native capacity.

Towards *Genuinely Useful* Accounts of "Authenticity" in AE …

So what have we learnt from our successful and unsuccessful efforts in achieving authenticity in our AE? First, we refute absolutely the criticism that this is lazy work or no work at all. For both of us this intellectual journey has embodied hard graft and application of a wide range of tools of scholarship. We also believe that such a line of criticism is unworthy of our trade and that it is fundamentally unprofessional to assume that the working practices of others are somehow easier than those one personally favours.

The methodological vulnerabilities of this kind of work do not need elaborating (Holt, 2003; Dashper, 2015; Delamont, 2007; Strathern, 1987; Tolich, 2010), but we have written about our experiences as selves in evolving social processes, which we are coming to understand. Is this work authentic and is this of value? According to Delamont, it is probably not. We disagree (see Table 8.1).

These stories wrote us as much as we wrote them, and we are able to put all that felt experience behind us when we don our research hat. Is this a weak choice, which somehow diminishes the authenticity of our accounts, or a fact of our total life as scholars and as persons?

If there was in these experiences some "anguish," it was not a motivator. We did not wish to experience it then nor to profit from it now: these insights were not the products of a conscious choice, but having gone through and reflected on our experience of *what happens* (Stewart, 2013), we are required to bring our trained perceptions and analytic craft to bear on the issues uncovered in our experience, including our pain.

Delamont's critique directs attention to the downside of "egocentric" AE where the voice of the speaker is louder than that of potentially more interesting or relevant others and where the author is always the leading legend in his/her own lunchtime: we concur that such accounts are tiresome and too "confessional" (Van Maanen, 1988).

In Wacquant's (2003) boxing notebooks, our attention is held because we know that this writing is the product of personally lived encounters that we have not shared but as a result of our trust in the narrative can come to empathize with. Bauman (2003, p. 1) describes it as "A poem in prose, a work of love and wisdom rolled into one: this is how ethnography should be written, were the ethnographers capable of writing like that." Bauman's dismissal of ethnographers is pejorative and unworthy because good ethnographers (e.g. Wacquant) can and often do write like that, but Bauman implies that there is in some writing too little poetry, too little anguish, and too little connection of the personal trouble with the public issue.

In our work we do not claim to be heroes and over-emphasize our successes: significant others play their parts, not just as a backdrop to our story. All of our accounts are up for grabs. Anybody else who was there can have their say, but as we *were* there, our claims should at least be accounted as honest reportage and stand until they can be disproved, standing or falling on their own merits testifying where we were, where we

148   D. WEIR AND D. CLARKE

were coming from, and what we have, so far, made of it all. Daniel was here. David was here. Kilroy *was* here (Kilroy, c1942).

Personal experiences comprise learning opportunities and privileged experiences, once they are shared in a scholarly, supportive environment, offering personalized accounts as authentic templates for other framings. Over-correction towards sentimentality or retrofitting the plain story into a Procrustean theoretical frame is misleading because "to wish to make a thing look pretty or look smart is to think poorly of it in itself and to want it more conventional, and to try to improve it is to weaken and perhaps destroy it" (Ransom, 1938, p. 81).

Delamont's dismissive references to "anguish" imply some negative position on the role of emotion and affect in AE, but this criticism is not restricted to AE but to other consequences of immersion in a field experience. Per contra, does emotional identification with a field site and its participants necessarily compromise "authenticity" or is it a very likely concomitant of serious long-term engagement with a chosen field? The loving recall of "capoeiristas and the strange musical instruments they carry" (Delamont, 2007, p. 2) and the self-reflexive query about the Cloisterham bar scene of "why don't I feel scared in this dangerous neighbourhood?" (Delamont, 2007, p. 3) are equally implicated with emotional freight. But this is not an opportunity for disparagement or abnegation but for respect for the implied human vulnerability. "The smell and taste of things remain poised a long time, like souls, ready to remind us, waiting and hoping for their moment, amid the ruins of all the rest" (Proust, 2006, p. 48).

AE is not a monolithic entity and all reportage is not interesting. Much self-reflexivity can be mere navel-gazing, but our ultimate justification may be that we had at the time of the experience fewer methodological choices than we thought. Things happen (Dawes, 2016; Seely, 2010) and in the quest to understand what has happened, it is necessary to lose the illusion of control (Langer, 1975). But this does not imply an avoidance of learning, and the processes of reflective functioning or mentalization are intrinsic to the realization of self-hood (Fonaghy, Gergely, & Jurist, 2004).

As these things happened to us in the emergence of ourselves, we have tried to be faithful to our experience so we dealt with it by writing about it. Not to gain promotion or to publish in a prestigious academic journal but to make sense for ourselves. Hopefully, the end product is of value to wider communities of scholarship and experience and that optimism has been justified by subsequent experience of the reaction of others.

We share the ethnographic creed (Van Maanen, 2011, p. 219), but a deliberate intention to "do fieldwork" in the style of a trained researcher is not the only manner in which experience occurs, and this ethnographic stance is both a matter of deliberative cognitive choice and also one of recognizing that through some process or set of events that may be completely beyond personal choice or preference, one has entered a different space, and the driving-force has been an unwilled, uncontrolled emotional vector.

Affect, even anguish, are not explanations or criteria for authenticity, but they may be helpful *markers* of these desiderata or offer clues to other kinds of relevance. Anguish can be a marker that something has happened or is happening to change a framing, maybe one that has never previously been interrogated. According to current neurophysiological research, it is affect that drives cognition, not the other way round as rational actor theories presume (Damasio, 1994).

After the epiphanic experience, one is now on the *other* side of the mirror (or even at the bottom of the rabbit hole) from which a way out has to be sought, and it is this understanding that constitutes both the beginning of meaningful work and of the possibility of an *authentic AE* giving rise to a new structure of learning opportunities. Sometimes the account of the journey becomes as valuable in the transmission to others of useful knowledge about deep experience as the presentation of the findings or data (Carolan, 2003) and while a claim of authorial presence can be destabilizing to other accounts, it has to be respected at least (Alvesson et al., 2008, p. 489)

AE is certainly not everything, but carefully and craftfully done, including the anguish (if that is how it all starts or is triggered), definitely can become something authentic. The autoethnographer does not seek univocality and knows this can never be achieved for as Derrida asks "How many voices intersect, observe, and correct one another, argue with one another, passionately embrace or pass by one another in silence? Are we going to seek one final evaluation?" (Derrida, 2001, p. 50). The social scientist as honest enough reporter even of personal emotional experience is still of value. It is only one voice but the voice of one who was there. Some stories write themselves because they have to be written.

REFERENCES

Adams, T. E., Holman Jones, S., & Ellis, C. (2013). Conclusion: Storying Our Future. In S. Holman Jones, T. E. Adams, & C. Ellis (Eds.), *Handbook of Autoethnography* (pp. 669–677). Walnut Creek, CA: Left Coast Press.

Adams, T. E., Holman Jones, S., & Ellis, C. (2015). *Autoethnography Understanding Qualitative Research*. Oxford: Oxford University Press.

Alvesson, M., Hardy, C., & Harley, B. (2008). Reflecting on Reflexivity: Reflexive Textual Practices in Organization and Management Theory. *Journal of Management Studies, 45*(3), 480–501.

Alvesson, M., & Skoldberg, K. (2000). *Reflexive Methodology: New Vistas for Qualitative Research*. Thousand Oaks, CA: Sage.

Alvesson, M., & Spicer, A. (2016). (Un)conditional Surrender? Why Do Professionals Willingly Comply with Managerialism. *Journal of Organizational Change Management, 29*(1), 29–45.

Anderson, L. (2006). Analytic Autoethnography. *Journal of Contemporary Ethnography, 35*(4), 373–395.

Archer, M. S. (2003). *Structure, Agency and Internal Conversation*. Cambridge: Cambridge University Press.

Auric, G. (1952). Theme from Moulin Rouge: Recorded by Percy Faith and Also by Mantovani, in 1953: No 1 and Best-Selling Song in the UK in 1953.

Barley, S. R. (2015). 60th Anniversary Essay: Ruminations on How We Became a Mystery House and How We Might Get Out. *Administrative Science Quarterly, 61*(1), 1–8.

Bauman, Z. (2003). Cover Review of Wacquant, Loic. *Body and Soul: Notebooks of an Apprentice Boxer*. New York: Oxford University Press. Retrieved April 17, 2016, from https://www.amazon.co.uk/Body-Soul-Notebooks-Apprentice-Boxer/dp/0195168356?ie=UTF8&*Version*=1&*entries*=0

Bernard-Donals, M. (2001, October). Beyond the Question of Authenticity: Witness and Testimony in the Fragments Controversy. *PMLA Journal of the Modern Language Association of America, 116*(5): 1302–1315.

Berry, K. (2008). Promise in Peril: Ellis and Pelias and the Subjective Dimensions of Ethnography. *The Review of Communication, 8*(2), 154–173.

Boje, D. (1991). The Storytelling Organization: A Study of Story Performance in an Office-Supply Firm. *Administrative Science Quarterly, 36*, 106–126.

Boje, D. (2008). *Storytelling Organizations*. London: Sage.

Boncori, I., & Vine, T. (2014). "Learning Without Thought Is Labour Lost; Thought Without Learning Is Perilous": The Importance of Pre-departure Training for Expatriates Working in China. *International Journal of Work Organization and Emotion, 6*(2), 155–177.

Boyle, M., & Parry, K. (2007). Telling the Whole Story: The Case for Organizational Autoethnography. *Culture and Organization, 13*(3), 185–190.

Brinkmann, S. (2014). Doing Without Data. *Qualitative Inquiry, 20*(6), 720–725.

WHAT MAKES THE AUTOETHNOGRAPHIC ANALYSIS AUTHENTIC? 151

Buchanan, D., & Bryson, A. (2009). *The SAGE Handbook of Organizational Research Methods.* London: Sage.

Carolan, M. (2003). Reflexivity: A Personal Journey During Data Collection. *Nurse Researcher, 10*(3), 7–14.

Clarke, D. W. (2010, May 19–22). *Transitions in Identity at the Intersection of Multiple Life Narratives.* 10th European Academy of Management Conference (EURAM), Tor Vergata University, Rome Italy.

Couser, G. T. (2004). *Vulnerable Subjects: Ethics and Life Writing.* Cornell: Cornell University Press.

Damasio, A. (1994). *Descartes' Error: Emotion, Reason, and the Human Brain.* New York, NY: Putnam Publishing.

Damasio, A. (2000). *The Feeling of What Happens: Body and Emotion in the Making of Consciousness.* New York: Mariner Books.

Dashper, K. (2015). Revise, Resubmit and Reveal? An Autoethnographer's Story of Facing the Challenges of Revealing the Self through Publication. *Current Sociology July 2015, 63*(4), 511–527.

Daskalaski, M., Butler, C. L., & Petrovic, J. (2016). Somewhere In-Between: Narratives of Place, Identity, and Translocal Work. *Journal of Management Inquiry, 25*(2), 184–198.

Dawes. (2016). Things Happen: *All Your Favourite Bands.* Produced by David Rawlings.

Delamont, S. (2007, September 5–8). *Arguments against Autoethnography.* Paper presented at the British Educational Research Association Annual Conference, Institute of Education, University of London, pp. 1–7.

Dennett, D. (1988, September 16–22). Why We Are All Novelists. *Times Literary Supplement.*

Derrida, J. (1988). *Limited Inc.* Chicago: University of Chicago Press.

Derrida, J. (2001). *The Work of Mourning* (Pascle-Anne Brault & Michael Naas, Eds.). Chicago: University of Chicago Press.

Ellis, C. (1999). Heartful Autoethnnography. *Qualitative Health Research, 9*(5), 669–683.

Ellis, C. (2007). Telling Secrets, Revealing Lives: Relational Ethics in Research with Intimate Others. *Qualitative Inquiry, 13*(1), 3–29.

Ellis, C. (2009, Fall). Fighting Back or Moving On: An Autoethnographic Response to Critics. *International Review of Qualitative Research, 2*(3), 371–378.

Ellis, C. (2010). *Final Negotiations: A Story of Love, and Chronic Illness.* Philadelphia, PA: Temple University Press.

Ellis, C. (2013). Carrying the Torch for AE. In S. Holman Jones, T. E. Adams, & C. Ellis (Eds.), *Handbook of AE* (Preface, pp. 9–12). Walnut Creek, CA: Left Coast Press.

Ellis, C. & Adams, T. E. (2014). The Purposes, Practices, and Principles of Autoethnographic Research. In P. Leavy (Ed.), *The Oxford Handbook of*

152   D. WEIR AND D. CLARKE

Qualitative Research (chap. 13, pp. 254–276). New York, NY: Oxford University Press.

Fonaghy, P., Gergely, G., & Jurist, E. L. (2004). *Affect Regulation, Mentalization and the Development of the Self.* London: Karnac Books.

Foucault, M. (1977). *Discipline and Punish: The Birth of the Prison.* New York: Vintage.

Foucault, M. (1980). *Power/Knowledge.* New York: Pantheon.

Gabriel, Y. (2016). The Essay as an Endangered Species: Should We Care? *Journal of Management Studies, 53*(2), 244–249.

Gingrich-Philbrook, C. (2013). Evaluating (Evaluations of) Autoethnography. In S. Holman Jones, T. E. Adams, & C. Ellis (Eds.), *Handbook of Autoethnography* (chap. 31, pp. 609–626). Walnut Creek, CA: Left Coast Press.

Goffman, E. (1974). *Frame Analysis: An Essay on the Organization of Experience.* New York, NY: Harper & Row.

Gray, C., & Sinclair, A. (2006). Writing Differently. *Organization, 13*(3), 443–453.

Hall, L., Jones, S., Hall, M., Richardson, J. & Hodgson, J. (2007). Inspiring Design: The Use of Photo Elicitation and Lomography in Gaining the Child's Perspective. *Proceedings of HCI 2007. The 21st British HCI Group Annual Conference* (pp. 1–10). University of Lancaster, UK. Retrieved from http://www.bcs.org/server.php?show=ConWebDoc.13322

Harding, N. (2008). The "I", the "Me" and the "You Know": Identifying Identities in Organisations. *Qualitative Research in Organizations and Management: An International Journal, 3*(1), 42–58.

Harding, N., Ford, J., & Gough, B. (2010). Accounting for Ourselves: Are Academics Exploited Workers? *Critical Perspectives on Accounting, 21*(2), 159–168.

Haynes, K. (2006). A Therapeutic Journey? Reflections on the Effects of Research on Researcher and Participants. *Qualitative Research in Organizations and Management: An International Journal, 1*(3), 204–221.

Hecht, A. (2001). *Home Possessions.* Oxford: Berg.

Holt, N. L. (2003). Representation, Legitimation, and Autoethnography: An Autoethnographic Writing Story. *International Journal of Qualitative Methods, 2*(1), 18–28.

Hull and East Yorkshire. (2016). Artistic Inspiration on the Yorkshire Wolds. David Hockney: A Bigger Picture. Retrieved November 14, 2016, from http://www.visithullandeastyorkshire.com/yorkshire-wolds/hockney.aspx

Humphreys, M. (2005). Getting Personal: Reflexivity and Autoethnographic Vignettes. *Qualitative Inquiry, 11*(6), 840–860.

Humphreys, M., & Learmonth, M. (2012). Autoethnography in Organizational Research: Two Tales of Two Cities. In G. Symon & C. Cassell (Eds.), *Qualitative Organizational Research: Core Methods and Current Challenges* (chap. 18, pp. 314–327). London: Sage.

Ingold, T. (2011). *Being Alive: Essays on Movements, Knowledge and Description.* London: Routledge Agreed.

WHAT MAKES THE AUTOETHNOGRAPHIC ANALYSIS AUTHENTIC? 153

Jackson, A. (Ed.). (1987). *Anthropology at Home*. London: Tavistock.

Kilroy (c1942). Kilroy Was Here: A Phrase Attributed to J Kilroy a Welding Inspector at the Fore River Shipyard in WW2 to Note that He Had Indeed Inspected Welds and Was Able to Check on Exaggerated Work Claims by Welders. Retrieved April 23, 2016, from https://en.wikipedia.org/wiki/Fore_River_Shipyard; https://en.wikipedia.org/wiki/Kilroy_was_here

Langer, E. J. (1975). The Illusion of Control. *Journal of Personality and Social Psychology, 32*(2), 311–328.

Lindstrom, M., & Kotler, P. (2010, February 2). *Brand Sense: Sensory Secrets Behind the Stuff We Buy*. New York: Simon and Schuster.

Lummis, T. (1988). *Listening to History: The Authenticity of Oral Evidence*. Lanham, MD: Rowman & Littlefield.

Lyotard, J. (1984). *The Postmodern Condition: A Report on Knowledge* (G. Bennington & B. Massouri, Trans.). Minneapolis: University of Minnesota Press.

Macklin, G. M. (1998). Epiphany, Identity, Celebration: Towards a Definition of the Rimbaldian Poème-fête. *Neophilologus, 82*(1), 19–31.

Magee, B. (2004). *Clouds of Glory: A Hoxton Childhood*. London: Pimlico.

McMahon, J., & Dinan-Thompson, M. (2011). A Malleable Body: Revelations from an Australian Elite Swimmer. *Healthy Lifestyles Journal, 55*(1), 23–28.

Mills, C. W. (1959). *The Sociological Imagination*. New York: Oxford University Press.

Nicol, J. J. (2008). Creating Vocative Texts. *The Qualitative Report, 13*(3), 316–333.

Ogbonna, E., & Harris, L. C. (2004). Work Intensification and Emotional Labour Among UK University Lecturers: An Exploratory Study. *Organization Studies, 25*(7), 1185–1203.

Potkins, & Vine, T. (forthcoming). Women, Bullying and the Construction Industry: Twisted Gender Dynamics in a Male-Dominated Work Environment.

Proust, M. (2006). *Swann's Way* (K. Scott-Moncrieff, Trans.). London: Wordsworth Edition.

Ransom, J. C. (1938). *The World Is Body*. New York and London: Scribner's.

Reed-Danahay, D. E. (1997). *Auto/Ethnography: Rewriting the Self and the Social*. Oxford: Berg.

Roth, W.-M. (2002, September) Grenzgänger Seeks Reflexive Methodology. *Forum: Qualitative Social Research: Sozialforschung, 3*(3, Art. 2).

Seely, H. (2010). *Pieces of Intelligence: The Existential Poetry of Donald H. Rumsfeld*. New York: Simon and Schuster.

Sparkes, A. C. (2009). Ethnography and the Senses: Challenges and Possibilities. *Qualitative Research in Sport and Exercise, 1*(1), 21–35.

Stewart, K. (2013). An Autoethnography of What Happens. In S. Holman Jones, T. E. Adams, & C. Ellis (Eds.), *Handbook of Autoethnography* (chap. 34, pp. 659–668). Walnut Creek, CA: Left Coast Press.

Strathern, M. (1987). The Limits of Auto-Anthropology. In A. Jackson (Ed.), *Anthropology at Home* (pp. 16–37). London: Tavistock.

154 D. WEIR AND D. CLARKE

Synott, A. (1991). A Sociology of Smell. *Canadian Review of Sociology/Revue canadienne de sociologie, 28*(4), 437–459.

Taylor, S. S., & Ladkin, D. (2009). Understanding Arts-Based Methods in Managerial Development. *The Academy of Management Learning and Education, 8*(1), 55–69.

Tolich, M. (2010). A Critique of Current Practice: Ten Foundational Guidelines for Autoethnographers. *Qualitative Health Research*. https://doi.org/10.1177/104973 2310376076. Published Online before Print July 21, 2010.

Van Maanen, J. (1988). *Tales of the Field: On the Writing of Ethnography*. Chicago: University of Chicago Press.

Van Maanen, J. (2011). Ethnography as Work: Some Rules of Engagement. *Journal of Management Studies, 48*(1), 218–234.

van Maanen, M. (1997). From Meaning to Method. *Qualitative Health Research, 7*(3), 345–369.

Verney, J. (1955). *Going to the Wars*. London: Collins.

Wacquant, L. (2003). *Body & Soul: Notebooks of an Apprentice Boxer*. Oxford: Oxford University Press.

Wall, S. (2006). An Autoethnography on Learning about Autoethnography. *International Journal of Qualitative Methods, 5*(2), 146–160.

Wall, S. (2008). Easier Said Than Done: Writing an Autoethnography. *International Journal of Qualitative Methods, 7*(1), 38–53.

Weir, D. T. H. (2008). *Journeyman*. Published in Bards in the Bog. Shetland Library Association.

Weir, D. T. H. (2009a). Eating Together on the 1950s Farm: An Ethnographic Account of Food, Communality and Reward in 1950s Agriculture. *Presentation to Track on Food, Power and Resistance in Organizations*. CMS6 Warwick University July 13–15, 2009.

Weir, D. T. H. (2009b). Putting the "I" Back into Ethnographic Practice: An Ethnographic Account of Food, Communality and Reward in 1950s Agriculture: *Keynote Address to Ethnography Symposium*: Liverpool University August 24–26, 2009.

Weir, D. T. H. (2015). *John Macmurray's Personalist Philosophy as a Helpful Re-positioning for Organisational Analysis*. Paper given at the conference of The John Macmurray Society at York St John University, October 2015.

Whyte, W. F. (1955). *Street Corner Society*. New York: Holt, Rinehart and Winston.

Whyte, W. F. (1994). *Participant Observer: An Autobiography*. Cornell: Cornell University Press.

Woolley, L. (1929). *Ur of the Chaldees*. Ernest Benn, Ltd., 1929, Penguin Books, 1938, revised 1950, 1952.

Wright, J. K. (2009). Autoethnography and Therapy Writing on the Move. *Qualitative Inquiry, 15*(4), 623–640.

CHAPTER 9

Saying the unsayable: An Autoethnography of Working in a For-Profit University

Katie Best

> *I am an ethnographer.*
> *I am not an ethnographer.*
> *I am an ethnographer.*
> *I am not an ethnographer.*
> *It has never been clear what I am. I conduct workplace studies, which are a fusion of conversation analysis, ethnomethodology, and ethnography.*
>
> *But I wear other labels. I have also been labelled a mother, a student, a researcher, a lecturer, an academic, a consultant, a qualitative researcher, a strategist.*
>
> *I was more ethnographer than at any other time when I worked at BPP as MBA Director. It was the easiest qualitative research label to apply to myself in an environment short of people who knew what I was talking about.*
>
> *I'm now a qualitative researcher, consultant, lecturer, and trainer. I'm self-employed. I'm mother (to a daughter), wife, and resident of Stoke Newington. And I'm still not sure if I'm an ethnographer.*

K. Best (✉)
Independent Lecturer and Consultant, London, UK

© The Author(s) 2018
T. Vine et al. (eds.), *Ethnographic Research and Analysis*,
https://doi.org/10.1057/978-1-137-58555-4_9

156 K. BEST

For a while, I wasn't sure if I was going to be able to write a chapter for this anthology. My initial pitch was for a chapter centred around my autoethnographic work during my time working at BPP, first as a Senior Lecturer, then as Programme Leader for the MSc Management, and then as MBA Director. I would look at some unusual qualities of the work and conduct an analysis of the (auto)ethnography.

But the more I tried to write it, the more I became stuck for a range of practical, ethical, and personal reasons. How does someone who is planning to have a career in consultancy present an exposé of a former workplace and expect it to be well-received, or have any clients left at the end of it? How does someone whose friends and colleagues from BPP still work there embrace and deal with the status of interloper that I'm projecting on myself? How do I protect myself from the negative fallout of saying things that might be taken as critical by a city law school when I work for myself and not a university that might protect me? And how do I cope, ethically, with the ramifications of talking about an organisation that largely treated me very well in a way that might be seen as negative by others?

I contacted the editors, who encouraged me not to give up. They felt there was something of worth in the very idea of an (auto)ethnography that was hard to write, that it meshed with the themes of the book that were developing around (saying the unsayable, being an autoethnographer, parallel 'truths', having things to say that others don't want to hear). They were convinced that there might be a way through, that it could be of use and they convinced me, but I knew that I had to find a way to do it.

Autoethnographic stories are 'stories of/about the self, told through the lens of culture'(Adams, Jones, & Ellis, 2014, p. 1). They confront 'the tension between insider and outsider perspectives, between social practice and social constraint' (ibid.). In examining my role as organisational ethnographer, and then as writer of organisational ethnography in an ethical and practical fix, this paper becomes more autoethnographic with each turn of the lens, towards and away from myself. It's an outline of my experiences of trying to cope with having written something quite sensitive about an organisation of which I'm no longer a part and how to reconcile that with my career and myself.

According to Ellis, Adams, and Bochner (2011), autoethnography allows the researcher to become subject and turn the analytic lens upon herself, writing herself in as a 'key player' (Allen-Collinson, 2014). As the author of an autoethnographic work, I thus split the role of participant and researcher, or analyst and analysed. But this is an artificial divide and it echoes what I'll be talking about for some of the time below—a split between different roles, and being required to be 'bilingual' in order to navigate this divide. The chapter now proceeds by telling a largely chronological story of my time at BPP, picking out the salient stories and areas which I feel are worth sharing in this chapter. As the BBC would say, other tellings of my time there are available.

My Early Days: Ringing the Changes

My interview at BPP goes badly. I feel as though I don't click with the people in the room and they ask about my research but seem totally disinterested. And I'm confused. I *thought* I was applying for a job somewhere that was more about teaching than research. Are they asking me questions about conversation analysis and tour guides in museums (what my PhD was about) because they think that's what I want to hear. I throw my high-heeled shoes in the bus stop bin on the way home in protest. They're too uncomfortable. I don't want to work in the sort of place where they want me to dress like a corporate whore. I hate suits. I talk myself out of it.

It's fine. When they don't phone me in the next few days, I realise that I haven't got the job anyway.

A month later, a phone call while I'm at my parents' house. 'We'd like to offer you the job.' 'I don't think I can take it. I've said I'll stay where I am as a research assistant'.

Then the talk about money begins; they offer almost double my salary. I bounce up and down with glee. 'When would you like me to start?'

I feel a bit cheap, a bit dirty, try to justify it to my mum in ways she doesn't understand. She's not from the academic world and doesn't get why I'm apologising for wanting to do this job, but I feel as though I'm giving up on research, on the reason that I did a PhD. I tell myself it's just for the time being; if I don't like it, I can leave.

I start at BPP in November as a Senior Lecturer in Management. They're the UK's first for-profit company with degree awarding powers. I'm excited and nervous as I enter the glass-fronted building in the legal area of London. It looks nothing like the Russell Group university that I've come from. The people who are called academics are in open-plan offices with one or two personal shelves. There is a clear desk policy (yawn) and a free fruit service twice a week (yay!). There is toast and jam available in the kitchen bought by BPP. More often than is sane, there are lots of leftover Pret à Manger sandwiches from some meeting or another. There are on site caterers who rattle the trolley down the corridor with chocolate biscuits (Penguin bars, Taxis, two-finger Kit Kats: the sorts of chocolate biscuits that make you nostalgic for your childhood). We go for lunch with clients in nice-ish city restaurants, have meetings in Starbucks to get away from the open-plan space. I feel grown-up, all of a sudden, sitting in a place next to lawyers and businesspeople doing their work, instead of in an academic cubicle.

> I think: *this does not feel like academia. I am not sure how long I want to stay. But there are lots of young people here who go for drinks. We get taken out for lunch. We have clients. I like the corporate feeling. I think I will stay for the time being.*

I realise that the space in BPP is training me to think about my work differently. In my early days, that is what I notice: spatial differences, differences in artefacts. Open-plan offices, corporate dress, toast in the kitchen. I feel the differences tangibly, in the layout of the space (Dale & Burrell, 2008), the artefacts in it. I've done lots of research on workspace. I know that it shapes what we do and how we feel about ourselves (Best, 2012; Fayard & Weeks, 2011). But I know that if I (we) try hard enough, I (we) can break out of it (Dale & Burrell, 2008). I barely listen to the clear desk policy. My desk is a mess. My friend leaves her Celebrity Academic top trumps out on her desk in spite.

But BPP's ideology in wanting clear desks is to allow us to share an open-plan space harmoniously. We're not about having our own caves in which to think big thoughts surrounded by books and the artefacts of first-hand research. It is an identity workspace (Petriglieri & Petriglieri, 2010) that tells us we should endeavour to create degree programmes which pass validation and which enough students want to do to make BPP financially viable/desirable.

One artefact is certainly different: food. I'm not sitting in a circle in the common area with other academics eating homemade sandwiches or maybe something from the artisan bakery. Instead, I go *out* for lunch, buy coffees, am given free bread and fruit. This is a world where there are excessive sandwiches and the promise of something free most of the time. It serves not just as a way to enchant clients but also staff, both tactically and strategically (Lugosi, 2014). Here, the 'third space'—Starbucks, restaurants—are used a lot to socialise, conduct meetings, and work with clients (Oldenburg & Brissett, 1982). I don't think I chose to go to a coffee for a meeting, or had the decision made for me, in my time at King's College London. *Has my world changed, or have I?*

The first challenge when I arrive at BPP to prepare documentation for the validation panel for the MSc Management. I was handed a textbook by Matt, the programme leader (and my manager) and asked to write a validation outline for an Innovation Management module. I had never studied innovation management. 'This book should help', he said, chuckling. The room laughed sarcastically, a noise that told me we were all supposed to be fed up with what a joke it was around here, that this wasn't how universities ran.

I learn on my third day that I just needed to copy down the headings from the chapters of the main textbook in the area. But I wanted my work to matter (I am not totally estranged from Maslow despite being an academic who teaches it) so I took my time. I kept working until I felt that I had done a good job. But I still ended up, more or less, with those chapter titles as my headings.

I tell my mum on the phone. She's an arts and crafts teacher, a role which she has excelled at despite only finding it in the latter years of her career. She consoles me. 'Well, even the best teachers are only ever one chapter ahead in the textbook. If you've read the whole textbook you know more than most'.

I realise a few days in that I'm not required to present an expert image. I don't have to act as though I know about Innovation Management, I don't have to study the textbook and nod as though I'm just reminding myself how things are in the world. Knowledge is no longer so valuable that we have to pretend we have it when we don't. I'm not a fraud if I don't know something. This isn't a world where all thoughts are only possible if they have emerged from hours of personal, first-hand research and scholarship (Boyer, 1990). We are allowed to trust our textbooks. We are allowed to write down headings. We default to someone's greater wisdom and it saves us hours. The irrationality of the other way of doing things, of trying to reinvent the wheel, hits me with its idiocy.

Is Being Commercial a Problem?

We go to validation. The innovation management module and the other three I've written get commended at validation, where other parts of the MSc that Matt had asked people to design were dragged through the mud, in particular the careers programme and the dissertation. I feel celebratory, proud. I have achieved something quickly. I have made progress. This isn't an academic paper that has taken years of crafting. This is tangible, there will be students taking the course in September. This is real.

Around 3 weeks after this chaotic validation, I was called into a room by the Dean and the Deputy Dean of the business school. The conversation (paraphrased) went something like this:

> Would you be interested in becoming the Director of the MSc Management?
> But what about Matt?
> We're going to be getting rid of him anyway. He's not on message any more. Would you like his job when he goes?
> Yes.

Research goes from the back seat to the car boot. I don't have the time or the inclination at the moment. Work is fun. I'm designing an MSc, and an MBA, and meeting clients, and making friends.

Nigel Savage, head of the College of Law who have historically been BPP's biggest rivals (BPP's cash cow has always been—and still is at time of writing—their law school), says in the Law Gazette that BPP is akin to a sausage factory. The suggestion seems to be that BPP are maximising their returns by churning out standardised education on an industrial scale.

Sausage factories are probably not nice places. Think of all the rubbish that goes into a sausage. I look up the expression. It turns out Marx said it. I cut and paste it into a document:

> Capitalist production is not merely the production of commodities, it is essentially the production of surplus-value. The labourer produces, not for himself, but for capital. It no longer suffices, therefore, that he should simply produce. He must produce surplus-value. That labourer alone is productive, who produces surplus-value for the capitalist, and thus works for the self-expansion of capital. If we may take an example from outside the sphere of production of material objects, a schoolmaster is a productive labourer when, in addition to belabouring the heads of his scholars, he works like a horse to enrich the school proprietor. **That the latter has laid out his capital in a teaching factory, instead of in a sausage factory, does not alter the relation**. (Marx, 1867 (1990), Chap. 16, para. 3)

I emphasise the last line. I call the file 'research ideas'. I close it down.

How intentionally, I'm not sure, but I start to gather some ethnographic data, notes, pictures. Things which make me think of factories. It is fun to be doing some simple research again. It feels exciting and quirky.

I find that Ritzer has something to say about this idea, too. And I love George Ritzer, forcing the McDonaldisation thesis down my students' throats whenever possible:

> The university operates in an increasingly efficient manner, its operations are more and more profitable, it relies more than ever before on quantifiable measures (often to the detriment of quality) and it utilizes an increasing number of nonhuman technologies that control and even replace professors. Furthermore, the acceleration of these processes...brings with it a...decline in the quality of education. (Ritzer, 2002, p. 19)

I want to agree with them. But, I think, what's the matter with making standardised sausages? If the ingredients are good and they taste good and the students are being sold gourmet sausages, not being told that they're buying fillet steak, then what's the problem?

I write this idea down too and churn it over.

It might be a good thing that I've started to care about research again, because the Academic Council (AC) are getting increasingly concerned that there's not enough scholarship going on at BPP. (At BPP, there's a board of directors (BoD) which look after the commercial life of the company, and an AC which looks after the academic life of the college, in particular safeguarding the academic standards. The academic council are made up of senior academics from other institutions (still appointed or retired) and members sit in on validation panels, attend quality meetings, and advise on issues such as scholarship. They are able to advise and recommend, as well as provide feedback to the QAA if BPP, including the BoD, are not listening to their advice. On this matter, the Academic Council don't feel that we're listening to their advice. It puts me back in mind of the sausage factory and seems to put them in mind of these sorts of ideas too. One academic says that we are dumbing down the quality of education if we don't do scholarship (or words to that effect—I wish I'd written down exactly what he said). Our Dean recycles the argument from Boyer (1990)—that there are at least four types of scholarship, and academic first-hand research is only one of them. Some of the AC agree, some don't. Those that do agree don't think that there's enough of the other sorts of scholarship going on, either.

Sausage factory, sausage factory, sausage factory. I take more notes.

I do some 'scholarship': I read what others have written, I have a think.

I realise that there has been a longstanding concern with the standardisation of education. A leap has been made between standardisation and diminishment of quality. This is not a leap that needs to be made, with plenty of standardised goods being of a very high quality. I could look in my cupboards and tell you about the lifetime guarantee on my Le Creuset saucepans or the high quality of a sofa from sofa.com or the solidity of my daughter's IKEA colouring-in table and chairs, which, years in, show no material signs of wear). The Omega workshop, run by the Bloomsbury set in the early 1900s, could speak volumes of the problems of making nonstandardised goods and having to learn the rules of engagement with each new curve of table or chair. There is hardly anything left made by them. Personalisation or individuation can lead to bad quality furniture. There is no inherent link between the quantity produced and the quality produced.

Why Is Education Any Different?

I find out when I look that traditional universities have also been called sausage factories. Whilst Marx might have been prescient, and Ritzer might have been talking about the US market where there's a plethora of HE vehicles including a range of different types of private concerns (charities, not for profits, businesses), there have still been noises in UK academia about this cranking up and dumbing down of higher education. It reaches all the way from the mainstream press (Hodges, 2009; Nordling, 2010) via industry-specific publications (e.g., Baty, 2006; Taylor, 2009) to academic journals (Greaves, Hill, & Maisuria, 2007; Lomas, 2007; Ritzer, 2002). We are all making sausages, it would seem.

I start to talk about the concern (was it increasing, or was I just noticing it more?) with the quality of education coming from BPP. But the interesting thing is, why's it always a bad thing? By seeking to routinise and rationalise parts of the production of education, BPP may be able to deliver the spectacular as routine. Why not? It's not impossible, is it? And it may be this which is getting in the way of being able to see the benefits of espousing the qualities of rationalisation and routinisation within the mainstream university sector.

SITTING ON THE FENCE

In my time there, BPP keeps changing. Why wouldn't it?

It gets taken over, changes its name, its logo, takes in undergraduates who fill the swishy building that was designed as a postgraduate business school with their bodies, and bags and budget supermarket sandwiches (from the sandwich factory?).

All that seems to stay the same is the tension between the AC and the BoD. The pressure to be academic. The pressure to make money. Perhaps I am noticing it because I have widened my lens, out from the sausage factory to the college as a whole. What can I see, examine, analyse, photograph? First I try to remove myself but then realise that my perspective is irrevocably entwined with the story. Whatever I produce needs to be some sort of (auto)ethnography.

I seem fixated on the dual structure. I Google (Scholar) it, but find little. Most of what's written on a dual board structure is talking about the separation of the role of CEO and Chairman or a supervisory board versus a management board (as is common in Germany and Finland, I find out). Is that because I'm using the wrong search terms or because nowhere else has this structure? I've asked accountants and lawyers and academics who study organisational structure. They don't know. They've not heard of it. They shrug in a way that tells me it might be loosely interesting, although not as interesting as if they'd come across it themselves.

I take more notes. I jot down 'Constitutionally irresolvable tensions'. It seems true: they can never both be happy unless someone finds a way for conventional academic research in the field of business (not medicine, or science, which can be different, I am led to understand) to pay its way. This conflict means that the balance is in a constant state of being tested and rebalanced. It's a set of scales. No, it's not, because it's in constant flux. I search around for another metaphor. A see-saw? Yes, but there, both parties are working together for the fun of it. It's a pushmi-pullyu, the two-headed beast from Doctor Doolittle. Wait a minute, isn't there a god with two faces? Janus? Is it Janus. Yes. *Janus-faced*. That feels right. Lots of academic papers talk about things being Janus-faced but mainly compounds or molecules which seem to simultaneously help and harm some biological process. I find one paper which talks about how, in a not-for-profit, there is Janus-faced activity as members of the volunteer organisation try to act as both workers and friends (Golden-Biddle & Rao, 1997). Bingo!

And then someone hands the answer to me: the head of the Instructional Design and Development team, who sits on the board of directors under a different job title (which I'm not going to tell you because either (a) it's confidential or (b) she's a friend or (c) I feel as though that could get me in trouble in some abstract way I'm not sure of, or (d) all of the above). Instructional Design and Development are a team of instructional designers (people who are experts in designing teaching material) and at BPP at this time, they were given the responsibility for getting programme con-

164   K. BEST

tent formatted and online. It meant that much of the materials development was being removed from the academics and put into the hands of people who were experts at instructional design but not at the subjects in question. This process was advocated by the BoD but controversial with the AC who were concerned about the quality as a result. Their boss said to me about this process:

> When I'm speaking to the academic council, I call it 'professionalise'; when I'm speaking to the board, I call it 'industrialised'. And I try not to get the two things muddled up.

People who played this duality seemed to prosper. It was less of a duality of action and more a duality of language, or framing. In most cases, you could past one activity off as being in line with the strategy of the BoD and the AC, as long as you could change the language you used, the subtleties, and thus as long as they weren't both in the room at the same time.

Duality is a common theme in qualitative research, exposing juxtapositions and/or contradictions between different ideologies (e.g., Parker, 2000) or different aspects of the self (e.g., Golden-Biddle & Rao, 1997).

But what is perhaps different is the way in which, at BPP, the tensions are endemic and irresolvable because the conflict is built into the organisational structure. I could argue that this is always the case in all organisations—as soon as you comprise a BoD of people with different primary motivations—marketing, finance, information, staff; you are forcing a set of different ideologies to figure it out. However, the importance here is that they can all agree to follow the same set of organisational objectives. In the sentiment of Collis and Rukstad (2008), they are iron filings lined up in the same direction, pointing towards the same strong magnet. They may just have disagreements (Advertise! Get better staff! Save money!) about how to get there.

But in the case of the AC and the BoD, nowhere are the AC required to think about marketisation of the degree or the college. They can if they want, but they're not obligated to. Whereas commerciality and some form of resource maximisation (how short-termist or long-termist the board were could be debated, I think, by anyone not sitting in that room) are the primary motivations of the BoD.

Secondly, staff are being forced to play a linguistic game. They can only do one set of work, but if they want to keep everyone happy, they need to get good at presenting it in two different ways. Members of staff start by talking to the AC and changing what they're doing and then talking to the BoD and changing again and then talking to the AC and changing again. Eventually, they just get good at talking the language.

The End of the Story?

No. Not yet. But the end of the story does begin when I decide that I'd like to leave BPP. I want to have another go at being a 'proper' academic. Why? Well, I thought I might like to have another go at all that proper research I've been missing out on.

A kind and highly regarded senior academic brokered a conversation between me and London School of Economics, and I was offered a job there. I moved almost exactly three years after starting at BPP. I carried on talking about BPP, taking papers to conferences on the subject and planning to write something for a journal. But time passed, and I had a baby, and the idea of this book was suggested, and by then, I was working for myself as a freelance lecturer and researcher. Guess what? I discovered I didn't want to be an academic researcher after all, or not in its entirety. For me, journal articles aren't fun to write. Writing journal articles is a laborious and political process and a game that I didn't want to spend a large part of my working life sighing with frustration at having to play (Adler & Harzing, 2009). Quoting this person or asking this person to review it or including this theory because the editors happen to like it despite the fact it doesn't fit with anything that I've found. I know I'm not saying anything new, but it was new to me and I didn't want to do it.

But then, I'm committed to writing an ethnography for this book. I say I can't do it, because I'm not protected by an institution anymore. What if BPP hate it and get angry about it? What if the clients for my commercial research and consultancy don't like the idea of me saying something frank about a previous employer in case it reflects a character flaw in me?

And so I try to opt out of the publication. 'Dear Tom, I'm really sorry, but I don't think I can contribute to the anthology. I'm not sure that I can say something about what I was going to write about without getting in trouble'.

Perhaps I'm being too sensitive and too risk-averse. Is it a real or imagined sense of danger that I am feeling? Is there really a chance that BPP or a future client might take exception with what I'm saying, or little chance at all? Will any potential clients be reading an academic text on the subject of ethnography?

Tom suggests reframing it. If I say the unsayable, I will not be alone as it seems to be an emergent theme of the book. If I can face it, it would be nice to have someone in the anthology being honest about the tensions and the difficulties of being a researcher. Particularly when that researcher is now outside the protection of an academic job and an academic institution prepared to defend my right to do research that may verge on the critical.

I stole the phrase 'saying the unsayable' from Tom. Theft is one unsayable in this piece but there are lots more. Janus-faced. Sausage factory. And, in the context, bilingual and marketisation have a critical bent, too. They are terms that I 'found' when I was supposed to be 'at work' on behalf of BPP. Things which aren't meant to be critical, but might sound that way, that are poised to get a reaction, to be publishable, to have me remembered. Just as my vanity may be what leads me to present myself as the (anti)hero of this story, so it might lead me to think things in ways which are antagonistic, designed to challenge.

Autoethnography can be about saying the unsayable (Denshire, 2015), and it's allowed to be because it escapes the tight academic confines to weave stories from researchers' worlds. It pinches together some unknowable reality with an unknowable world-view, and the output is something that can be published because it has names and dates in brackets tying it to some accepted academic convention.

But now, as I'm writing this, I find myself questioning whether any of it is really unsayable. Or, because it's a story that I've experienced, written from my perspective, owned, does it mean that I'm allowed to do it? And who gives permission for me to tell my own truth, or the version of truth that I would like you to see? Am I being critical? Is the distance a problem? Do I sound as though I'm being mean, a disgruntled ex-employee, saying I never wanted to work there, anyway? Weeks before publication, I change the title, worried how my friends and colleagues in private universities might perceive the earlier title (which used the term sausage factory and thus seemed critical to a level that the rest of this chapter isn't at all).

Autoethnography could be cathartic if you'd like it to be (Douglas & Carless, 2013). But how to be honest when what it says can be twisted? I'm not at BPP anymore where I can be strong and positive in my views because I'm there, living them and living with them. I'm no longer at LSE where I am protected by the behemoth academic system which helps me to say what I'd like to without repercussions.

Autoethnography is often used as a critical tool, to break down hegemony and expose structural prejudices (Adams & Ellis, 2014). But having my word on the page telling a version of my time at BPP, whilst exposing some of the criticisms of the institution, is itself hegemonic and encourages the reader to take on the same structural prejudices I have (can you guess what they are?).

In autoethnography, the writer is required to say something approximating their truth (Tullis, 2013). 'The writer'. Did I just say that? What distancing language I'm typing—'the writer'. As though I am casting blame elsewhere, as though I am disowning my own work? I can't help it. I'm just a 'writer' telling something that might be conveniently labelled 'the truth' but might more accurately be referred to as 'my attempt to approximate something approaching my truth'.

If I'm not working for a university directly does that mean that I'm not required to follow ethical guidelines? What would be the ethics of this, anyway? What about my own ethical code? Does my ego and desire to be published outweigh my need to protect? By changing names and job titles, is it enough, or is it just a cover for something deeper at the heart of this which is giving other people's secrets away? I wonder whether I think that applying the label of autoethnography voids me from this accusation.

Perhaps the biggest lie of all is (my) narrative.

Everything I've said is presented in a linear fashion—when no story is really linear—it's chaos, or, as Burrell (1997) labelled it, 'pandemonium'. It's just the main way that we can digest stories in the western tradition of storytelling (Yorke, 2013). Anything else is avant-garde and, as a result, highly suspect. I could have written it in columns down the page, could have turned the words into threads and tangled them like a plait across the white space, making something as ostensibly clever as a jazz poem but as indigestible as a bird cage. Stories change and can be wilfully changed. We do something to the reader in that action. I've shaped you. I'm shaping you now. As a writer, it's my job. *You know that, don't you?* And yet, you can't hold the thought of what I'm saying and the sense that you're being manipulated in your head, easily, at the same time (Kahneman, 2011). And so at some point you have to relax and absorb my words and then, there you are, ready for me to try to convince you. But this means that in some way, you the imagined reader are shaping me. As are the editorial board, and the publishing company, and the institutions of academia.

Perhaps the biggest narrative lie is putting myself as the (anti-)hero. Autoethnographer, MBA director, spy. They're all the most rock'n roll variations of usual jobs (researcher, business school lecturer, someone who works for the government). You might question who it is that I want you to see. But I'm not the hero of anyone else's story, only my own. Autoethnography gives me an excuse to present myself as the hero, but is it excusable? Or is it the only way that we can attempt to present 'the truth'? I think our own story may be the only story we have any kind of licence to tell.

Saying that an organisation is 'structurally unbalanced' and can only function when it has employees who can act as though they're Janus-faced doesn't sound particularly positive. It is this material which made me nervous about publishing this paper. I am a freelance teacher, consultant, researcher. I am not an ethnographer. I am an ethnographer. Perhaps I should have just dropped it. But the editors of this book thought it was a good idea.

REFERENCES

Adams, T. E., & Ellis, C. (2014). Trekking Through Autoethnography. In S. D. Lapan, M. T. Quartaroli, & F. J. Riemer (Eds.), *Qualitative Research: An Introduction to Designs and Methods* (pp. 189–212). San Francisco: Jossey-Bass.

Adams, T. E., Jones, S. H., & Ellis, C. (2014). *Autoethnography: Understanding Qualitative Research*. Oxford: University Press.

Adler, N., & Harzing, A.-W. (2009). When Knowledge Wins: Transcending the Sense and Nonsense of Academic Rankings. *Academy of Management Learning and Education, 8*(1), 72–95.

Allen-Collinson, J. (2014). Autoethnography as Engagement. In S. H. Jones, T. E. Adams, & C. Ellis (Eds.), *Handbook of Autoethnography*. Oxford: Routledge.

Baty, P. (2006). Sausage Factory Culture Puts the Squeeze on Ideas. *Times Higher Education* [Online]. Posted on 5 May, http://www.timeshighereducation.co.uk/story.asp?storyCode=202912&sectioncode=26

Best, K. (2012). Strategy as Practice. In J. Verity (Ed.), *The New Strategic Landscape: Innovative Perspectives on Strategy*. London: Palgrave Macmillan.

Boyer, E. L. (1990). *Scholarship Reconsidered: Priorities of the Professoriate*. New York: The Carnegie Foundation for the Advancement of Teaching.

Burrell, G. (1997). *Pandemonium: Towards a Retro-organisational Theory*. London: Sage.

Collis, D. J., & Rukstad, M. G. (2008, April). Can You Say What Your Strategy Ixs? *Harvard Business Review*.

Dale, K., & Burrell, G. (2008). *The Spaces of Organisation and the Organisation of Space: Power, Identity and Materiality at Work*. London: Palgrave Macmillan.

Denshire, S. (2015). An Auto-ethnographic Research Degree: Crafting Twice-told Tales of Practice in Dialogue with Your Published (or unpublished) Writings. Retrieved August 3, 2016, from https://www.researchgate.net/file.PostFileLoader.html?id=56790c1b6307d9e0548b457c&assetKey=AS%3A309380770140173%401450773531930

Douglas, C., & Carless, D. (2013). A History of Autoethnographic Enquiry. In S. H. Jones, T. E. Adams, & C. Ellis (Eds.), *Handbook of Autoethnography*. Oxford: Routledge.

Ellis, C., Adams, T. E., & Bochner, A. P. (2011). Autoethnography: An Overview. *Forum Qualitative Social Research, 12*(1), Article 10.

Fayard, A. L., & Weeks, J. (2011, July–August). Who Moved My Cube? *Harvard Business Review*.

Golden-Biddle, K., & Rao, H. (1997). Breaches in the Boardroom: Organizational Identity and Conflicts of Commitment in a Nonprofit Organization. *Organization Science, 8*(6), 593–611.

Greaves, N., Hill, D., & Maisuria, A. (2007). Embourgeoisment, Immiseration, Commodification – Marxism Revisited: A Critique of Education in Capitalist Systems. *Journal for Critical Education Policy Studies*. Retrieved August 3, 2016, from http://www.jceps.com/index.php?pageID=article&articleID=83

Hodges, L. (2009). American Owner of McDonald's of Higher Education Gets Foothold in UK Market. *The Independent Online*. Posted on September 3, http://www.independent.co.uk/news/education/higher/american-owner-of-mcdonalds-of-higher-education-gets-foothold-in-uk-market-1780552.html

Kahneman, D. (2011). *Thinking, Fast and Slow*. London: Penguin.

Lomas, L. (2007). Are Students Customers? Perceptions of Academic Staff. *Quality in Higher Education, 13*, 31–44.

Lugosi, P. (2014). Hospitality and Organizations: Enchantment, Entrenchment and Reconuration. *Hospitality & Society, 4*(1), 75–92.

Marx, K. (1990). *Capital: A Critique of Political Economy*. London: Penguin.

Nordling, L. (2010, February 2). A Lego University – Is This Another Brick in the Wall? *The Guardian Education Supplement, 9*.

Oldenburg, R., & Brissett, D. (1982). The Third Place. *Qualitative Sociology, 5*(4), 265–284.

Parker, M. (2000). *Organisational Culture and Identity: Unity and Division at Work*. London: Sage.

Petriglieri, G., & Petriglieri, J. (2010). Identity Workspaces: The Case of Business Schools. *Academy of Management Learning & Education, 9*, 44–60.

Ritzer, G. (2002). Enchanting McUniversity: Towards a Spectacularly Irrational University Quotidian. In D. Hayes & R. Winyard (Eds.), *The McDonaldization of Higher Education* (pp. 149–165). London: Sage.

Taylor, M. (2009, April 27). End the University as We Know It. *The New York Times*.

Tullis, J. A. (2013). Self and Others in Autoethnographic Research. In S. H. Jones, T. E. Adams, & C. Ellis (Eds.), *Handbook of Autoethnography*. Oxford: Routledge.

Yorke, J. (2013). *Into the Woods: Why Stories Work and How We Tell Them*. London: Penguin.

CHAPTER 10

An Autoethnographic Account of Gender and Workflow Processes in a Commercial Laundry

David Weir

I had submitted a brief biography but was asked to change it because it was very conventional with much emphasis on posts held and achievements recorded. As I reread it, it became clear that this very act of biographising had become a static, structured, stereotyped ritual and that it told the reader rather little about me as the author of what had been written. Then I saw how self-revelatory were the alternatives offered by my colleagues. OK, so here goes.

My mother died when I was 6 years old, and my two sisters were three: increasingly I realise that this was a turning point in my life: the end of innocence and the start of uncertainty driving a need for enquiry. After a school career where I excelled in sport, especially athletics, I won a History scholarship to Oxford, discovered politics and changed to Politics, Philosophy, and Economics moving to Sociology for graduate study. My father died in my first year at university, and I now see that to an extent my career choices have involved a restitution of his life as much as a set of choices for myself.

My first working decade was as a sociologist and I still want to know how society works but never questioned what I had been learning about

D. Weir (✉)
York St John University, York, UK

© The Author(s) 2018   171
T. Vine et al. (eds.), *Ethnographic Research and Analysis*,
https://doi.org/10.1057/978-1-137-58555-4_10

172   D. WEIR

> *myself until I had been a professor and then Director of Business Schools*
> *for over 20 years. A stopped train on a summer afternoon changed my*
> *life utterly and I suddenly understood that "each venture is a new*
> *beginning" and that it was time to start raiding the inarticulate.*
> *Then it became gradually clear that there was another person bubbling*
> *along beneath the superficials of role, status, and public persona: this*
> *person had been learning different tasks and trades all the time—it is*
> *too late to become again a farm worker or a laundry hand, but maybe*
> *I could become a poet?*

The commercial laundry is of interest as an important institution because it stands at the fulcrum of organised industrial society's concern with cleanliness and the need to regularly purify clothing, linen, and table coverings and make them fit for social use again. The function of a laundry is to make dirty things clean and re-fit them for their proper function in a social order in which cleanliness is a virtue. This case study uses Douglas' framework of Purity and Danger to illustrate the central significance of gender and the distinction between heavy and light tasks in mapping the flow of work through the organisation. The methodology is unusual and definitely not above legitimate criticism, as the study is based on contemporary participant observer-derived material recalled some 50 years later: there are issues of identity and authenticity and the corrigibility of recalled events to be dealt with. Once this study is in the public domain, it will hopefully stimulate comparative research. Meantime it may be illuminating to compare it with the findings of other, more mainstream research if such exists.

Purity, Danger, and Gendered Relations in the Workplace

In all societies, some work is clearly gendered and some work is classifiable as "dirty" or "clean" (Bolton, 2005). Douglas' framework of Purity and Danger emphasises the centrality of the categorisation structures that invest the notion of "dirt" relating order to disorder (Douglas, 1966, p. 6). Purity in organisational terms has been applied to the work of lawyers (Sandefur, 2001), police (Hunt, 1984), physicians (Barr & Boyle, 2001), care work (Isaaksen, 2002) "exemplary work" (Ten Bos & Rhodes, 2003), and food production (Domosh, 2003; Scapp & Seltz, 1998). Purity applied to gendered relations with an explicit or implicit sexual content may have religious or ritual connotations (Bashford, 1998; Bolton, 2004; Fonrobert, 2002; Wasserfall, 1999), and these issues are theoretically complex (Nayak & Kehily, 2006).

The commercial laundry, a relatively understudied locale, stands at the fulcrum of organised industrial society's concern with cleanliness and the need to purify clothing, bed-linen and table coverings and make them fit for social use again (Van Herk, 2002). Laundry makes dirty things clean and re-fits them for their proper function in a social order in which cleanliness is a virtue.

"Where there is dirt there is system" (Douglas, 1966, p. 36), and the laundry is a sociotechnical system (Trist & Bamforth, 1951), serving a symbolic as well as practical role in a complex social order.

"Dirty work" often refers explicitly to tough manual occupations, though is sometimes by analogy applied to broader social and political actions (Hughes, 1962) and identifies "occupations that are viewed by society as physically, socially, or morally tainted" (Ashforth, Kreiner, Clark, & Fugate, 2007). Being a dirty worker implies identity threat and among organisational theorists tends to be relatively understudied (Ashforth & Kreiner, 1999); perhaps because of the "moral taint" that surrounds such occupations or because as Delamont suggests, organisational scholars may prefer to study the powerful rather than the powerless (Delamont, 2007). Identity dynamics in these situations are possibly "incomplete" (Irigaray, 1985) or "abject" (Kristeva, 1980) and oppositional strategies to demeaned identity are common (Kreiner, Ashforth, & Sluss, 2006).

The laundry was a focus of political and social conflict around the fundamental nature of "women's work" in Sweden where the "laundry issue" was a central theme in social and demographic politics in Swedish politics in the 1930s and 1940s as "washing by hand was presented as a woman's chore in the home that was well suited to simplification and rationalisation" (Rosen, 2008, p. 1). Fundamentally, the laundry is "a meeting point between filth and cleanliness" (Donaldson-Evans, 1992, p. 159).

Laundry Work, a Geographical and Historical Universal

Laundry work is one of the oldest documented occupations and in some cultures is a publicly visible occupation and a very central aspect of the contemporary Indian city (Cook, 2012). Washing other peoples' clothes has typically been an "underclass" job, and laundries became a prominent

174   D. WEIR

feature of the late nineteenth-century urban built environment in Europe and North America. Air pollution from the urban laundries was a nuisance comparable with that from urban factories (Hall, 2002), and the need to control the spread of Chinese laundries in burgeoning Californian cities was an important spur to the town planning movement (Hall, 2002, p. 60). The hand laundries of the earlier Victorian period were followed by the mechanised steam-powered laundries of the twentieth century, a "society-shaping institution" (The Economist, 2003, vol. 367).

Most establishments were relatively small in scale with under 40 employees though they concentrated in venues like the "soap suds island" of Kensal Green and the "laundry land" of Notting Dale (Ball & Sunderland, 2001, p. 324).

Where the profession of domestic "laundress" in early Victorian society had connotations of prostitution, the large laundry of the workhouse and asylum redressed the moral balance by constraining women in a harsh cycle of heavy, manual work through which in purifying the dirt of respectable society they could become morally cleansed themselves (Walkowitz, 1982). Closer to our own times, laundry work was central to the institutional structures of the enforced purging of sexual guilt of young Irish women in the Magdalene institutions (Finnegan, 2001).

METHODOLOGICAL ISSUES

In my teenage years, I worked during a summer vacation in a town of 20,000 inhabitants, in a laundry serving a total area in West Yorkshire of about 60 square miles with hotels, hospitals, and nursing homes and industrial premises. The company's business model was predominantly focussed in the domestic market and the customer base and organisation of operations quite characteristic of such enterprises. Dirty clothes were collected weekly in bundles prepared by the customers, normally of course housewives, in vans that serve a different district each day, then washed, dried, ironed, parcelled up and delivered back by the same van 1 week later.

The methodology is based on contemporary participant observerderived material recalled some 50 years later. This was my first encounter with a quasi-factory environment, and the experience was striking but of course at that stage in my life, I had no formal experience or training for ethnographic research nor probably any idea that such a metier existed: indeed the application of ethnographic methods to contemporary urban and work situations was by no means widespread (Plotnicov, 1973).

But having looked seriously for more methodologically pure and *authentic* literature on this topic to benchmark my report against, very little exists either in historical or contemporary accounts. The style of this presentation is descriptive, and the author has tried to avoid the extremes of reflexivity as confession, catharsis, or cure (Pillow, 2003). This is a descriptive workplace ethnography of the emic genre privileging the frames of reference and discourses of the native participants in a lifeworld, creating a palimpsest of rich description (Geertz, 1973) rather than focussing on what is generic or scientifically comparable in the situation (Triandis, 1996).

Memory is a variable capability, not a standard item, equally valuable or available to all. *But memory is not without its methodological benefits.* Age and increasing understanding derived partly from one's own evolving professionalism in ethnographic work, systematic and serendipitous reflection on that work, and greater awareness of the work of others and comparative reflection on it makes it possible to reposition the archives of memory in a more coherent if less fresh framework. Many respected anthropological monographs rely for their data on interviews, informal and over a long, perhaps intermittent, time frame with the "elders" of a social group whose recollections are assumed to bear the stamp of verisimilitude. The methodological implications of relying on personal memory in ethnographic work of this kind have been dealt with in another paper (Clarke & Weir, 2016, this volume).

The setting of the commercial laundry has features in common with factory work as a workplace in which the tight constraints of technology and time permit a strong framing in which areas of control and conflict can be identified (Mars, 1982), also informal groupings and interpersonal rituals and discourse including the important role of humour in the workplace (Roy, 1959).

In a conventional commercial laundry, for a variety of reasons, the fundamental technologies have remained relatively stable over a considerable time period, but this research site has appeared remarkably unattractive to ethnographers. We may know from the literature more about the Chinese laundry than about the regular commercial laundry in the United Kingdom (Yang, 1999) possibly because of the apparently exotic nature and culturally comic implications (Wang, 2004). For many reasons Chinese laundries and Chinese people in general were often stereotyped in popular representations like George Formby's "Limehouse Chinese Laundry Blues" (Formby-Cottrell, 1932).

The Flow of Work

The work flow in this locale imposed a strong temporal and spatial structure, starting with the delivery of bundled dirty washing to the back door, by the van drivers where the bundles were opened and labelled with a heat and water proof tag identifying it as part of the order of a specific customer. Each customer was allocated a colour-coded numbered tag, ensuring a specific identification for items. The colour code changed during the course of a day roughly each hour to accord with a "journey" signifying a notional hour's worth of work.

A parallel system of processing existed for a secondary and cheaper grade of service, the "bagwash" (in the USA sometimes referred to as "bobwash") which consisted of white items that went through the washing cycle in their laundry-provided bag but were only part dried and returned to the customer, without being fully dried and ironed (see Cryer, 2016).

There are balancing problems in the work flow as the "journey" progresses because not every incoming bag of laundry contains precisely the same proportions of different kinds of clothes, in terms of sheets, pillowcases, blankets, shirts, socks, underwear, and so on. Every kind of laundry category requires a distinct treatment, and items should be washed, spun, and dried with others of the same category. There are some cardinal sins in handling these items as they pass through the laundry like mixing coloured items with white or wools with cottons, and so on, exactly as in a domestic washing machine situation. White garments of course could never be mixed with coloureds and fabric types should be separated, but by control of wash temperature and timings, small advantages could be achieved that could cumulate during the course of the day.

The sorting room gave the superficial appearance of disorder with dirty clothes on the floor in rough piles but was in fact highly ordered as women worked fast to open the bundles, tag each item, and throw them into open boxed partitions in a floor to ceiling metal structure with different drawers for each type of item. When an appropriate amount for a notional "journey" is ready, the women push the load through a metal flap divider secured by a hinge at the top. By this time if all has gone according to plan, there will be empty space on the other side as the previous "journey" will have been passed through into a washing machine.

From the start of the working day, one is continuously aware of the time/loading balancing required. One journey represents a *notional* hour's work and thus there should be eight journeys of each class of item in a day's work. But at the end of the shift one has to leave one journey *and no more* in the hoppers so you can start the next day with an hour's worth of work. Any more and you will create a start of the day backlog and always be behind; any less and you will have empty machine time. On a light day it is possible to make an early start, get ahead of the journey allocation and keep up to speeds to enable an early finish, sometimes even of half an hour.

But if there has been blockage or delay in the washing, spinning, or drying parts of the subsequent cycle of operations, there may be still clothes in the other side and the operative will incur rough words from the other side that indicate displeasure. One cannot always see through the pile of dirty clothes in the shelves, and disembodied voices are the mode of communication. Likewise if a machine is empty, ready for a further load, and there is nothing in the hopper, "get me a load" and "hurry up!" "Stop kallin'on" would be shouted the other way. (To "kall" spoken with a short "a" as in "flat" is a Yorkshire dialect word for gossiping, from the Old Norse). Dialect words were common then at work and in the community so your lunch was your "bait" or for country cousins "lowance", and the latch was a "sneck"; "laikin" was playing or to be out of work; if someone or something bothered you, you were "mithered", if you looked in a bad mood you were "mardy"; if you messed about you were "faffing", possibly because you were "gormless", and in the laundry, sticky dirty clothes were "clarty". If you explained a point to a colleague you would start or finish by exclaiming "sithee" (BBC, 2016).

The governing controls of this system are based on the temporal rhythms of the work flow, which, although it is based on a notional amount of work to be done in an hour's approximate duration, is still variable according to the unpredictable volumes of work arriving through the door.

The sorting room therefore represents a double interface, with the outside world of the vans and drivers and the inside world of the laundry's gendered processes. The van drivers are men and the sorters are women who thus receive their work from men and pass their work on as input to the work operations of other men, who are in charge of the wet and steamy work at the washing machines.

The incoming washing varies in dirtiness, and some dirty laundry has evidently been pre-washed to make it not unpleasant for others to handle, while some is appalling in its filthiness and disdain for the sensibilities of the sorting women. Some sheets have been pissed on and worse: little hard

178 D. WEIR

Table 10.1 Dirty and clean areas

Dirty	Clean
Sorting	Spinning
Washing	Drying
	Folding
	Ironing
	Mending
	Packing

Table 10.2 Heavy and light areas

Heavy	Light
Washing	Woollens
Spinning	Ironing
Sheets	Folding
Blankets	Packing
Tumbling	Office

brown turds rolling round the sorting room floor was a not uncommon hazard. "Mucky kecks wi' skid marks" were standard occurrences. For both the women on the sorting team and the men on the washing side, pulling clothes from the hopper is "blind" work as you have to get in it up to your elbows before you know what you are among! In those days, fleas were common, and flea-bites and some arm slapping were part of the job (Table 10.1).

The next task of the men on the washers is loading the machine (Table 10.2):

The men on the washers were each responsible for loading their machines and emptying each hopper before the next journey was pushed through. This was a judgement call and, because of the varying mix of work in the incoming distribution of the sorting room, not always got right. The pressure to remain slightly ahead of the next journey was akin to the pressure of the assembly line characterised by Baldamus and its twin characteristics of Tedium and Traction where "traction" is "a feeling of being pulled along by the inertia present in a particular activity" (Baldamus, 1961, p. 58). As in assembly line work, small gains against the relentless pressure of tempo were much valued.

There were four roughly similar machines on a similar washing cycle for general washing and one separate slower one for woollens. The workforce at the washing station consisted of one foreman, myself plus one other boy of my age, and one senior man a little older. The senior man ran his share of the regular machines but also the specialist woollen washer. Thus the team did not map on a one-to-one basis because the woollen washer stood slightly apart and in normal operation three other men were managing four washers and four spinners. It was a cardinal sin to have a washer standing empty at the height of the day's work. The foreman would shout injunctions like "gerr' on, Lad, Get your washer filled".

Opposite each washer was a large spin dryer, driven by a belt from an overhead spindle that rolled continuously during the working day. Each large spin dryer had a number of internal divisions, normally four, though one spinner had three and was thus difficult to balance. The clothes go into the spinner fully wet and come out dry enough for the next stage of the process. The spinners provided the time-balancing opportunity.

The balancing had to be done evenly, and great care was needed to get the weight distribution as accurate as possible. A bad distribution can cause severe problems of oscillation; in the worst case this can throw off the belt and this is very dangerous, because a flying belt can cut a person's head off and all processes have to be stopped, the work area cleared, and the engineer has to reattach the belt. This causes great dislocation, and everybody hates the person whose incompetent work has caused this massive inconvenience. Everybody goes home late. Even worse, the oscillation can directly affect the spinner and break it off its mountings. A large metal tub hurtling across the floor can kill or maim anybody in its way. The routine dangers of washing were less terrifying though still not pleasant: you can be scalded by hot water or suds and you can be burned with bleach or can get hands caught in moving parts. Burns and scalds were an everyday occurrence.

Tempo drives everything in a laundry. The pace is relentless, but times have to be kept up because at 12:00 precisely the laundry hooter will go and the power ceases soon and the workforce will be expected to be ready to restart at 13:00. If you have a load still spinning, it is your own time you are using. It might have been expected that the group of men on the washers and spinners would be strong, burly types, but this was not the case. Even though I was a schoolboy and a year younger than the youngest of the three others, I was by far the fittest physical specimen.

After the spinning phase, the semi-dry clothes are separated and the big items, sheets, and pillow cases go to the Calendar. This is a big machine in the middle of the working area, staffed by women who feed the sheets

180   D. WEIR

through a large heated roller. If the sheets are still too wet they may have to go through more than once and the women will give negative feedback to the man who has taken the sheets out of his spinner too soon and has thus passed them on too wet for the Calendar, requiring to be put through twice.

At this stage the bagwash loads exited the system before completing the full drying cycle, normally to be collected by their owners, usually women who lived within walking distance of the laundry.

The men delivered the spin-dried clothes in a basket that had to be pulled across the floor to the area in front of the Calendar, where it was removed by two women and laid on the Calendar rollers. This was a major interface between types of work: it was also a male–female gender interface.

This interface gave opportunity for verbal exchanges usually of a sexual nature. Typical comments include "You've pulled it out too soon!", "Your thing's still wet…look it's dripping over t' floor", "Oh, he allus does that, but he'll learn", "Aah'll learn 'im fast enough!". Sometimes gratuitous advice would be shouted across to one of the men packing a spinner: "push it in 'ard, lad…gerrit all't way in….,Heh! Heh!" (Table 10.3).

Other clothes go to the tumblers, a bank of one horizontal tumbler dryer and two upright ones. Usually you keep one upright tumbler for shirts that only need a quick tumble to get them ironing dry and they are then passed to the ironing tables. If they are too dry, the ironing women complained volubly though without the overt sexual innuendo of the Calendar girls. The input interface between the spinners and the tumblers was male–male, but the output–tumbler interfaces were male–female.

Table 10.3 Male and female areas

Male	Female
Washing	Sorting
Spinning	Sheets in Calendar
Drying	
Tumbling	
Woollens	
Blankets washing	
Folding	
Blankets drying	
Packing	

The tumbler operator was an older man who was on most days very much better before lunch (BBL) because his lunchtimes were invariably spent in the pub 30 yards from the laundry. After lunch he joshed the women to whom he had the responsibility for delivering their work and was responded to again with thinly disguised derogatory, sexual innuendo. Thus if the shirts especially were overcooked and not damp enough for a good crisp iron, there would be feedback on the lines of "that's all dried up, like you Jim! Can't you give me summat I can get a bit o' stiffenin' into?" As he staggered sometimes noticeably in the afternoon session, this would be noticed and commented on, not always in a kindly fashion. Williams (1995) suggest that men who "do women's work" can become the butt of jokes and demeaning discourse, but there seemed to be no such generic implications of the verbal jesting between the sexes. Jim was laughed at because he was old, usually the worse for his lunchtime wear, intermittently incompetent and therefore laughable.

Change of Role and Observational Opportunity

After I had been working at the laundry for a month, this tumbler operator injured himself in an unnecessary accident of a rather unpleasant type. As this incident occurred after lunch and he had clearly been imbibing incautiously ("nobbut a couple of pints" he explained), he was suspended from all duties before being sent to the hospital. But he would obviously be off work for a while so I was rapidly promoted on the spot to tumbler operations, having been severely warned not to put my arm up the back. I did not need the warning: I had seen the incident and helped the injured colleague to the ambulance. He was despite his afternoon jocularity, not an especially popular colleague because his weakness for the electric soup made him unreliable and unpredictable and not merely a danger to himself, so the general opinion was that "he had it coming", "'e were Kaylied!", and "it's a bad day for him but he's been found out, daft bugger".

This promotion signalled a subtle change in status because as the tumbler man I was not only in charge of my own bank of machines but was also put into the role of being the primary interface between the male and female arenas of the laundry. This role transition was immediately seized on both by my former groupmates on the washers and spinners and also by the females with whom there was now more direct contact delivering dried or semi-dried part-finished work as inputs to their finishing processes of folding, ironing, mending, and finally if any tags had come off, as they intermittently did, to the sorting table where untagged items were reconciled with their other halves in the case of socks and to the customer package of which they were a part. This new role opened up a gateway to the female side of the arena, as a new stage in a moral career (Goffman, 1961).

Behind and adjacent to the tumblers but with direct access to the female side was the blanket room where big slow drying items like blankets were hung on lines. It was dark, steamy, and warm, and I had of course been in it before to hang up cotton blankets from my machines. But there was surprise when one of the older women advised at the start of one lunch break that "someone wants to talk to you". When I asked "who?" and "where?", I was told "you'll find out in t' blanket room". I did, and (as Michelin would advise) discovered that the experience was "vaut bien le détour".

This event is by no means merely of personal anecdotal significance because it was clear that the blanket room did function as a locus for such encounters. The literature on sexual encounters at the workplace has recently been somewhat dominated by the trope of sexual harassment, but the literature on consensual sexuality at the workplace is massive (see, for example, Florence & Fortson, 2001; Gutak, Nakamura, Gahart, Handschumacher, & Russell, 1980; Williams & Dellinger, 2010), and van Herk notes that "the laundry came to be associated with sexual experimentation and freedom" (van Herk, 2002, p. 897). The sexual geography and territoriality of workplace inter-gender relations is explored by Hearn and Parkin (1995) who identify the ways in which organisations construct sexuality and create opportunity and discourse around it. The blanket room was a "backstage" area, and my role as a temporary worker created a double liminality of space and role. There is not much about these aspects of behind the scenes activity in the ethnographic literature, but the novelist Michele Roberts captures the scene brilliantly (Roberts, 1994, pp. 128–129).

GENDER AND CONTROL

The women at the ironing tables and in folding and packing were perceived as of higher social status than the sturdy women on the Calendar who were deemed a "rough bunch" handling this heavy work. They worked as two at each side and another two women folded the dry sheets,

AN AUTOETHNOGRAPHIC ACCOUNT OF GENDER AND WORKFLOW... 183

Table 10.4 Interface areas

Van-sorting	M–F
Sorting to washing	F–M
Washing to spinning	M–M
Spinning to tumbling	M–M
Spinning to Calendar	M–F
Tumbling to ironing	M–F
Ironing to packing	F–F
Folding to packing	F–F

working as a coherent group of six. The Calendar stood at the centre of the floor, and these women, by their central position and noisy behaviour, dominated the work space with their laughing and "carrying on". Many worked in curlers, covered by a scarf, whereas the ironers and still more so the folders, packers, and menders dressed their hair more neatly and appeared more conventionally feminine in that their street clothes under their overalls were better presented.

There were areas of interface where work passed between males and females but no areas where both genders worked on shared tasks (Table 10.4).

The van drivers were all men, and initial sorting was by women only: all of the washing and spinning was male only. All of the ironing, mending, sorting, and packing work was undertaken by women. Within each of these "zones of control" the groups were single gendered.

The canteen was technically available to all *but only the women ate there*. I brought sandwiches daily but only ate them once in my first week in the canteen, where it was obvious that my presence transgressed some unspoken norm.

After that one experience, I joined the other men taking our bait into the bleach room, where bleach, detergents, and equipment spares were stored, where we sat more uncomfortably on upturned boxes and were "not bothered" with the women's conversation (Table 10.5).

But beyond the partition wall that separated the laundry from the office and ultimately the front desk where customers could pick up their finished, packaged washing if they needed to recover it before the weekly van delivery was a different world, where the clerical, accounting, and management offices were located. An intense class and status differentiation existed in that era in practically every place of work.

184   D. WEIR

Table 10.5   Zones of control

Sorting	Women only
Wool wash	Men only
All washing and spinning	Men only
Calendar	Women only
Ironing and folding	Women only
Canteen	Notionally mixed but actually usually dominated by women
Blanket room	Mixed

The distinction between the male and female areas demonstrates the social controls on behaviour and the front-stage and backstage opportunities for contravening these constraints. In particular the blanket room incident (incidents actually because there was more than one) illustrate the way in which the role of the "stranger" segues into that of the "newcomer" (Schutz, 1944) and permits a systematic testing of moral boundaries in a tightly organised social structure illuminating the use of backstage areas for sexual purposes by mutual tolerance. I had found a new *recipe* (Schutz, 1944).

The work flow is divided between a number of regions in terms of distinctions between "male–female", "wet–dry", "heavy–light", "team–group", and "loose–tight". While areas of men's and women's work are strictly defined, they do not follow the obvious patterns of heavy or light work or clean and dirty or wet and dry.

Much of the "women's work" is in fact either "heavy" as in the case of the Calendar or "dirty" as in the sorting room. Conversely while the men's work can be both "heavy" as in the washing and spinning, and also quite dangerous, in practice the most dangerous processes are on the Calendar (female) and on the tumblers (male). Much of the *heavy* work was in fact done by females on the Calendar and much of the *dirty* work of initial sorting was also female. But men and women did not work together on the same types of dirty or heavy work. Females and males nowhere worked together on the same type of task.

Much of the male work, while also heavy and wet, in fact involved opportunities for quite fine operations of judgement about timing and pacing that directly affected the opportunities for others down the line to control or be controlled by the work flow. Much of the work flow offered opportunities for "traction" though the inherent variability in the items and their balancing through the processes meant that "tedium" was unusual (Baldamus, 1961). As David T, my oppo on the next washer, observed "it's all right here, there's allus summat comin'off. It's not allus t' same bloody thing".

The affective tone of most of the work space was set by the separate groups in each different space. The noise in the men's washing area was overwhelming, and it was several days before in a quiet lull on all four machines together I realised that music from a central radio loudspeaker was playing and could evidently be heard in the folding, ironing, and packing area. The role of music among women employed in the factories of World War II has been documented by Korczynski and others and continued to be a feature of factory and laundry work for years after the War (Korczynski, Robertson, Pickering, & Jones, 2005). The men talked intermittently and understood each other in part by lip reading. There was no singing along: indeed when one day for no particular reason, I started to whistle along to a tune I had just caught a snatch of, I was instantly asked what I was on about and wasn't there enough bloody racket in here?

A delay at the washers has implications for the whole system and makes the larger group of the women ultimately dependent on the smaller group of the men. The Calendar women seemed to operate most coherently as a group and their collective presence was obvious. The tight structure of the work flow and its tight but marginally controllable timing constrained all in the work space. The tempo of the whole laundry is governed by the "journey" framing of the workload. In practice, all dirty laundry is washed, pressed, and packed the same day and with rather few exceptions is ready for delivery or collection within 2 days. Customers who chose or needed to reclaim their laundry early could usually do so at the front counter.

In my temporary role of tumbler operator I had opportunities for interface activities that were not available to the other men. Throughout the work areas of the laundry but especially at the interface areas between male and female tasks, the conversation was regularly infused with humour and banter often with overt sexual implications. The women in the laundry, in particular the strong women at the Calendar in the centre of the workplace, formed the core of the social climate of the laundry and did not appear to evidence the "incompletenesses" described by Irigaray (1985). Per contra they had bold presence and visible energy. And despite their low social status in the outside world (Kristeva, 1980), they were not *abject*.

In the laundry there is an implicit timing process symbolised by the notional mapping of a "journey" onto approximately an hour's worth of work, but this mapping has to be flexible because there is in fact considerable variability in the actual mix of work and therefore many opportunities to exercise local control and judgement. These decisions have implications

186 D. WEIR

for others further down the workflow. Judgement calls on mix, timing, and effort have to be continually made on more than one dimension as while the machines do work to a determinate cycle, the settings and the start and finish times may be more loosely defined, and there is scope for operator-induced variability. But this does not approach the "fiddle" behaviour described by Mars (1982) because there is no financial benefit. Time is the real boss of everyone.

The gender structure of the workplace, and also the tropes of "heavy" as distinguished from "light" work, and of "dirty" contrasted to "clean" and "wet" to "dry, does not distinguish work tasks in a binary way either by gender or status but form a more complex matrix of overlapping mappings in which status, purity and power distinctions, while significant, do not operate on uniform lines because "organisations and especially large, complex ones are characterised by contradictory social and spatial processes" (Hearn & Parkin, 1995). Nonetheless, "laundry's endless resonance challenges the creative scholar to rethink the dominance of the wider metaphorical sweep of the domestic and to focus on the telling detail of women's work" (van Herk, 2002, p. 899). And men's work also.

Earlier versions of this chapter have had the benefit of very helpful critique and feedback from colleagues and especially from Natalie Paleothodorous and Perri 6. As author I take full responsibility for the final product.

REFERENCES

Ashforth, B. E., & Kreiner, G. E. (1999). "How Can You Do It?": Dirty Work and the Challenge of Constructing a Positive Identity. *The Academy of Management Review, 24*(3), 413–434.

Ashforth, B. E., Kreiner, G. E., Clark, M. A., & Fugate, M. (2007). Normalizing Dirty Work: Managerial Tactics for Countering Occupational Taint. *Academy of Management Journal, 50*(1), 149–174.

Baldamus, W. (1961). *Efficiency and Effort.* London: Tavistock.

Ball, M., & Sunderland, D. (2001). *An Economic History of London, 1800–1914, 1800–1914.* London: Routledge.

Barr, D. A., & Boyle, E. H. (2001). Gender and Professional Identity: Explaining Formal and Informal Work Rewards for Physicians in Estonia. *Gender & Society, 15*(1), 29–54.

Bashford, A. (1998). *Purity and Pollution: Gender, Embodiment, and Victorian Medicine.* New York: St Martins Press.

BBC. (2016). Voices: North Yorkshire. Retrieved March 15, 2016, from http://www.bbc.co.uk/northyorkshire/voices2005/glossary/glossary.shtml

Bolton, S. C. (2005). Women's Work, Dirty Work: The Gynaecology Nurse as 'Other'. *Gender, Work & Organization, 12*(2), 169–186.

Cook, S. (2012). *Top 10 Mumbai Attractions: The Best Things to See and Do in Mumbai: About.com – India Travel.* Retrieved August 17, 2012, from http://goindia.about.com/od/whattosee/tp/mumbai-top-attractions.htm

Cryer, P. (2016, March 16). The Bagwash: Forerunner of the Laundrette. http://www.1900s.org.uk/1940s60s-bagwash.on

Delamont, S. (2007). *Arguments Against Auto-Ethnography.* Paper presented at the British Educational Research Association Annual Conference, Institute of Education, University of London, September 5–8.

Domosh, M. (2003). Pickles and Purity: Discourses of Food, Empire and Work in Turn-of-the-Century USA. *Social & Cultural Geography, 4*(1), 7–26.

Donaldson-Evans, M. (1992). The Morbidity of Milieu: L'Assomoir and the Discourse of Hygiene. In A. Tourmayon (Ed.), *Literary Generations: A Festschrift in Honour of Edward D. Sullivan* (pp. 150–162). Lexington, KY: French Forum.

Douglas, M. (1966). *Purity and Danger: An Analysis of Concepts of Pollution and Taboo.* New York: Praeger.

Finnegan, J. (2001). *Do Penance or Perish: Magdalen Asylums in Ireland.* Oxford: Oxford University Press.

Florence, M., & Fortson, E. (2001). *Sex at Work: Making Sense of Attraction, Orientation, Harassment, Flirtation and Discrimination.* Aberdeen: Silver Lake Publishing.

Fonrobert, C. E. (2002). *Menstrual Purity: Rabbinic and Christian Reconstructions of Biblical Gender.* Stanford: Stanford University Press.

Geertz, C. (1973). *The Interpretation of Cultures.* New York: Basic Books.

Goffman, E. (1961). *Asylums. Essays on the Social Situation of Mental Patients and Other Inmates.* Harmondsworth: Penguin.

Gutak, B. A., Nakamura, C. Y., Gahart, M., Handschumacher, I., & Russell, D. (1980). Sexuality and the Workplace. *Basic and Applied Social Psychology, 1*(3), 255–265.

Hall, P. G. (2002). *Cities of Tomorrow: An Intellectual History of Urban Planning and Design in the Twentieth Century.* Oxford: Wiley-Blackwell.

Hearn, J., & Parkin, W. (1995). *Sex at Work: The Power and Paradox of Organisation Sexuality.* Basingstoke: Palgrave Macmillan.

Hughes, E. (1962). Good People and Dirty Work. *Social Problems, 10*(1), 3–11.

Hunt, J. (1984). The Development of Rapport Through the Negotiation of Gender in Field Work Among Police. *Human Organization, 43*(4), 283–298.

Irigaray, L. (1985). This Sex Which Is Not One (trans. Porter, Catherine). New York: Cornell University.

Isaaksen, L. W. (2002). Toward a Sociology of (Gendered) Disgust: Images of Bodily Decay and the Social Organization of Care Work. *Journal of Family Issues, 23*(7), 791–811.

188   D. WEIR

Korczynski, M., Robertson, E., Pickering, M., & Jones, K. (2005). 'We Sang Ourselves Through That War': Women, Music and Factory Work in World War Two. *Labour History Review, 70*(2), 185–214.

Kreiner, G. E., Ashforth, B. E., & Sluss, D. M. (2006). Identity Dynamics in Occupational Dirty Work: Integrating Social Identity and System Justification Perspectives. *Organization Science, 17*(5), 619–636.

Kristeva, J. (1980). Powers of Horror: An Essay on Abjection (trans. S. Roudiez, Leon). New York: Columbia University Press.

Mars, G. (1982). *Cheats at Work: A Typology of Workplace Crime.* London: Allen and Unwin.

Nayak, A., & Kehily, M. J. (2006). Gender Undone: Subversion, Regulation and Embodiment in the Work of Judith Butler. *British Journal of Sociology of Education, 27*(4), 459–472. Special Issue: Troubling Identities: Reflections on Judith Butler's Philosophy for the Sociology of Education.

Pillow, W. (2003). Confession, Catharsis, or Cure? Rethinking the Uses of Reflexivity as Methodological Power in Qualitative Research. *International Journal of Qualitative Studies in Education, 16*(2), 175–196.

Plotnicov, L. (1973). Anthropological Field Work in Modern and Local Urban Contexts. *Urban Anthropology, 2*(2), 248–264.

Roberts, M. (1994). Laundry. In *During Mother's Absence* (pp. 121–129). London: Virago.

Rosen, U. (2008). *Rational Solution to the Laundry Issue: Policy and Research for Dayto-Day Life in the Welfare State.* No. 133 Cesis Series the Royal Institute of Technology Centre of Excellence for Science and Innovation Studies (CESIS), Sweden.

Roy, D. F. (1959). Banana Time: Job Satisfaction and Informal Interaction. *Human Organization, 18*(04), 158–168.

Sandefur, R. L. (2001). Work and Honor in the Law: Prestige and the Division of Lawyers' Labor. *American Sociological Review, 66*(3), 382–403.

Scapp, R., & Seltz, B. (1998). *Eating Culture.* Albany, NY: SUNY Press.

Schutz, A. (1944). The Stranger: An Essay in Social Psychology. *American Journal of Sociology, 49*(6), 499–307.

Ten Bos, R., & Rhodes, C. (2003). The Game of Exemplarity: Subjectivity, Work and the Impossible Politics of Purity. *Scandinavian Journal of Management, 19*(4), 403–423.

Triandis, H. C. (1996). The Psychological Measurement of Cultural Syndromes. *American Psychologist, 51*(4), 407–415.

Trist, E., & Bamforth, K. (1951). Some Social and Psychological Consequences of the Longwall Method of Coal Getting. *Human Relations, 4,* 3–38.

Van Herk, A. (2002). Invisibled Laundry. *Signs, 27*(3), 893–900.

Walkowitz, J. R. (1982). *Prostitution and Victorian Society: Women, Class, and the State.* Cambridge: Cambridge University Press.

Wang, J. (2004). Race, Gender, and Laundry Work: The Roles of Chinese Laundrymen and American Women in the United States, 1850–1950. *Journal of American Ethnic History, 24*(1), 58–99.

Wasserfall, R. R. (1999). *Women and Water: Menstruation in Jewish Life and Law.* UPNE.

Williams, C. L. (1995). *Still a Man's World: Men Who Do "Women's Work".* Berkeley, CA: University of California Press.

Williams, C. L., & Dellinger, K. (2010). *Gender and Sexuality in the Workplace: Contributions to Technological Advancement: Volume 10 of Research in the Sociology of Work Series.* Bingley: Emerald Publishing.

Yang, J. (1999). Vanishing Sons: The Chinese Laundry Workers at 1813 Seventh Street Sonoma, California. M.A. thesis submitted to Sonoma State University

CHAPTER 11

The Salience of Emotions in (Auto) ethnography: Towards an Analytical Framework

Ilaria Boncori

I became interested—almost obsessed actually—with ethnography during my PhD in Management Studies. I was especially fascinated by the opportunity to include my own experience, understanding, and emotions in research projects through the use of autoethnography. The processes linked to the use of autoethnography centred on reflexivity, self-questioning, ethical concerns, and emotion management did not come without intellectual struggles for me. But I believe that it made me a better scholar. Now, as a senior lecturer in Management, Marketing, and Entrepreneurship, I support students in their ethnographic studies and continue to value ethnography in the research I write, examine, read, and take part in. My interdisciplinary background (language and linguistics, marketing and communication, management, and organisation studies) has allowed me to experience different cultures, contexts, and 'lifeworlds'. But almost fifteen years ago I chose to leave the 'real' business world to become an academic in order to follow my passion for learning, an insatiable curiosity that I hope will never be fulfilled. To me

I. Boncori (✉)
University of Essex, Colchester, UK

© The Author(s) 2018
T. Vine et al. (eds.), *Ethnographic Research and Analysis*,
https://doi.org/10.1057/978-1-137-58555-4_11

ethnography offers the ideal methodology and methods to generate deeper understandings in different places, spaces or fields, to experience a more kaleidoscopic form of learning and to live research in a way that continues to titillate my 'intellectual buds'.

Ethnographic research methods have gained increased popularity within the field of organisation studies (Brannan, Pearson, & Worthington, 2007; Yanow, 2009). Organizational Ethnography (OE), which I consider as ethnographic work focused on the specific setting of the organisation, the organised, and the organising, has become increasingly popular over the past two decades. Although it has often been used to signify the use of a methodology or method (Dahles, Höpfl, & Koning, 2014), more contemporary discourses are exploring OE as a paradigm, a way of investigating phenomena through sociological imagination (Van Maanen, 2011) and a mode to explore research that is messy, dirty, critical, or at the margins of more traditional qualitative research. Ethnographic studies are growing in popularity within the field of organisation studies as they allow for 'thick descriptions' (Geertz, 1973) of a particular environment or culture, achieved by the researcher through a rich and detailed exploration of a certain setting and the meaning systems therein that shape people's understanding of the world, create relationships with the environment around them, and guide their actions. This chapter seeks to emphasise how emotions add an invaluable layer of meaning and understanding to the richness of ethnographic research, and argues that the emotional experience should take its neglected place on the centre stage of ethnographic research.

Notwithstanding the developments in the use and understanding of ethnographic studies, ethnography is often still believed to be a challenging approach in the current research market and publishing arena, specifically in organisation studies, especially in the UK where the Research Assessment Framework (REF) seems to favour more mainstream methodologies or approaches. As Prasad (2013, p. 937) explains, academia is a 'game' that requires us to 'accept and follow its pre-established rules' where academics are acutely aware of the 'politics of academia, or the politics of publishing' (Koning & Ooi, 2013, p. 28). Researchers need to be very aware of the classification of their outputs to be successful in this academic game and have their publications recognised as being of a high quality and international standard, but also in order to achieve tenure, progress in their career, or maintain a strong research profile. This in turn means that, in the UK and other countries where the criteria of quality publications are strongly guided, or in some cases controlled, by journal rankings, academics are often obliged to tailor their outputs for publication towards specific journals that may not consider favourably ethnographic research that pushes boundaries. Although an increasing number of researchers are now breaking the 'academic journal ceiling' by publishing ethnographic papers in highly ranked journals whilst sticking to their areas of interest and practice (see, for instance, a recent article published by Harriet Shortt in Shortt, 2014 in Human Relations that is based on photoethnography), this is yet to become the norm. Qualitative researchers, although no longer necessarily required to prove 'real facts' are still often expected to present 'objective observations', and to ignore, silence, or veil their failures and doubts as professionals (Koning & Ooi, 2013). Researchers in organisation studies often tend to conceal or overlook emotions because these emotional experiences may seem too subjective and not 'scientific enough' given the rational/objectivist tendency still strong within ethnography (Foley, 2002; Gilmore & Keeny, 2014) in mainstream research. In line with what could be deemed as a more traditional positivist approach rather than one stemming from an interpretive perspective, Douglas and Carless (2012) point out the need for separation between the researcher and the phenomena in order to avoid: (a) biases from the researcher, (b) disturbance of the natural setting, and/or (c) contamination of the results. This is in line with Gubrium and Holstein (1997) who highlight the need to maintain distance during ethnographic research, which I consider somewhat of a paradox.

In ethnographic studies reflexivity is used to negotiate closeness and distance in the relationship between the researcher and the phenomena. Reflexivity is an important aspect of qualitative research (Cassell & Symon, 2004), as while it allows researchers to step back in order to gain some distance and become more engaged in the reflection upon themselves in relation to the circumstances they observe or become part of (Burkitt, 2012), it also helps the ethnographer magnify and dissect their own personal experience. In an article titled 'Surviving Ethnography: Coping with Isolation, Violence and Anger' Harris (1997) highlights how acknowledging the emotional impact of work done in the ethnographic field allows the researcher to engage reflexively with an analysis of the differences between one's own values and those of others. Although this point is relevant, I maintain the need to liberate (but not dissociate) the emotional experience of ethnography from the confines of reflexivity and methodological contributions in order to let it have a more prominent place in ethnographic narratives and academic discourses. Owton and Allen-Collinson (2013, p. 1) also argue that 'emotional involvement and emotional reflexivity can provide a rich resource for the ethnographic researcher, rather than necessarily constituting a methodological "problem" to be avoided at all costs'. In many cases, even reflexive ethnographers might be reluctant to express their feelings about the field, especially those who don't fit with the narrative of the good ethical researcher and are 'nasty emotions' (see Lazarus, 1999). Although as ethnographers we might make emotions and embodiment the main topic of our studies, the researcher's experience of 'dark' emotions tends to remain private (Fineman, 2005; Pullen, 2006). Anger towards participants (Kleinman & Copp, 1993, p. 49), jealousy of collaborators who might be more evocative storytellers, or envy towards those we observe tend to be hidden emotions unless justified by self-righteousness and ethical or moral stances. One exception is Kleinman and Copp (1993), which highlights the researcher's emotions as a central topic. In their article, emotions and feelings are not only allowed a central place but the ways these can be used for the purposes of data analysis is explicitly acknowledged:

> As I look back, my anger served as an inequality detector. This detector however, is fallible; we should use it to test whether or not we are witnessing an injustice. But we can only test this hypothesis if we first acknowledge such feelings as anger. Facing my worst fear, that I was unempathic, led me to articulate my analytic position and explain why it fit the data better than some other perspective. (Kleinman & Copp, 1993, p. 51)

Johnson and Duberley (2003) identify three types of reflexivity: epistemic, methodological, and deconstruction/hyper reflexivity. In order to effectively engage with emotions, ethnographers should also consider the importance of *emotional reflexivity* (Burkitt, 2012) as 'emotion colours reflexivity and infuses our perception of others, the world around us and our own selves' (p. 458), and it 'is central to the way people in social relations relate to one another: it is woven into the fabric of the interactions we are engaged in and it is therefore also central to the way we relate to ourselves as well as to others' (p. 459). Burkitt advocates reflexivity that is embodied and not just based on knowledge (cognitive processes). Although reflexivity is understood as an 'internal conversation' and the mental capacity to consider oneself in relation to the social context (Archer, 2003), emotional reflexivity must be relational in its conversation with emotions related to the researcher and others (Burkitt, 2012, p. 464). I see emotional reflexivity not as a medium that allows us to 'stand back' but as a way to develop an even more engaged, reflexive, and holistic understanding of ethnographic work.

Within organisational ethnographic studies, the last decade has seen the emergence of autoethnography and its more frequent use in various disciplines (Boncori & Vine, 2014; Ellis, 2004; O'Reilly, 2009). Cloke, Crang, and Goodwin (1999, p. 333) define autoethnography as 'the process by which the researcher chooses to make explicit use of [their] own positionality, involvements and experiences as an integral part of ethnographic research'. Although, as mentioned before, ethnography has often been condemned for not being 'scientific' enough, it is widely accepted as being an interpretive rather than simply subjective or objective methodology (Agar, 1986, p. 19). This helps move away from concerns of 'real' representations of phenomena and frame ethnographic work as a negotiated interpretation. In agreement with Atkinson (2006) and Coffey (1999), I believe that all ethnographic studies include autoethnography to a certain extent, due to the fact that the researcher's self is always somewhat involved in the research process and inevitably interacting with and affecting the settings under analysis. For instance, the oxymoron of 'participant observation' in ethnography highlights the reflexive interplay between the researcher's participation and distance from the phenomena. Learmonth and Humphreys (2012) highlight the contribution of autoethnographic accounts in organisation studies as a new source of empirical data and valuable unorthodox approaches. Researchers have been urged to deconstruct their experiences and expose the messiness of their own biases, beliefs, expectations, emotions, and tensions that permeate the research process (Johnson & Duberley, 2003). If we accept that ethnographers are themselves always part of the studied phenomena through their presence, understanding, interpretation, and experience, surely the ever-present and inevitable emotional aspect of their research should be embraced, made explicit, and discussed. Autoethnographic accounts or vignettes expose experiences, issues, and emotions that researchers live through at different stages of their careers or projects. However, the very subjective and personal nature of ethnography makes the uncovering of this multifaceted experience an even more controversial and somewhat troublesome approach to research, particularly in the

196   I. BONCORI

study of organisations from a business perspective, and also a risky choice especially for early career academics trying to establish themselves within institutionalised practices.

Ellingson and Ellis (2008, p. 448) explain that 'autoethnography becomes a space in which an individual's passion can bridge individual and collective experience to enable richness of representation, complexity of understanding and inspiration for activism'. Autoethnographic stories are then seen as examples of creative non-fictional texts (Narayan, 2007) pervaded by emotional, aesthetic, and almost literary forms of writing in order to provide a vivid account that allows others to enter a specific personal phenomenon. As these narratives are about the personal, embodied, situational, and emotional experience of the researcher, the use of first person pronouns (I, we) seems the most appropriate, like in this chapter. The use of first person pronoun in research articles has been explored in various linguistics studies (see, for instance, Mur Dueñas in the field of business management, 2007) which highlight how the frequency of the first pronoun is very sensitive to subject-specific practices. However, in the case of OE, the use of impersonal language and the distancing of the author from the text in *auto*ethnographic accounts would seem an epistemological oxymoron that contradicts the very nature of the contribution. The act of writing research is in itself an artefact of reflexivity (Alvesson, Hardy, & Harley, 2008). Emotions, reflexive accounts, and personal experiences permeate the autoethnographic negotiations between subject/object 'I/me' and the researcher 'I'. The ethnographic style of writing is a vehicle that exposes, inspires, and generates emotions. It is generally believed that autoethnographic stories should be evocative and written in such a way that readers get drawn into the plot by a less academic and more literary type of language. This style of writing therefore bridges the world of emotions between the researcher and the reader who can then empathise with the author while reading the text. Jago's (2002) autoethnographic account of going through depression manages to draw in the reader through the use of emotional introspection as a methodology through a disarmingly evocative narrative. Nonetheless, while in some of the social sciences (particularly in sociology and anthropology; see, for instance, Heather Montgomery's work on child prostitution in Thailand, 2007) the exploration of emotions is fairly common, in business studies the exploration of the researcher's emotional lifeworld, although

THE SALIENCE OF EMOTIONS IN (AUTO) ETHNOGRAPHY: TOWARDS... 197

increasingly popular, can still be considered as 'embarrassing' and something 'to be avoided' in the production of the academic output to be published as part of the 'ultimately and utterly private' (Lutz, 1988, p. 41), and is thus often silenced (Brannan, 2011; Gilmore & Keeny, 2014)—with some exceptions such as Kondo's (1990) ethnographic work in a sweet factory and Brannan's (2011, p. 324) account of his 'emotional encounter' in the study of a UK call centre. Gilmore and Keeny (2014, p. 56) suggest that 'researcher self-reflexivity is now taking center stage and becoming a requirement in this kind of research', and they see 'the emotional engagement of the ethnographer with the research experience' as an under-explored aspect of the reflexive process. Although emotional understanding and analysis of ethnographic work requires a particularly enhanced reflexive approach, I would argue that the emotional experience in qualitative research should be treated in its own right rather than as a mere mode of reflexive engagement or methodological point for the ethnographer in relation to the researched individuals, phenomena, environment, and organisations.

In this chapter the practice of ethnography is explored as emotionally embodied by drawing from theory in the field of psychology through Lazarus' (1999) contribution to the study of emotion, which will be used as the main theoretical framework. I argue that, as the practice of psychology is premised on an individual's ability to study and reflect on their own emotions, those engaging in Organisational Ethnography might benefit from the use of techniques and analytical frameworks borrowed from psychology and psychoanalytic studies in order to enhance their research practice and reflexive engagement with emotions. From my experience as an autoethnographer, established ethnographic literature (see, for example, Coffey, 1999; Ellis, 2004), and recent accounts from researchers in the field of organisation studies (for instance, through informal contributions to discussions conducted at the Ethnography stream at EGOS, 2014), it has become apparent that ethnography is a highly emotional practice. I highlight how this methodology is not only associated with but drenched in a number of positive and negative emotions that will be firstly identified and then discussed in the following section, which will start by drawing from theories in psychology to provide a discussion on emotions and appraisal, and will then be linked more specifically to a framework of emotions in ethnography.

Emotion and Appraisal

Emotion is generally understood as a feeling state involving thought, physiological changes, and an outward expression or behaviour. Stemming from physiological, behavioural, or cognitive points of origin, different theorists have debated the issue of which of these components comes first and which aspect is a cause of the other (see, for instance, Lazarus' Theory, the James-Lange Theory, and the Schachter-Singer Theory) to ascertain whether events cause an emotional response that is mediated by reasoning or whether mental and emotional processes happen simultaneously. In his history of the philosophy of emotions, Solomon (2008) highlights how a number of philosophers throughout history (from Aristotle to Spinoza, Hume, Nietzsche, and then more developed and detailed theorisations in the twentieth century) have investigated emotions in some form or other to identify and understand positive and negative ones. Lazarus (Lazarus, 1991; Smith & Lazarus, 1993) argues that people's experience of emotion depends on the way they understand, appraise, or evaluate the events surrounding them. Stanley and Wise (1993, p. 196) suggest that 'emotions, the product of the mind, can be separated, at least at the level of theoretical discussion, from feelings, rooted in the responses of the body; cold and pain are feelings, love and envy are emotions'. Emotions are an integral part of ethnographic research that needs to be espoused and explored rather than ignored or put aside as being just a methodological rather than content matter, or 'not academic enough': emotional fatigue or strain is believed to be commonly experienced by ethnographers (Frank, 2005; Rager, 2005) as they often engage in 'emotion work' (Hochschild, 1983) or emotion management in the display (of real or faked emotions that are in/appropriate to the setting) or concealment of their emotions while conducting field research.

Before exploring the different emotions that can be associated with ethnographic work, it is worth clarifying some terminology, specifically with regards to the different uses of affect, emotions, and moods. The term 'affect' is very broad and has been generally used to refer to emotions, moods, and preferences. In contrast, the term 'emotion' tends to be applied to rather fleeting but intense experiences, although it can also be used in a wider sense. Finally, 'mood' or 'state' are terms generally used to describe low-intensity but more prolonged experiences. In addition to these categorisations, according to Parkinson (1994), people's emotional experience can also be classified based on four separate but interdependent factors: (1) appraisal of some external stimulus or situation, which is generally accepted as the most important out of the four factors, and was the one particularly emphasised by Lazarus (e.g., 1991), (2) reactions of the body (e.g., arousal), (3) facial expression, and (4) action tendencies. In this chapter my understanding of the emotional experience is of an event that involves cognitive, affective, and physical processes that are interlaced and interdependent without a prescribed or fixed chronological relationship. I understand the affective realm as inseparable from bodily experience and from thought. Affects (emotions) can be *transitive* in their interaction with external or internal objects (Guattari, 1996, p. 9); *transformational*, or *transitional*, due to their constant variation through the ongoing 'passage from one state to another' (Deleuze, 1988, p. 49); *cross-temporal* (Bertelsen & Murphie, 2010, p. 138) in their ability to connect and often blur memories of the past, expectations of the future, and present experience; and *active* and *passive* in their power of affecting and being affected. In addition, Massumi (2002, p. 217) suggests that affect is also 'trans-situational …the invisible glue that holds the world together'. Emotions can therefore be understood as a multidirectional bridge between bodily and cognitive experience; on the other hand, these two realms of experience (of the mind and the body) can also be considered as indivisible parts of a process that does not necessarily follow a prescribed unidirectional chronological order of cause and effect.

In order to offer a framework that can help ethnographers engage with emotional reflexivity, we can draw from theories in the field of psychology which were originally developed by Lazarus (1982). These 'appraisal theories' can be used in order to understand and distinguish between emotions. In contrast with categorical and dimensional appraisal theories of emotions (see, for instance, Smith & Ellsworth, 1985 for an overview of different theoretical approaches to emotions) that tend to present emotions as an unstructured or inter-related collection of distinct entities, respectively, cognitive appraisal theories pose that emotional differences inevitably involve differences in the way a person appraises their environment (see, for instance, Arnold, 1960; James, 1950; Scherer, 1982). According to Lazarus (1982), cognitive appraisal can be sub-divided into three more specific forms that can be engaged with both at the conscious and the unconscious level (Lazarus, 1991, p. 169):

- Primary appraisal—whereby an external/environmental/social situation is perceived as being positive, stressful, or irrelevant to well-being
- Secondary appraisal—which highlights the resources available to the individual in order to cope with the situation
- Re-appraisal—the monitoring of the stimulus and the coping strategies implemented to address the situation, and changes that are implemented to the two former forms of appraisal if necessary

In ethnography the personal experience and interaction with the environment can be seen as primary appraisal, while several cognitive and methodological measures (such as, for instance, the sharing of vignettes for feedback, the cathartic use of field notes and diaries) can be seen as secondary appraisal. Reflexive engagement and writing practices can then be used as a form of re-appraisal. In a later development of this theory, Smith and Lazarus (1993) suggested six appraisal components, two involving primary appraisal and four involving secondary appraisal. These can all be linked to the practice of ethnography in an academic context:

- Primary appraisal components

  - motivational relevance (related to personal commitments—that is, publishing a paper, contributing to co-authored research)
  - motivational congruence (consistent with the individual's goals—that is, job security, increased salary, successful achievement of tenure)

- Secondary appraisal components

  - accountability (credit or blame—e.g., concerns and claims regarding a researcher's status and reputation, quality of the work)
  - problem-focused coping potential (to ascertain whether the situation can be resolved—that is, issues of trust and external validation, access, funding, lack of knowledge or understanding, conflict with theoretical traditions)
  - emotion-focused coping potential (the likelihood that the situation can be handled psychologically—that is, unpredicted discoveries, self-doubt, ethical or moral issues in data collection)
  - future expectancy (the likelihood that the situation will change—that is, career progression, higher profile in the profession)

In order to unpick emotions that can sometimes blur into each other and create confusion, we can investigate their relationship with different forms of appraisals to create a more immediate blueprint for emotional reflexivity. Smith and Lazarus (1993) state that different emotional states can be identified depending on which of the primary or secondary appraisal components are involved and how they are involved. For example, they posit that guilt, anxiety, and sadness all possess the primary appraisal components of motivational relevance and motivational incongruence (these emotions only occur when goals or objectives are hindered or stopped). However, they differ in terms of secondary appraisal components—so guilt, for instance, involves self-accountability, while anxiety involves low or uncertain emotion-focused coping potential, and sadness involves low future expectancy for change. Moreover, Smith and Kirby (2001) suggest that various types of appraisal processes (the associative processing through primary appraisal and activation of memories; reasoning through deliberate thinking; and appraisal detectors that monitor associative and reasoning processes and determine the emotional state an individual experiences at any given moment) can happen at the same time. It should be noted that the link between cognitive appraisals and an individual's specific emotional experience may in some cases be weak because a specific emotion can be produced by various combinations of appraisals. An appraisal does not necessarily have to be a lengthy reasoned cognitive process but can involve very rapid associative processes happening below the level of conscious awareness (Chartrand, van Baaren, & Bargh, 2006; Smith & Kirby, 2001), which can therefore arise across the boundaries of primary or secondary components. While it is believed that cognitive processes are at some level always linked with emotions, appraisals do not necessarily have to be the cause of emotion but can also become a consequence for it. It should also be acknowledged that the two are discursively separate but in reality appraisal and emotional experience often blur into each other as the latter has a strong influence on information processing. Scheff (2015, p. 111) highlights the difficulties in understanding and explaining emotions: 'The meaning of words that refer to emotion are so confused that we hardly know what we are talking about [...]Both lay and expert disagree on almost everything about emotions'.

These frameworks can support the engagement of ethnographers with their emotional reflexivity through a more processual and detailed approach to their emotional experience. Another distinct emotional trait of ethnographies can be traced to the element of surprise in ethnographic fieldwork. It could be assumed that while often in ethnographic studies researchers go into the field without knowing what to expect, the use of autoethnography and emotional self-reflexivity would involve personal knowledge and therefore fewer surprises. However, both the autoethnographer and the reflexive ethnographer, especially the more inexperienced one, might be subject (and simultaneously object) to even stronger emotions generated by novelty arising through research that is introduced in the taken for granted knowledge of the self. In other words, bigger surprises might actually come from revelations brought by new insights on the researcher's own beliefs, actions, values, etc. The 'awkward encounters' in ethnographic fieldwork (Koning & Ooi, 2013) can also occur within the inner emotional work of researcher, and bring along, or bring back, complex emotions and unexpected insights. Research has highlighted the difference between emotional labour (the management of one's emotions to appear appropriate when externally portrayed; see, for instance, Hochschild, 1983; Mann, 1999) and emotional work (a more private endeavour). In line with Owton and Allen-Collinson (2013) I maintain that the boundary between the two is often blurred. This is especially the case in autoethnographic studies where the personal and external faces of the Janus-researcher blend together. Negotiating this dual role can be in itself a very emotional experience for the researcher. The exploration of these emotional nodes in ethnographic studies, whether positive or negative, can generate interesting data and reflections through the critical engagement with the academic challenge, the emotional involvement with the unexpected, the bridging of the conscious and unconscious self-experience. For instance, when I decided to focus my doctoral research conducted in the UK on Italian expatriates in China (Boncori, 2013) and to use my own experience as well as interviews to investigate this phenomenon, I had not anticipated the revelations I was to unlock throughout my PhD journey in relation to my own marital situation, career aspirations, and personal choices. These unexpected discoveries created considerable emotional turmoil and resulted not only in increased consciousness but also in practical changes to my life. Locke, Golden-Biddle, and Feldman (2008, p. 916) urge scholars to become more self-aware and embrace doubt and self-reflexivity as central to the research process. The identification of emotions and the use of primary and secondary appraisal components through reflexive engagement with the affective experience of ethnography can be a beneficial way of enhancing self-awareness and enriching the ethnographic account.

Evaluating Emotions in Ethnography

Having considered various types of appraisals that can help investigate the autoethnographer's emotional experience, I now turn to a discussion of specific emotions and how those can be related in practice to ethnographic work. The past four decades have seen the development of many theories of emotions (see Lewis, Haviland-Jones, & Barrett, 2008 for an overview of various theories and approaches) and disciplines (see, for instance, Stets & Turner, 2007, as well as Harris, 2015). While a number of early studies in psychology have focused on the biological physical expressions of stress and emotions, others have considered the internal or external physiological manifestations of emotions in connection with their psychological sphere. Further developments took into account the interplay and power relations between emotions, cognitive processes, and motivation. This interest in the theory of emotion from a psychological and psychoanalytical viewpoint also generated several classifications of emotions. Research conducted by Ekman and his colleagues (Ekman, 1984) concluded that happiness, fear, anger, disgust, surprise, and sadness are universal emotions, while others such as Greenberg (2002) later differentiated between 'primary emotions' that are the result of people's gut-level responses to situations and 'secondary emotions' that are subsequent to other more primary internal processes; in addition, 'adaptive' and 'maladaptive' emotions are those learned responses that are appropriate or non-appropriate to certain situations. Building on work by Ortony, Clore, and Collins (1988), Briner (1999) provides a list of 22 emotions (with 52 sub-emotions) that may be experienced by people in the workplace. In another classification offered by Lazarus (1999, p. 216), 15 'negatively or positively toned' emotions are divided into 5 groups: the nasty emotions (anger, envy, and jealousy), the existential emotions (anxiety, fright, guilt, and shame), emotions provoked by unfavourable life conditions (relief, hope, sadness-depression), the empathic emotions (gratitude and compassion), and emotions provoked by favourable life conditions (happiness, pride, and love). The emotional work and labour that can occur in the embodied, felt, and thought practice of ethnography offers various examples of the emotional experience related to this methodology. Any classification of emotions is bound to be an artificial and limited representation of a very complex experience: emotions are rarely clear cut and set within rigid boundaries as they can indeed change, overlap, grow in intensity, and mask themselves through our cognitive filters. However, a number of emotions (this list is by no means exhaustive) seem to be particularly common in ethnographic research work, here followed by some contextual examples:

Self-Reproach (Embarrassment, Guilt, Shame)

> Traditionally emotions in ethnographic work are recorded in field diaries where one can express secret 'non-academic feelings', fears, and affects that are often not included in the final writing of ethnographies as not 'properly measurable' or not appropriate for the type of publications and outputs academics are required to produce. Self-doubt frequently arises in relation to one's interpretation of a phenomenon, the relevance of one's findings to the academic discourse, and also the 'impostor syndrome' many researchers suffer from (Clance & Imes, 1978; Rippin, 2003). In a current research project, I have felt fairly guilty while talking to a participant describing his life story as I know that I am probably going to use a theoretical framework that will somehow highlight the negative aspects of his business practice. I feel that I could not have disclosed that intention prior to the meeting, otherwise he would have tried to appear different in his account, which fits almost perfectly with the intended theoretical framework. While I did not provide any false information, I feel somewhat ashamed of my omission and I am experiencing guilt for two reasons: for failing to disclose my 'negative' theoretical approach, and for the ulterior motive behind my questions and the fact that he fell into my 'academic research trap'.

Gratitude (Feeling Indebted, Thankful)

Researchers often feel gratitude towards participants who have allowed them to join their world, whether knowingly or not. This is also true for 'the others' who are part of ethnographic narratives as they give us their stories and trust us with what are in some cases painful secrets which can on one hand help us contribute to our research field, but also work advantageously to benefit our own careers. This emotion can in some cases generate a psychological conflict whereby researchers who feel indebted towards their participants are reluctant to put them on the spot, ask difficult questions, set 'academic traps', or feel torn as to whether they should disclose organisation-wide policies or practices that could be detrimental to individuals. I am currently transcribing some interviews conducted for a research project, and I have noticed how in most cases at the beginning or the end of the conversation I express how 'I am really grateful for your time and for your kindness in sharing your story in a research that I know is very personal'. This was also the case in my doctoral research, especially when I interviewed friends who entrusted their stories to me and provided me with other participants through snowballing. I undoubtedly owe my participants my PhD as securing access otherwise to appropriate individuals would have required significant amounts of time and money spent on travel abroad, neither of which I could afford at the time.

Anger (Annoyance, Fury, Outrage)

Having the validity, reliability, and academic quality of ethnographic studies questioned can bring about feelings of anger, especially for those who operate in more traditional academic contexts where this can generate career obstacles in applications for promotions, grants, or funding.

Also, anger can be generated during the data collection process as fieldwork tends to be chaotic, more often than not digressing from plans and expectations, within temporal and financial constraints and periods when nothing 'useful' seems to be happening.

I have recently experienced anger, to some extent, in relation to research. A few weeks ago a colleague approached me to discuss the potential of an empirical situ for a collaborative research project. She had met a key participant by chance and proceeded to describe him to me in a bemused tone as a fairly self-absorbed and self-obsessed business person. We decided to schedule a formal meeting to discuss a possible collaboration with the businessman and, mindful of being fairly young female foreign academics, we decided to turn down his offer to meet for a coffee in a bar in town and asked him to come to our university instead. Ignoring the references in our business cards and email signatures to our professional titles (Doctor, Lecturer, Senior Lecturer, Director) he addressed us as 'you lovely ladies' during the meeting, referred four times to his genitalia throughout the approximately 90-minute conversation, and offered a number of times to teach us some fairly basic English expressions while imparting his speech, which ended with 'there it is, lesson over'. I suspect that he would not have used that same language and level of familiarity had he been talking to

206 I. BONCORI

a middle-aged male colleague of mine with similar professional credentials.

Remorse (Anger at Self, Penitence)

In the case of covert studies, one can easily feel remorse for what may be perceived (by participants as well as researchers) as a betrayal enacted for academic purposes, a fake friendship, a malicious omission. This, and revelations or discoveries made even in overt studies, may lead to the exclusion of some of the data from the published material to avoid negative consequences on the lives of participants (see, for instance, Li, 2008). I myself decided to exclude some juicy details from my autoethnographic work on expatriates (Boncori, 2013) as, though academically salient, the information would have damaged the reputation and status of someone I had worked with. Also, China in the late 1990s and early 2000 was a 'small world' of professional expatriates, so anonymity would have been difficult to protect.

Mistakes in administrative processes resulting in delays, procedural errors that make data unusable, and poor time management in relation to other professional commitments that take away time from research can all result in remorse. For instance, when co-authoring, I am very mindful of the timeliness, amount, and quality of my input, even more so than when working alone. This means that my collaborations are generally prioritised over my 'solo research'. At the moment I have probably taken on too many research projects and spread myself too thin, which makes me angry and disappointed as I am the one to blame for the subsequent overload and tiredness and also for the little time I have to dedicate to my loved ones. This amount of work, the weekend distractions from research that I am entitled to and still feel guilty for, the numerous co-authored projects, and my average typing speed resulted in what was supposed to be my 'main research project' for this year being pushed backstage. I felt really remorseful when a participant asked me if the papers would be coming out soon, stating how keen she was to read the results of the research she had contributed to, while I knew that I had caused a delay in the process myself.

Joy (Delight, Cheerfulness, Happiness)

Conducting ethnographic work, submerging oneself in the field, and analysing the lived experience of the self can be deeply satisfying and joyful. Re-reading a good piece of ethnographic writing and thinking 'did I write that? It's good stuff!', getting ethnographic work published notwithstanding obstacles, shedding light on new avenues of inquiry, and creating novel insights can all bring positive feelings of joy. I have often experienced a moment of small—perhaps even childish—triumph when data in the field seemed to lead to a great discovery, or confirm my initial hopes. The same frequently happens when I can spot a really powerful quote while listening to a participant talk, and I then mentally cut and paste it onto my future article with a silent 'happy dance' in my heart. In a few occasions, I was delighted to receive emails or comments from respondents whereby they thanked me for giving them the opportunity to tell their story, and explained how they had found our conversation cathartic or instrumental in order to understand some aspects of their experience or make decisions in their personal lives.

Distress (Distraught, Uneasiness, Shock, Misery, Discomfort)

Witnessing pain, unfair treatment, discrimination, and other phenomena in the field without being able to contribute positively to resolution of the issues can bring considerable distress, which can last long after the fieldwork or analysis is concluded. In a recent article, Brewis (2014) investigates the ethics of 'using' friends as respondents in organisation studies and mentions feelings of 'discomfort' (p. 656) in relation to the ethical implications of her convenience sampling. Research becomes more emotional when it is or becomes personal. Nothing is more personal than autoethnographic studies, where one of the most difficult negotiations to be made is just how much one wants to disclose, how deep one wants to analyse and bare. The autoethnographer is both the living subject and the stage, and the researcher may face difficulties or genuine risk when providing too much personal information as 'once a story is told it cannot be called back. Once told, it is loose in the world' (King, 2003, p. 10). Researchers then have little control over the growth of the story, its possible transformations, and development, while their identity and life events become crystallised on paper and interpreted, developed, and co-created by readers.

208   I. BONCORI

Inspired by an article by Barry, Berg, and Chandler (2006) on gender and managerial identities in organisational life within academic settings in the UK and Sweden that identifies various types of academics (namely the Stressed Professor, the Managerial Advocate, the Administrative Patrician, the Accidental Female, the Academic Chameleon, and the Resolute Researcher), I thought it may be a good idea to do something similar with the data collected for one of my current research projects. However, I then started having internal debates as to whether it would be appropriate to reduce my respondents to characterisations and two-dimensional 'research stereotypes', especially regarding a research topic that is very private and required participants to share very intimate details of their lives. Contrary to what Brewis (2014) reports, although I had friends, colleagues, and strangers amongst my interviewees, I felt more responsible towards the latter and decided not to be tempted with any cleverly worded labels that would have over-simplified their stories and lives. Which is a pity, because it could have made a really interesting little article.

Fear (Apprehension, Anxiousness, Worry)

It is common for ethnographers to suffer from separation anxiety from the field (Halstead, Hirsch, & Okely, 2008) or to find themselves in dangerous situations (Howell, 1990). Although not all empirical sites involve real danger, stress is very common in ethnographic work when securing access to data; sacrificing time and relationships while conducting long-term fieldwork; trying to decide whether the data collected is 'enough'; managing ethical and moral dilemmas in the field; and constraints in terms of publications and professional reputation. For example, while discussing the challenges of ethnography with a PhD candidate, he reported high levels of stress during his fieldwork as he knew that while on the one hand using a voice recorder would have deterred his participants, reliance on memory recall on the other would compromise accuracy. He had toyed with the idea of using a hidden recorder, or even a hidden camera, but felt that this would have been unethical and also possibly damaging for him in the future as the fieldwork was done in his home country. In addition, this created anxiety as he was scared of being questioned by his external examiner on this lack of detail and that his work would have been deemed unworthy.

Loneliness is not mentioned in the classification by Ortony et al. (1988). Nonetheless, I feel that this emotion warrants discussion in the future, as it is particularly relevant to ethnographic work (Woods, Boyle, Jeffrey, & Troman, 2000). Interestingly, Erickson and Stull (1998: iv) advocate the use of team ethnography in order to avoid the 'the lone ranger' scholar syndrome (Scales, Bailey, & Lloyd, 2011) which is often experienced by (auto)ethnographers who feel isolated while in the field.

In a recent study, Briggs (2011, p. 2 citing Ridge et al., 1999) highlights the functional use of having awareness and understanding of emotions: 'accepting one's emotional disposition and understanding the emotional involvement in the field can be beneficial to how research is written up and designed for future work'. Over the past 20 years authors have increasingly explored emotion, in various fields such as medical, criminal, or clinical studies (Burr, 1995; Campbell, 2002), while others have highlighted the ethnographic study of emotion in numerous disciplines but especially in anthropology, sociology, and cultural studies (see, for instance, Hochschild, 1983; Lutz & White, 1986). However, its research is still limited in organisational ethnography. Although there is growing awareness that undertaking qualitative research can have emotional consequences for the researcher (Dickson-Swift, James, & Liamputtong, 2008) the importance of emotions in auto/ethnography needs further attention in academic publications in the field of organisational studies.

Conclusions

This chapter has advocated the need for ethnography, especially in its more personal autoethnographic form, to explore and expose the emotional labour and emotional work embedded in its practice as a central component of academic scholarly production. In organisation studies the exploration of the process of negotiating relations and positionality between the researcher and the researched is rarely explored as the main focus (Cunliffe & Karunanayake, 2013; Whittle, Mueller, Lenney, & Gilchrist, 2014). I recommend that emotions are embedded within the exploration of such accounts of relational perspectives and positionality. We conduct ethnographies to be surprised and to discover the multifaceted unexpected in the social world—we enter the field, explore, drill, dig, uncover, turn the soil, plant seeds, and get dirty with research through a methodology where emotions cannot be avoided. Emotional awareness and the management of emotions though analytical or instinctual processing (whether in the field or later during data analysis) can lead to such discoveries and surprises. As emotions are interwoven with cognitive and physical experiences in people's lives, researchers in the qualitative sphere should dare to bare their emotional experience and bring that to the forefront in academic outputs in order to allow for more kaleidoscopic, reflexive, holistic accounts of lifeworlds. As ethnographers we can learn from our emotions, which can help uncover themes and questions and to manage nodes of tension in the environment, process, or organisation. Emotions can be considered as lenses through which one can get a deeper understanding of the social phenomena under investigation, the researcher's own knowledge, and mental processes by shedding light on issues we struggle with, emphasising feelings and making moments more memorable. It is through the personal ethnographic account that exposure of our sensitivities, emotions, doubts, and imperfections as researchers in the field allows the contamination between the messy, confusing, multifaceted, and non-linear experience of life and the cognition that is then turned into rich academic insights which contribute to social understandings. Based on what I have discussed above, I would therefore encourage a different approach to emotions in organisation studies both in terms of the centrality of subject matter of ethnographic research and from a methodological viewpoint whereby researchers engage with e*motional reflexivity* (Burkitt, 2012). This needs to be addressed if ethnographers truly want to engage with reflexivity not just as a box-ticking exercise to testify the rigorousness of their academic research practice but as a means of unveiling layers of understanding and unlocking areas of meaning. The appraisal framework identified offers a blueprint towards exploration and implementation of emotional reflexivity. Emotions should be further considered as an integral part of ethnographic methodology that seeks to produce rounded, rich, and kaleidoscopic studies of human phenomena in organisational research. Emotional reflexivity will then become an established practice for researchers to explore their conscious and unconscious emotional experience in connection to phenomenon, environment, and the people involved in their ethnographic work.

I owe a huge vote of thanks to the VIDA network and Professor Joanna Brewis for her invaluable feedback on the first draft of this book chapter.

REFERENCES

Agar, M. (1986). *Speaking of Ethnography.* Qualitative Research Methods Series, no. 2. Sage: London.

Alvesson, M., Hardy, C., & Harley, B. (2008). Reflecting on Reflexivity: Reflexive Textual Practices in Organization and Management Theory. *Journal of Management Studies, 45*(3), 480–501.

Archer, M. S. (2003). *Structure, Agency and the Internal Conversation.* Cambridge: Cambridge University Press.

Arnold, M. B. (1960). *Emotion and Personality* (Vol. 2). New York: Columbia University Press.

Atkinson, P. (2006). Rescuing Autoethnography. *Journal of Contemporary Ethnography, 35*(4), 400–404.

Barry, J., Berg, E., & Chandler, J. (2006). Academic Shape Shifting: Gender, Management and Identities in Sweden and England. *Organization, 13*(2), 275–298.

Bertelsen, L., & Murphie, A. (2010). An Ethics of Everyday Infinities and Powers: Félix Guattari on Affect and the Refrain. In M. Gregg & G. J. Seigworth (Eds.), *The Affect Theory Reader* (pp. 138–157). Durham, NC: Duke University Press.

Boncori, I. (2013). *Expatriates in China: Experiences, Opportunities and Challenges.* Palgrave Macmillan.

Boncori, I., & Vine, T. (2014). Learning Without Thought Is Labour Lost, Thought Without Learning Is Perilous: The Importance of Pre-departure Training and Emotions Management for Expatriates Working in China. *International Journal of Work Organisation and Emotion, 6*(2), 155–177.

Brannan, M. J. (2011). Researching Emotions and the Emotions of Researching: The Strange Case of Alexithymia in Reflexive Research. *International Journal of Work Organization and Emotion, 4*(3/4), 322–339.

Brannan, M. J., Pearson, G., & Worthington, F. (2007). Ethnographies of Work and the Work of Ethnography. *Ethnography, 8*(4), 395–402.

Brewis, J. (2014). The Ethics of Researching Friends: On Convenience Sampling in Qualitative Management and Organization Studies. *British Journal of Management, 25*(4), 651–874.

Briggs, D. (2011). Emotions, Ethnography and Crack Cocaine users. *Emotion, Space and Society.* Retrieved September 20, 2014, from http://hdl.handle.net/10552/1615

Briner, R. B. (1999). The Neglect and Importance of Emotion at Work. *European Journal of work and Organizational Psychology, 8*(3), 323–346.

Burkitt, I. (2012). Emotional Reflexivity: Feeling, Emotion and Imagination in Reflexive Dialogues. *Sociology, 46*(3), 458–472.

Burr, G. (1995). Unfinished Business: Interviewing Families of Critically Ill Patients. *Nursing Inquiry, 3*, 172–177.

Campbell, R. (2002). *Emotionally Involved: The Impact of Researching Rape.* London: Routledge.

Cassell, C., & Symon, G. (Eds.). (2004). *Essential Guide to Qualitative Methods in Organizational Research.* London: Sage.

Chartrand, T. L., van Baaren, R. B., & Bargh, J. A. (2006). Linking Automatic Evaluation to Mood and Information-Processing Style: Consequences for Experienced Affect, Impression Formation, and Stereotyping. *Journal of Experimental Psychology: General, 135,* 7–77.

Clance, P. R., & Imes, S. (1978). The Imposter Phenomenon in High Achieving Women: Dynamics and Therapeutic Intervention. *Psychotherapy Theory Research and Practice, 15*(3), 1–8.

Cloke, P., Crang, P., & Goodwin, M. (1999). *Introducing Human Geographies.* London: Arnold.

Coffey, A. (1999). *The Ethnographic Self: Fieldwork and the Representation of Identity.* London: Sage.

Cunliffe, A., & Karunanayake, G. (2013). Working Within Hyphen-Spaces in Ethnographic Research: Implications for Research Identities and Practice. *Organizational Research Methods, 16*(3), 364–392.

Dahles, H., Höpfl, H., & Koning, J. (2014). *Organizational Ethnography: The Theoretical Challenge.* EGOS 2014 Conference, Sub-theme 15 Call for papers, Rotterdam.

Deleuze, G. (1988). *Spinoza: Practical Philosophy.* (trans. Hurley, R.). San Francisco: City Lights Books.

Dickson-Swift, V., James, E., & Liamputtong, P. (2008). *Undertaking Sensitive Research in the Health and Social Sciences: Managing Boundaries, Emotions and Risk.* Cambridge: Cambridge University Press.

Douglas, K., & Carless, D. (2012). Membership, Golf and a Story About Anna and Me: Reflections on Research in Elite Sport. *Qualitative Methods in Psychology Bulletin, Sports and Performance I, 13,* 27–35.

Ekman, P. (1984). Expression and the Nature of Emotion. In K. Scherer & P. Ekman (Eds.), *Approaches to Emotion* (pp. 319–343). Hillsdale, NJ: Erlbaum.

Ellingson, L., & Ellis, C. (2008). Autoethnography as Constructionist Project. In J. A. Holstein & J. F. Gubrium (Eds.), *Handbook of Constructionist Research.* New York: Guildford.

Ellis, C. (2004). *The Ethnographic I: A Methodological Novel About Autoethnography.* Walnut Creek: AltaMira Press.

Erickson, K. C., & Stull, D. D. (1998). *Doing Team Ethnography: Warnings and Advice* (Vol. 42). Thousand Oaks, CA: Sage.

Fineman, S. (2005). Appreciating Emotion at Work: Paradigm Tensions. *International Journal of Work Organisation and Emotion, 1*(1), 4–19.

Foley, D. E. (2002). Critical Ethnography: The Reflexive Turn. *Qualitative Studies in Education, 15*(5), 469–490.

Frank, A. (2005). What Is Dialogical Research and Why Should We Do It? *Qualitative Health Research, 15*(7), 964–974.

Geertz, C. (1973). *The Interpretations of Cultures*. New York: Basic Books.

Gilmore, S., & Keeny, K. (2014). Work-Worlds Colliding: Self-Reflexivity, Power and Emotion in Organizational Ethnography. *Human Relations*, 1–24. Retrieved July 15, from http://hum.sagepub.com/content/early/2014/06/26/0018726714531998

Greenberg, L. S. (2002). *Emotion-Focused Therapy: Coaching Clients to Work Through Their Feelings*. Washington, DC: American Psychological Association.

Guattari, F. (1996). *The Guattari Reader*. London: Blackwell.

Gubrium, J. F., & Holstein, J. A. (1997). *The New Language of Qualitative Method*. New York: Oxford University Press.

Halstead, N., Hirsch, E., & Okely, J. (2008). *Knowing How to Know: Fieldwork and the Ethnographic Present*. New York: Berghahn Books.

Harris, J. (1997). Surviving Ethnography: Isolation, Violence and Anger. *The Qualitative Report 3*(1). [Online]. Retrieved September 20, 2014, from http://www.nova.edu/ssss/QR/QR3-1/harris.html

Harris, S. R. (2015). *An Invitation to the Sociology of Emotions*. New York: Routledge.

Hochschild, A. (1983). *The Managed Heart: The Commercialisation of Human Feeling*. Berkeley, CA: University of California Press.

Howell, N. (1990). *Surviving Fieldwork: A Report of the Advisory Panel on Health and Safety in Fieldwork*, American Anthropological Association.

Jago, B. (2002). Chronicling an Academic Depression. *Journal of Contemporary Ethnography, 31*(6), 729–757.

James, W. (1950). *The Principles of Psychology* (Vol. 2), New York: Dover Publications. (Original work published in 1890).

Johnson, P., & Duberley, J. (2003). Reflexivity in Management Research. *Journal of Management Studies, 40*(5), 1279–1303.

King, T. (2003). *The Truth About Stories*. Toronto: Anansi Press.

Kleinman, S., & Copp, M. (1993). *Emotions & Fieldwork*. Thousand Oaks, CA: Sage Publications.

Kondo, D. (1990). *Crafting Selves: Power, Gender and Discourses of Identity in a Japanese Workplace*. Chicago, IL: University of Chicago Press.

Koning, J., & Ooi, C. (2013). Awkward Encounters and Ethnography. *Qualitative Research in Organizations and Management: An International Journal, 8*(1), 16–32.

Lazarus, R. S. (1982). Thoughts on the Relations Between Emotion and Cognition. *American Psychologist, 37*, 1019–1024.

Lazarus, R. S. (1991). *Emotion and Adaptation*. Oxford: Oxford University Press.

Lazarus, R. S. (1999). *Stress and Emotion: A New Synthesis*. New York: Springer.

Learmonth, M., & Humphreys, M. (2012). Autoethnography and Academic Identity: Glimpsing Business School Doppelgängers. *Organization, 19*(1), 99–117.

Lewis, M., Haviland-Jones, J. M., & Barrett, L. F. (Eds.). (2008). *The Handbook of Emotion* (3rd ed.). New York: Guilford.

Li, J. (2008). Ethical Challenges in Participant Observation: A Reflection on Ethnographic Fieldwork. *The Qualitative Report, 13*(1), 100–115.

Locke, K., Golden-Biddle, K., & Feldman, M. (2008). Making Doubt Generative: Rethinking the Role of Doubt in the Research Process. *Organization Science, 19*(6), 907–918.

Lutz, C. (1988). *Unnatural Emotions: Everyday Sentiments on a Micronesianatoll and their Challenge to Western Theory*. Chicago, IL: University of Chicago Press.

Lutz, C., & White, G. M. (1986). The Anthropology of Emotions. *Annual Review of Anthropology, 15*, 405–436.

Mann, S. (1999). Emotion at Work: To What Extent Are We Expressing, Suppressing or Faking It? *European Journal of Work and Organizational Psychology, 8*(3), 347–369.

Massumi, B. (2002). *Parables for the Virtual: Movement, Affect, Sensation*. Durham, NC: Duke University Press.

Montgomery, H. (2007). Working with Child Prostitutes in Thailand: Problems of Practice and Interpretation. *Childhood, 14*(4), 415–430.

Mur Dueñas, P. (2007). 'I/we Focus On...': A Cross-Cultural Analysis of Self-Mentions in Business Management Research Articles. *Journal of English for Academic Purposes, 6*(2), 143–162.

Narayan, K. (2007). Tools to Shape Texts: What Creative Nonfiction Can Offer Ethnography. *Anthropology and Humanism, 32*(2), 130–144.

O'Reilly, K. (2009). *Key Concepts in Ethnography*. London: Sage.

Ortony, A., Clore, G., & Collins, A. (1988). *The Cognitive Structure of Emotions*. New York: Cambridge University Press.

Owton, H., & Allen-Collinson, J. (2013). Close But Not Too Close: Friendship as Method(ology) in Ethnographic Research Encounters. *Journal of Contemporary Ethnography, 43*(3), 283–305.

Parkinson, B. (1994). *Emotion*. In A. M. Coleman (Ed.), *Companion Encyclopaedia of Psychology* (Vol. 2). London: Routledge.

Prasad, A. (2013). Playing the Game and Trying not to Lose Myself: A Doctoral Student's Perspective on the Institutional Pressures for Research Output. *Organization, 20*(6), 936–948.

Pullen, A. (2006). Gendering the Research Self: Social Practice and Corporeal Multiplicity in the Writing of Organizational Research. *Gender, Work and Organization, 13*(3), 277–298.

Rager, K. (2005). Self-Care and the Qualitative Researcher: When Collecting Data Can Break Your Heart. *Educational Researcher, 34*(4), 23–27.

Rippin, A. J. (2003). Big, Fat Phoney: How the Massified, Modularised System Creates Incompetence. *BBS Teaching and Research Review, 6,* 1–9.

Scales, K., Bailey, S., & Lloyd, J. (2011). Separately and Together: Reflections on Conducting a Collaborative Team Ethnography in Dementia Care. *Enquire, 6,* 24–49.

Scheff, T. (2015). Toward Defining Basic Emotions. *Qualitative Inquiry, 21*(2), 111–112.

Scherer, K. R. (1982). Emotion as Process: Function, Origin and Regulation. *Social Science Information, 21,* 555–570.

Shortt, H. (2014, October 6). Liminality, Space and the Importance of 'Transitory Dwelling Places' at Work. *Human Relations,* Published online before print. https://doi.org/10.1177/0018726714536938

Smith, C. A., & Ellsworth, P. C. (1985). Patterns of Cognitive Appraisal in Emotion. *Journal of Personality and Social Psychology, 48,* 813–838.

Smith, C. A., & Kirby, L. D. (2001). Toward Delivering on the Promise of Appraisal Theory. In K. R. Scherer, A. Schoor, & T. Johnstone (Eds.), *Appraisal Processes in Emotion: Theory, Methods, Research.* Oxford: Oxford University Press.

Smith, C. A., & Lazarus, R. S. (1993). Appraisal Components, Core Relational Themes, and the Emotions. *Cognition and Emotion, 7,* 233–269.

Solomon, R. C. (2008). The Philosophy of Emotions. In M. Lewis, J. M. Haviland-Jones, & L. Feldman Barrett (Eds.), *The Handbook of Emotions* (3rd ed., pp. 3–16). New York: The Guildford Press.

Stanley, L., & Wise, S. (1993). *Breaking Out Again: Feminist Ontology & Epistemology.* London: Routledge.

Stets, J. E., & Turner, J. H. (Eds.). (2007). *Handbook of the Sociology of Emotions.* California: Springer.

Van Maanen, J. (2011). *Tales of the Field: On Writing Ethnography.* Chicago: University of Chicago Press.

Whittle, A., Mueller, F., Lenney, P., & Gilchrist, A. (2014). Interest-Talk as Access-Talk: How Interests Are Displayed, Made and Down-Played in Management Research. *British Journal of Management, 25,* 607–628.

Woods, P., Boyle, M., Jeffrey, B., & Troman, G. (2000). A Research Team in Ethnography. *International Journal of Qualitative Studies in Education, 13*(1), 85–98.

Yanow, D. (2009). Organizational Ethnography and Methodological Angst: Myths and Challenges in the Field. *Qualitative Research in Organizations and Management, 4*(2), 186–199.

CHAPTER 12

It's More Than Deciding What to Wank Into: Negotiating an Unconventional Fatherhood

John Hadlow

I had never considered myself to be an ethnographer, let alone an autoethnographer. In my background in educational research I had always adopted a more traditional form of qualitative research. In teaching qualitative research to undergraduates I was always a little uneasy that autoethnography could look a little like storytelling. I was eventually 'forced' into autoethnography because of the difficulties I found in recruiting men like me to my research. I would have been much happier with lots of interviews. However, during a teaching session with my sociology students at university we were talking about my PhD and my experiences as a sperm donor father. I was explaining how my own experiences had formed the basis of my research into the subject. One student remarked that she thought it was really weird that I would reflect on my particular role as a somewhat unusual father and immediately see this as something that could be developed academically into a PhD. She felt that this was the difference between, as she put it, 'you academics that spend your life in books and the rest of us'. She said, 'a normal person wouldn't think "this will make a great PhD", they would just get on with doing it'. I think I had been an autoethnographer all along.

J. Hadlow (✉)
University of Suffolk, Ipswich, UK

© The Author(s) 2018
T. Vine et al. (eds.), *Ethnographic Research and Analysis*,
https://doi.org/10.1057/978-1-137-58555-4_12

> *It is my son James' 10th birthday and he has decided he wants to invite all his friends to a paintball day. He has invited me as well. He has lots of his school and football friends there together with a smattering of dads. I don't know any of them. We are all moving from one combat area to another. We are all dressed in anonymous combat clothes with full face masks. In front of me are three of his friends talking. One says, 'who is the guy who came on a motorbike?' (This is me). 'That's James' dad' replies one of them. 'Can't be' says the third 'James doesn't have a dad'. There's a silence of a few seconds. 'Not a real one'.*

Making a PhD Out of My Life

I think it takes a particular attitude to turn a key aspect of your life into an academic exercise. I am not sure if this is a good thing. I have a well-practised narrative that I have formed over a number of years when people ask me what my PhD is about. I tell the story of being asked, in causal encounters, if I have children. I note that for most people this is a perfectly ordinary and unproblematic question that can have a straightforward answer. However, for me this was not a simple question. In the way I tell the story the question presents me with a dilemma. I say that I am the biological parent to two children, but they weren't conceived through a sexual relationship. The conception didn't happen through a sperm donor clinic. It was an 'informal' arrangement that involved self-insemination. I point out that the question 'do you have children?' made me realise that my own situation was a very interesting one. My dilemma in answering the question 'do I have children'? is that to say 'yes' is to invoke in the mind of the questioner a whole set of assumptions and meanings around fatherhood that my role often doesn't conform to. However, to say 'no, I don't have kids' feels like betrayal of my relationship with my children. 'Sort of' was often my reply, which required considerable explanation. It was this realisation that my position as a father was problematic and required unpacking that made me think there was the possibility of an interesting research issue relating to this form of fatherhood. I was looking for a PhD topic and had explored many other ideas. However, my own experiences looked like they would offer the perfect subject matter.

This is the story I tell to explain my research focus. Many universities now ask their PhD students to give three minute presentations on their research. Some have even turned this into a competitive event. This is the narrative I tell whenever I am asked to participate in these. It is a neat story and one which clearly makes me and my questions on my status as a father the centre of my research. My experiences initiate my PhD focus and help form some of the key questions. While it seemed that there were many ways in which men experience fatherhood in contemporary society none of these really matched my way of being a father. Was I an example of something new in fatherhood? My own personal experiences provided the rationale for the identification of a research topic and helped me to ask if something socially significant is occurring which is captured in my own problematic experiences of fatherhood. My original plan was to use this as the start point for additional research. I believed, and was encouraged in this by my supervisors, that my own experiences would quickly be left behind and my project would become a traditional piece of qualitative sociological research initiated by my experiences but not really informed by them as the research developed and progressed. My narrative would form part of a wider project that was going to look at the way fatherhood was socially constructed in the context of sperm donation to lesbian mothers. This proved to be very hard. I only managed to recruit one other man who had an experience similar to mine. It became clear that with limited resources I would be unable to develop research around a qualitative interview model. I was 'forced' into considering autoethnography or abandoning my research. I had to place my own narrative not just as the starting point for more research but at the very crux of the data collection itself.

AUTOETHNOGRAPHY?

The majority of accounts of autoethnography are written from the perspective of seasoned researchers seeking to make use of a methodology that fully grasps the opportunities that have arisen from what Ellis, Adams, and Bochner (2011) have called an ontological and epistemological 'crisis of confidence inspired by postmodernism in the 1980s' (p. 1). This introduced new and abundant possibilities to reform social science and reconceive the objectives and forms of social science inquiry. My journey into autoethnography was less decisive. In fact, I didn't even recognise my unconscious attempts to form a research focus for my PhD as autoethnography until this was pointed out in a PhD colloquium. One of the things that made me realise that autoethnography could be more than a 'fallback' position given the failure of my original research idea was my reflection on the rather too neat narrative I had constructed. I wanted to reflect on whether I could do more than offer a personal account. I also wanted to go beyond my own experiences and find the stories of others who had followed a similar path. I was keen not to stop at my own story. It seemed that what I needed was a much more detailed, deep, and honest reflection on my own experiences that delved into the interlocking narratives of my family in much more detail than my self-contained three minute talk offered (Rosaldo, 1993). I was moving away from the original idea of offering a level of self-reflection that initiated the research and some key questions, and then was left behind. While I wanted to do justice to the complexity of my narrative and to the narratives of others I wanted to avoid what Geertz (1988) calls a 'sociological self-absorption' and author saturated texts. I am not sure if I have achieved this and I am aware that this is exactly what may be developing. I feel there is a need for my own narrative to illuminate aspects of family life, fatherhood, and parental complexity that can be seen in the wider cultural landscape. It has yet to be seen if I will achieve this. However, I hope that by exploring the concept of negotiation in the emerging ways in which I am a father and linking this to wider cultural and social concerns over fatherhood, sexuality, parenting, and family I may get close. Ellis et al. (2011) argue, 'Autoethnography is one of the approaches that acknowledges and accommodates subjectivity, emotionality, and the researcher's influence on research, rather than hiding from these matters or assuming they don't exist' (p. 3). For me the value of autoethnography lies in its ability for practitioners to use their methodological tools and literature to analyse experience. At the heart of autoethnography is the directive to use personal experience to illustrate facets of cultural experience, and, in so doing, make characteristics of a culture familiar for both insiders and outsiders. So, my research seems to sit somewhere in the domain of a reflexive ethnography. Ellis et al. (2011) claim that reflexive ethnographies document ways a researcher changes as a result of doing fieldwork. Reflexive/narrative ethnographies exist on a continuum ranging from starting research from the ethnographer's biography, to the ethnographer studying her or his life alongside cultural members' lives, to ethnographic memoirs (Ellis, 2004; Ellis and Bochner, 2000) or 'confessional tales' (Maanen, 1988) where the ethnographer's backstage research endeavours become the focus of investigation (Ellis, 2004). Atkinson (2015) notes that it is now common to employ these techniques that, 'blur with those of biographical work' (p. 165). He goes on to say that this trend, 'moves the personal from the marginal notes of the confessional tale to occupy the central place of sociological or anthropological analysis' (p. 165). The resulting texts can appear as highly charged, personal accounts of experiences, memories, and actions that can be significant for the reader as well as the author. That sounds like me.

The more I read about autoethnography the more I realised that my carefully constructed narrative about not only why I chose my PhD but also the ways I represented how I behaved as a father failed to do justice to the complexity of the situation. I grew in the belief that I didn't want to simply use my narrative as the justification for the research and then allow it to fade into the background to be overtaken by a body of data taken from interviews, even if I could find the interviewees. Atkinson, Coffey, and Delamont (2003) captured this when they argued for an approach in which researchers,

> frame their accounts with personal reflexive views of the self. Their ethnographic data are situated within their personal experience and sense making. They themselves form part of the representational processes in which they are engaging and are part of the story they are telling. (Atkinson et al., 2003, p. 62)

I felt I needed to really reflect on not only my narrative but that of others who had been involved in the process: my wife; the mother of my children and her partner; my wife's parents, especially her mother; and the immediate families of the children's mothers. For example, my mother-in-law has pictures of the children on the walls in her living room. She sees them as her grandchildren (sort of) and yet has no biological connection to them. This seems to be a clear display of family practises. (Morgan, 1996, 2011). For her 'family is not a thing, but a way of looking at, and describing, practices which might also be described in a variety of other ways' (Morgan, 1996, p. 199). She chooses to look at and describe my children as her grandchildren; they are part of how she defines family. It does not matter to her that this family may be seen by some as unconventional. Family practices, Morgan writes, 'are not simply practices that are done by family members in relation to other family members but they are also constitutive of that family "membership" at the same time' (p. 32). The narratives of extended relatives are pertinent here too. There was therefore a whole set of narratives that were absent in my 'neat' account. I increasingly believed these had to be heard if the real social significance of this experience of fatherhood and family form was to be understood.

222   J. HADLOW

My goal is to achieve a wider cultural significance for my experiences. Chang, Ngunjiri, and Hernandez (2013) describe the use of personal stories as 'windows to the world' (p. 18) through which autoethnographers are able to interpret how their selves are connected to their sociocultural contexts and how these contexts give meaning to their experiences and perspectives. The aim is to transcend mere narration. Marowitz's and Morrison's warnings of the dangers of placing one's own experiences at heart of everything seems particularly ironic given the method of conception under discussion here. The actual mechanics of my method of conception remains unstated in my developing thesis. Maybe because it seems obvious. However, I tend to the idea that it is simply embarrassing. The most honest question I ever received was from a Sixth Form A level sociology student who, in response to the story of how I became a father, asked 'Who decided what you would wank into?' I was disconcerted by these sorts of frank questions. However, as Ellis reminds us:

> honest autoethnographic exploration generates a lot of fears and doubts—and emotional pain. Just when you can't stand the pain anymore, well that's when the real work has only begun. Then there's the vulnerability of revealing yourself, not being able to take back what you have written or having any control over how readers interpret it. (Ellis p. 738 cited in Freeman, 2015)

These fears run through the very process of writing this account of my novice approach to autoethnography. How honest do I really want to be in describing how I thought about fatherhood before the event when there is a strong possibility my children will one day read this? And, layer upon layer, I can't really talk about why I fear talking about it for the same reasons.

There is, in my narrative of parenting, a complex and fluid interplay of meanings around fatherhoods which draw on the many contemporary experiences of fathering rather than the dominant normative familial ideological role of heterosexual, married, breadwinner. However, my way of being a father is constructed around these norms and does not simply replicate them. My role as a sperm donor seems to give me a 'get out of jail card' that isn't available to other fathers. If I negotiate to be only marginally involved in some aspects of my children's lives I seem to receive no criticism from those I explain my situation to. Whereas the same marginal involvement may label me as 'deadbeat dad' if I had arrived at fatherhood by another means. In this sense I have considerable agency over the sort of father I want to be as do the women who are mothers to our children. However, this may be only apparent and a result of my desire not to be too involved (Hobson and Morgon, 2002). I feel that had I pushed harder to engage in more than emotional connections with my children and demanded more say in aspects of decision-making over their lives this would have produced resistance from their mothers. To avoid self-absorption I need to show how my experiences relate to broader questions and fatherhood, family and gay parenting, as well as attitudes to same-sex relationships.

My way of being a father was clearly being negotiated in relation to the diversity of ways of being a father that have developed and are developing in contemporary Britain. Within the dynamic of my emerging family I had a number of roles of play. One aspect of it is clearly transgressive: enabling a same-sex couple to have children; having no sexual relationship with either of the parents; an ambiguous role for my wife. However, other aspects are equally conformist. Michelle and Sarah actively negotiated a specific role for me as father, which has some characteristics of conventional fatherhood while they retained autonomy over James and Lilly. My social identity as a father was thus contested and has to be negotiated to fit a number of agendas notably for my wife and me, as well as for Sarah and Michelle, in a broader social context made up of schools, social services, other family members, friends, and neighbours.

While I no longer wanted to leave my story behind as I moved onto traditional qualitative research I am also hoping to transcend a mere narration of experience and use data from my own life story to gain an understating of society (Chang, 2008; Morse, 2002). Anderson suggests that analytic autoethnography is a value-added quality of not only truthfully rendering the social world under investigation but also transcending that world through broader generalisation. I was taken by Karp (1996) who saw the importance of the subjective, expressive quality in sociology but who also saw that valuable sociology 'requires more than an important topic and the goal of informative description. That's a good start, but the value and vitality of a piece of research depend on its providing theoretical illumination of the topic under investigation' (Karp, 1996, p. 14). I felt I was increasingly settling on the analytical side of autoethnography. I went to read as much of the work around fatherhood that had come from the evocative tradition as I could find (Anonymous, 2015; Gale, 2012; Goodall, 2012; Pelias, 2012; Poulos, 2012; Sparkes, 2012; Wyatt, 2012; Wyatt & Adams, 2012, 2014). I also looked at work by Denzin, Ellis,

Holman Jones, and others. I do not consider myself to be very widely read in this area, but I just couldn't see this form of ethnography as valid (Guyote and Sochacka, 2016). They seemed to present what Atkinson (2006) describes as, 'the elevation of the autobiographical to such a degree that the ethnographer becomes more memorable than the ethnography, the self more absorbing than other social actors' (p. 402). For Atkinson, the problem stems from a tendency to promote ethnographic research on writing on the basis of its experiential value, its evocative qualities, and its personal commitments rather than its scholarly purpose, its theoretical bases, and its disciplinary contributions. This position reflects my own uneasy feelings about the method.

Potential Problems

I am aware also that I am missing many other stories. The idea that the complexity of this form of family life can be told through one narrative is long gone. I need to find a way to allow the narratives of many others to be told. Do I tell their stories on their behalf? Do they tell their own story? Will they want to and will they have the skill to fit their story into the particular format demanded of academic writing? To what extent will fitting the stories into the style of a PhD distort the meaning? When I take this beyond my own experiences and bring in the stories of those not connected to me I need to find the right way to do this. Interviews seem inadequate. I want to capture the same complexities in others that I feel are there with me in my situation. And then I want to connect it to theoretical developments. I want to generalise beyond my own experiences. I want to do what Anderson describes (Anderson, 2006): 'When I suggest that there is value in using ethnography to analyse social life, it is for the purpose of exploring how people come to construct social worlds, what the consequences are, and how we might construct better worlds and enrich our collective lives in the process' (p. 459).

In a set of notes provided by the editors on an early draft of this paper they stated that 'There is much in this chapter about emotions—fear, for example'. That is true. My process of reflection on the subject of my PhD has made me wonder if I am a good father. Should I be more involved with my children? I am also fearful of how this approach exposes you and others. As Allen and Piercy (2005) wrote, 'By telling a story on ourselves, we risk exposure to our peers, subject ourselves to scrutiny and ridicule, and relinquish some sense of control over our own narratives' (p. 156).

Chatham-Carpenter (2010) capture this when they say doing autoethnography can simultaneously create anxiety, vulnerability, and maybe even pain (Chatham-Carpenter, 2010 cited in Adams & Manning, 2015 p. 361). I want to reach an audience. I sent a copy of my PhD proposal to my sister for comments. She is a historian who writes in a manner immediately accessible to a non-specialist audience. Her comment was that it was good but no one would ever read it written like that. No one can, or wants to, read sociology other than other sociologists. The subject matter is great but the language, tone, and structure are a barrier. At the time I felt this was right but I had no choice. I would have to write a second version of the whole research to speak to an audience other than the one the PhD was intended for. Now, maybe I feel more confident in writing in a different way for my PhD audience. I am able to use conversational and descriptive language that we felt would invite a reader to travel alongside me as I attempt to unpack and interrogate our experiences. I do not feel a draw to a fully evocative autoethnography (Ellis, 1999) but I do feel inspired to bring myself, my position, and my vulnerabilities into my writing. Anderson (2006) indicated one of the five essential criteria for analytic autoethnography as being a 'full member in the research ... setting' (p. 375) or what he calls a complete member researcher.

So, I have taken my first steps into autoethnography. It seems very daunting.

From Father to Daddy

I am the father of two children, James and Lilly. James is 11 and Lilly is 5. James and Lilly have two primary care giving parents, a lesbian couple, Sarah and Michelle. Sarah is their birth mother.

James and Lilly's conception might be considered by some as unusual, and my role as their father is unconventional. James and Lilly are the result of self-insemination with sperm donated by me. To a large extent the story of my PhD, my research, and my interaction with autoethnography is the story of how I became a father.

Sarah and Michelle had known my wife, Sue, for many years as they all worked in the same school. I had met them on a few occasions but couldn't say that I knew much about them other than that they were a friendly, outgoing gay couple. I meet a lot of Sue's work colleagues and didn't really think that much about it. A few years later, after Sue had stopped working there, she met up with them and was told the lengthy story of their failed attempts to conceive. My subsequent research into the literature revealed that their experiences of dodgy websites, odd individuals, and large expense was not untypical. Sue was keen that we help them and suggested the possibility of me being a sperm donor. As she put it at the time, 'it's not like we have any other use for it is there'. We had no desire for children of our own. I had never wanted to be a father and Sue has always told me she has no desire to be a mother. Sue and I had married late. I had been in previous relationships where my partners had had young children so I had some experience of a sort of parenting. I had enjoyed this and formed close relationships with the children while the relationships lasted. My greatest regrets were the loss of the contact with the children when the relationships ended. But this had not provoked in me a desire for 'my own' children. My decision to donate sperm to Sarah came from a desire to enable her and Michelle to become parents, not for me to become a father. There was no desire from either Sue or me to become parents and I had no desire for fatherhood. In the initial discussions between ourselves Sue and I assumed that we would be making parenthood possible for Sarah and Michelle and not taking on any sort of parenting role ourselves. We had no ambition for this. Consequently, we saw no point in negotiating our involvement with Sarah and Michelle as we envisaged little direct participation in bringing up the child. We joked that one day there would be a knock on the door and a young man would be standing there who would say 'I think you're my dad'. Just like in a movie. However, it felt like the right thing to do.

Sarah and Michelle had become adamant that they didn't want to go through the medical profession and be forced into a formal, legal arrangement to become parents. They wanted an informal arrangement they could be in charge of. This formal/informal distinction seemed to be very important. When Sue and I discussed with Sarah and Michelle it was clear that one of the things that they had felt burnt by in their previous attempts to conceive using clinics was the lack of control they felt. For Sarah and Michelle going down an informal route offered many benefits. It allowed them the chance to not only control the conception process but also to create the meanings of parenthood that would develop. I don't feel that this was done consciously at the start. I feel this developed over time, but that Sarah and Michelle felt that the potential for this was only going to be found if they had an informal arrangement. This is reflected in the literature where for many lesbian women owning and managing the process outside of medical and legal systems was a way of gaining control (Ryan-Flood, 2009). It seems that Sarah and Michelle had deliberately opted for an informal process of conception in this context because it offered the greatest degree of de-medicalisation and control. Chabot and Ames (2004) show in their research that increasingly lesbian couples are choosing to become parents without the help of medical personnel. Instead the research on lesbian women in this area seems to confirm some key aspects of 'my mothers' that many couples choose to step outside formal, institutionalised methods and adopt a 'self-help' approach drawing on support from gay and lesbian community resources (Oswald, 2002).

The process of attempting conception took place sometimes in our house, sometimes in Michelle and Sarah's with our respective partners 'assisting' in the process. This had the potential to be embarrassing. However, we all just treated it as normal. The exact timing would be determined by Sarah for when she was most fertile. I had even started looking at websites to see what a man could do to make his sperm more likely to conceive. I was eating fresh fruit, avoiding alcohol, and wearing loose pants. We would meet and chat as if we were just getting together for drinks. Then Sue and I would go off to produce the sperm. When this was delivered Michelle and Sarah would go off for the insemination. The involvement of the partners was very important. Sue's part in the process made it feel less sordid and more a product of love and affection.

When James was born Sarah's mother gave Sue a scarf she had knitted. We didn't know her mother well at all. She said when she gave it to Sue that it was 'for everything she had done to make James possible'. I remember thinking immediately, it was my sperm, 'where's my scarf'? However, I also recognised that this was an acknowledgement of Sue's role in making it possible and wanting it to happen. Any sense of reluctance on her part would have made it all impossible. Sarah conceived after a few attempts. We were happy for them but I felt little sense of fatherhood at this stage. I remember having a sense of masculine pride that 'my boys' had proved so potent it only took a couple of goes. James was born a very healthy baby. We visited them at home when James was only a few weeks old. I held the baby, awkwardly. Photos were taken. That was really the end of my direct involvement. At this stage there was no sense that I would move beyond simply being a biological father.

We saw James with Michelle and Sarah on a more frequent basis for the next few years. As part of this contact my in-laws were becoming part of the family. My mother-in-law in particular bought gifts for James and had many pictures of him displayed prominently in her house. I don't think this is something we were consciously aware of at the time. There was a pivotal moment when James, aged four, started calling me 'Daddy John'. My daughter has dropped the 'John' and now calls me just 'Daddy'.

228   J. HADLOW

The negotiation of my fatherhood with James was at an emotional rather than a practical level. I was not very involved in James' care and everyday life. However, when we were together much work went into establishing an emotional bond. James drew pictures for me and we played together a lot. It is interesting to reflect on how this transition took place. I was not becoming a 'traditional' dad, but I was becoming more involved. Sarah and Michelle were instrumental in this. They introduced me as James' dad to their friends and neighbours. I was invited to birthday parties, school activities, and other social events and always given the status of dad. Sue and I were involved in discussions about school. I read with James and put him to bed whenever we were there. However, while the emotional aspect of fatherhood was being developed there was no sense that I was an equal in any decision-making process over James' life. This suited Sue and I. We were developing a form of fatherhood that suited all of us.

Around this time Michelle and Sarah said they would like to try for another baby. My wife and I discussed our feelings and agreed once again. Lilly was the result.

Lilly followed on calling me Daddy John. Although she soon dropped the John and calls me 'Daddy' now. I get father's day cards and we visit each other all the time. My change in name seemed to be important. I had gone in my own mind from being a donor to a father and then to a dad. My children call me 'Daddy' or 'Daddy John'. Language matters. All the way through this research I have struggled with finding the 'appropriate language' to describe the people involved. Wittgenstein, Heidegger, Saussure, Derrida, and many others have explored the complexities of language, reification, logocentrism, meaning fluidity, and other concepts. Despite a familiarity with these philosophers and their work I still struggle to see where I fit. The terms to identify parents seem to me to be a poor 'fit' with my own experiences of being a parent. Many of the revisions that have taken place to this account requested by the editors have involved clarifications of what I mean by certain terms and expressions. I feel I am constantly trying to lock down a meaning. I have now arrived at a status as a 'sort of father' that sits somewhere between a dad, a divorced dad, and uncle. This complexity of language, of my exact role as a father, creates a whole series of questions. In the story I tell of how I arrived at my research focus it is this lack of a readily available, short-hand account of my form of fatherhood that made me realise that there was maybe something new and interesting going on, albeit it similar to other non-normative family formations and roles.

I came to realise that my role has elements of conventional fatherhood with some specific differences. Dempsey (2004, 2012) argued that it is important to distinguish between patriarchal concepts of relatedness that connote entitlement to authority, what she terms 'proprietoriality' or legal rights over children, and the various other dimensions of affinity men in her research revealed, including that predicated on biological relatedness. This idea really resonated with me. I was not being offered, and indeed did not want, any formalised legal say in the decisions to be made around my children's lives. It was not suggested that I would have a moral right to this as a consequence of the nature of how I became a father. I was offered a relationship based on the biological connectedness I had with my children.

For me donor fatherhood offered the opportunity to construct fatherhood as an ongoing and iterative process. It is a form of continually negotiated fatherhood that can change with circumstances. 'Just a donor' was all I had expected to be. This doesn't mean I regret it but it does force a continual process of reflection on the sort of father I am and where I should look for role models. Fatherhood crept up on me as my first child got older. I feel I have little power in the process of becoming a father but I am not sure if I really wanted more power. I am aware that for men with a much stronger procreative consciousness than me (Berkowitz, 2007; Mallon, 2004; Murphy, 2013; Tasker & Patterson, 2007) this process can involve something of a power struggle, which necessitates negotiation and interaction with interested parties. On reflection it seems that I could be described as a man who has gone into it extremely unprepared without having thought it through. However, this is not a unique situation. What may be different is that my decision to embark on this process was not to enable me to become a parent; I had rejected this in my life. It was to enable someone else to become parents. I have now become a parent. I think it is different. It feels different. It is this experience that has become the basis of my PhD and is the reason for my nervous encounter with autoethnography.

It was my son who got me thinking about my form of fatherhood as something that could be the subject of sociological research. He started calling me 'Daddy John' at the age of five or so. The 'Daddy' part placed me in a traditional fatherhood role; the addition of 'John' made it clear that there was something else going on. My son is now 11 years old. Recently, when asking if I wanted a cup of tea, he jokingly called me 'father Jonathon'. He has an awareness that there has always been something different about my role as a dad and he likes to play with it. Recently he seems to be avoiding using any title. I see this as his developing awareness as he gets older of the ambiguity and complexity of our relationship which struggles to find expression in the 'father' langauge available to both of us.

Autoethnography has allowed me to use my own experiences as the basis for wider, analytical social thinking. I make no claims about my experiences being typical or speaking to a general truth. (Delamont, 2009). Rather, they provide the basis for key questions about the nature of fatherhood, choice, reflexivity in family life, change, and continuity. Autoethnography has allowed me to explore fundamental questions about fatherhood based on my own experiences. I am also worried. When my son called me 'father Jonathon' my immediate thoughts were about how I could use this in my research, what does it mean, and what does it say sociologically. Does this mean that I now see every interaction with my children as data? I fear that autoethnography may mean that every aspect of life as a father becomes research. I worry that my children may resent being the subject of my research and I wonder what they will think of it as they grow older. These fears are not put to rest by the most careful ethical considerations built into the research process.

My own degree students often comment that studying sociology makes you look at everything in a different way. One said, 'you can never just watch the TV anymore; you're always looking at it as a sociologist'. Having studied sociology for so many years I had forgotten what this revelation was like, I felt as if I had always looked at everything as a sociologist. Now I am positioning myself as an autoethnographer, I am powerfully reminded of the changes that studying sociology has on individuals and the transformative nature of this critical way of seeing the world. Now I find myself unable to just pick my son up from school without looking at the other parents and thinking 'I could use this'.

References

Adams, T. E., & Manning, J. (2015). *Autoethnography and Family Research. Journal of Family Theory & Review, 7*(4), 350–366.

Allen, K. R., & Piercy, F. P. (2005). *Feminist Autoethnography*. In D. H. Sprenkle & F. P. Piercy (Eds.), *Research Methods in Family Therapy* (pp. 155–169). New York: Guilford Press.

Anderson, L. (2006). *Analytical Autoethnography. Journal of Contemporary Ethnography, 35*(4), 373–395.

Anonymous, S. F. (2015). Father Figuring: An Autoethnography of Fatherhood. *Qualitative Inquiry, 21*(1), 11–19.

Atkinson, P. (2006). Rescuing Autoethnography. *Journal of Contemporary Ethnography, 35*(4), 400–404.

Atkinson, P. (2015). *For Ethnography*. London: Sage.

Atkinson, P. A., Coffey, A., & Delamont, S. (2003). *Key Themes in Qualitative Research: Continuities and Change*. Walnut Creek, CA: AltaMira Press.

Berkowitz, D. (2007). *A Sociohistorical Analysis of Gay Men's Procreative Consciousness. Journal of GLBT Family Studies, 3*(2/3), 157–190.

Chabot, B., & Ames, B. (2004). *"It Wasn't 'Let's Get Pregnant and Go Do It':" Decision Making in Lesbian Couples Planning Motherhood via Donor Insemination. Family Relations, 53*(4), 348–356.

Chang, H. (2008). *Autoethnography as Method*. Abingdon: Routledge.

Chang, H., Ngunjiri, F. W., & Hernandez, K. C. (2013). *Collaborative Autoethnography*. Walnut Creek, CA: Left Coast Press.

Chatham-Carpenter, A. (2010). "Do Thyself No Harm": Protecting Ourselves as Autoethnographers. *Journal of Research Practice, 6*, 1–13.

Delamont, S. (2009). *The Only Honest Thing: Autoethnography, Reflexivity and Small Crises in Fieldwork. Ethnography and Education, 4*, 51–63.

Dempsey, D. (2004). *Donor, Father or Parent? Conceiving Paternity in the Australian Family Court. International Journal of Law, Policy and the Family, 18*(1), 76–102.

Dempsey, D. (2012). *More Like a Donor or More Like a Father? Gay Men's Concepts of Relatedness to Children. Sexualities, 15*(2), 156–174.

Ellis, C. (1999). Heartful Autoethnography. *Qualitative Health Research, 9*(5), 669–683.

Ellis, C. (2004). *The Ethnographic I: A Methodological Novel About Autoethnography*. Walnut Creek, CA: AltaMira Press.

Ellis, C., Adams, T. E., & Bochner, A. (2011). Autoethnography: An Overview. *Forum: Qualitative Social Research, 12*(1), Art. 10.

Ellis, C., & Bochner, A. P. (2000). *Autoethnography, Personal Narrative, Reflexivity: Researcher as Subject*. In N. K. Denzin & Y. S. Lincoln (Eds.), *The Handbook of Qualitative Research* (2nd ed., pp. 733–768). Newbury Park, CA: Sage.

Freeman, J. (2015). *Trying Not to Lie...and Failing: Autoethnography, Memory, Malleability*. The Qualitative Report. 20, 6, 918-929. How To Article 3.

Gale, K. (2012). *Knowing Me, Knowing You: Becoming Father, Becoming Son in the Fluid Play of Memory, Affect, and Intuition. Qualitative Inquiry, 18*(2), 149–152.

Geertz, C. (1988). *Works and Lives: The Anthropologist as Author*. Stanford, CA: Stanford University Press.

Goodall, H. L. (2012). *The Fatherland Museum. Qualitative Inquiry, 18*(2), 203–209.

Guyote, K. W., & Sochacka, W. (2016, January–December 1–11). Is This Research? Productive Tensions in Living the (Collaborative) Autoethnographic Process. *International Journal of Qualitative Methods, 15*(1), 1–11.

Hobson, B., & Morgon, D. (2002). Introduction: Making Men into Fathers. In B. Hobson (Ed.), *Making Men into Fathers Men, Masculinities and the Social Politics of Fatherhood*. Cambridge: Cambridge University Press.

Karp, D. (1996). *Speaking of Sadness*. New York: Oxford University Press.

Mallon, G. (2004). *Gay Men Choosing Parenthood*. New York: Columbia University Press.

Morgan, D. J. (1996). *Family Connections: An Introduction to Family Studies*. Cambridge: Polity Press.

Morgan, D. J. (2011). *Rethinking Family Practices*. Basingstoke: Palgrave Macmillan.

Morse, J. M. (2002). *Writing My Own Experience. Qualitative Health Research, 12*, 1159.

Murphy, D. (2013). *The Desire for Parenthood: Gay Men Choosing to Become Fathers Through Surrogacy. Journal of Family Issues, 34*(8), 1104–1124.

Oswald, R. F. (2002). *Resilience Within the Family Networks of Lesbians and Gay Men: Intentionality and Redefinition. Journal of Marriage and Family, 64*, 374–383.

Pelias, R. J. (2012). *Archiving Father and Son. Qualitative Inquiry, 18*(2), 144–148.

Poulos, C. N. (2012). *Stumbling into Relating: Writing a Relationship with My Father. Qualitative Inquiry, 18*(2), 197–202.

Rosaldo, R. (1993). *Culture and Truth: The Remaking of Social Analysis*. Boston: Beacon.

Ryan-Flood, R. (2009). *Lesbian Motherhood: Gender, Families and Sexual Citizenship*. Basingstoke: Palgrave Macmillan.

Sparkes, C. (2012). *Fathers and Sons: In Bits and Pieces. Qualitative Inquiry, 18*(2), 174–185.

Tasker, F., & Patterson, C. (2007). *Gay and Lesbian Parenting in Context. Journal of GLBT Family Studies, 3*(2/3), 9–34.

Van Maanen, J. (1988). *Tales of the Field: On Writing Ethnography*. Chicago: University of Chicago Press.

Wyatt, J. (2012). *Fathers, Sons, Loss, and the Search for the Question. Qualitative Inquiry, 18*(2), 162–167.

Wyatt, J., & Adams, T. E. (2012). *Introduction: On (Writing) Fathers. Qualitative Inquiry, 18*(2), 119–120.

Wyatt, J., & Adams, T. E. (2014). *On (Writing) Families. Autoethnographies and Presence and Absence, Love and Lose*. Rotterdam: Sense Publishers.

CHAPTER 13

Hate the Results? Blame the Methods: An Autoethnography of Contract Research

Will Thomas and Mirjam Southwell

Will: I've always been hesitant to describe myself and my academic practice—although my initial 'training' is as a scholar of politics and of moral philosophy. I now work in a business school where I find myself interested in business ethics, leadership, critical management and, of course, in research methods. This diversity reflects my interest in learning and an insatiable curiosity in the world around me and was also why I enjoyed my time as a contract researcher. As I worked on projects across a wide range of disciplines I was able to satisfy my own intellectual inquisitiveness—and develop my skills in research practice and management. I aspire to follow my own advice to students and to select research approaches by focussing on the best tools for the job although the truth is that I will usually take jobs that demand approaches which are interpretivist and focus on individuals' sense-making and experiences. Increasingly I am more comfortable with the idea of myself as a philosopher whereby my contribution is often in helping others to understand and examine the underpinning assumptions or practice.

W. Thomas (✉)
University of Suffolk, Ipswich, UK

M. Southwell
Independent Researcher, Ipswich, UK

© The Author(s) 2018
T. Vine et al. (eds.), *Ethnographic Research and Analysis*,
https://doi.org/10.1057/978-1-137-58555-4_13

> *Mirjam: I am perhaps a reluctant academic and dislike having to position myself in research terms. However, when pushed, I describe my research practice as 'bricolage'—utilising methods from many and various sources but always focusing on the research question and the lived experience of the research participants. In part this comes from my original background in industrial design where I rarely waivered from the principle of form follows function.*

The story presented in this chapter relates a painful and embarrassing moment in our research careers that occurred during the final stages of a piece of contract research. On the presentation of the final report from a large piece of qualitative research the quality of the work was publically challenged and we were told that many of the findings were 'not true'. We have reflected on our experiences at length helping us to move on and, we hope, to become better researchers. We also hope that it has helped us to become more adept at working with external partners and in navigating some of the challenges that can be raised in those relationships. Our story is offered in the hope that readers might find it interesting, useful, and thought-provoking. This chapter presents both an account of our experience and reflections from related literature in order to analyse what happened and reflect on what we should learn as researchers operating in a 'contract research' environment.

The approach taken is autoethnographic—although given that there are two authors perhaps we might better term this *symethnography*. At the time of the research described in this chapter neither author had the intention of producing an autoethnographic account of the experience. This work is therefore autoethnography *a posteriori* (Boncori & Vine, 2014) with a focus on supporting a process of reflection and, to some degree at least, making sense of the experiences that are recounted below.

Collaborative writing presents challenges for the autoethnographer; since the events recorded in this chapter we have reflected on our experiences both alone and together and discussed what happened whilst writing formal responses and consoling each other. What is presented here is the result of these shared and individual reflections. We have tried to show where thoughts are ours (shared) or where they are those of one or other of us. Language is critical in these descriptions and this is perhaps the hardest aspect of collaborating in this type of writing. For an individual, the choice of words is a matter for oneself: getting it 'right' requires only that one is honest with oneself and careful about selections. In a joint project such as this, the choice of words is difficult largely because only one person can be writing at any one time—the choice of words *is* that of one person, even if the intent is to describe feelings which were shared and about which there is general agreement. We believe that this risks stripping the text of some of the emotion and vibrancy that a piece authored by one person might contain. Of course, we have endeavoured to avoid this as best we can by discussing and agreeing the language we have used, trying to relate the events and our reactions to them with honesty. Nevertheless, we recognise that collaboration of this sort presents a real problem as we seek to recall and describe how these events made us feel and our emotions as we look back upon them.

Autoethnography as Reflection

The process of self-reflection is one that educators and professionals are familiar with using in order to enhance practice. Indeed, it is a method and a skill that we are keen to ensure that students develop during the course of their studies. However, there is a danger that reflection, particularly self-reflection, does no more than acknowledge one's perspective (Pillow, 2003) and does not sufficiently engage with critique or analysis. The work of authors such as Delamont and Ellis remind us that the self and self-observation are legitimate focuses of study. Therefore what we are doing is more than noting down what happened, or wallowing in self-pity (Delamont, 2007; Ellis, 1991; Sparkes, 2000). Yet it is also true that the autoethnographic approach allows for a meaningful evaluation and critique of one's actions (Duncan, 2004); in our case, in the hope that we can better understand our experience and improve on our future 'performance'. Explicitly, we reject the criticism of Delamont (2007) who accuses autoethnographers of focusing on the powerful rather than the powerless—the narrative presented here illustrates a lack of power and influence in two researchers who expected and assumed far greater control of their situation. We also have the chance to reveal something about the way in which the phenomena is not just experienced, but about how it is co-created by the interaction of researcher and their object of research (Alvesson & Sköldberg, 2009; Moustakas, 1990) picking out the issues which are personally important and seeking to explore the social context of their existence (Holt, 2001; Sparkes, 1996).

In this chapter we weave together a narrative account of our experiences of conflict and rejection in a contract research setting with reflection based on an understanding of related literature. It is this combination that Ellis and Bochner (2006) suggest is most useful in harnessing an autoethnographic approach to reflection (Wall, 2006), noting that simply telling a good story is not enough (Josselson, 1993). In doing so, we hope to start to understand the interaction between our intentions, assumptions, and actions and the social world in which we conduct our work. Both Van Maanen (2011) and Reed-Danahay (1997) highlight the usefulness of autoethnography in this task as we seek to uncover or to expose something of the conditions under which our knowledge is produced (Skeggs, 1997), interpreted, and responded to.

After describing our position relative to the analysis we recount a brief sketch of our experiences in a contract research project that 'went wrong'. The analysis that follows is split into three main sections, each dealing with a question that we asked ourselves in the time following the study's conclusion.

Positioning

At the time of the study, we worked together in a research centre in which our primary function was to undertake 'contract research'. The majority of this work was undertaken for local authorities and other public sector organisations and took the role of evaluation studies and research projects. These were completed either as desk-based work or through primary data collection, primarily, but not exclusively, using qualitative methods. The topics varied but we were clear that our expertise and 'offer' to those that commissioned work from us was in bringing academic skills and knowledge to the process of research. At the time of this study we had more than 10 years combined experience in running similar sorts of studies. In addition, we had both taught research methods at undergraduate and postgraduate levels. We both hold PhDs—one in International Policy, the other in Philosophy.

As such, we felt confident and competent in our skills and ability to produce a credible study that drew upon our academic skills and met the expected outcomes of the commissioning body. We felt that it was implicit (although it was never made explicit) that we had been asked to do the work because of a degree of expertise—not necessarily in the subject matter but in project development, management, and research skills.

Whilst in the analysis that follows we maintain this positionality we hope that the reader will see that our certainty in our position is not unwavering. Through reflecting on our own position we begin to question the degree to which we should have made assumptions about our skills and experience. We know that it would be foolish to claim that we can be fully self-aware (Clough, 1998) or that the choices and descriptions we choose to present here are not affected by assumptions, prejudices both implicit and explicit, and our own self-interest (Stivers, 1993; Wolcott, 1999). Nevertheless, we present this account not as a deliberate attempt to position ourselves as 'experts' or as 'right' but rather as practitioners reflecting on experience in an attempt to improve their future work.

Another aspect of our positioning in relation to this piece of work is the extent we deliberately, or inadvertently, take an overly defensive or offensive position in relation to the other actors in the story. Wall (2008) refers to this in her account of writing an autoethnography in which colleagues encouraged her to consider whether her writing was becoming too defensive. For her, the solution was twofold: to be mindful of the danger that had been highlighted and to be conscious of trying to avoid it; and ensuring that her piece was engaged with the literature. The same techniques are useful in our current case, but perhaps are not enough. We found ourselves in a situation of conflict and high emotion where both sides took up offensive and defensive positions in relation to each other. The account must therefore reflect this and is consequently more personal than we might otherwise choose to be.

What Happened?

In the summer of 2008 we were sub-contracted to undertake a major piece of research intended to support the development of economic policy in the area. We were commissioned by a small public sector group responsible for inward investment and the promotion of the area as a business destination, acting on behalf of the 'partnership group'. This group consisted of local authority representatives, other public sector actors, and representatives of the private sector (both companies and membership organisations). We reported to the organisation that commissioned us, but lines of responsibility quickly became blurred. A steering group was established with representation from the research team, the commissioning organisation, and a representative of the partnership group (who was employed by the upper tier local authority for the area). On a day-to-day basis we worked directly with our commissioners and the representative of the partnership group. The study was completed and a draft report was produced by December of the same year.

Oversight of the project was the responsibility of the small steering group. The partnership group was represented by an officer from the upper tier local authority, an organisation that dominated many of the discussions within the partnership group. We met several times in the first weeks of the project and then approximately monthly during the latter stages, communicating by email throughout. This group agreed the methods and approach for the study, although importantly these were somewhat different in terms of balance than those in the original brief document and in the tender that was submitted.

The main section of the project was a series of in-depth interviews with senior business people, owners, directors, and managers each lasting approximately 45 minutes. All were recorded, transcribed, and analysed to draw out themes which would be used to inform a discussion on ways in which the partnership group, and its members, might act to promote the economic development of the area. We coded interview transcriptions firstly in a descriptive manner and then more analytically to highlight and define common themes. We could therefore be confident that the conclusions we drew from the data could be related back to interviews and that the process could reasonably be described as 'reliable'. To validate the conclusions we took from our data, we also reviewed existing literature to ascertain the extent to which the themes we identified were in line with existing work. We were confident that whilst we could not claim that the resulting findings were statistically significant, they gave a reliable and valid insight into the views of leading business people operating in the area.

As the project neared its conclusions we discussed the preliminary findings within the steering group and then presented a draft report for comment and feedback. We had some comments from the representative of the partnership group, mostly in terms of presentation, wording, and typos. We were therefore confident that the resulting report would be viewed as useful and supportive by the partnership group as a whole when we presented it back to them having reviewed the notes we received.

> Extract from email from steering group representative of partnership group (on first draft of report, dated 09/12/2008):
> 'Thank you for the draft—a very interesting piece of work, thank you.
>
> ...
>
> There are some points that sound very negative and will put people on the defensive rather than see them as ways for improvement... as you can see from my reaction in the comments...I think they are constructive points to make and positives can be brought out of them so they may need approaching in that light...I don't want to lose the feedback as it is real but also want everyone to be receptive and open to the report.
>
> ...
>
> The comments from businesses provide excellent support and feedback for the [specific named project]'

When we returned from the Christmas break, expecting to prepare to present our findings to the partnership group, we learnt that a senior member of the group 'had issues' with the report. Unable to get clarification on what these issues were before the meeting, we had no alternative but to go ahead with the presentation knowing that someone had concerns (but not what they were). At the presentation, in front of a large meeting of the whole partnership, we were told that the conclusions drawn from the interviews were 'not true' and therefore the work we had done was invalid. At the time we were shocked, embarrassed, and angry both at the way that this situation had been handled and the implication our work was unsatisfactory, but we were determined to try to address the concerns of the senior member.

> Extract from email from representative of commissioning organisation (following 4 months of revisions and meetings to revise the work, dated 30/04/2009):
> 'It is evident that [upper tier local authority's] expectations of the work don't match what has been delivered. I would suggest that this relates to the very loose nature of the brief. Whilst you have delivered as both you and I interpreted it, their interpretation was that

> the results would be more quantitative in nature (revisiting the brief it is difficult to argue that either side is wrong). They feel that in its current form they won't be able to use the report as they had originally hoped. Again, my view is that if the intended uses had been clearly stated at the start we may not be in this position'.

Despite considerable further work on the report and rewording of the conclusions, we were not able to address the concerns fully and work finally stopped on this project in late May 2009. Consequently, the report and its findings have not, to our knowledge, been circulated or used to inform the creation of new economic development strategies as was originally intended. With the exception of the outburst during the meeting this happened quietly and without ceremony. As we reflect back on this it suggests guilt on behalf of the partnership group—an acknowledgement that if things had gone wrong there was some shared responsibility. At the time this was the very opposite of the message that we were given.

Subsequent weeks and months featured much self-reflection and many cups of coffee as we tried to make sense of the experience and to consider how it shapes our self-identity as professional researchers. In the end, we identified three 'questions' which we asked ourselves and which are presented below.

Naivety and Inexperience

We asked ourselves the extent to which the problems that we had faced in this project were a reflection of our political naivety and inexperience of the realities of the process of policy formulation. We entered into the project confident in our abilities and knowledge of research methods and techniques, knowing that we could produce a piece of work that generated interesting insight into the views and opinions of our research participants. This confidence perhaps led us to ignore some of the complexities of the project. In presenting this as a potential example of naivety or of inexperience we hope to reinforce our attempt to produce a useful and valuable piece of work and our commitment to trying to find a way to reconcile the competing interests and views of the parties involved.

Choice of Methods

For researchers who subscribe to a pragmatic approach to the selection of methods, in which we seek guidance not from dogmatic adherence to a methodological paradigm but to working out what suits the project best, the choice of methods (and methodology) is frequently difficult. We made a conscious decision to suggest a qualitative, interpretivist approach to this project because the challenge appeared to be one of understanding not just what barriers, problems, and opportunities there *are* for businesses but also how these are *perceived*. It was not enough, for example, to know how many businesses made use of a particular support service; we wanted to know how and why they did so, whether it helped, and what it might do differently or better. Crucially, there is a distinct difference between wanting to know whether the services available to support businesses are useful and understanding the challenges that businesses face and how they might be supported. Our approach, agreed with the steering group, was the latter—in-depth, detailed understanding that comes from experts and that can be triangulated with the literature.

We are not so naive as to think that the choice of methods is one that is value-free; we would both freely admit that our preference would always be to take an interpretivist approach. Such values come into play not just at this stage of the process, but in the selection of priorities and questions posed by the funder which are the result of politics and context (Cheek, 2011; Walker, 2007). Assumptions are made about the possible outcomes of research work and about the scope of a particular approach to answer a specific question. Our experience of this reinforces a view that practitioners (in this case policy-makers) are frequently misguided about the nature and scope of social-science knowledge in assuming it can resolve key questions in a straightforward manner (Pollitt, 2006). It also serves to highlight that researchers forget or fail to appreciate the extent to which politics is often a messy mix of negotiation, ideology, and bureaucratic satisficing tactics (Walker, 2007).

An implication of our selection of method, familiar to those that undertake qualitative research of all types, is its tendency to result in complex answers and results. As Klein notes (Klein, 2003, p. 430) 'evidence, even scientific evidence, rarely speaks with a single clear voice about complex public issues'. As researchers we are somewhat used to contingency and uncertainty, perhaps even tentativeness, in presenting our findings—for policy-makers though, this may only serve to cloud the decision-making processes (Petticrew, Whitehead, Macintyre, Graham, & Egan, 2004) and perhaps limit its direct usefulness.

Negotiation and Evidence in Decision-Making

It is all too easy for researchers without experience of engagement in a policy-making process to assume that their input is a vital part of the decision-making that surrounds a particular initiative. Indeed, we made an assumption of this sort in thinking that our project was intended to support a process of policy-development rather than to act as an evidence base to support initiatives that were either already ongoing or that had already been decided upon.

Black (2001) reminds us that policy-making at a local level is more reliant on negotiation and compromise than politics at national level and so the degree to which research can influence the process is much more limited. One of the sources of critique for our report was a lack of explicit support for programmes (including economic development plans, investment in specific projects, and the prioritisation of work streams) which had already been placed in a public arena or where they had received public funds.

One assumption from the senior member of the commissioning group was that we had not asked about these programmes—perhaps assuming that had we asked, the positive endorsement of the project would surely follow. In fact, we had a range of specific initiatives and had found either no support or an outright rejection of ideas as being misguided. In the end though, our being right (or in the right) was not enough.

Concurrent Work

We were aware, right from the outset of the research, that it was one of a number of pieces of work that were running concurrently. There were a variety of projects, including those that looked at very specific proposals for developments or support for individual sectors. A key question for us was whether and how we should engage with them. In the end, this question proved to be another example of the complexity of the policy-making environment and one which highlighted to us the difficulties faced by researchers working in this field.

Notes from a meeting on 28th July 2008 show that we had agreed to focus on the agriculture sector as a primary producer rather than on the more complex 'food and drink' production. We were aware that work was already starting on a separate study in this area. On the 22nd August notes from a further meeting confirm that we were not expected to make contact with those conducting the sector-specific study as the representative of the partnership group felt the two projects 'don't sit particularly close together'. Nevertheless, by the time we reached 15th January 2009 the senior member of the partnership group commented that her colleague had asked for (and not had) input into the business development for this sector-specific project.

It is too easy to simply put this example down to poor communication within the partnership group and the organisation within which both the steering group member and senior representative work. Whilst this may be part of the problem the example also serves to illustrate Rist's (1994, p. 1002) point 'Policy making is often multidimensional and multifaceted. Research is but one (and often minor at that) among the number of frequently contradictory and competing sources that seek to influence what is an ongoing and constantly evolving process'. Managing this range of sources is not easy but researchers working in this environment must be aware that the foundation on which they work is built is unlikely to be strong or unwavering.

Value of 'Independent' Research

Petticrew et al. (2004) point out that researchers would like to feel that their work will influence policy and that action will be taken on the basis of the conclusions or recommendations that they draw. Indeed, it is frequently the case that universities are approached when partners are looking for an independent research team to provide an important piece of insight especially when a degree of impartiality is valued. This distance and objectivity, as well as a perceived (and hopefully actual) expertise in the process of data collection and analysis, can be a vital factor in securing the work.

Our experiences suggest that the reality of the situation may not be as clear and straightforward. Certainly academic staff would like to think of themselves as independent and skilled, but they may be perceived as distant or too far removed from practice (or the 'real world') by those that commission work from them and, as a result, simply interested in pursuing their own interests. The conflict in the meeting at which we presented our findings certainly led us to rethink our position in relation to the project. We started out understanding ourselves to be 'experts', not necessarily in the subject of the work, but in the process and mechanisms by which we would collect and analyse data. Following a period of reflection we began to appreciate that the quiddity of 'good' research is not a matter of academic debate that occurs within peer-reviewed journals and conference halls, but also relates to the 'political fit' that a report has to its context. In this case, it was not sufficient that the project was conducted according to principles of sound academic research. We had not reported support for projects that had already been made public or were underway and this led to the report being described as poor research. The judges of quality in this case are not our community of peers but a selection of organisations that have political concerns (whether relating to voters, shareholders, or other stakeholder groups) and for whom the degree to which the findings of the report correlate to interests is as great a concern as more abstract considerations of research design and execution.

With the distance that time provides we still believe in the quality of the work that we undertook and in the value of the themes and conclusions that we presented in the report. However, the notion of 'independent research' is inaccurate: all projects of this sort are the result of a relationship between the funder or commissioner of the work and those that undertake the project. If we had chosen to see ourselves as partners in the research rather than a commissioned team of independent researchers, we may have reached a more satisfactory outcome.

The Research Process

In reflecting upon the way in which we conducted the research project we wondered how we might have used the research process to mitigate or avoid problems. It seemed to us that a flawed process was always likely to lead to a flawed outcome; and equally that a better process may have improved the outcome of the study. In that regard, although we remain happy with the quality of the work that was produced we also acknowledge that there are ways in which the study might have been run more effectively.

The Steering Group

Lomas (2000) reminds us that the involvement of the commissioners in the steering group for the project offers the chance for them to influence both the scope of the project and the areas of focus, but also the mechanisms by which data will be collected. Indeed, we assumed that by giving the partnership group a say in these decisions we would be immune from later questions and problems resulting from the discussions in the steering group. We were amazed to receive emails that questioned the interpretation of the brief, the way in which interviews were conducted, and the choices about the participating individuals including names and numbers. We assumed that by discussing and agreeing these within the steering group we would avoid these issues. On reflection we draw two conclusions:

Firstly, the partnership group was represented by one individual on the steering group but had more than 20 members each with competing interests, ideas, and concerns. It was perhaps impractical to assume that one individual could adequately reflect this plurality of views in such a way that all members would feel that they had been represented. The outpouring that occurred at the presentation was in part a reflection of this difficulty. As Campbell et al. (2007, p. 29) note, 'If the findings sounded reasonable and fitted with the policy maker's understanding of the world, they were more likely to trust, and therefore use, it'. We suggest two alternatives: either our efforts were always doomed to cause some people to disagree with our findings, or by representing more of the members on the panel we may have avoided some of the problems we faced.

Secondly, there was a failure in communication between the partnership group and its representative on the steering group. Most problematically for us, the steering group member did not communicate adequately with the senior official that later caused problems for us. A clear example of this is in the feedback provided on initial drafts of the report where none of the problems that were raised later were highlighted. We have come to identify several concerns: the lack of proper delegated authority; the lack of proper understanding of the concerns of the partnership group or its constituent members; and the lack of adequate reporting mechanisms. As a result, the steering group simply could not have navigated the group in the correct direction with any more reliability than a ship with a broken compass.

Choice of Methods

We come to consider issues that relate to the communication of qualitative research in this setting in the final section. Here, we consider the choice of methods and approaches used to gather and analyse data in this study.

Whilst neither of us would consider ourselves to be strongly attached to any particular method or methodology we have a preference for qualitative, interpretivist approaches where this suits the project.

It is too easy to lay the blame at one party's door and forget that communication must be understood as a complex process in which failures are rarely the fault of one party alone. This stage of the project was hurried in order to meet the deadlines from the partnership group and was not given the care that it should have had with none of the parties taking appropriate time to understand the concerns of others. Some of the advice we offered the commissioners demonstrates awareness of both what makes good research and the needs of those using the research to be able to rely upon its accuracy. One example of this was emails that explain why datasets that had relevance at a County-wide level were not suitable for use in a smaller geography. Had we understood the ways in which the final report was intended to be used, the advice we offered could have taken these into account. A more careful and considered approach at the start of the project may have helped avoid these problems. As a result we learnt a very valuable lesson in project initiation and ensured that in future projects we took greater care to understand the function of the research output and not just the 'question' to be answered.

We also learnt that an important aspect of expertise and training in research methods is being able to communicate the reasons behind, and implications of, choices in project design to partners who may not have the same background, knowledge, and experience. There was a failure of communication between researchers and those commissioning and funding the process: we did not do enough to support our choices and recommendations with clear justifications. Our confidence that the choices we made would deliver a project that met the needs of the partnership group did not translate into confidence in the quality of the conclusions that might be drawn from them.

Communication of Qualitative Research

The final broad question that we asked ourselves was whether there were aspects of the way that we had communicated our (qualitative) research that contributed to the problems that we faced. We wondered whether by giving deeper thought to this aspect of the work we might have been able to avoid some of the challenges we faced and learn something about the way in which we work in the future.

Hate the Results? Blame the Methods

The nature of some of the criticism that we received at the time of the presentation suggests that some of those reading our report understood 'research quality' in terms more appropriate to the consideration of a quantitative study. Issues such as reliability and validity clearly have a place in qualitative work. However, we are also aware that within a study such as ours it is harder to convince a non-expert audience of the quality of the work than it might be in a quantitative study where statistics often give an audience confidence (even though this may be misguided). In asserting that 30 interviews was not enough to produce reliable results, the senior official demonstrated an understanding that 30 survey responses may not be sufficient in a quantitative study but did not show that the same thinking could not be applied to a piece of qualitative work. She failed to take into account the care with which we identified companies to contact and recruited participants, the skill with which the interviews and subsequent analysis was undertaken, or the fact that we compared our findings with previous similar studies as part of the literature review. This misunderstanding was incredibly frustrating for us, particularly when careful attempts to explain the situation were not taken on board.

Lomas (2000) cites a study in which it was shown that when presented with data that does not match with pre-existing views the research subjects were likely to criticise the methods by which the data was collected rather than the data itself. The response that we experienced in the presentation of our report is, we believe, an example of the same phenomenon. The lack of support in our study for projects that had commitments from members of the partnership board led to a reaction against the study—expressed as a criticism of the methods themselves. More than 30 years ago, Miles (1979) noted that this tendency was greater when the research was qualitative rather than quantitative—that audiences are more likely to reject quotes than statistics.

Qualitative Research Is 'Unreliable'

We found ourselves asking whether presenting the findings of the project more effectively would have eased the issues we faced. We already knew there was a risk that qualitative research could be regarded as 'susceptible to "cherry picking"' (Scott, 2002, p. 929) or open to accusations of 'anecdotalism' (Silverman, 2005, p. 176). The natural response for most academics would be to write long, detailed, research methods sections that lay out the details of the approach used. However, in the case of our project, as with much contract research, we were steered away from such sections and asked to focus on the content that mattered most to the audience. Whilst we do not believe that officials wish to gloss over complex issues (Campbell et al., 2007) getting the most from qualitative research requires active participation by the reader (Labuschagne, 2003) in a process that might be described as 'art' (Vicsek, 2010). Here, we attempted to make our report more accessible to the audience for whom it was intended, and in doing so did not give the amount of detail that might have convinced them of the quality of the work (had they read the section).

Our reflections on both the process and our experiences led us to consider how we might convince the audience to trust in our skills and integrity as researchers. We knew that the interview data that we had collected represented the views and insights of leading business people in the area and that hearing their voice(s) was a valuable benefit of the process we had led. We came to believe that a commitment to preserving the anonymity of the participants exacerbated some of the problems we experienced. The group was asked to take our word for the fact that those we spoke to were knowledgeable business leaders—aside from the sectors that they represented they did not know any more about them (we did not disclose the companies we spoke to either). Without hearing the conversations that we had with the participants the audience had to trust that our analysis had drawn out important themes and not cherry-picked soundbites, perhaps for our own agenda.

Had we been able to organise a public meeting at which the participants presented their own words or even had we been able to name those that we spoke to and attribute quotes we felt that the research would have carried greater weight. We might have been able to shape the writing and presentation of our work to meet the 'sense-making priorities of our audience' (Silverman, 2010, p. 417) had our ethics approval permitted naming participants.

However, we had not asked permission to name our participants; in the time that has passed it is impossible to say whether this was because we did not expect permission to be granted by our ethics panel (as Pollitt, 2006; Wiles, Coffey, Robison, & Prosser, 2012 suggest is likely) or whether we simply did not consider the benefits that it might have brought. Regardless, our reflection on this experience leads us to conclude that an unthinking assumption that research should always be conducted in an anonymous way may do little to help the audience of qualitative work, perhaps threatening the value and impact of the words themselves.

CONCLUSIONS

In the time following the conclusion of this project we both experienced periods of anger, insult, embarrassment, and desperation. We sought to reconcile our efforts, the reactions of the audience, and a desire to protect our own reputation and that of our institution. The process of writing has certainly helped with the first of these tasks. Others have previously noted the value in reflection and how writing an autoethnography can facilitate the therapeutic quality of making sense of our experiences (for example, see Ellis, Adams, & Bochner, 2011; Esterling, L'abate, Murray, & Pennebaker, 1999). Having experienced the public rejection of our work as a pair there is no doubt that we were able to help each other through the resulting hurt. We worked closely together at the time and were therefore able to discuss what happened informally and without the need to schedule meetings. Having shared the experience we did not need to explain or describe what happened. Had this not been the case, had either of us been operating alone, we believe the 'fall out' would have hurt much more and taken longer to fade.

Working as a pair, the discussions also prompted deeper reflection on the experience. We could not hide from what happened or seek to avoid it as one might if working along. The shared nature of the experience meant that whilst we could support each other we were also unable to hide from what had occurred.

When the ideas presented here were first discussed at a small conference we were applauded for honesty and a willingness to talk about experiences that many of those that have engaged in research have had but kept hidden. We hope that this account demonstrates the effectiveness of some principles taken from autoethnography in shaping reflection in such a way that it helps to further our practice, and that of those who read our words. Indeed, accounts that seek to uncover or expose hidden experiences (those that might otherwise remain unspoken) may have particular value in supporting and consoling the reader as much as the writer (Ellis & Bochner, 2006).

Many of the issues that we faced in this work are the result of communication that was 'less than ideal'. A single point of contact with the partnership group, at the end of the project, was certainly one of the clearest examples of poor practice on our part. Had we taken the advice of Neal (2010) and engaged the audience throughout the process we may have avoided many of the concerns that were raised when the project was complete.

To avoid a reoccurrence of these experiences and in seeking closure, we present these conclusions. We have learnt a painful lesson about the importance of ensuring that the purpose of the research (that is, what it is to be used for, not what information is sought) should be understood by the researchers and by the commissioners. The first part is obvious but it is all too easy to forget that research can be commissioned some time before it is understood *why* it has been commissioned. We have also seen that all those involved in the project have to understand how the choices of approach and methods relate to meeting the objectives of the work. For example, if a relatively small-scale qualitative study is to be undertaken, how confident can those who commission the work be that the findings will meet their requirements? Lastly, the communication needs of the audience must be considered early on and well before the report is drafted. Whether we engage the audience in the process directly (Silverman, 2010) or explore creative ways to understand complexity (Campbell et al., 2007) it is critical that efforts at communication are the result of conscious decisions rather than habit or accident.

What of (auto)ethnography? We have sought to use an ethnographic approach to bring together snippets of reflection from our experiences with insight from the literature. Alone, each would have value but together the effect is more dramatic and considerably more insightful. In the same way that Wall (2006, p. 39) suggests her autoethnography allowed her to consider 'personal and social motivators and enablers', this project allows us to bring together, acknowledge, and understand the personal, social, and political aspects that coalesced creating the experience that we related above.

REFERENCES

Alvesson, M., & Sköldberg, K. (2009). *Reflexive Methodology: New Vistas for Qualitative Research*. London: Sage.

Black, N. (2001). Evidence Based Policy: Proceed with Care. *BMJ (Clinical Research ed.), 323*(7307), 275–279.

Boncori, I., & Vine, T. (2014). 'Learning Without Thought Is Labour Lost, Thought Without Learning Is Perilous': The Importance of Pre-departure

Training and Emotions Management for Expatriates Working in China. *International Journal of Work Organisation and Emotion, 6*(2), 155–177.

Campbell, S., Benita, S., Coates, E., Davies, P., & Penn, G. (2007). *Analysis for Policy: Evidence-Based Policy in Practice*. London: Government Social Research Unit.

Cheek, J. (2011). *The Politics and Practices of Funding Qualitative Inquiry* (p. 251). London: The Sage Handbook of Qualitative Research.

Clough, P. T. (1998). *The End (s) of Ethnography: From Realism to Social Criticism*. Newbury Park, CA: Peter Lang Pub Incorporated.

Delamont, S. (2007). *Arguments Against Auto-ethnography*. Paper presented at the British Educational Research Association Annual Conference.

Duncan, M. (2004). Autoethnography: Critical Appreciation of an Emerging Art. *International Journal of Qualitative Methods, 3*(4), 28–39.

Ellis, C. (1991). Sociological Introspection and Emotional Experience. *Symbolic Interaction, 14*(1), 23–50.

Ellis, C., Adams, T. E., & Bochner, A. P. (2011). Autoethnography: An Overview. *Historical Social Research/Historische Sozialforschung, 4*, 273–290.

Ellis, C. S., & Bochner, A. P. (2006). Analyzing Analytic Autoethnography: An Autopsy. *Journal of Contemporary Ethnography, 35*(4), 429.

Esterling, B. A., L'abate, L., Murray, E. J., & Pennebaker, J. W. (1999). Empirical Foundations for Writing in Prevention and Psychotherapy: Mental and Physical Health Outcomes. *Clinical Psychology Review, 19*(1), 79–96.

Holt, N. (2001). Beyond Technical Reflection: Demonstrating the Modification of Teaching Behaviors Using Three Levels of Reflection. *Avante-Ontario, 7*(2), 66–76.

Josselson, R. (1993). A Narrative Introduction. In R. Josselson & A. Lieblich (Eds.), *The Narrative Study of Lives* (Vol. 1, pp. xi–xv). London: Sage.

Klein, R. (2003). Evidence and Policy: Interpreting the Delphic Oracle. *Journal of the Royal Society of Medicine, 96*(9), 429–431.

Labuschagne, A. (2003). Qualitative Research-Airy Fairy or Fundamental? *The Qualitative Report, 8*(1), 100–103.

Lomas, J. (2000). Connecting Research and Policy. *Canadian Journal of Policy Research, 1*(1), 140–144.

Miles, M. B. (1979). Qualitative Data as an Attractive Nuisance: The Problem of Analysis. *Administrative Science Quarterly, 24*, 590–601.

Moustakas, C. (1990). *Heuristic Research: Design, Methodology, and Applications*. London: Sage Publications.

Neal, S. (2010). Engaging in Effective Dialogues: How Can Qualitative Researchers, Policy Makers and Practitioners Talk Better to Each Other? *Qualitative Research for Policy Making*, Merlien Institute, 14–15 January.

Petticrew, M., Whitehead, M., Macintyre, S. J., Graham, H., & Egan, M. (2004). Evidence for Public Health Policy on Inequalities: 1 – The Reality According to Policymakers. *Journal of Epidemiology and Community Health, 58*(10), 811–816.

Pillow, W. (2003). Confession, Catharsis, or Cure? Rethinking the Uses of Reflexivity as Methodological Power in Qualitative Research. *International Journal of Qualitative Studies in Education, 16*(2), 175–196.

Pollitt, C. (2006). Academic Advice to Practitioners—What Is Its Nature, Place and Value Within Academia? *Public Money and Management, 26*(4), 257–264.

Reed-Danahay, D. (1997). *Auto/Ethnography: Rewriting the Self and the Social.* New York: Berg.

Rist, R. C. (1994). Influencing the Policy Process with Qualitative Research. In N. K. Denzin & Y. S. Lincoln (Eds.), *Handbook of Qualitative Research* (pp. 545–557). Thousand Oaks, CA: Sage.

Scott, D. (2002). Adding Meaning to Measurement: The Value of Qualitative Methods in Practice Research. *The British Journal of Social Work, 32*(7), 923–930.

Silverman, D. (2005). *Doing Qualitative Research: A Practical Handbook.* Thousand Oaks, CA: Sage.

Silverman, D. (2010). *Doing Qualitative Research.* Thousand Oaks, CA: Sage.

Skeggs, B. (1997). *Formations of Class & Gender: Becoming Respectable.* London: Sage.

Sparkes, A. C. (1996). The Fatal Flaw: A Narrative of the Fragile Body-Self. *Qualitative Inquiry, 2*(4), 463–494.

Sparkes, A. C. (2000). Autoethnography and Narratives of Self: Reflections on Criteria in Action. *Sociology of Sport Journal, 17*(1), 21–43.

Stivers, C. (1993). Reflections on the Role of Personal Narrative in Social Science, Signs. *Journal of Women in Culture and Society, 18*(2 Winter, 1993), 408–425.

Van Maanen, J. (2011). *Tales of the Field: On Writing Ethnography.* Chicago: University of Chicago Press.

Vicsek, L. (2010). Issues in the Analysis of Focus Groups: Generalisability, Quantifiability, Treatment of Context and Quotations. *The Qualitative Report, 15*(1), 122.

Walker, D. (2007). Is Evidence for Policy Good for Democracy? *Public Money and Management, 27*(4), 235–237.

Wall, S. (2006). An Autoethnography on Learning About Autoethnography. *International Journal of Qualitative Methods, 5*(2), 146–160.

Wall, S. (2008). Easier Said Than Done: Writing an Autoethnography. *International Journal of Qualitative Methods, 7*(1), 38–53.

Wiles, R., Coffey, A., Robison, J., & Prosser, J. (2012). Ethical Regulation and Visual Methods: Making Visual Research Impossible or Developing Good Practice? *Sociological Research Online, 17*(1), 8.

Wolcott, H. F. (1999). *Ethnography: A Way of Seeing.* Lanham, MD: Rowman Altamira.

CHAPTER 14

Collaborative Autoethnography: Enhancing Reflexive Communication Processes

Ngaire Bissett, Sharon Saunders,
and Carolina Bouten Pinto

Ngaire—Having studied many in-depth ethnographies throughout my
social science education and contrasted this with my PhD research
interrogation of the positivist quantitative fetish, I believe it is actually
qualitative research methodologies that substantiate our everyday life
experiences. Teaching MBA managers too, I see them respond keenly to
narrative accounts that help to explain the contradictory spaces they
inhabit in organisations. Recently, a PhD student I supervised relayed
several reflexive autoethnographic (AEG) tales of her experiences as a
company executive, revealing more understanding of top-down
leadership practices than any quantitative survey could surface. As a
meaning-making process, AEG bridges potential personal-professional
divides in my life too.

Sharon—I have always been interested in how others view the world
and how perceptions of reality and identity are formed. Ethnography
and undertaking an ethnographic study during my PhD provided me
with a formalised and legitimised name and approach to what I
deemed to be a natural curiosity. In my current role as the Director of

N. Bissett (✉)
Canberra University, Bruce, ACT, Australia

S. Saunders • C. Bouten Pinto
Griffith University, Nathan, QLD, Australia

© The Author(s) 2018
T. Vine et al. (eds.), *Ethnographic Research and Analysis*,
https://doi.org/10.1057/978-1-137-58555-4_14

254   N. BISSETT ET AL.

*a Graduate School, I rarely disclose my ethnographic and
autoethnographic tendencies but know that they are guiding my
everyday practice, decision-making processes, and analysis of self.*

*Carolina—As an inclusion and diversity practitioner and consultant
for many decades, autoethnography and its associated reflexivity have
enabled me to work with others in illuminatory ways. Theories are more
lucidly exposed, explained, and reframed, and nuances become more
clearly defined, stories have more impact, and new frameworks of being
and becoming emerge. Currently, nearing the end of my PhD journey
marks only the beginning of my expression of these expansive modes of
engagement, located at the nexus between theory and practice.
Expansively then, reflexive autoethnography allows us to stay in the
question to explore a rich panoply of possibilities.*

Setting the Stage, the Scenes, and the Narratives

Autoethnography occupies a diverse grounding involving: personal lived narratives (Chang, 2008; Denzin, 1989; Muncey, 2010), reflexive ethnography (Adams & Holman Jones, 2011; Wall, 2006), emotionalism (Chandler, 2012), critical ethnography (Bissett, 2006; Cann & de Meulenaere, 2012), and autobiographical ethnography (Scott-Hoy & Ellis, 2008). Despite the differences in the way that autoethnography is characterised, a common strand involves recognition of the relationship between notions of inner, vulnerable and often resistant, expressions of selfhood, along with attention to the cultural, social, and political contexts within which our lived experiences are encountered. This chapter responds to the potential and discipline of the situated embodied integration aspect of autoethnography by narrating a preliminary collaborative written encounter amongst three 'critical management studies' researchers who have a shared interest in enhancing their teaching and facilitation practice.

The chapter is thus framed by the personal narratives of the authors who reflect openly on concerns they hold in relation to their experiences teaching/facilitating in higher education and industry contexts pertaining to institutional expectations and constraints. In narrating their subjective vignettes, the authors seek to contribute to a growing scholarly dialogue regarding the complex, relational, and emergent nature of our intersubjective social experiences (Cunliffe, 2009). Autoethnography allows us to engage techniques of 'critical reflexivity' (Warren, 2011) to imagine how we might draw on in the moment interactions with participants/students to enhance learning processes. A key objective of the chapter therefore is to show how autoethnography can facilitate such collaboration.

> This article is an unusual reflective text. It has 2 authors, 2 voices, 2 embodied experiences, and 2 sociological biographies in dialogue...The dualities of the collaborative and contrastive engagement are explored...focusing on how to do fieldwork in an embodied manner. (Stephens & Delamont, 2006, p. 317)

This quotation is representative of recent attempts to create more authentic and rigorous ethnographic readings/understandings following a prolonged wave of critical commentary, which began in the 1960s (see Birnbaum, 1971; Clifford, 1983; Clifford & Marcus, 1986; Douglas & Ney, 1988; Gertz, 1973; Mitchell, 1969), pointing out that by maintaining the researcher as the sole voice of scientific authority, ethnographic research has contributed to the colonising of 'subjects' legacy (Schneider & Wright, 2013). Hence, like Stephens and Delamont, this chapter has an emancipatory objective, where the authors attempt to demonstrate the substance of providing space for multiple participants to engage in the knowledge construction process. As well as for research purposes, we draw on our everyday autoethnographic stories as a means of exploring the dynamic learning possibilities to be gained from a focus on the grounded character of workplace cultures. The intention is to reclaim a sense of embodied humanity to these often alienating spaces. This is achieved by demonstrating that the integration of intellectual activity, feelings and emotions, and the imagination (Burkitt, 2012; Leach, 1984; Turner, 1974; Worsley, 1997) is always present in our deliberations, albeit traditionally downplayed.

Moreover, emphasising the value of collaborative, relational 'leaderful' (Uhl-Bien & Ospina, 2012) learning encounters to make sense of institutional contexts allows us to challenge the dominance and ir/relevance of top-down leadership constructions. Indeed, our narratives serve as a vehicle from which to reimagine leadership as relationally embedded situated practice and in the process objectivist views of leadership practice, linked to singular individualised performance, can be contested. In addition, by rereading our texts through a critical reflexivity lens, our collegial endeavour reveals the limits associated with 'entitative' (Raelin, 2016) leadership conceptions.

256 N. BISSETT ET AL.

Accordingly, the structure of the chapter involves our personal sketches being initially relayed followed by a discussion of how the imagery created by autoethnographic texts can serve as rich sources of organisational/ research/teaching material when complemented by critically reflexive analysis. The presentators seek to demonstrate that the in-depth, embodied focus of autoethnographic can provide an effective model of inclusive relational practice that all manner of organisations could benefit from, not just individual contributors.

As well as silencing the respondent, Dauphinee (2010) argues traditional research denies the presence of the selfhood of the researcher too. The starting point for this endeavour involves engaging 'through the mirror' (Bolton, 2010) writing, which is described as intuitive and spontaneous, with an objective of self-illumination and exploration rather than the creation of a finished product. However, the result can be 'unsettling' in revealing insights into why we act in the ways that we do; where our sets of assumptions, mental models, and values are exposed to scrutiny and contemplation. In sharing the following vignettes we reveal our vulnerable selves to stimulate discussion in the spirit of cooperative enquiry (Reason, 1988), This reflects our deeply held belief that the 'practice' of teaching through a facilitation approach, where participants and facilitators jointly engage in dialogue and exploration, represents a genuinely 'embodied' process, in terms of sense-making being both emotive and intellectual. We choose autoethnography as a vehicle for this objective because:

1. we believe it produces evidence not typically surfaced by other methods.
2. reflexive autoethnographic scripts are not simply confessional tales but rather represent an evocative and provocative way of weaving practice orientated stories with theoretical insights.
3. by acting out our collaborative autoethnographic scripts, our conversations demonstrate the kind of ethical partnering respectful model of mutual learning we are suggesting autoethnography facilitates.

In the following sketches we attempt to demonstrate these claims.

*   *   *

Sharon's Vignette: *Doing What's Expected of Me*

I am writing about my experiences facilitating a number of workshops that I have developed and market under a 'bitesize self-leadership for researchers' banner. The underpinning ethos for the workshops is that as individuals we need to be responsible for, and proactive, in managing our own career/life, seeking out mentors for support, for example, and initiating collaboration with others. I explain to participants that the world of academe is becoming tightly regulated and monitored as funding is linked to publication rates and researchers are expected to bid for their research projects to be supported in an extremely competitive environment. Therefore, learning how to work in a multidisciplinary team is valuable because research councils and funders are more likely to fund such collaborations due to the increased innovation potential. Hence, there are external drivers influencing the way we need to think about our careers as researchers and the 'outputs' that we need to produce.

The participants in the workshops are university research associates and senior research associates who are typically on 2–3-year research only contracts. They usually work for a principal investigator/academic supervisor on large research projects, often funded by millions of pounds. It's interesting for me to find myself working at this particular university and to hear the reactions of others when they find out that I work for this institution. The workshops that I run are in a building next door to a restaurant called Browns that I loved to visit in my teenage years. I used to get the train to Cambridge from the village that I lived in with my parents and remember my first taste of independence. I liked Browns as it had big ceiling fans like those I had seen in Raffles Hotel in Singapore—on TV of course. I dreamed of going there one day, as it seemed far away and exotic (I have since been to Raffles and was disappointed). I loved the buildings in Cambridge, the parks, the river, the posters on the railings advertising the concerts and plays you could see. It seemed a world away from my tiny village—so grown up and sophisticated.

When I was 17, my history teacher, Mr Mills, told me that I could study at Cambridge University. I was on track with my grades. I did get the grades but had already decided that I wouldn't survive the Cambridge environment. I was worried that the people I would meet would be from different worlds to me and I made the assumption that I would struggle to keep up with the work. This was the story going on in my head; the tale I told others was that Cambridge was too close to 'home'. I wanted to find a university in the north away from where I grew up. This was a major life decision as I wrote myself out of going to Cambridge University through this mental chatter. It doesn't matter now of course because my life story has brought me to where I am today, but I am interested in the power of mental chatter to affect fundamental life decisions. This is one of the messages that I emphasise in the self-leadership workshops: as how we think about a situation (our mental chatter) influences the actions that we do or do not take. So best to notice what that mental chatter is telling us and to change it if it is not serving us well. This seems so simple but has such a profound impact upon the way I think and the actions that I now take. I do worry that people will think I'm evangelical about this but it has been my most significant life learning thus far.

I am transported back as a teenager as I stand at the front of a room with researchers who may have been some of the people I might have met if I had gone to Cambridge University. I smile to myself about the irony of this situation. Shall I share this story with them as an icebreaker? I'd better not this time. I feel more comfortable sticking to 'the plan'. I am worried that it might ruin my credibility as being the one who has worked out this 'self-leadership' thing; the one who has got over her teenage insecurities, but really is the one who still struggles with imposter syndrome. Is this a good story to illustrate the point I am making? I will try and be brave next time and tell it.

Many of the participants in the workshops I facilitate are scientists and work in a laboratory setting, 'at the bench'. I must admit this is where I start to feel anxious about my ability to connect to their reality, as I have no experience of doing research in either a lab environment or as part of a large research group. They talk to me about it being really competitive because there are many researchers all working on a project; all trying to get breakthrough results to make their mark. They talk about how they have to come to the lab in the middle of the night to check their experiments; tricky for one woman who was breastfeeding her newborn baby. They talk about PIs who ask them, 'no' tell them, to complete experiments in unreasonable timeframes and they tell stories about not knowing how to have conversations with their PI about authorship on their papers; they have done all the work but their PI wants to have their name on the paper—should they say anything? They talk about the uncertainty they feel about the temporality of their employment contracts and how they feel vulnerable because they don't have a secure position at the university or in their job; they tell me they will have to leave the country soon because their visa expires unless their PI gets more grant funding that can support another project they could be invited to work on.

These are real situations that participants face daily. Is it ok to say that you just have to change your mental chatter about the scenarios you describe and everything will be ok? I start to feel anxious about this 'self-leadership' message in the context of these other realities. Am I still going to have credibility when I reverse their statements to read as (1) everyone has a chance to shine and I need to take responsibility for how this might happen for me; (2) if I enjoy what I am doing, I need to take responsibility for finding a way to make it work; (3) if I have genuinely done the work, it is my personal responsibility to tell my academic supervisor that I think it is unfair that they are the first authors.

I realise through writing this vignette that my teaching/facilitation approach is to seek to understand notions of reality as the participants experience them so that we can jointly unpack their assumptions and concerns. My purpose is to open up new/different windows through which others can look so that they can make 'choices' about how to reinterpret a situation, event, or idea. I consider that to be a good facilitator/teacher, participants need to feel that their issues, concerns, and context are all appreciated. So how come I assume that when someone bothers to spend a couple of hours out of their day attending my workshop that it is my job to ensure that they leave the room feeling they now have the means by which to see the problem differently or to feel that they have the confidence to do something to change the situation? How ridiculous that I think it is 'my job' and cast myself in this starring 'all knowing' leadership role when deep down I believe that sense-making is a relational and embodied process. I am caught up in the notion that I need to be seen as 'the expert' rather than a facilitator of meaning, but I can't seem to get past this. That's interesting to me—I didn't know this until I wrote it down.

* * *

CAROLINA'S VIGNETTE—MEETING EXPECTATIONS...

Can you provide cultural awareness training for our staff? We do this every so often, when we don't forget, or when we think it is about time.

This is the message that was embedded in a conversation with a client preceding four three-hour cultural awareness sessions held over two days. In excess of one hundred participants from a variety of backgrounds work for this organisation who provide a myriad of social services to people from increasingly culturally diverse backgrounds. My questions regarding staff's experiences and any presenting issues largely go unanswered. It is assumed that I will just 'know' what they need when I get there. And also, 'can I do this in three hour sessions, as it is really hard to get people away from what they are doing?' I used to get indignant with requests like that. 'What do people expect to get in three hours? How will they ever be able to get their heads wrapped around all of this?' Not anymore, I have given up on convincing people that three hours is probably not enough to engage participants in meaningful ways regarding the complexity of culture, or that a workshop itself may not be the most effective way to enable people to develop new insights and understandings. I give them what they ask for. Not because I am lazy or indifferent; I have realised that it does not matter what I believe, that it is about what the client and, ultimately, the participants believe, and that my challenge is to start from there and take them on a journey.

So I reach for my usual outline; an experience, debrief, theoretical concepts interwoven with narratives, discussions, and time to reflect and connect all of it to the workplace, something for each learning style, and lots of opportunity for interaction. Thus far this line-up has been well received elsewhere, so I don't expect resistance. The theoretical concepts I use are oldies: Hall's 'Theory of Context' (Hall, 1976) and Hofstede's 'Individualism/Collectivism' concepts (Hofstede, 1991). Although both engage binary concepts I present them as potentially operating simultaneously and on a continuum for each individual, rather than being representative of any particular culture. I am aware of the challenges associated with presenting cultural concepts in what could be perceived as reductionist and instrumental ways. People tend to position bipolar models as 'truths' about cultures and the door is left open for stereotypes to be perpetuated. I try to manage this by demonstrating the subjectivity of binary thinking through an experiential exercise and stories I draw from my own personal experiences and those the participants are willing to share. In this way, most of the time, I think I enable people to expand their understanding of the complexity of culture, as operating in the moment, influencing interactions and affected by numerous factors.

Until today. She was sitting in the back of the room; and seemed disinterested in being there, responding to my 'hello, my name is Carolina, what is yours' with a churlish 'Kate'. Normally I am un-phased by these types of responses from participants. I realise that ultimately, people will walk into workshops with their own perspectives regarding the value of, and reasons for, being there. I simply aim to ensure that people don't feel they wasted their time and come away with something to think about. This time was no different, and after welcoming Kate, I continued going around the room greeting other participants.

So we complete the simulation and discussion abounds. It never ceases to amaze me how this one fairly simple exercise invokes such emotion and insight regarding the influence of unconscious assumptions on our sense-making in relation to others. It proves again to be an effective way to begin to unpack the influence of values, beliefs and worldviews as the underpinnings of everyday behaviours. Aided by a picture of Kohl's iceberg (Kohl & Knight, 1994) and paired with the story of the sinking of the Titanic, I reinforce the affective experience and get the point across from a cognitive perspective. The basic message is that: 'it is not just the words and actions that create misunderstanding; it is what we think these words/actions represent, and that this is coloured by what <u>we</u> think is important, appropriate, imperative,—hence from our world view'. This then leads me to introduce Hall's theory of 'context' and Hofstede's 'individualism/collectivism' concepts as examples of such sense-making perspectives, defining: what we deem as important; how we differentiate between right and wrong, and our ideas about how we relate to others, and what that looks like behaviourally.

And this is where Kate, quite abruptly, holds me to account regarding why I am unpacking these concepts in such abstract, binary terms rather than providing specific contextualised managing diversity information. In addition, she points out that these concepts are gendered and narrow and therefore, according to Kate, I am perpetuating stereotypical, either/or ways of thinking about culture that fails to address its complexity. This is when I know I have failed Kate in particular. I agree with her. I wrongly assumed that by using stories as illustrations, the complexity would become more visible. I understand her point about gender; indeed there are discussions in the intercultural field regarding the masculinist character of such treatises and how they continue to perpetuate a legacy of colonisation. However, I disagree with her about providing specific how-to information, for exactly the same reasons. And so I agree with her publicly on the former point. I do not engage her in discussion around the latter point, because I introduced the workshop as not being about specific how-to cultural information. I do remind her though that this is a three-hour workshop with a large number of participants representing a broad range of understandings. However, I do ask her if she can briefly elaborate on her perspectives. She chooses not to do so, and I wonder then to what extent I have impeded her doing so by raising the issue of time and context. I realise though, that obviously whatever I brought to the table, it did not meet Kate's expectations. Upon reflection, there are a number of things I could do differently:

- Maybe I need to be more probing in attaining information from the client.
- Maybe, I need to develop deeper insights into the profile of the organisations I work with, and to gauge the different levels of cross-cultural understanding, within the groups, more carefully.
- Maybe I do need to have some additional back-up material that I can refer to that goes beyond 'the basics'.
- Maybe I could have engaged with Kate more effectively.

In the model I introduce to participants, I stress the importance of getting an understanding of the context in which you work in order to engage effectively, to check out your assumptions, to engage in dialogue … maybe I need to heed my own advice more soundly.

*   *   *

NGAIRE'S VIGNETTE—ACADEMIC SUPERVISION: MODELLING AN AUTOETHNOGRAPHIC ETHOS

de Lauretis 'bases her conception of subjectivity on real practices and events [recognising that] language is not the sole source and locus of meaning, that habits and practices are crucial in the construction of meaning, and that through self analysing practices we can rearticulate [an embodied form of] subjectivity'. (précised in Alcoff, 1988, p. 431)

Thus far we've heard the voices of my colleagues operating as facilitator consultants. The role I will discuss reflects a more conventional academic PhD pedagogical one. However, I will endeavour to show that in responding to the needs of my students, I embrace a more deliberative partnering relationship-centred style of engagement than is traditional. I document the mutualist benefits that arise in terms of a fuller corporeal, intersubjective human experience and, importantly, the associated resultant rigour of scholarship (Bissett & Saunders, 2015).

My story, as a business school academic, invokes my relationships with the mature practitioner PhD students I supervise, whose ages range from the 30–50. My account is of a different order to the preliminary stream-of-consciousness reflection scripts delivered by my colleagues, as it details the next phase of interrogation that autoethnography engages to ensure a degree of substance underpins the dynamic critical reflexivity process I pursue. When the students check me out as a prospective supervisor inevitably they reveal that they are driven by a need to know more about a problematic issue related to an organisational environment they are associated with and wish to pursue an agenda of change. Invariably I learn about this content through the relaying of richly layered, personal autobiographical tales that identify relationship-centred issues and structural concerns (though the latter are not named as such).

As a relational leadership, and managing diversity researcher, with specialist training in qualitative research philosophy and methods, the students' approach me with a predetermined decision to pursue a qualitative research methodology approach. My training has led me to believe that while quantitative approaches can provide useful 'data' regarding relevant numerical and macro issues; the most viable way to gain in-depth insights into the everyday workings of intersubjective, processual, and systemic organisational relationships and structures is by close observational studies of the auto/ethnographic kind. Throughout my career I have frequently witnessed deeply engaged students become increasingly disconnected from the relevance of the material they are studying when being supervised in an autocratic manner where they are expected to obsess more about the validity, reliability, and generalisability of the technical measurement procedures utilised than the empirical matters under scrutiny (Bissett, 2017).

This legacy gives rise to Van Maanen's (1995, p. 139) frustrations:

> I am appalled at much of organization theory for its technocratic unimaginativeness. Our generalizations often display a mind-numbing banality and an inexplicable readiness to reduce the field to a set of unexamined, turgid, hypothetical thrusts designed to render organizations as systematic and organisation theory as safe science.

I also reject the prevailing assumption that the supervisor should take control and direct the choice of philosophy and/or methodology, to be pursued with little meaningful input from the student. In effect the student is commonly treated as an empty vessel, an apprentice awaiting enlightenment at the feet of the (most often) male professorial scholar. This exposure, and my own affiliation with the field of 'critical management studies', has made me aware of the need to value the different kinds of knowledge sources academics and practitioners bring to an issue (Bissett, 2004). Hence, my approach is to pursue a more open, partnering, relational foundation to the supervisory relationship to maintain ethical integrity, mutual respect, and shared learning outcomes (Dauphinee, 2010). I also believe such affiliations are crucial; to be effective in addressing the intricate issues organisations face today, due to the inevitable partiality of our respective inputs.

Auto/Ethnography as a 'Situated Curriculum' Framework

Autoethnography should be ethnographical in its methodological orientation, cultural in its interpretive orientation, and autobiographical in its content orientation. (Chang, 2008)

Similar to the one-on-one PhD relationships, I have utilised ethnographic texts as postgraduate coursework material to help students move from a top-down managerialist perspective, where employees are regarded as subjects to be controlled, to an appreciation of the benefits of developing a 'community-of-practice' collegial approach (Liedtka, 1999). In the reflective learning journal assignment I set to facilitate this kind of interrogation, I encourage the students to document their direct experiences of the workplace whilst linking/integrating these with *analysis* of the ethnographic analytical material. All manner of students' comment that this integrative reflective approach facilitates a significant mindset shift for them in relation to their understanding of the organisational realm (Bissett & Saunders, 2015). It also translates into increased quality of scholarly work, as their first-hand accounts enable them to practise expressing their newfound appreciation of the connections between practice and theory. The following student's script speaks to the level of sophistication attained:

At high school I studied mathematics, physics and chemistry. These disciplines relied heavily on positivist methods of research and proof. As a police officer, I was trained to be objective in my approach to investigation. The principles behind an ethnographic approach seemed to fly in the face of my understanding of effective research methods. After reading the literature and being able to see vivid examples of its application by authors such as Knights and Willmott (1999), I began to consider the possibility that perhaps there was some merit in an ethnographic approach. As I progressed through the literature, I could see the application of the theories and findings in my own working environment. In some instances, the authors could have just as easily been describing experiences in my own organisation. [He describes ethnography as] allowing the researcher to look underneath the 'skin' of an organisation, past the carefully constructed and managed corporate image, to the meanings individual employees give to the routine, mundane, day-to-day activities that make up our working lives, and the processes involved in developing those meanings.

Over the years as I marked such richly layered scripts I began to see that the documented insights were not just derived from the coursework texts but reflected the unique personal responsive accounts the students' contributed when describing their own intersubjective daily encounters (Spry, 2011). The ethnographic scripts provided the students with a way to name their own embodied life in the organisation and, in so doing, allowed them to recognise/acknowledge the glaring gap between the traditional heroic representations of management and leadership, as individually owned characteristics (leadership as 'product'), and the more dynamic emergent process revealed in the ethnographic texts and their own daily relationships.

This pedagogical experience led me to realise that facilitating their autoethnographic endeavours was providing scope for the students to name the immediacy of their complex immersion in the managerial role and thereby to performatively explore 'identity politics' issues in their own working lives (Bissett, 2017). The students would invariably respond that this initially represented a frightening awakening for them but then became a profoundly liberating experience. These elements largely related to my analytical pedagogical input and that of the critical management studies material provided to the students, which challenged the hegemonic, overly voluntarist, individualistic, agency discourse, by drawing attention to the constraining aspects of associated deterministic structures. Gherardi et al. (1998, p. 279) describe this approach as introducing 'situated curriculum [defined] as an order or pattern of activities that enable a "novice" to become a fully participating member practising a particular role', in this case critically reflexive autoethnography.

Ellis and Bochner (2000, p. 737) frame the autoethnographic method thus:

> I start with my personal life. I pay attention to my physical feelings, thoughts and emotions. I use what I call systematic sociological introspection and emotional recall to try to understand an experience I lived through. Then I write my experience as a story.

Ellis and Bochner draw our attention to the need for the rich descriptions of emotive immersion to be contextualised by intellectual rigour if autoethnography, as a methodology, is to be a genuinely embodied representational form. As the approach has been trenchantly critiqued as narcissistic and superficial, preoccupied with simple nostalgia (Strangleman, 2012), then in terms of analysis it is important to compliment the experiential account with a critical reflexivity reference point. This is where I see my partnership role coming into play in drawing attention to the potential limits of everyday ways of knowing, and pointing to the positive contribution critical theorising can make to enhance autoethnographic methods, by increasing understanding of relational connections and providing the emancipatory impetus that the participants in the learning process seek (Warren, 2011).

Following this performativity focus, we will now attempt to situate the two preceding narratives of Sharon and Carolina's through reference to a Critical Management Studies perspective. This will involve demonstrating the benefits of linking particularist personal reflections with a disciplined critical reflexivity manoeuvre to substantively inform a preferred 'situated [leadership] practice' model (Kempster & Stewart, 2010). This approach is based upon a relational epistemology that advances a deeper understanding of informed practice developed through 'situated activity'.

AUTOETHNOGRAPHY EXPLORATION PROCESS: SITUATING FIRST-HAND EXPERIENCE

> Autoethnography allows the researcher to adopt a hyper-reflexive stance where the autoethnographer is encouraged to conduct a study within a study that involves depth of self-disclosure and analysis. (Kempster & Stewart, 2010, p. 206)

While an initial reading of Sharon and Carolina's expressive, personally reflective, texts may seem to relay common issues surrounding the limits of everyday communication processes, a deeper CMS reflexive reading of each script reveals a great deal about the current constraints of hierarchically structured institutions and the elitist precepts surrounding teaching and facilitation practice. As Holman Jones (2010) points out, the conditions and consequences of the telling process that autoethnography facilitates are inevitably political, inseparable from the story in terms of its contingency, limitations, and potential. Hence, each of Sharon and Carolina's scripts anxiously refer to the organisational expectations imposed on them to perform in top-down, directive ways; to concentrate on instrumental preoccupations; and to proffer overly individualistic behaviourist and cognitive explanations for what, in reality, are culturally embedded encounters. The intention here is not to critique the authors' point of view but rather to demonstrate their discomfort with the imposed 'identity politics' order, which underpins classical perceptions of the teacher/facilitator role. Secondly, to offer an alternative reflexivity perspective that builds on the important 'situational' content potential present in the autoethnographic texts.

In revealing the insecurities associated with individual sense-making processes, Sharon and Carolina also surface the leadership representational codes where the performance of the individual is key to maintain status, efficacy, and most importantly, control (Bissett, 2017). Each narrator identifies the overwhelming pressures they feel to come up with the goods and act in ways that are expected (hence their titles are fitting), despite their inclination to work more collegially. We see the paradox that results then when Kate both expects to be 'led', by the formally appointed facilitator, and yet, calling on her own clearly well-informed understanding of the limits of behaviourist constructions, resists any such perceived imposition.

The middle managers Ngaire teaches report a similar sense of burden and refer to the disjuncture between the formal disembodied representation of their role and the more informal, emotively connected, current reality of their day-to-day management-employee relations. The former emphasises the heroic leader as always ready to articulate 'the' strategic vision, while the latter makes visible the more ad hoc, confused, and often arbitrary mode of human engagement, which relies on reciprocal input to maintain some sense of order. We see elements of this in Sharon's account of the junior researchers' concerns over their formerly portrayed, 'follower-led' situation, in relation to their senior supervisors, when the reality is they carry the major load in terms of taking 'the lead' regarding the day-to-day research practice.

268 N. BISSETT ET AL.

We learn that for all the rhetoric surrounding team participation and the valuing of innovative input, the system only formally recognises the expertise and contribution of the formally appointed leader (in Sharon's example it is the PIs in relation to research grant applications). Equally, the senior managers who engage Carolina and provide her consultancy brief make it clear that space for the voices and views of the employees don't figure in their expectation of her restricted timetable. Rather the assumption is that she will deliver on her role as a leader/facilitator, being both a product herself, in terms of performance attributes that they are purchasing, but also that she will achieve a predetermined set of results—namely: transformational change—(despite such an impossibility given the lack of context/time to be able to build worthwhile relational encounters).

The sets of command-and-control demands are thus multilayered. We also witness this with Sharon's engagement, where she is expected to demonstrate (perform) a positive (positivist) solutions-fixated, self-disciplining mode of self-leadership. In the process, it is anticipated that she will 'influence' her followers in ways that ensure their collective concerns are reduced to an individualistic focus. The emphasis on imagined voluntary 'choice' thus leads to a conundrum where participants are told they can be in control of areas that are, in reality, being significantly impinged upon by structural issues. This then downplays the existence of systems of inequitable institutional power and politics, and, in 'identity performance 'terms, is designed to preserve an order (appearance) of compliance and continuity.

By unpacking embedded belief structures we understand why the gap between traditional leadership/teacher/facilitator depictions and the complexity and unpredictability of everyday relationally embedded encounters leads to the sense of vulnerability that both Carolina and Sharon give voice to, and which many managers experience, but feel they must hide to retain their formal identity position. We also observe that the myth of the in-control leader prevents us from engaging a more productive processual understanding of the immense leaderful potential that lies dormant in organisations. This is visible in Carolina's account where the 'wealth' of cultural diversity present, in terms of the identity of the employees, is unable to be drawn on as a resource and her awareness that workshopping complex identity issues may not be best handled through such a format.

In Sharon's vignette she declares: 'it is my job to ensure that they leave the room feeling that they now have the means by which to see the problem differently or to feel that they have the confidence to do something to change the situation'. In stating this, she demonstrates that, though seeking to adopt a facilitator role, she feels constrained to take on the individualist self-contained leader identity role to deliver measurable outcomes for the groups she works with. Engaging the potential of autoethnography, in terms of its embodied character, could help such presenters raise awareness of the ordinariness of human frailty in relation to such identity politics issues. Ancona, Malone, Orlikowski, and Senge's (2007) *Incomplete Leader* paper is a useful reference point in this regard as they dispel the myth of the 'all knowing' leader. Utilising the storytelling aspects of autoethnographic texts could also provide an entry point to demonstrate that meaning making is collectively derived. Rather than the formally appointed leader taking responsibility for such input, expectations of change could then be set by the participants, with the presenter guiding/facilitating the dialogue.

In addition adopting an autoethnographic relational philosophical stance means the 'situational practice' orientation all for the identification/addressing of inequitable employment relations issues. For example, displacing the anticipated prescriptive macho theories (like Hall and Hofstede) with more tentative, openly subjectivist, situational accounts could encourage the likes of Kate to enter the collaborative reflection dialogue process. Indeed, creating space for multiple interpretations does not undermine the forging of key insights; on the contrary impressionistic experiential input is more likely to draw out the complexity through the close readings they provide. Applying autoethnographic methods in the workplace therefore has potential for empowering prospects because the needs/concerns of all participants are valued and made visible. The tendency to apathy on the part of employees, who are constantly told what needs to happen in terms of change, and their part in it, could be overcome through such a mutual respect approach.

Challenge and Reward: The Dis-ordered Autoethnographic Process

However, as Cann and de Meulenaere (2012, p. 2) point out, this kind of 'work is messy and complicated; [therefore] it would be disingenuous to write a sanitized version of it from a falsely objective and dispassionate distance'.

Hence, behind the scene, the initial response of both Sharon and Carolina to the collective unpacking of the texts in this critically reflexive manner was to initially express a sense of frustration regarding the gap that they experience in terms of their understanding of the theory of the situation and their capacity to address the limits imposed in practice. Nonetheless, following our intense discussions they decided they like the idea of sharing an autoethnography text with their respondents, as a starting point for discussion and dialogue, rather than simply providing the theories and models which tends to encourage passivity.

Through the co-produced autoethnographic process, we created a space for a genuine shared conversation amongst ourselves where we explored the value of autoethnographic for enhancing the application of teaching and facilitation processes. This performance piece is the result of our mutually respectful, three-way partnership relationship where our different forms of know-how have contributed to an enlarged picture (Watson, 2012, p. 683). We consider our sense of ongoing companionate connectedness represents a source of educational inspiration for each of us and provides a meaningful corporeal working model of teaching and facilitating 'relational leaderful' practice. We hope the reader/s agree.

References

Adams, T. E., & Holman Jones, T. (2011). Telling Stories: Reflexivity, Queer Theory, and Autoethnography. *Cultural Studies Critical Methodologies, 11*(2), 108–116.

Alcoff, L. (1988). Cultural Feminism Versus Post Structuralism: The Identity Crisis in Feminist Theory. *Signs, 13*(31), 405–436.

Ancona, D., Malone, T. W., Orlikowski W. J., & Senge, P. M. (2007, February). In Praise of the Incomplete Leader. *Harvard Business Review*, 94–100.

Birnbaum, N. (1971). *Toward a Critical Sociology*. New York: Oxford University Press.

Bissett, N. (2004). Diversity Writ Large: Forging the Link Between Diverse People and Diverse Organisational Possibilities'. *Journal of Organizational Change Management, 17*(2), 315–325.

Bissett, N. (2006, July). The Pedagogy of Critical Ethnography: An Organisational Trojan Horse? *Current Developments in Ethnographic Research in the Social and Management Sciences*. Liverpool University Management School Conference, United Kingdom.

Bissett, N. (2017). Beyond Subjectless Abstractions: A Feminist Praxis Contribution. In A. Pullen, N. Harding, & M. Phillips (Eds.), *Dialogues in Critical Management Studies*. Bingley, UK: Emerald Publishing Ltd.

Bissett, N., & Saunders, S. (2015). Criticality and Collegiality: A Method for Humanizing Everyday Practice? *Journal of Management Education, 39*(5), 597–625.

Bolton, G. (2010). *Reflective Practice Writing & Professional Development.* London: Sage.

Burkitt, I. (2012). Emotional Reflexivity: Feeling, Emotion and Imagination in Reflexive Dialogues. *Sociology, 46*(3), 458–472.

Cann, C., & de Meulenaere, E. J. (2012). Critical Co-Constructed Autoethnography. *Cultural Studies Critical Methodologies, XX*(X), 1–13.

Chandler, A. (2012). Self-injury as Embodied Emotion Work: Managing Rationality, Emotions and Bodies. *Sociology, 46*(3), 442–457.

Chang, H. (2008). Autoethnography as Method: Raising Cultural Consciousness of Self and Others. In *Electronic Magazine of Multicultural Education.* Walnut Creek, CA: Left Coast Press. http://www.eastern.edu/publications/emme

Clifford, J. (1983). On Ethnographic Authority. *Representations, 1,* 118–146.

Clifford, J., & Marcus, G. E. (1986). *Writing Culture: The Poetics and Politics of Ethnography.* Berkeley, CA: University of California Press.

Cunliffe, A. L. (2009). Retelling Tales of the Field: In Search of Organizational Ethnography 20 Years On. *Organizational Research Methods, 13*(2), 224–239.

Dauphinee, E. (2010). The Ethics of Autoethnography. *Review of International Studies, 36*(3), 799–818.

Denzin, N. K. (1989). *Interpretive Biography.* Newbury Park, CA: Sage.

Douglas, M., & Ney, S. (1988). *Missing Persons: A Critique of the Social Sciences.* Berkeley, CA: University of California Press.

Ellis, C., & Bochner, A. P. (2000). Autoethnography, Personal Narrative, Reflexivity. In N. K. Denzin & Y. S. Lincoln (Eds.), *Handbook of Qualitative Research.* Thousand Oaks, CA: Sage.

Gertz, C. (1973). Thick Description: Toward an Interpretive Theory of Culture. In *The Interpretation of Cultures: Selected Essays* (pp. 3–30). New York: Basic Books.

Gherardi, S., Nicolini, D., & Odella, F. (1998). Toward a Social Understanding of How People Learn in Organizations: The Notion of Situated Curriculum. *Management Learning, 29*(3), 273–297.

Hall, E. T. (1976). *Beyond Culture.* Toronto: Anchor Books/Double Day.

Hofstede, G. (1991). *Culture: Software for the Mind.* New York: MacGraw-Hill.

Holman Jones, S. (2010). Burnt: Writing Torch Singers and Torch Singing. *Cultural Studies Critical Methodologies, 10*(4), 283–294.

Kempster, S., & Stewart, J. (2010). Becoming a Leader: A Co-produced Autoethnographic Exploration Situated Learning of Leadership Practice. *Management Learning, 41*(2), 205–219.

Knights, D., & Willmott, H. (1999). *Management Lives: Power and Identity in Work Organizations.* London: Sage.

Kohl, L. R., & Knight, J. M. (1994). *Developing Intercultural Awareness.* Intercultural Press.

Leach, E. R. (1984). Glimpses of the Unmentionable in the History of British Social Anthropology. *Annual Review of Anthropology, 13*, 1–24.

Liedtka, J. (1999). Linking Competitive Advantage with Communities of Practice. *Journal of Management Inquiry, 8*(1), 5–16.

Mitchell, J. C. (1969). *Social Networks in Urban Situations.* Manchester: Manchester University Press.

Muncey, T. (2010). *Creating Autoethnographies.* London: Sage.

Raelin, J. A. (2016). *Leadership-as-Practice: Theory and Application.* New York: Routledge.

Reason, P. (Ed.). (1988). *Human Inquiry in Action: Developments in New Paradigm Research.* London: Sage.

Schneider, A., & Wright, C. (2013). *Anthropology and Art Practice.* New York: Bloomsbury Academic.

Scott-Hoy, K., & Ellis, C. (2008). 11 Moving Pictures, Discovering Heartfelt Autoradiography. In J. G. Knowles & L. Cole (Eds.), *Handbook of the Arts in Qualitative Research, Perspectives, Methodologies, Examples and Issues.* London: Sage.

Spry, T. (2011). *Body, Paper, Stage: Writing and Performing Autoethnography.* Walnut Creek, CA: Left Coast Press.

Stephens, N., & Delamont, S. (2006). Balancing the Berimbau: Embodied Ethnographic Understanding. *Qualitative Inquiry, 12*(2), 316–339.

Strangleman, T. (2012). Work Identity and Crisis? Rethinking the Problem of Attachments and Loss at Work. *Sociology, 46*(3), 411–425.

Turner, V. (1974). *Dramas, Fields and Metaphors: Symbolic Action in Human Society.* Ithaca, NY: Cornell University Press.

Uhl-Bien, M., & Ospina, S. (Eds.). (2012). *Advancing Relational Leadership Research: A Dialogue Among Perspectives.* Charlotte, NC: Information Age Publishing.

Van Maanen, M. (1995). On the Epistemology of Reflective Practice. *Teachers and Teaching: Theory and Practice, 1*(1), 33–50.

Wall, S. (2006). An Autoethnography on Learning About Autoethnography. *International Institute for Qualitative Methodology (IIQM), 5*(2), 146–160.

Warren, J. T. (2011). Reflexive Teaching: Toward Critical Autoethnographic Practices of/in/on Pedagogy. *Cultural Studies Critical Methodologies, 11*(2), 139–144.

Watson, T. J. (2012). Making Organisational Ethnography. *Journal of Organizational Ethnography, 1*(1), 15–22.

Worsley, P. (1997). *Knowledges: Culture, Counterculture, Subculture.* New York: The New Press.

CHAPTER 15

Methodology: From Paradigms to Paradox

Tom Vine

In my native field, I have noticed an emerging trend for highly politicised analysis, particularly in what has become known as 'critical management studies'. It is a personal preference, but I have lost my appetite for discussions of power and politics. Critical management studies seems to have become a one-stop shop for all things leftist. It also appears to have created a straw man of mainstream management studies. This is not to say that I consider myself a right wing conservative. I don't. My reservation here is that leftist politics should not have a monopoly on all things critical.

An example may help. In the final year of my doctoral programme, my university won a research grant to explore the concept of ecological resilience from various disciplinary perspectives. I was recruited as part of the team. Unexpectedly, my data revealed that small-scale organic farming methods can be more destructive than large-scale non-organic methods. It seemed that economies of scale—in one sense at least—gave rise to ecologies of scale. My paper was rejected on the basis that it 'did not contribute to the message that we want to send'. I was flabbergasted. I knew this sort of thing happened in newsrooms, but at universities?

At the time, I found solace in writers such as Jeffrey Pfeffer, Gerald Salancik, and Karl Weick and, more generally, in what might be considered the proto-critical management discourses of the 1970s. However, unlike their contemporary counterparts (for whom power and

T. Vine (✉)
University of Suffolk, Ipswich, UK

© The Author(s) 2018
T. Vine et al. (eds.), *Ethnographic Research and Analysis*,
https://doi.org/10.1057/978-1-137-58555-4_15

> *politics repeatedly trump other considerations), their intellectual methods instead prioritised ontology, subtlety, and complexity. And notably, though by no means explicit, I detected in their work an analytical sensitivity to paradox. Paradox does not sit easily in contemporary critical management discourses because it would, in effect, undermine the ideological proclivities of the movement. And I suspect an analytical focus on paradox would undermine ideological convictions found elsewhere in the academy.*

Introduction

Since the publication of Burrell and Morgan's seminal text on sociological paradigms in 1979, the framing of social science research methods has remained largely unchanged. Though illuminating in so many ways, their thesis has had the effect of entrenching ideological positions (see, e.g., Hammersley, 1992, p. 182). If we are to propel our understanding of human behaviour to new pastures, we need to initiate an analytical shift away from paradigms. This chapter argues that ethnography represents an excellent vantage point for both experiencing and understanding paradox. As part of this discussion I consider why it is that we find paradox so troubling, before presenting a case for its alternative methodological and pedagogical potential in a world dominated—both on the left and right—by linear cause-and-effect ontologies.

I begin by exploring the literature on paradox before conceptualising as paradoxes several familiar challenges to the ethnographer. These include the apparent impossibility of internalising an 'exotic' culture while simultaneously maintaining professional distance, and the expectation for ethnographers to concurrently convey to their subjects both empathy and honesty. Although similar concerns have been extensively debated under the rubric of ethics, this is not the intention for this discussion. Instead, the emphasis here is on both justifying and bolstering the quality and reliability of ethnographic data. To this end, it is argued that paradox must be celebrated rather than concealed or maligned since it is, for the most part, representative of social interaction itself.

In a rather curious twist, paradox is paradoxically indicative of methodological strength. To illustrate this another way, Alvesson and Deetz (2000, p. 66, emphasis added) have suggested that 'interpretivists and others often labelled as "subjective" often have the *better claim to objectivity* through the way they allow alternative language games and the possibility of alternative constructions arising from existing communities denying both research community conceptions and preferred methods as privileged and universal.' Since interpretivists (of whom ethnographers are perhaps the most notable given their direct engagement with their subjects) are more sensitive to social constructions and research bias, they ultimately produce more 'objective' data than their positivist counterparts. And this, of course, becomes the definitive methodological paradox.

A Personal Interest in Paradox

As a master's student in the early 2000s, my research focussed on the conceptual parameters of utopia and dystopia. I soon noticed a peculiar quality to the concepts. Although habitually understood as polar opposites, a more nuanced interpretation revealed them not as opposites but as concepts with a tendency to morph into one another. On an academic level, at least, this was to be my first encounter with paradox and this is where my scholarly interest in the concept most likely stems from. From here, however, my growing intellectual curiosity for paradox is closely linked to ethnography; that I became an ethnographer meant that, sooner or later, I would be grappling with the concept. Nothing is quite as it seems when conducting an ethnography. As Holliday (1995, p. 17) reminds us: 'Textbooks on methodology can never quite prepare researchers for the actual experience of doing [ethnographic] fieldwork.' The ethnographer finds herself in this peculiar position of simultaneously belonging and not belonging. It is a sort of limbo or liminal state, as several of the other chapters in this book have illustrated. The point is, of course, paradox is much more noticeable when actively and consciously carrying out an ethnography because you are living, experiencing, participating, *and* observing all at once. The expectations of ethnography force us to pay attention to what is happening rather than simply accepting it without question. As we will see, paradox is endemic to everyday life and this—of course—is the reason it pervades ethnographic experience.

Beyond the boundaries of particular research projects, my reading with attention to paradox has taken me on a more extensive ethnographic journey; the more I read, the more it seems that paradox is unavoidable. It permeates experiences across academic disciplines. This is part of the reason why books such as the one you are reading are so revealing. By sharing knowledge between disciplines these experiences, frustrations, inconsistencies, and contradictions with which each of us is all too familiar on a personal level are brought into the open where they can be formally acknowledged and—hopefully—better understood.

Some of the questions tackled in this chapter have been previously explored by philosophers. However, I cannot ignore the fact that it is my ethnographic experience that has driven my curiosity for paradox and shaped my conceptual enquiries. Indeed, such an approach affords a fresh vantage point. I wonder how many English language idioms and phrases are based on paradoxes: 'the grass is always greener on the other side,' 'you don't know what you have until it's gone,' 'try to please all and you end up pleasing none,' and so on. There is something alarming about the implication that unschooled wisdom appears to have a better handle on these ironies than does abstract philosophical thought.

Understanding Paradox

The *Oxford English Dictionary* defines paradox as 'a seemingly absurd or contradictory statement or proposition which when investigated may prove to be well founded or true'. The *Oxford Companion to Philosophy* delineates multiple uses of the word but asks ultimately: 'is there any common feature marked by this term?' In response, it suggests that 'part of any feature would be the idea of conflict.' By recourse to synonym, then, paradox refers to a manifestation of contradiction or conflict. For the purposes of this chapter, however, I would like to deemphasise these aspects, not to deny their relevance but to reconstruct paradox as something with unique pedagogical potential. Put simply, in assuming an ideological position (either consciously or implicitly), we automatically open ourselves up to unintentionally lending support to the opposite position. In this sense, we are better off taking steps to distance ourselves from ideology, and incorporating this as part of our methodological framing. There is, perhaps, a lesson here: where we seek to occupy a particular ontological and epistemological position, perhaps we ought to convey to the reader the preventative steps we are taking to ensure such a framing doesn't descend into ideological conviction?

Two final points of caution. First, my intention here is not reductionist. I am not attempting to do for paradox what others have attempted to do, for example, for class (Marx), power (Nietzsche), or pleasure (Freud). Rather I see paradox as a concept with analytical potential across the full range of scholarly pursuits, irrespective of whether our particular orientation is intellectual, emotional, or ethical. Second, we do well to ask ourselves the following question: is analysis focussed on paradox likely to yield anything different to analysis focussed on dialectics? Certainly, Hegel's notion of the dialectic might legitimately be considered a precursor to the idea that paradox is a central concept to all of life (see, e.g., Singer, 2009, p. 13). Indeed, operationalised under Marx, dialectics described the way in which contradiction elicits progress (see, e.g., Stent, 1978, p. 119). However, this should not suggest that my own observations are little more than a repackaging of Marx. For Marx, contradiction spurred evolution (and this argument has been lent new currency by Harari, 2011). My ethnographic experiences and readings of the experiences of others have demonstrated something else: that contradiction seems to be either ignored or attempts are made to either resolve or dissolve the contradiction. Both reactions, I argue, are problematic. Furthermore, for Stent, 'these conflicts and contradictions are unlikely to be resolved within the context of a western tradition' (ibid., p. 146). My position is notably different: paradox appears to be endemic to the human condition and hence, most likely, *ir*resolvable, irrespective of whether eastern or western traditions are authorised. Indeed, the desire to resolve contradictions reveals our difficulty in comprehending paradox; paradox transcends cause-and-effect ontologies and hence the suggestion it can be resolved loses traction.

PARADOXICAL EXPERIENCES IN ETHNOGRAPHY

As Atkinson and Hammersley (1994, p. 256) have previously observed, 'paradox lies at the heart of the ethnographic endeavour and of the ethnography as a textual product.' Contemporary ethnography 'explores the discontinuities, paradoxes, and inconsistencies of culture and action [and does so] not in order to resolve or reconcile those differences' (ibid.). I here expand on this interpretation and in so doing identify ten paradoxes inherent to the ethnographic experience. These are the participant-observer paradox, the familiarisation paradox, the insider-outsider paradox, the honesty paradox, the consensus paradox, the all-too-human paradox, the certainty paradox, the plagiarism paradox, the linguistic construction paradox, and the autoethnographic paradox.

278   T. VINE

The Participant-Observer Paradox

There is a categorical paradox immanent in ethnography. The implication that the researcher is expected to, concurrently, participate *and* observe is problematic. As Boncori has observed (see Chap. 11), this very essence of ethnography is a paradox—or contradiction—*par excellence*. Barnes too (see Chap. 7) echoes Punch's (2005) concern as regards the ethnographer's capacity for observation when preoccupied with participation: 'One of the key objections to relying upon participant observational data is that it raises the question about how effectively a participant observer can observe the group if they are participating fully.' This dilemma is brought into relief if conceptualised slightly differently: the apparent impossibility of internalising an 'exotic' culture while simultaneously maintaining professional distance. Boggis (see Chap. 5), for example, reports that 'immersing myself within the culture of a community in order to study it, raised tensions in respect of distance and the maintenance of objectivity.' My own experience at Findhorn (see Chap. 2) is noteworthy too in this respect. Prior to my own ethnography at the community, sociologist Carol Riddell had visited Findhorn. However, it would appear that she rapidly 'went native'. In 1991, with the support of Findhorn's own press, she published a book entitled *The Findhorn Community: Creating a Human Identity for the 21st Century*. On the back cover, her biography reads as follows

> Carol Riddell lectured in sociology at Strathclyde and Lancaster Universities until 1978, after which she studied healing, clairvoyance and herbalism. She has lived in the Findhorn Community since 1983 and is a devotee of Sai Baba.

Riddell was, it seems, unable to transcend the paradox; she was unable to internalise an 'exotic' culture while simultaneously maintaining professional distance. Now, there may be many reasons for this. Unlike mine, for example, I am unsure whether or not her first visit to Findhorn was consciously intended as an ethnography. This aside, however, she was apparently unable to reconcile her credentials as a sociologist with her newfound New Age identity. But this begs the question: must we always choose? Intellectual curiosity is, by definition, roused by the unknown. Uncertainty, as Barnes ultimately acknowledges (see Chap. 7), is at its core. All too often, academic researchers *are* expected to choose and it is presumed that

METHODOLOGY: FROM PARADIGMS TO PARADOX   279

they will select the rational at the expense of the emotional. For futurist, Alvin Toffler:

> Science first gave man a sense of mastery over his environment, and hence over the future. By making the future seem malleable, instead of immutable, it shattered the opiate religions that preached passivity and mysticism. Today, mounting evidence that society is out of control breeds disillusionment with science. In consequence, we witness a… revival of mysticism. Suddenly, astrology is the rage. Zen, yoga, séances, and witchcraft become popular pastimes. Cults form around the search for Dionysian experience, for non-verbal and supposedly non-linear communication. We are told it is more important to 'feel' than to 'think', as though there were a contradiction between the two. Existentialist oracles join Catholic mystics, Jungian psychologists, and Hindu gurus in exalting the mystical and emotional against the scientific and rational. (Toffler, 1970, p. 406)

Toffler describes the difficulty we have in reconciling the emotional and the rational and the extent to which each camp responds to this difficulty by entrenching themselves ideologically. History suggests this appears to be our default response. Of the participation paradox, Jackson (1989, p. 135, cited in Rose, 1990, p. 58) comments that:

> Many of my most valued insights into Kuranko social life have followed from comparable cultivation and imitation of practical skills: hoeing a farm, dancing (as one body), lighting a kerosene lamp properly, weaving a mat, consulting a diviner. To break the habit of using linear communication model for understanding bodily praxis, it is necessary to adopt a methodological strategy of joining in without ulterior motive and literally putting oneself in the place of other persons; inhabiting their world. Participation thus becomes an end in itself rather than a means of gathering closely observed data which will be subject to interpretation elsewhere after the event.

If you genuinely participate you will, in effect, *observe*. Equally, observation can readily be construed as participation, in the sense that the observer 'constructs' the observed. Here we might invoke myriad studies of surveillance or, indeed, the *observer effect* in physics. In sum, participation and observation and not mutually exclusive; for our purposes at least, participation (when conceptualised as an end in itself) is effective 'observation'. By concurrently participating *and* observing; by internalising 'exotic' cultures *while at the same time* maintaining professional distance,

280   T. VINE

the ethnographer has a unique opportunity and, I argue, a unique duty. Quite simply, it is a question of intuiting balance.

The Familiarisation Paradox

Expertise is typically understood by virtue of familiarity with a subject area. As scholars, perhaps above all else, we are expected to be *familiar*. In ethnography, it is rarely this straightforward. Silverman (2007) points out that ethnography actively seeks out both the mundane in the remarkable and the remarkable in the mundane. Another way of looking at this is to either render the 'exotic' familiar (i.e., to familiarise ourselves with a new culture to understand it from that perspective) or to make the familiar 'exotic' (i.e., to 'defamiliarise' our existing culture to gain a fresh perspective). Bell (1999, p. 21) comments of this process in my native field: '[Some] organizational ethnography involves a process of defamiliarization, through which concepts like "strategy" and "human resource management" are made strange.' The notion of deliberately defamiliarising oneself is, of course, paradoxical, but Hammersley and Atkinson (2007, p. 9) argue that it is necessary 'in an effort to make explicit the presuppositions he or she takes for granted as a culture member'. This paradox of familiarisation is likely part of the broader concern academic ethnographers experience in terms of expertise. As academic ethnographers we are simultaneously expected to be an expert (as befits the expectations of our students or subjects) while at the same time each of us is, at times, doubtful of our own abilities, not least in terms of *in*experience. The notion of *imposter syndrome* therefore takes on an interesting guise under the vicissitudes of ethnography. Do all ethnographers suffer perpetually from imposter syndrome? To complicate matters further, Hammersley and Atkinson (1983, pp. 84–85, as cited in Holliday, 1995, p. 28) have suggested that in many ways the most favourable role for a participant observer to adopt in the early stages of fieldwork is as a 'socially acceptable incompetent'. Rather than present oneself as an expert, which may have the corollary effect of condescension, intentionally presenting oneself as foolish may well be more appropriate. It is probably part of the reason that ethnographers can't help but lie (Fine & Shulman, 2009, p. 193). However, as Vine (2010, p. 646) has commented of the same text, 'this thoroughly disheartening thought is alleviated, at least in part, with the hope that fibs too can be creative': the ethnographer's falsehoods create ethnographic realities. But is this any different outside the experiential flow of ethnography? No. As Sharon notes in her vignette (see Chap. 14), reflecting on her professional experience as a career coach, 'I am caught up in the notion that I need to be seen as "the expert" rather than a facilitator of meaning, but I can't seem to get past this.'

The Insider-Outsider Paradox

For Rose (1990, p. 10), ethnography represents a 'democratic epistemology' implying that 'the thinking of the ethnographer and those studied inhabit the same historical moment.' Atkinson and Hammersley (1994, p. 256) explain that

> prolonged immersion in 'the field' and the emphasis on participant observation commit the ethnographer to a shared social world. He or she has become a 'stranger' or 'marginal native' in order to embark upon a process of cultural learning that is predicated on a degree of 'surrender' to 'the Other'. The epistemology of participant observation rests on the principle of interaction and the 'reciprocity of perspectives' between social actors. The rhetoric is thus egalitarian: observer and observed as inhabitants of a shared social and cultural field, their respective cultures different but equal, and capable of mutual recognition by virtue of a shared humanity.

Most students of ethnography will be familiar with this 'egalitarian' approach. However, we have a problem. In approaching ethnography in this way, do we prevent ourselves from obtaining an external perspective? Atkinson and Hammersley go on to acknowledge that the classic texts of ethnography often inscribed a distinction between the Author and the Other as a means of securing this external perspective. So which approach is better? To 'talk the talk' of egalitarian rhetoric (in the interests of securing insider status), or to preserve outsider status with the perspective advantages that may bring but risk accusations of superiority? You're damned if you do and you're damned if you don't. Furthermore, for those already considered insiders in one sense or another (by the virtue of skin colour, perhaps, or some other shared demographic) Ganga and Scott (2006, p. 1) identify another complication:

> [T]o a large extent, interviewing within one's own 'cultural' community— as an insider—affords the researcher a degree of social proximity that, paradoxically, increases awareness amongst both researcher and participant of the social divisions that exist between them.

In the sphere of organisational ethnography, Holliday (1995, p. 26) suggests that 'The process of managing one's identity as a researcher—and the more complex schizophrenic identity of researcher-cum-employee—is itself very stressful, involving continual renegotiation.' This is relevant as it demonstrates how the researcher is both insider and outsider simultaneously, and echoes the 'professionally-induced schizophrenia' described by Mascarenhas-Keyes (1987, p. 180). And how uncanny a resemblance does this have to life more generally! Most of us will be accustomed to the experience of the first few months in a new job with a new employer. This schizophrenic positionality is thoroughly familiar. But, even beyond that immersion period, though not necessarily by name, many of us will be aware of the 'pronoun test'. For Rousseau (1998) the pronoun test is acutely relevant to conceptualisations of identity: do employees refer to the organisation for which they work (or are a member) as 'we' or 'us', or as 'they' or 'them'? Or to what degree do participants use both, at different times, depending on how they might feel about the organisation? Certainly, my own experience of working for the University of Suffolk alternates between a desire to belong to it and a desire to distance myself from it. Holliday (ibid.) continues:

> Initial entry to the field can involve 'learning on the job' to be done during the period of fieldwork. Thus, it is possible to be both insider and outsider as a not yet fully fledged member of the organisation. The initial focus of fieldwork is concentrated around learning how to do the task, leaving little room for reflection. Later, when the job is learnt and a position within the firm consolidated, it is possible to take a more detached view of the study setting.

What could be more effective, then? Without even trying, an ethnographer is getting multiple perspectives of her setting simply by virtue of the learning process. Indeed, this interpretation need not be restricted to the context of work. We could easily substitute the business for wider family, community, school, social club, gang, and so on.

I return, once again, to my own experience at Findhorn. I believed that was perceived by my subjects as a 'mainstreamer' in their 'alternative' community. To some extent, this was probably self-consciousness. But what was I to make of the situation? I had read extensively on ethnography and although aware of the diverse approaches within the method, I certainly knew one thing: I didn't want to emulate the colonial tradition of cultural superiority. But I faced a problem. So conscious was I to secure insider status that I began to denigrate mainstream culture and I did so with 'born again' vigour. I engaged in what might be described as *ethnomasochism*. Worse still, I didn't really believe what I was saying, at least not without qualification (which I withheld). I was, in effect, engaging in the egalitarian rhetoric Hammersley and Atkinson describe. At the time I felt dreadful. But in the years that have passed since, I have accepted this. I see it less as deceptive and more as representative of real life. When introduced to new people in *any* situation, we rarely take issue with their beliefs. We search instead for common ground and, in so doing, inevitably compromise—and subconsciously re-evaluate—our own beliefs. My conduct at Findhorn was no different. In order to secure insider status, I had no choice but to *Other* the outsider. This felt like a natural response. The outsider (and her ritual denigration) was essential to securing insider status. The two were intertwined. Notably, Cooper and Law (1995, p. 244) draw on the work of Starobinski to argue that there is a false distinction between inside and outside:

> inside and outside are not separate places; they refer to a correlative structure in which "complicity is mixed with antagonism... No outside would be conceivable without an inside fending it off, resisting it, 'reacting' to it." (Starobinski, 1975, p. 342)

Later in the same text, they draw on the words of Latour and in so doing explain that 'the inside and the outside world can reverse into one another very easily' (Latour, 1985, p. 154, as cited in Cooper & Law, 1995, p. 244). The field of psychology is especially revealing in this sense. Jackson and Carter (1985, p. 22) remind us that Lacan rejects the idea of an autonomous unitary Self, in favour of a subject mediated by the preexisting world of the Other. Or as Bowie (1979, p. 135) puts it: 'The subject is made and re-made in his encounter with the Other.' There is something decidedly paradoxical about the relationship between the individual and the collective. The absence of autonomy is posited as an unfillable *lack* at the centre of our being. Furthermore, in *The Abilene Paradox*, Harvey (1988, p. 96) reflects on the fact that for Jung *any* dimension of human behaviour can also be expressed in its opposite form. It is also worth noting that it is within the field of psychology that we can readily observe the paradox between social identity and cognitive dissonance. On the one hand, social identity theorists suggest it is usual to possess conflicting views about something. In their study of women construction students, Powell et al. (2010, p. 573),

284   T. VINE

for example, conclude that 'identity is often contested ground for women construction students who, while subscribing to an ideal that the sector is accessible to all those who want to work in it, uphold gendered stereotypes about women's suitability for so-called masculine work such as construction.' And yet on the other hand, theories such as cognitive dissonance suggest to possess conflicting views is deeply unsettling.

The Honesty Paradox

The term is not used, but Gans (1962) in Bryman and Bell (2011, p. 124) reveals a paradox when exploring the ethics of ethnography: 'the researcher must be dishonest to get honest data.' Indeed, Denzin (1968), cited in the same volume, argues for an 'anything goes' stance as long as it does not harm participants or damage the discipline. More recently, during the ethnography stream at the European Group for Organizational Studies (EGOS) (2014) conference I made a note of the words presenters used to describe their experiences of conducting ethnography. In addition to those which we are by now quite accustomed, these included *aggressive, betrayal*, and *deceptive*. This seems to be a world away from the descriptions brokered in the often brief sections on ethnography in research methods textbooks. Related to this is the question as to whether ethnography ought to be covert or overt. While the 'observer effect' implies that overt ethnography will most likely modify subjects' behaviour (notably, Barnes experiences this for himself; see Chap. 7), covert ethnography presents ethical problems. Inevitably, since the ethnographer is all too human (see The All-Too-Human Paradox, below), she will most likely do a bit of both. However, crucially, this in no way represents a departure from real life since we present ourselves differently in accordance with circumstances; our behaviour is contingent on our environs. I cite, once again, my own experience at Findhorn. Given the highly emotive and contingent experience in a New Age community, the solicitation of permission to use a voice recorder was not only impractical but—notably—would have been extremely insensitive. I therefore did use a voice recorder, but kept it concealed in a pocket. When you are immersed in the field for weeks on end, there are times when the researcher's capacity for recall is bound to be compromised. I was, at various times, tired, frustrated, or confused. The voice recorder was essential to assist in the collection of relevant data. I acted dishonestly to acquire honest data. Of photographic documentation, too, how often does an ethnographer go through the process of securing formal permission to photograph her subjects? To do so would render the process ungainly, bureaucratic and—by implication—create 'dishonest' representations of those photographed. A dishonest strategy is essential if we are to generate truer photographic data. To this end, Prince and Riches (2000: xi) suggest that their camera was used principally in situations whereby its use 'could pass for tourist snaps'.

The Consensus Paradox

As researchers new to ethnographic field work, we are schooled in sensitivity. We are schooled, in effect, to be sensitive and empathetic to our subjects as a means of avoiding conflict. The wording on your university's ethics approval process will most likely prime you to orient your research in this way. By implication, consensus between the researcher and her subjects reigns. But Janis's (1972) teachings in respect of *groupthink* (in which a prevailing desire for harmony results in dysfunctional decision-making) or the story Harvey (1988) recounts in *The Abilene Paradox* (in which a group of people collectively decide on a course of action that is counter to each of their preferences) caution against unbridled empathy. Consensus has an unmistakable allure, but it is through conflict that progress typically unfolds. We learn through our mistakes. Even catastrophe can be considered paradoxical since without it we become complacent. And complacency leads to further—and perhaps more damaging—mistakes. The concept of apocalypse is especially pertinent. Translated from the Ancient Greek for 'an uncovering', apocalypse describes a disclosure of knowledge; a lifting of the veil; a revelation. On the one hand, we are enlightened; on the other catastrophe unfolds. When conceptualised through the lens of apocalypse, then, knowledge or enlightenment elicits a deep-seated tension. We may therefore ask ourselves: will ethnography *without* conflict and *without* mistakes achieve anything truly insightful?

The All-Too-Human Paradox

As part of the review process, my Findhorn chapter was read by various people. Without exception, each of these reviewers (both formal and informal) has passed comment in respect of the hot tub scene. The circumstances of the environs were not especially relevant to the point I was trying to make at the time (in respect of Sofie's work life), but I decided to leave in the detail, conscious that I would reflect upon it in this chapter. Sofie was an attractive woman and similar in age to myself. In spite of the professional expectations of academic research, I will not overlook the fact that I was physically attracted to her. We were alone in the hot tub and were both naked, as was conventional at Findhorn. The simple fact of the matter is that bathing nude in a hot tub was an erotic experience. However, at the time, I did not report this in my field notes. Why not? Perhaps it wasn't strictly relevant to my research endeavours. Perhaps, as a student, I felt compelled to maintain some sort of unspoken scholarly respectability. But in respect of intellectual insight, what a wasted opportunity! How many of us can claim to have gone through our many years of education, for example, without ever having an all-consuming crush on a teacher or classmate? How many of us have not felt considerable discomfort in respect of medical procedures which in some way invade our sense of the erotic? How many of us can say that our attraction to a colleague at work has not affected (for better or for worse) our ability to do our job? Such experience is intrinsic to the very fabric of our social lives and so as ethnographers to ignore it, or—worse still—repress it, is only going to compromise that insight.

During that same visit to Findhorn, I overslept one morning. I wanted to reflect on this as part of my research (notably that I was for the first time completely relaxed), but my supervisor commented to me back on campus that such a 'confession' was tantamount to sloppy ethnography and would imply to the reader a 'disinterested researcher'. It would paint me as 'lazy', he said, and that would not do. I yielded to his authority. In some respects I regret this because on a personal level it demonstrated that I felt at ease with life in the community. Surely, as ethnographers we have a responsibility to convey experiences beyond the parameters of what they might imply on a surface or 'respectability' level?

The Certainty Paradox

One of the recurring themes across the contributions in the book is that of existential uncertainty. Indeed, for several of our authors this concept of uncertainty has constituted a preoccupation. In an early draft of his chapter, by way of a preface to his own experiences transitioning from a positivist researcher to an ethnographer and the sense of existential doubt this elicits, Barnes (Chap. 7), for example, opened with a quote from Rilke's *Letters to a Young Poet*: 'Have patience with everything that remains unsolved in your heart... live in the question.' This is pertinent. Historically, our approach to paradox has been to view it as an inconvenience; we have preoccupied ourselves with how best to resolve or dissolve the paradox. But is this necessary or indeed desirable? Most of us will be familiar with the philosophical truisms that underpin these experiences: 'the only thing we can be certain of is uncertainty'; 'the only constant is change', and so on. In turn, these find an analytical lineage dating back to Heraclitus of Ephesus's observation that 'you cannot step into the same river twice.'

But what, if anything, is the ethnographer to make of this? The certainty (or lack thereof) reported in this book is more practical than existential. Strudwick (Chap. 6), for example, airs concern that in her native discipline of radiography there was a danger that ethnographic research may be seen as un-scientific, lacking rigour and therefore easily dismissed. She utters the following questions: How much should I ask? How much should I participate? Should I simply observe? There is, of course, no straight answer.

As part of this exploration, several of the authors in this volume have tackled the concept of liminality. These ethnographic experiences at the liminal state seem to imply on the part of most, if not all, a sense of both fear and fascination as two sides of the same coin. For Dale and Burrell (2011, p. 113), architectural ruins are emblematic of this peculiar coupling: 'Fear comes from the significance that ruins hold for the integrity of our own world whilst the fascination with ruins lies in their liminal status between organisation and disorganisation, architecture and dust, order and chaos, humanity and nature. They materialise tensions in temporality and spatiality, survival and decay.' Fear and fascination inevitably disorientate. Drawing on the research of both Rosen (1991) and Foster (1990), Holliday (1995, p. 21) comments thus:

> ethnography allows the researcher to drift and formulate ideas in the research setting, and to explore uncharted ground. While at times this may feel like losing one's way, it in fact produces a far more dynamic and processual view of the research setting. Further it shows clearly how research itself is processual, and that in this way issues which may not have been thought of at the outset emerge through the fieldwork, and can rise to prominence.

It is a common concern among early career ethnographers that they feel as though they are losing their way. But this, once again, is what life is like: ethnographic methods mirror verisimilitude. A little further on, Holliday (1995, p. 30) refers to the 'chaotic nature of my experiences', and further normalises this experience. Indeed, it reflects in its entirety the picture of organisational life famously painted in *The Nature of Managerial Work*, by Henry Mintzberg in 1973. Management is not about command,

288   T. VINE

control, and coordination, as convention would have it. On the contrary, management is about muddling through, getting interrupted, and keeping your head above water. Uncertainty propels inquiry. It is the backbone of intellectual endeavour. But just try declaring that on your next ethics application form!

The Plagiarism Paradox

We live in a world where plagiarism is scorned and yet, in research—particularly ethnography—it is the dangers of *inverse* plagiarism that are the more arresting. For Fine and Shulman (2009, p. 185):

> [Ethnographers] engage in the inverse of plagiarism, giving credit to those undeserving, at least not for those precise words. To recall the exact words of a conversation, especially if one is not trained in shorthand is impossible [or indeed if you are not using a voice recorder; see *The honesty paradox*]. This is particularly applicable with those who maintain the illusion of 'active' or 'complete membership' by not taking notes within the limits of the public situation.

In this sense, paradoxically, the more 'genuine' your ethnography, the less likely you are to accurately represent your subjects since your note-recording capacity is inhibited by immersion. Perhaps, therefore, and given the scholarly tradition of 'accuracy' in respect of sources, inverse plagiarism is inevitable. However, and once again, it need not detract from the strength of the ethnography. Inverse plagiarism is another inevitability of everyday lives (e.g., when embellishing stories in the interests of effect). An inspiring book, a provocative film, an engaging lecture, each will likely involve inverse plagiarism, hyperbole, and embellishment. A dull one most likely will not.

The Linguistic Construction Paradox

For Humphries and Watson (2009, p. 40), 'ethnography is writing'. More specifically we might argue that ethnographic writing is reportage. As Liamputtong (2009, p. 42) reminds us, 'Through conversation… individuals have an opportunity to know others, learn about their feelings, experiences and the world in which they live. So if we wish to learn how people see their world, we need to talk with people.' However, given the centrality of writing to ethnography, the biases associated with linguistic construction affect ethnography more, perhaps, than any other research method. In this sense, then, every word the ethnographer transcribes and every word she uses as part of her interpretation, both enhances our understanding of a phenomenon *and* creates further bias. As Best (see Chap. 9) writes, 'I've shaped you. I'm shaping you now.'

Vocabulary, too, is relevant. My own experience at Findhorn revealed a divisive vocabulary. To outsiders, Findhorn was most definitely a 'commune'. To insiders, the word commune was never used; 'community' was preferred. How was I to describe Findhorn? Which term would I use, or would I use a different term altogether? The academic literature had long abandoned commune in favour of intentional community, but this is in no way neutral. In abandoning the term 'commune' the discourse says, quite firmly, that it wishes to dissociate itself from those who regard such collectives derogatorily. This is clearly about identity. I felt that the use of 'intentional community' would prove rather ungainly throughout the entire narrative and so, ultimately, settled on 'community'. However, intentionally or not, this set out an allegiance. It carved out an identity, a political position, and I wasn't entirely comfortable about this. It is much the same in respect of the relatively recent move by the academy to distance itself from the terms 'prostitute' (in favour of sex worker) or 'gypsy' (in favour of traveller). The terms 'sex worker' and 'traveller' are no less biased than their counterparts (prostitute and gypsy); they merely represent a shift in political position (or, more accurately, a shift in the labelling of such positions). Boggis's research in this volume reveals something interesting in respect of disability, too. Boggis (see Chap. 5) explores Oliver's (1983, p. 261) observation that for some 'the term "people with disabilities" should be used in preference to "disabled people" because this prioritises people rather than disability'. However, for others, it seems, 'disabled people' is the preferred terminology of those within the disabled movement because it makes a statement: they are not 'people with disabilities', but people who are disabled or disadvantaged by society's responses to their differences.

The Autoethnographic Paradox

As Weir and Clarke have argued in Chap. 8, there is unquestionably an authenticity of knowing oneself. To this end, they defend autoethnography in light of Delamont's (2007) critique. However, one may choose to point out that common sense suggests that the worst person to ask about me is me. This is, of course, part of the reason dating websites such as *mysinglefriend.com* have been so successful. Rather than engage in the uncomfortably narcissistic exercise of marketing yourself to potential partners, the task is delegated to a friend.

Notably, this is—I think—slightly different to the argument regarding the purported inability to 'fight familiarity' proffered by Delamont (2007). It is about perspective, yes, but it's not that the autoethnographic perspective is *wrong*; it's just different. It's no less valid. The point I'm trying to make is that there is a wonderful tension here. It's foolish to denigrate the tradition on the basis of an inability to fight subjectivity since it is that same subjectivity that enables the different perspective. Notably, for Jeffcut (1991, p. 13, cited in Holliday, 1995, p. 22) 'the objective of [ethnographic] interpretation is to bring us into touch with the lives of strangers, [and] one of those strangers is inevitably ourself.'

The experience of autoethnography will likely be unsettling for generations of researchers to come. But this doesn't invalidate it; on the contrary, it underscores its vitality. The autoethnographer is not an objective scribe. Rather, what's revealing about autoethnography is the sense of change and transformation; tension and contradiction. For Learmonth and Humphries (2012), for example, 'Throughout our adult lives we have both been haunted by a sense of doubleness—a feeling of dislocation, of being in the wrong place, of playing a role... Presenting ourselves as objects of research, we show how, for us, contemporary academic identity is problematic in that it necessarily involves being (at least) 'both' Jekyll and Hyde.' Finally, there's the perennial accusations of narcissism. Narcissism was explored in autoethnography as early as William Whyte's *Street Corner Society*. And, yes, writing about oneself *is* narcissistic. That is inescapable. But, once again, therein lies its significance.

THE DEFINITIVE METHODOLOGICAL PARADOX

For Denzin and Lincoln (1994, p. 15), research endeavours are 'defined by a series of tensions, contradictions and hesitations'. Ethnography is no different. Indeed, in ethnographic research, these tensions hint a much deeper basis: a paradox which lies at the very heart of the objective-subjective binary. Addressing the related discourses of truth, objectivity, and cause-and-effect in turn, I here conceptualise the definitive methodological paradox.

Truth

Truth and methodology have an awkward relationship. I have lost count of the number of undergraduate dissertations I have read in which in their methodology section reads something like this: *I have chosen a positivist approach because I am interested in the truth.* Although most likely a result of misunderstanding the purpose of methodological framing, that students fall into this trap is hardly surprising. We are primed to think of objectivity as 'good' and subjectivity as 'bad'. Objectivity, we are told, means truth. But even the hardest of hard sciences has no legitimate claim to the truth. We continue to teach Newtonian physics in our schools even though—by the perspectives of Einstein or quantum theory—Newtonian physics is wrong. But does this mean that Einstein or quantum theoretical approaches are correct. No. Semiotician Umberto Eco hints at as much in his novel *The Name of the Rose:*

> Perhaps the mission of those who love mankind is to make people laugh at the truth, *to make truth laugh*, because the only truth lies in learning to free ourselves from insane passion for the truth. (Eco, 1984, p. 491, original emphasis)

Nietzsche [1887] (1989, p. 151) has said, 'Strictly speaking, there is no such thing as science without any presuppositions.' Rather, (ibid., p. 119) 'there is *only* a perspective seeing; *only* a perspective knowing; and the *more* affects we allow to speak about one thing, the *more* eyes, different eyes, we can use to observe one thing, the more complete will our "concept" of this thing, our "objectivity", be.' Ethnographers are best placed to be the myriad eyes Nietzsche describes, each—in turn—contributing by way of a unique perspective to the collective ethnographic record. In this way, truth is more legitimately described as something subjective; something *emotional* (Bochner & Ellis, 2016, p. 85), and as something we *feel* rather than acknowledge (ibid., p. 218).

Objectivity

Henry Mintzberg (1979, p. 583) asks us some pertinent questions:

> What is wrong with small samples? Why should researchers have to apologize for them? Should a physicist apologize for splitting only one atom? A doctoral student I know was not allowed to observe managers because of

the 'problem' of sample size. He was required to measure what managers did through questionnaires, despite ample evidence that managers are poor estimators of their own time allocation. Was it better to have less valid data that were statistically significant?

Twenty-seven years on we are *still* forced to apologise for the same. In spite of the ideographic orientation of their research, Thomas and Southwell (see Chap. 13) were forced to apologise for their 'small sample' of twenty. And what of the circumstances when we have a sample size of one; a single datum? In qualitative research methods classes, I am asked this question perhaps more than any other: *How many interviews do I need to do?* Inevitably, I respond with three pieces of advice: (1) I ask the student 'How long is a piece of string?' (2) I suggest they revisit the concepts of ontology and epistemology. (3) I point them to this brief passage in Holliday's (1995, p. 17) ethnography of a small business:

> At the very outset [of my research] I began to worry that I had not really seen the inside of a small manufacturing firm and so had no idea what kind of questions I would need to ask when I began my fieldwork. If I had been researching by questionnaire, of course, I might *never* have seen the inside of a small business.

These three pieces of advice are normally enough for the student to figure out that a small sample size is frequently advantageous. For Gelsthorpe (1992, p. 214) 'a rejection of the notion of "objectivity" and a focus on experience in method does not mean a rejection of the need to be critical, rigorous and accurate; rather, it can mean making interpretive schemes explicit in the concern to produce good knowledge.' The point here I think is that it is better to caveat (and say 'this is my story') than to control for variables (and so deny the existence of a story). As Becker (1967, p. 239) explains, it is impossible 'to do research that is uncontaminated by personal and political sympathies'. And to quote Alvesson and Deetz (2000, p. 66, emphasis added), once again: 'interpretivists and others often labelled as "subjective" often have the *better claim to objectivity* through the way they allow alternative language games and the possibility of alternative constructions arising from existing communities denying both research community conceptions and preferred methods as privileged and universal.'

Linear Cause-and-Effect

We are schooled from an early age to think in terms of 'cause-and-effect' or—in the humanities—'beginning-middle-end'. Such instruction is, of course, a gross over-simplification. For Marsden (1993, p. 115), for example, 'There can be no power without resistance because it is the relationship between A and B that causes the behaviour of both.' In reflecting on her ethnographic story, Best (see Chap. 9) says: 'Everything I've presented is in a linear fashion—when no story is really linear—it's chaos.' Only the very simplest of story would adhere to the expectations of linearity. Are 'stories' in the natural sciences any different? No. In *Paradoxes of Progress*, Stent (1978, p. 148) writes: 'Provided that the questions one asks of Nature are not too deep, satisfactory answers can usually be found. Difficulties arise only when… the questions become too deep and the answers that must be given to these questions are no longer fully consonant with rational thought.' Where analysis remains shallow, cause-and-effect ontologies (or 'stories') tend to operate effectively; it is where we dig a little deeper that paradox emerges. As a result, we become fearful of deeper analysis.

However, in spite of what we've said about truth, objectivity, and cause-and-effect, we live in a world where there is a bias towards analytical simplicity, or 'elegance' (as has become the popular term). We are told frequently that 'Simplistic explanations are the most effective' (BBC, 2016). Certainly, most positivist/quantitative research strives for simplicity. But this is a fundamental problem because our world is far from simplistic. 'Successful'—by which we really mean 'popular'—explanations are rarely accurate. Turning once again to my native discipline, theoretical models tend to come in the form of 2×2 typologies. Examples include Porter's diamond, the Boston matrix, and even Burrell and Morgan's sociological paradigms. Why is this? Is there some underlying elegance to the universe that favours such a configuration? It seems unlikely. A more likely explanation for the prevalence of 2×2 typologies is that they are simple. Furthermore, although typologies may purport to reflect, in practice they tend to *reinforce*; typologies are a way of organising. They are inevitably associated foremost with positivist/quantitative methodologies. By actively resisting a temptation to 'typologise', and instead pursuing research sensitive to a grounded theoretical approach, effective ethnography can rise above these concerns.

294   T. VINE

Let's look at this another way. Ethnography might be described as the *method acting* of academic research. Method acting traces its origins to Stanislavski's philosophy, a philosophy which was part of the theatrical realist movement based on the idea that good acting is a reflection of truth, mediated through the actor. For Shakespeare, of course, all the world's a stage and we are 'merely' actors. For Gephart (1978, p. 556), the methods by which social actors construct everyday life are important:

> Such actors are viewed as engaged in constructing and reconstructing social realities through generating and using meanings to make events sensible. A dramaturgical metaphor is often employed; actors must manage appearances and constantly ad lib essentially vague social roles in an emergent stream of existential being and awareness. A basic assumption is that social reality is not merely a stable entity but passively entered and apprehended, but one which requires actors (members) to work at accomplishing this 'reality for all practical purposes'.

'Real' life is, paradoxically, an act. For, Deloria (1969, p. 146) 'irony and satire provide much keener insights into a group's collective psyche and values than do years of [conventional] research.' Ultimately, of course, 'human behaviour is based upon meanings that attribute people to and bring to situations, and that behaviour is not "caused" in any mechanical way, but is continually constructed and reconstructed on the basis of people's interpretations of the situations they are in' (Punch, 2014, p. 126).

Scientists simply cannot be external to their experiments. A biologist himself, Stent (1978, pp. 212–213) reminds us that

> the kind of impersonal and objective science on behalf of which authority is claimed is only a myth and does not, in fact, exist. Since scientists are human beings rather than disembodied spirits, since they necessarily interact with the phenomena they observe, and since they use ordinary language to communicate their results, they are really part of the problem rather than part of the solution. That is to say, scientists lack the status of observers external to the world of phenomena, a status they would have to have if scientific propositions were to be truly objective.

Further on, Stent shifts attention away from the objective and to the intersubjective:

an individual's moral judgements arise by a transformational process operating on an innate ethical deep structure. But despite their subjective source, his moral judgements are not seen as arbitrary or completely idiosyncratic by others, because the innate ethical deep structure is a universal which all humans share. (ibid., p. 226)

Notably, intersubjective insight is the bread and butter of ethnography. Crang and Cook (2007, p. 37), for example, argue that 'to talk about participant observation should not be to separate its "subjective" and "objective" components, but to talk about it as a means of developing intersubjective understandings between the researcher and the researched.' 'Ethnography is neither subjective nor objective. It is *interpretive*, mediating two worlds through a third' (Agar, 1986, p. 19, emphasis added). One way in which I encourage my students to recognise this is by positing the concept of the collective unconscious. The collective unconscious is determined by recurring primordial behaviour throughout history. In this sense Jung was fascinated with, for example, the occult, religion, and parapsychology not because of their particular ontologies, but what their very existence as cultural artefacts tells us about humankind and its predispositions. In this sense, any attempt to educate ourselves out of these artefacts is likely to be existentially troubling. An empirical focus on intersubjectivity also enables ethnography to generate understanding in respect of *process* rather than *result* (see Cooper & Law, 1995, p. 238). And this is why ethnography has a unique responsibility. Ethnography is non-finite; it is live; it is dynamic; it unfolds; it is 'flying by the seat of your pants' (Van Maanen, 1988, p. 120). It is forever 'in process'.

Earlier in this book, Boggis (Chap. 5) drew on the pertinent words of Stanley and Wise. I restate them below:

Whether we like it or not, researchers remain human beings complete with the usual assembly of feelings, failings and moods. All of these things influence how we feel and what is going on. Our consciousness is always the medium through which research occurs; there is no method or technique of doing research other than through the medium of the researcher. (Stanley & Wise, 1993, p. 157)

Although supposedly objective research seeks to distance the researcher from her experiment or study, the 'reality' is that this mediation is likely the only thing 'true' about the research. Herein lies the paradox.

Paradox as Pedagogical Device

For, Rappaport (1981, p. 121) 'the most important and interesting aspects of community life are by their very nature paradoxical; and [so] our task as researchers, scholars, and professionals should be to "unpack" and influence contemporary resolutions of paradox.' It is my belief, however, that attempts to resolve (or dissolve) paradoxes are misplaced. That is not to say that I believe instead we should work carefully to avoid paradox. No, paradox is an important part of life. But academics are reluctant to engage with paradox because to do so would undermine our role as 'experts', since 'expertise' invariably assumes logic. However, we have—I hope—debunked the concept of the 'expert' (in terms of familiarity), earlier in this chapter. So how might we use paradox by way of pedagogical device? Take the paradox associated with identity. Liberal-minded academics (and ethnographers are perhaps a case in point) are fond of lending voice to marginalised groups. But how desirable is this? The pressures of identity politics, for example, seek overt recognition of minority groups such as, for example, LGBT. But to what extent does this further marginalise minorities from forming part of an integrated community? Drawing on Oliver's work, Boggis (see Chap. 5) recognises something similar in respect of disabled groups and how they are labelled. The point, of course, is *not* for the pedagogue to suggest that LGBT designations are destructive, or that a particular nomenclature in respect of the disabled is warranted; rather the point is to suggest that any research that smacks of ideological closure should be viewed with suspicion, irrespective of how noble its ambitions appear to be.

What Now?

Paradox is pervasive: from the theory of relativity (Einstein, 1916) to the pursuit for world peace (Mosley, 2009). Paradox exists *between* disciplines too. Although usually considered in binary opposition, science and religion rest upon comparable causal ontologies. Indeed, they are frequently invoked to justify one another. Isaac Newton, for example, held that absolute space and absolute time are constituted by the omniscience and omnipotence of God, as his 'Sensorium' (Powers, 1982, p. 31).

That paradox is pervasive means ethnographers must proceed with extreme caution. Although—ironically—we have demonstrated that ethnography often has the better claim to objectivity, there is no room for complacency or self-righteousness. For Yanow (2010, p. 1400):

> ethnography entails a complex interchange between the researcher's prior conceptual boxes and the field data generated—and one can only hope, from an interpretative methodological perspective, that the data are not being force fitted into those conceptual boxes but rather that the shape and content of the boxes are being allowed to develop into a bottom-up fashion in light of those generated, non 'given' data.

And this is crucial. The sensitivity built into the ethnographic enterprise does not guarantee it will be deployed. One concern is that while positivists may be blissfully ignorant of the biases underpinning their frameworks, interpretivists—who are not—may be using these to their advantage. After all, paradox manifests itself in both directions. As Atkinson and Hammersley (1994, p. 253) imply, positivism may actually be more sensitive to participant well-being than interpretivism: 'It is suggested that by its very nature anthropology (and the point can be extended without distortion to ethnographic work in general) involves "representation" of others even when it does not explicitly claim to speak for or on behalf of them.'

Ours is a brave new post-paradigms ontology and it is one in which ethnographers have a formidable responsibility.

References

Agar, M. (1986). *Speaking of Ethnographies.* London: Sage.

Alvesson, M., & Deetz, S. (2000). *Doing Critical Management Research.* London: Sage.

Atkinson, P., & Hammersley, M. (1994). Ethnography and Participant Observation. In N. Denzin & Y. Lincoln (Eds.), *Handbook of Qualitative Methods.* London: Sage.

BBC. (2016). Retrieved January 27, 2017, from http://www.bbc.co.uk/news/magazine-35311422

Becker, H. (1967). Whose Side Are We On? *Social Problems, 14*(3), 239–247.

Bell, E. (1999). The Negotiation of a Working Role in Organizational Ethnography. *International Journal of Social Research Methodology, 2*(1), 17–37.

Bochner, A., & Ellis, C. (2016). *Evocative Autoethnography: Writing Lives and Telling Stories.* London: Routledge.

Bowie, M. (1979). Jacques Lacan. In J. Sturrock (Ed.), *Structuralism and Since: From Levi-Strauss to Derrida*. Oxford: Oxford University Press.

Bryman, A., & Bell, E. (2011). *Business Research Methods*. Oxford: Oxford University Press.

Burrell, G., & Morgan, G. (1979). *Sociological Paradigms and Organisational Analysis: Elements of the Sociology of Corporate Life*. London: Heinemann.

Cooper, R., & Law, J. (1995). Organization: Distal and Proximal Views. *Research in the Sociology of Organizations: A Research Annual, 13*, 237–274.

Crang, M., & Cook, I. (2007). *Doing Ethnographies*. London: Sage.

Dale, K., & Burrell, G. (2011). Disturbing Structure: Reading the Ruins. *Culture and Organization, 17*(2), 107–121.

Delamont, S. (2007). *Arguments Against Auto-Ethnography*. Paper presented at the British Educational Research Association Annual Conference, Institute of Education, University of London, September 5–8.

Deloria, V. (1969). *Custer Died for Your Sins: An Indian Manifesto*. Norman, OK: University of Oklahoma Press.

Denzin, N., & Lincoln, Y. (1994). Introduction: Entering the Field of Qualitative Research. In N. Denzin & Y. Lincoln (Eds.), *Handbook of Qualitative Research*. London: Sage.

Eco U. (1984). *The Name of the Rose*. New York: Harcourt Inc.

Einstein A. (1916). *Relativity: The Special and General Theory*, (Translation 1920). New York: H. Holt and Company.

European Group of Organizational Studies (EGOS). (2014). Subtheme 15: (SWG) Organizational Ethnography: The Theoretical Challenge, Rotterdam.

Fine, G., & Shulman, D. (2009). Lies From the Field: Ethical Issues in Organizational Ethnography. In S. Ybema, D. Yanow, H. Wels, & F. Kamsteeg (Eds.), *Organizational Ethnography: Studying the Complexities of Everyday Life*. London: Sage.

Ganga, D., & Scott, S. (2006). Cultural "Insiders" and the Issue of Positionality in Qualitative Migration Research: Moving "Across" and Moving "Along" Researcher-Participant Divides. *Forum: Qualitative Research, 7*(3), Article 7.

Gelsthorpe, L. (1992). Response to Martyn Hammersley's Paper "On Feminist Methodology". *Sociology, 26*(2), 213–221.

Gephart, R. (1978). Status Degradation and Organizational Succession: An Ethnomethodological Approach. *Administrative Science Quarterly, 4*(23), 553–581.

Hammersley, M. (1992). *What's Wrong with Ethnography? Methodological Explorations*. London: Routledge.

Hammersley, M., & Atkinson, P. (2007). *Ethnography: Principles in Practice* (3rd ed.). London: Routledge.

Harari, Y. (2011). *Sapiens: A Brief History of Humankind*. London: Vintage.

Harvey, J. (1988). *The Abilene Paradox and Other Meditations on Management*. Oxford: Maxwell Macmillan.

METHODOLOGY: FROM PARADIGMS TO PARADOX   299

Holliday, R. (1995). *Investigating Small Firms: Nice Work?* London: Routledge.

Humphries, M., & Watson, T. (2009). Ethnographic Practices: From 'Writing-up Ethnographic Research' to 'Writing Ethnography'. In S. Ybema, D. Yanow, H. Wels, & F. Kamsteeg (Eds.), *Organizational Ethnography: Studying the Complexities of Everyday Life.* London: Sage.

Jackson, N., & Carter, P. (1985). The Ergonomics of Desire. *Personnel Review, 14*(3), 20–28.

Janis, I. L. (1972). *Victims of Groupthink.* New York: Houghton Mifflin.

Learmonth, M., & Humphries, M. (2012). Autoethnography and Academic Identity: Glimpsing Business School Doppelgängers. *Organization, 19*(1), 99–117.

Liamputtong, P. (2009). *Qualitative Research Methods* (3rd ed.). Oxford: Oxford University Press.

Marsden, R. (1993). The Politics of Organizational Analysis. *Organization Studies, 14*(1), 93–124.

Mascarenhas-Keyes, S. (1987). The Native Anthropologist: Constraints and Strategies in Research. In A. Jackson (Ed.), *Anthropology at Home.* London: Tavistock.

Mintzberg, H. (1973). *The Nature of Managerial Work.* Upper Saddle River, NJ: Prentice Hall.

Mintzberg, H. (1979). An Emerging Strategy of "Direct" Research. *Administrative Science Quarterly, 24,* 582–589.

Mosley, N. (2009). *Paradoxes of Peace.* London: Dalkey Archive Press.

Nietzsche, F. (1989[1887]). *On the Genealogy of Morals.* New York: Vintage.

Oliver, M. (1983). *Social Work and Disabled People.* Basingstoke: Macmillan.

Powell, A., Dainty, A., & Bagilhole, B. (2010). *Achieving Gender Equality in the Construction Professions: Lessons from the Career Decisions of Women Construction Students in the UK.* Retrieved May 17, 2013, from http://www.arcom.ac.uk/-docs/proceedings/ar2010-0573-0582_Powell_Dainty_and_Bagilhole.pdf

Powers, J. (1982). *Philosophy and the New Physics.* London: Methuen.

Prince, R., & Riches, D. (2000). *The New Age in Glastonbury: The Construction of Religious Movements.* Oxford: Berghahn.

Punch, K. (2005). *Introduction to Social Research.* London: Sage.

Punch, K. (2014). *Introduction to Social Research: Quantitative and Qualitative Approaches* (3rd ed.). London: Sage.

Rose, D. (1990). *Living the Ethnographic Life.* London: Sage.

Rousseau, D. (1998). Why Workers Still Identity with Organizations. *Journal of Organizational Behavior, 19*(3), 217–233.

Silverman, D. (2007). *A Very Short, Fairly Interesting and Reasonably Cheap Book About Qualitative Research.* London: Sage.

Singer, I. (2009). *Philosophy of Love: A Partial Summing-up.* Cambridge, MA: MIT Press.

Stanley, L., & Wise, S. (1993). *Breaking Out: Feminist Consciousness and Feminist Research*. London: Routledge and Kegan Paul.

Starobinski, J. (1975). The Inside and the Outside. *The Hudson Review, 28*, 333–351.

Stent, G. (1978). *Paradoxes of Progress*. San Francisco: W. H. Freeman & Co.

Rappaport, J. (1981). In Praise of Paradox: A Social Policy of Empowerment Over Prevention. *American Journal of Community Psychology, 9*, 1–25.

Toffler, A. (1970). *Future Shock*. London: Pan Books.

Van Maanen, J. (1988). *Tales of the Field*. Chicago: Chicago University Press.

Vine, T. (2010). *Book Review: Organizational Ethnography – Studying the Complexities of Everyday Life*. In S. Ybema, D. Yanow, H. Wels, & F. Kamsteeg (Eds.) London: Sage (2009). *Organization 17*(5), 645–649.

Yanow, D. (2010). Review Essay. *Organization Studies, 31*(9 & 10), 1397–1410.

CHAPTER 16

Conclusion

*Tom Vine, Jessica Clark, Sarah Richards,
and David Weir*

Reflecting on this collection of ethnographic works, on the one hand we find experienced ethnographers presenting illuminating, evocative and emotional accounts of their chosen topics. Vine takes us into a New Age community and with him we share 'sprinklings of light', hot tub liaisons and ultimately a search for some semblance of existential security. Through a vivid recollection of his apprenticeship in the 1950s, Weir reproduces for us the hot, steamy, dirty commercial laundry environment involved in the production of a clean sheet. Both these authors make use of ethnographic techniques to craft stories of the worlds which they inhabited. Here the value of ethnography as methodology and method is clear. In contrast, a number of the authors in this volume are not proclaiming to be 'intentional' ethnographers and are relatively inexperienced in its craft. Instead they have discovered that the approach fits rather nicely with their topic and/or field. Their writings thus reveal the opportunities ethnography can facilitate but also the anxieties and trepidation that its application can evoke. For example, Barnes's apprehensive journey into ethnography

T. Vine (✉) • J. Clark • S. Richards
University of Suffolk, Ipswich, UK

D. Weir
York St John University, York, UK

© The Author(s) 2018
T. Vine et al. (eds.), *Ethnographic Research and Analysis*,
https://doi.org/10.1057/978-1-137-58555-4_16

301

highlights the difficulties of applying a methodology to a discipline built around different epistemological assumptions. Meanwhile, Hadlow shares with us his anxieties about revealing elements of the self in an inherently personal account of the emergence of his unconventional fatherhood. In so doing, he discloses some reticence about using an autoethnographic methodology and how its use might be received. Other authors have experimented for the first time with collaborative ethnography and gained significantly from experience. Bissett et al., for example, demonstrate that a collaborative approach enables a fresh perspective of the researcher self not as a singular entity but as co-produced through relationships and interaction. Thus this book has revealed the possibilities for ethnography to transcend discipline, co-construct identity and enable multiple selves. As Weir and Clarke recognise: 'the stories wrote us as much as we wrote them'.

Our varying fields reveal something interesting. For those accustomed to traditional management research (Barnes) or the natural sciences (Driscoll-Evans and Strudwick), objectivity and distance have hitherto provided a degree of authority and legitimacy for the researcher. Perhaps more importantly, they have provided a sense of ontological certainty. Thus the analytical focus on uncertainty that preoccupies Barnes, for example, is not shared by those accustomed to the messiness and subjectivity of such approaches. Ultimately, certainty is counter-intuitive in ethnography.

Ontological certainty aside, concerns regarding authenticity are more pervasive across each of the chapters. Implicit here is a search for an 'authentic' identity. The notion of 'authentic identities' is primary throughout the experience imparted by Richards' account of English parents adopting Chinese children. What constitutes an 'authentic' identity for such children? The situation is not especially different for any of us. We are deeply uncomfortable with the notion of an authentic identity. Who is to say which parts of one's identity are authentic and which are not?

Related to this, the explicit revelation of self has constituted a key thematic throughout the book. Hadlow is a sociologist, informal sperm donor and emerging father. He has learned a great deal about himself and his professional craft from engaging in his autoethnographic reflection. This sort of revelation is found elsewhere. Boggis as a mother of a disabled child; Best experienced a flash pan career as a consultant (and horror of horrors, rather enjoyed it); Driscoll-Evans reveals explicitly his own sexuality; Clarke as a grieving son; and Weir as a poet. For Richards, her experience as an inter-country adoptive mother is pertinent. Richards is an academic in the field of social policy and childhood studies *and* an adoptive mother. For other methods, in which the researcher-role is ignored, distanced or suppressed, this would be of no consequence. But at what cost? Perhaps more so than anything else this is integral to Richards' sense of self and fundamentally intertwined with her professional role. Our multiples selves cannot be disentangled, and nor should they be. There's also a second more nuanced revealing of self that is exposed in the telling of ethnographic stories. This is less explicit; for example, Vine as the 'adopted son' of his subjects and Best as a skilled navigator of academic and commercial tensions despite her presumed anxieties. For many of us, it wasn't until we actually formalised our ethnographic scripts that we saw ourselves revealed in the data. As Sandra (in Bissett et al.) says in reflecting of her anxieties about being received as an expert: 'I didn't know this until I wrote it down.' To quote Weir and Clarke once again, 'the stories wrote us as much as we wrote them.' We might, at this point, usher in the relevance of the Foucauldian subject constructed through regulatory practices. But this is a well-rehearsed path. What's important here is perhaps easier to grasp: the self is both in flux and imperative to our role as researchers.

Anxiety: The Emerging Thematic

Nearly 30 years ago, Rose commented that research 'can be a superficial mess unless the way of life on which it is based is subjected to greater risks and thereby made truly experimental' (Rose, 1990, p. 16). We're not entirely sure if the risks Rose had in mind are the sort explored in this book. Nevertheless, without exception each of the writers in this book has engaged in risky situations. And with risk comes anxiety.

It would be delightfully convenient if we were able to glean from the experiences recounted here a series of recurrent themes, perhaps with the aim of revealing some underlying pattern which might then go on to form some sort of law-like insights as regards human behaviour. Predictably, we can't. The truth is, the human experience is gloriously multifaceted and apparently infinite in its variety. Indeed, it seems the only theme that transcends all chapters—both in terms of examined content and author reflection—is that of anxiety. In Chap. 2, the participants at the New Age community are attracted to it precisely because of the sense of insecurity they feel in their mainstream lives. In Chap. 3, Norfolk's MSM proxy themselves into an online existence in order to help mitigate anxieties regarding their sexuality. In Chap. 4, English adoptive parents of Chinese children feel elements of anxiety which are alleviated to some extent by a sense of belonging to a shared space with 'similar' families. In Chap. 5, in spite of the aid of well-intentioned technology, the acute frustrations of disabled children with alternative and more complex modes of communication with their carers are palpable. In Chap. 6, radiographers express doubt about their own clinical abilities and—perhaps without even knowing—are acutely reliant on the socialised aspects of the job to get them through the day. In Chap. 7, the transition from a schooling in positivist approaches to the 'boundarylessness' and 'drift' of ethnography is thoroughly—and perhaps even, irreversibly—unsettling. In Chap. 8, the criticisms levelled at autoethnography impose a sense of existential doubt but with it a determination to reassert the validity of the method. In Chap. 9, in a world in which universities must now fight at the rough edge of capitalism, reconciling both research interests and critical reflection with the demands of the bottom line has become increasingly anxiety-ridden. In Chap. 10, the tension between the grubbiness of the industrial laundry with the cleanliness of its product resonates beyond its irony. In Chap. 11, in spite of the relative pervasiveness of ethnography in studies of organisation, emotion—we are told—remains forever relegated to the analytical back seat. In Chap. 12, without sufficient precedent the informal sperm donor and 'accidental dad' persists in his quest to understand his—and his family's—journey. In Chap. 13, the palpable anxiety felt in light of rejected research findings is explicitly reflected upon in relation to the authenticity of researcher identity and authority. In Chap. 14, the insecurities associated with individual sense-making processes are brought into relief through collaborative techniques. Finally, in Chap. 15 paradox is lent analytical paramountcy and in so doing anxiety is, ultimately, normalised.

One question remains: Did we set out to write a book on anxiety? No. The chapters were considered on the basis of their individual merits alone. Transcending discipline and reflecting on the core concerns of identity and self were our aims. From here, we have arrived at anxiety. The data is there for you, dear reader, to infer from yourself. It's difficult to interpret otherwise. Does it mean, perhaps, that anxiety-stricken researchers are *led* to ethnography? This seems unlikely. On the contrary, as Barnes has illustrated, his anxiety didn't emerge until he was actually 'doing' the method. So perhaps ethnography should carry a health warning?

If risk, as Rose suggests, is essential to moving the field of ethnography forward. Then so too is anxiety. Indeed, as Stacey (1996, cited in

Streatfield, 2001) points out, both emotion and anxiety are fundamental enablers of the creative processes. Let us not forget 'to be alive is to be uncertain… ethnography should be celebrated and appreciated as *the genre of doubt*' (Bochner & Ellis, 2016, p. 246, original emphasis).

RECOMMENDATIONS FOR FUTURE RESEARCH

At first glance this may appear to be a rather bleak way in which to conclude our book. It isn't. As a practice, ethnography has brought each of us closer to both the grubbiness and the beauty of lived existence. That each of us, without exception, has experienced frustration, anger and anxiety was, frankly, unanticipated. On a practical level, producing ethnography serves as a form of what might be described as self-help. At a deeper level, however, this volume has enabled a mutual recognition of the socialised bases of our disparate disciplines. Each of us has felt a personal sense of the imposter syndrome. Does ethnography—in some respect at least—enable us to be more transparent in terms of our experiences, emotions and fears, especially as regards ethical norms? As previously noted, nearly 30 years ago Rose speculated on the future of ethnography, focussing particularly on the expectation for researchers to deliberately place themselves in unfolding situations. A generation on, we have done just that in this book and believe such experience has a salient place in the academy. A generation from now, it is difficult to envisage exactly how ethnography may have developed. However, we would like to speculate on the virtues of two broad possibilities:

Analytical Engagement with 'Ethnomasochistic' Anxieties

Unexpectedly, anxiety has constituted a key thematic in our book. We are keen to expand on this and in so doing ask ourselves some uncomfortable questions. Are we so anxious to reinforce our progressive credentials that we do so at the expense of our scholarship? Perhaps conscious of anthropology's colonial legacy, are we as twenty-first-century ethnographers all too keen to damn our own cultures? To date, the concept of ethnomasochism appears to have been addressed only by ultra conservative commentators as a means of chastising what they perceive to be the tendency for liberal-minded Westerners to celebrate cultures distinct from their own while concurrently condemning their own culture. Might ethnography have an opportunity to rescue the concept from these ultra conservative commentators? If so, in what ways? Best (see Chap. 9), for example, admits she has 'things to say that others don't want to hear'. Vine too (see Chap. 15) finds himself readily denigrating mainstream culture as a means of securing insider status. And let us not overlook the timeliness of our publication. We are living in the post-Brexit era, and one in which—against all odds—Donald Trump has secured victory in the US presidential election. Has ethnography, like the liberal arts more generally, for too long focussed on those we have chosen to construct as 'victims'? As Bochner & Ellis (2016, p. 239), suggest of autoethnography:

> It is no secret that autoethnography has a wide appeal to people on the margins (working class, LGBTQ and ethnic and racial minorities) because these populations have been silenced, objectified, left out, or oppressed by value-free, disembodied social science.

Certainly, the empirical focus of many of the chapters in this book follows in this trend: New Agers, gay men, inter-country adoption, children with disabilities and alternative fatherhood. But in deliberately—and exclusively—focussing on the supposedly 'powerless', do we inadvertently silence, objectify and leave out those on the political right? Are we, paradoxically, part of the problem? These groups should not be ignored by ethnographers, even if their examination elicits further identity anxieties on the part of the liberal-minded academic. On the contrary, it seems probable that the most interesting data will be realised by focussing on these largely ignored sections of the ethnographic potential. Perhaps we should expand our remit in a bid to understand—and perhaps even empathise with—the emotions, fears and insecurities of white, working class conservatives. Rose (1990, p. 14) himself commented that 'one assumes in a remarkably brief time the culture of anthropology or sociology in graduate school. The culture and the identity that goes with it are central for the qualitative researcher...' Like any other group, ethnographers are primed and socialised. So in addition to further refining the specifics of the ethnographic method, we might feasibly claim a grander objective: to dislodge ethnography from its liberal tract. And, of course, there is potential here for the autoethnographer. How exactly do we deal with, endure and reflect upon our individual ethnomasochistic anxieties? Ethnography has clearly become a popular tool for the progressive scholar, but we must do our very best to ensure our ideological proclivities don't adversely affect the reach of our craft. It is also worth noting that the majority of the chapters in this book were written by Western—specifically British—academics. This is clearly a limiting factor. Future research will, we hope, remedy this.

Enhanced Cross-Disciplinary Collaboration

This book has demonstrated that ethnography is pertinent across a diverse range of academic fields. As such, the book contributes to the continued relevance and increasing popularity of ethnography and highlights its application in places previously underexplored in this respect; for example Ruth (radiography), Paul (sexual health) and Sarah (social policy). We would like to encourage more joint research projects, where writers collaborate from different disciplinary backgrounds. This would help mitigate black box closure (where we resort to preconceived notions) enable a truly grounded approach to emerge. In this sense if, say, Richards and Vine worked together on a joint project in the field of organisational behaviour, they could then each tell their own story; Vine's from a native's point of view and Richards from a childhood or social policy perspective. It's worth noting that when reviewing each of the contributions received, each of the editors tended to be most impressed with those contributions not of their native discipline. This was doubtless because we each learned most from those outside our discipline. And this, perhaps, highlights more than anything else the extraordinary value of cross-disciplinary enterprise. Notably, our volume tentatively dipped its toe into potentially expansive waters where ethnography can be applied into alternative fields, including those found in the natural sciences. And the potential here is huge. Ethnomathematics, for example, shows significant promise (D'Ambrosio, 2006). Indeed, the study of the relationship between mathematics and culture will almost certainly yield further insight in respect of the methodological paradox Vine describes in Chap. 15. More generally, on the basis that the most interesting research tends to emerge at disciplinary boundaries, any move to enable further collaboration between social and natural scientists will likely yield formidable results. In 2016, the BBC aired *Aliens: The Big Think* which documented the modern search for extra-terrestrial life speculating, in particular, on alien technologies. The documentary focussed exclusively on scientists' views. From a social scientific viewpoint, there were noticeable flaws. For example, although there was some recognition of the tension between scientific advance and self-destruction, the contributors spoke uncritically about both 'civilisation' and 'technology'.

As such, there appeared to be an assumption that civilisations (alien or otherwise) would inevitably wish to continue to grow larger and more influential; none entertained the possibility of the Schumacherian 'small is beautiful' thesis, for example. Such a thesis would imply an alternative trajectory for civilisation (and perhaps help us understand better the Fermi Paradox). This is just one example of the myriad possibilities for further disciplinary cross-pollination. To this collaborative end, ethnographers must take a lead.

References

Bochner, A., & Ellis, C. (2016). *Evocative Autoethnography: Writing Lives and Telling Stories*. London: Routledge.

D'Ambrosio, U. (2006). *Ethnomathematics*. Rotterdam: Sense Publishers.

Rose, D. (1990). *Living the Ethnographic Life*. London: Sage.

Streatfield, P. (2001). *The Paradox of Control in Organizations*. London: Routledge.

INDEX

A

Academia, 10, 11, 137, 158, 162, 167, 192
Adoption, 54–60, 63, 65, 67, 69–72
 intercountry adoption, 9, 54, 302, 306
Affect, 89, 136, 139, 148, 149, 179, 198, 199, 204, 258, 289, 291, 306
All-too-human, 277
Anguish, 129, 131, 133, 139, 140, 147–149
Anthropology, 2, 4, 14, 122, 128, 196, 209, 297, 305, 306
Anxiety, 6, 8, 9, 11, 49, 55, 70, 115, 201, 203, 208, 225, 303–305
Appraisal, 197, 198, 203, 210
Augmentative and alternative communication systems (AACS), 10, 79, 85, 88, 90–92
Authenticity, 10, 128, 129, 132, 133, 142, 143, 145–149, 172, 289, 302, 304
Authorities, 15, 71, 82, 134, 229, 236–239, 245, 255, 286, 294, 302, 304

Autoethnography (AE), 2, 7, 11, 128, 129, 133, 135, 137–139, 142, 146, 156, 195, 196, 202, 219–225, 229, 230, 234–250, 254–270, 289, 290, 304, 306

B

Barley, S., 16, 133
Becker, H., 82, 83, 292
Belonging, 9, 31, 34, 53–73, 275, 304
 familial belonging, 9, 16, 55
Biography, 6, 220, 278
Boje, David, 128, 143
Boltanski, L., 16
Boundaries, 5, 10, 17, 50, 55, 57, 79, 124, 184, 193, 201–203, 275, 307
Burrell, G., 274, 293

C

Careful listening, 86, 87, 93
Celebration, 58, 62, 64, 68, 141
Change, 7, 17, 27, 32, 40, 41, 90, 114–116, 120–123, 137, 141,

© The Author(s) 2018
T. Vine et al. (eds.), *Ethnographic Research and Analysis*,
https://doi.org/10.1057/978-1-137-58555-4

310 INDEX

145, 149, 157–159, 162, 164, 167, 181, 182, 198, 200–203, 220, 228–230, 258, 259, 263, 268, 269, 287, 290
organisational change, 116
Chiapello, E., 16
Childhood
  children, 4, 27, 77, 80–82, 140
  diversity of childhood, 81, 93
Collaboration, 97–109, 205, 206, 235, 255, 257, 307, 308
Commune, 14, 18, 34, 289
Communication, 17, 44, 47, 78, 83, 85–89, 91, 92, 101, 177, 243, 245–250, 254, 279, 304
Community, 9, 14, 15, 17–20, 24, 26, 28–30, 33, 34, 38, 39, 41, 42, 45, 47, 49, 50, 83, 149, 177, 227, 244, 275, 278, 282, 284, 286, 289, 292, 296, 301, 303
Competency, 8, 81, 82
Complexity, 2, 3, 11, 54, 56, 98, 124, 196, 220, 221, 224, 228, 240, 242, 250, 260, 261, 268, 269
Conflict, 163, 164, 173, 175, 200, 204, 236, 237, 243, 276, 277, 285
Consensus, 277, 285
Contradiction, 2, 60, 141, 164, 275–277, 279, 290
Creswell, J. W., 115, 116, 119
Criteria, 129, 133, 149, 193, 225
Criticality, 6, 7, 10, 17, 57, 78, 79, 81, 108, 156, 166, 192, 202, 230, 234, 250, 254, 255, 266, 292, 304
  proto-critical, 273
Culture, 7, 8, 14, 17, 31, 32, 50, 54–59, 61–63, 65, 72, 98, 99, 103, 116, 117, 122–124, 136, 138, 156, 173, 192, 220, 255, 260, 261, 274, 277–281, 283, 305–307

professional culture, 98, 99, 108, 109

D
Dark humour, 107
Deem, R., 115
Defamiliarization, 280
Delamont, Sarah, 128–133, 143, 147, 148, 173, 221, 235, 255, 289, 290
Denzin, Norman, 54, 141, 223, 254, 284, 290
Dialectics, 277
Digital spacialities, 50
Dirt, 172–174
Disability, 1, 4, 79–82, 89, 90, 93, 289, 306
Discipline, 2–5, 114, 116, 122, 123, 143, 195, 203, 209, 254, 264, 275, 284, 287, 293, 296, 302, 304, 305, 307
Diversity, 2, 60, 61, 66, 81, 93, 223, 261, 263, 268
Dual board structure, 163
Dystopia, 275

E
Ecology, 273
Education
  doctorate in education, 114
  higher education, 162, 254
Ellis, Carolyn, 128–133, 135, 137, 139, 141, 156, 195–197, 219, 220, 222, 223, 225, 235, 236, 249, 254, 266, 291, 305, 306
Emotion, 70, 71, 108, 128, 134, 144, 148, 192–210, 224, 235, 237, 255, 261, 266, 304–306
  emotions framework, 197
Empathy, 8, 106, 196, 274, 285, 306
Epiphany, 136, 141

INDEX 311

Epistemology, 266, 281, 292
  democratic epistemology, 281
Ethics
  ethical subject, 3, 5
  ethical symmetry, 78
Ethnographies, 2–11, 14–17, 34, 46,
    49, 54, 55, 57, 73, 78, 80,
    98–100, 114, 115, 117, 119,
    122–124, 128, 142, 143, 147,
    156, 165, 175, 192–195, 197,
    200–204, 209, 220, 224, 254,
    265, 274, 275, 277, 278,
    280–282, 284–290, 292–297,
    301, 302, 304–307
Ethnomasochism, 283, 305
Ethnomathematics, 307
Evaluation, 78, 129, 132, 133, 146,
    149, 236
Exclusion, 78, 84, 92, 206
Exotic, 9, 14, 16, 34, 54, 67, 175,
    257, 274, 278–280

F
Family
  family surrogate, 30
  nuclear family, 16, 29, 30, 34
Fatherhood, 11, 218–230, 302, 306
Fieldwork, 3, 8, 9, 38, 39, 47, 50,
    103, 109, 131, 135, 202, 205,
    207, 208, 220, 255, 275, 280,
    282, 287, 292
Findhorn Foundation, 14, 18, 19
Fine, G., 280, 288
Framing, 128

G
Gender, 25, 26, 46, 57, 84, 88, 117,
    172–186, 208, 261
Goode, W., 30
Grief, 134, 137, 139
Grindr, 43, 45, 49

Groupthink, 285

H
Headwork, 135, 138, 141
Healthcare, 98–100
Heelas, P., 15, 17
Holden, S. S., 113
Holman Jones, Stacy, 128, 139, 267
Honesty, 3, 8, 11, 22, 24, 145, 147,
    149, 166, 220, 222, 235, 249,
    274, 277, 284, 285
Huberman, A. M., 116

I
Identity
  identity workspace, 158
  organisational identity, 30–34
  schizophrenic identity, 282
Ideology, 55, 158, 164, 241, 276
Imposter syndrome, 258, 280, 305
Industrialisation, 164
Insider, 82, 83, 116, 133, 134, 156,
    220, 281–283, 306
Integrity, 10, 248, 264, 287
Intersubjective, 84, 254, 263, 265,
    294, 295
Interview, 17, 47, 49, 85–87, 108,
    116, 120, 157, 175, 202, 204,
    219, 221, 224, 238, 239, 245,
    247, 248
  semi-structured interview, 38, 83,
    98
Irony, 138, 258, 294, 304

J
Janus-faced, 163, 166

K
Keefer, J. M., 122, 123

312 INDEX

Kinship, 7, 28
Knowledge, 4, 6, 7, 44, 54, 56, 59, 61, 62, 67, 72, 73, 80–84, 86, 91, 99, 100, 105, 106, 114, 132, 133, 136, 137, 140, 143, 149, 159, 194, 200, 202, 210, 236, 240, 241, 246, 255, 264, 275, 285, 292
  embodied knowledge, 255
Kunda, G., 16

L

Landscape, 41, 140, 144, 220
Laundry, 10, 172, 301, 304
Lazarus, R. S., 194, 197–201, 203
Leadership, 15, 34, 255, 259, 265–268
  relational leadership, 263
Lesbian, gay, bisexual, and transgender (LGBT), 38, 39, 46, 296
Life stories, 66, 204, 258
Liminality, 2, 122, 123, 141, 182, 287
Linear cause-and-effect, 274, 293–295
Linguistic construction, 277, 288, 289

M

Management, 4, 10, 11, 14, 39, 134, 156, 157, 159, 160, 163, 183, 196, 237, 265, 280, 287, 288, 302
  critical management studies, 142, 254, 264–266
Marginalisation, 79
Marx, K., 10, 160, 276, 277
McDonaldisation, 161
Mental health, 21, 22, 108
Men who have sex with men (MSM), 9, 38–45, 47, 49, 50, 303
Messiness, 195, 302
Methodology

metaphorical methods, 86
Miles, M. B., 116, 247
Mood, 84, 116, 177, 198, 295
Morgan, G., 274, 293
Motherhood/mothering, 19, 28, 73
Mourning, 15, 131, 136–138
Mowlabocus, Sharif, 40, 43–45
Multivocality, 129
Mundane, 9, 14, 60, 101, 102, 107, 265, 280

N

Naivety, 240
Narcissism, 290
Narrative, 2, 10, 11, 38, 39, 46, 49, 50, 54–58, 60, 61, 64, 65, 72, 73, 80, 82, 87, 129, 130, 132, 141, 143, 147, 167, 194, 196, 204, 218–222, 224, 235, 236, 254–256, 260, 266, 289
Negotiation, 196, 207, 220, 228, 229, 241, 242
New Age spirituality, 18
New Capitalism, 16, 27, 34
Nietzsche, F., 198, 276, 291

O

Objectivity, 6, 83, 84, 115, 145, 243, 278, 290–293, 297, 302
  objective-subjective binary, 290
Observation
  observer effect, 279, 284
  participant observation, 10, 38, 39, 58, 73, 121, 122, 124, 195, 281, 295
Ontology, 292, 297
Organisation, 1, 16, 17, 23, 30, 31, 33, 34, 39, 41, 42, 58, 114, 115, 117, 134, 156, 163, 164, 168, 172, 174, 182, 186, 192, 193,

195–197, 204, 207, 209, 210,
236–239, 243, 244, 256, 260,
262–265, 268, 282, 287
Outsider, 83, 106, 107, 116, 156,
220, 277, 281–284, 289

P

Paradigm, 11, 90, 130, 132, 192, 241,
274–297
post-paradigm, 297
Paradox, 2, 11, 193, 267, 274, 304,
308
methodological paradox, 275, 290,
307
Participant-observer, 115, 121, 172,
174, 277–280
Pedagogy, 5, 11, 262, 265, 274, 276,
296
collaborative pedagogy, 5, 11
Performance, 2, 9, 29, 54, 143, 255,
267, 268, 270
Person
first person, 6–8, 196
personal accounts, 219, 220, 302
personal experience, 79, 82, 133,
135, 148, 193, 196, 200,
219–221, 260
personhood, 9, 38–40, 47
third person, 6
Philosophy, 1, 198, 236, 263, 264,
276, 294
Plagiarism, 277, 288
inverse plagiarism, 288
Poetic representation, 128
Positionality, 2, 5, 54, 73, 84, 86, 105,
195, 209, 237, 282
Positivism, 123, 124, 297
Privilege, 132, 143, 144
Probability, 118
Professional, 108
professional distance, 274, 278, 279

professional support, 102
Protection, 166
Psychology, 7, 197, 199, 203, 283
Public sector, 236, 237
Purity, 172, 173, 186

Q

QAA, 161
Questioning technique, 119, 123

R

Radiography
diagnostic radiography, 98
radiographic imaging, 101
Rationalisation, 162, 173
Reflexivity
critical reflexivity, 254, 255, 263,
266
emotional reflexivity, 194, 195, 199,
201, 210
reflection, 6, 11, 44, 50, 79, 86,
119, 121, 141, 175, 193, 219,
220, 224, 229, 234–236, 240,
244, 245, 248–250, 262, 263,
266, 269, 282, 294, 302–304
Reframing, 128, 166
Rejection, 11, 242, 249, 292
Reliability, 84, 118, 143, 205, 245,
247, 263, 274
Religion, 18, 279, 295, 296
Research, 85
contract research, 234
research relationships, 50, 72
Researcher, 2, 3, 5, 6, 8, 9, 17, 18, 50,
54, 58, 78, 84, 86, 88, 93, 98,
99, 107, 109, 116, 118, 120,
137, 138, 149, 156, 165–168,
192–197, 200, 202, 204,
206–210, 219–221, 234, 235,
240–244, 246, 248, 250,

254–258, 263, 265–267, 275, 278, 281, 282, 284–287, 290, 291, 295–297, 302–306
Ritual, 3, 8, 54, 58, 59, 62–64, 66, 72, 173, 175, 283
Role
  researcher role, 6, 303
  role and identity, 6, 99
  role model, 229
Rousseau, D., 282
Routinisation, 162

S
Sausage factory, 160–166
Security
  existential security, 7, 16, 34
  organisational security, 16
Self, 2, 5–8, 84, 131, 136, 141, 143, 156, 164, 195, 202, 206, 207, 221, 224, 262, 283, 302–304
Sennett, R., 16
Sensorial acclimatisation, 77
Sensory approach, 78
Sexual, 4, 8, 182, 220, 302, 304
  sexual citizenship, 45
  sexual geographies, 44, 182
  sexual networking, 38, 45
Shulman, D., 280, 288
Silence, 71, 85–92, 133, 137, 145, 149, 193, 306
Situated practice, 57, 255
Social, 108
  social dissonance, 283
  socialisaiton, 10
  social policy, 1, 57, 73, 303, 307
Soundscape, 78, 85
Sperm donor, 11, 218, 222, 226, 302, 304
Stories, 8, 15, 49, 55–58, 60, 64, 66, 72, 80, 83, 100, 101, 106–109, 120, 129, 130, 132–149, 156,

157, 163, 165–168, 196, 204, 205, 207, 208, 218–225, 228, 234, 236, 237, 255–258, 260, 261, 263, 266, 267, 269, 285, 288, 292, 293, 301–303, 307
Storytelling, 2, 98, 101, 106–109, 128, 133, 167
Subjectivity, 2, 84, 220, 260, 262, 290, 291, 302
Subtlety, 274

T
Technology, 2, 38–50, 88, 99, 117, 120, 161, 175, 304, 307
Textwork, 128, 133, 135, 136, 138–140
Third space, 158
Transdisciplinary, 2–5
Truth, 56, 130, 132, 156, 166–168, 230, 260, 290, 291, 293, 294, 302, 303

U
Uncertainty, 8, 10, 57, 113–124, 133, 241, 258, 278, 286–288, 302
  existential uncertainty, 286
Universities, 5, 10, 26, 114, 116, 117, 122, 123, 138, 141, 156, 205, 218, 243, 257, 258, 278, 282, 285, 304
Utopia, 275

V
Validity, 10, 62, 84, 118, 119, 205, 247, 263, 304
Van Maanen, John, 10, 17, 128, 129, 132, 134–136, 138, 143, 147, 149, 192, 220, 236, 263, 295

INDEX 315

Verisimilitude, 175, 287
Vignettes, 11, 54, 60, 119–121, 124,
    143, 195, 200, 254, 256
  illustrative vignette, 134
Voice
  authenticity of voice, 85–86
  privileging voice, 81, 128
  quiet voice, 86
  unconventional voice, 81, 82, 92
  voice prosthetics, 91

W
Wall, Sarah, 134, 135, 237, 250, 254
Watson, Tony, 288
Worlding, 133
Writing
  craft of writing, 139
  lazy writing, 128, 139
  writing about writing, 137, 139
  writing for publication, 139
  writing story, 134